# STUDIES ON VOLTAIRE AND THE EIGHTEENTH CENTURY

A fully searchable index to over
fifty years of research published in *SVEC*
http://www.voltaire.ox.ac.uk/svec_index

Manuscripts should be prepared in accordance with the *SVEC* style sheet, available on request and at the Voltaire Foundation website (www.voltaire.ox.ac.uk). One paper copy should be submitted to the *SVEC* general editor at the Voltaire Foundation, 99 Banbury Road, Oxford OX2 6JX, UK; an electronic version, with a summary of about 750 words, should be sent to jonathan.mallinson@trinity.ox.ac.uk.

# Book illustration,
# taxes and propaganda:

## the Fermiers généraux edition of
## La Fontaine's *Contes et nouvelles en vers* of 1762

DAVID ADAMS

SVEC

2006:11

VOLTAIRE FOUNDATION

OXFORD

2006

© 2006 Voltaire Foundation, University of Oxford

ISBN 0 7294 0885 X
ISSN 0435-2866

Voltaire Foundation
99 Banbury Road
Oxford OX2 6JX, UK

A catalogue record for this book
is available from the British Library

The correct reference for this volume is
*SVEC* 2006:11

This series is available on annual subscription

For further information about *SVEC*
and other Voltaire Foundation publications see
www.voltaire.ox.ac.uk

This book is printed on acid-free paper

Typeset and printed in Europe by the Alden Group, Oxfordshire

# Contents

# Acknowledgements

MANY people have helped me to write this book. First, the scholars who have worked on French illustrated books of the eighteenth century, and without whose labours it would have been impossible to survey the field coherently. Second, the librarians who have placed their collections at my disposal, and who have been unfailingly courteous in dealing with my enquiries. Third, my colleagues and students at the University of Manchester, who have made many valuable comments on the ideas and opinions which are set out in this volume. To all of them I owe more than I can express in words.

I am no less grateful to the British Academy, which has funded the cost of reproducing the illustrations used in this study.

David Adams
Manchester, January 2006

# List of illustrations

T<small>HIS</small> summary list of the illustrations used in this study refers to three specific editions of La Fontaine's *Contes et nouvelles en vers*, which are described by René Lacroix de Vineux, comte de Rochambeau, *Bibliographie des œuvres de La Fontaine* (Paris, 1911, reprinted New York, 1970). Reproductions are from the author's private collection unless otherwise stated.

'De Hooghe': the 1732 edition ('Amsterdam, chez N. Etienne Lucas') in two volumes with illustrations designed by Romeyn de Hooghe (Rochambeau 62). The position of the headpieces given in this list indicates the page on which they appear.

'Cochin': the 1745 edition ('Amsterdam', no pub.), in two volumes, with illustrations designed by Charles-Nicolas Cochin (Rochambeau 71). The position of the headpieces given in this list indicates the page on which they appear.

'Eisen': the 1762 edition ('Amsterdam', no pub.) in two volumes, with illustrations designed by Charles Eisen (Rochambeau 79). The position of the plates given in this list normally indicates the page opposite which the engraving appears, except where two plates are inserted between facing pages.

## Illustrations to volume 1 of the *Contes et nouvelles en vers*

## Illustrations to volume 2 of the *Contes et nouvelles en vers*

## List of illustrations

# 1. Introduction: the French illustrated book in the eighteenth century

## i. Introduction[1]

FRENCH illustrated books of the eighteenth century have long been regarded as one of the finest achievements of the Ancien régime. Collectors have always prized them for the harmonious rapport between text and image, for the quality of the printing and for the superior bindings in which many copies are found.[2] More than half a century ago, informed commentators could write 'Le Livre du XVIIIᵉ siècle [...] devrait faire figure, non plus d'objet d'art, mais de véritable miracle.'[3] With rather less emphasis, but no less enthusiasm, Gordon Ray echoes this judgement, calling the French eighteenth century 'arguably the greatest of all periods of illustration'.[4] Such judgements could be multiplied, but would simply underline further the concerted view of historians of the book trade and bibliophiles that the illustrated books produced in France in the period 1700-1789 must be ranked very highly in any estimate of the artistic and cultural triumphs of the period.

There is less unanimity, of course, among those who seek to place in an order of merit the books which fall into this category. Even so, the edition of La Fontaine's *Contes et nouvelles en vers* published in 1762 is frequently accorded pride of place among the illustrated books produced in France at that time.[5] That reputation is founded essentially on the eighty or so[6] copperplate illustrations created for the work by Charles Eisen, and

---

1. See also my article 'Politics and illustration: the lower classes as depicted in the "Fermiers généraux" edition of La Fontaine's *Contes* of 1762', *British journal for eighteenth-century studies*, 26:2 (2003), p.155-66.

2. For a detailed discussion of individual illustrated books of the period, see, for example, Henri Cohen and Seymour de Ricci, *Guide de l'amateur de livres à gravures du XVIIIᵉ siècle*, sixième édition (Paris, 1912); Gordon Ray, *The Art of the French illustrated book from 1700 to 1914* (New York, 1986); Antony Griffiths, *Prints for books: book illustration in France 1760-1800*, The Panizzi Lectures 2003 (London, 2004).

3. Maurice Boissais and Jacques Deleplanque, *Les Livres à gravures au dix-huitième siècle* (Paris, 1948), p.14.

4. Ray, *The Art of the French illustrated book*, p.xiii.

5. The Goncourts called it 'une merveille et un chef d'œuvre, l'exemple sans égal de la richesse d'un livre' (E. and J. de Goncourt, *L'Art du dix-huitième siècle*, Paris, 1883, p.139); Cohen states: 'Parmi les livres illustrés du XVIIIᵉ siècle, cette édition des *Contes de La Fontaine* [...] est celle dont l'ensemble est le plus beau et le plus agréable' (*Guide de l'amateur de livres*, col.558). Gordon Ray calls it 'the collector's book *par excellence*' (*The Art of the French illustrated book*, p.56).

6. The figure is imprecise because some plates were discarded, or occur only in a few copies.

engraved by some of the most celebrated craftsmen of the day. Commentators have pointed out that, although a considerable number of illustrated books were produced in France in the middle years of the century, the drawings on which the illustrations were based were the work of only a handful of artists.[7] Consequently, there are strong 'family' resemblances between one set of illustrations and another, even when they occur in books with no obvious similarities of subject matter. In these circumstances, the reputation of the 1762 *Contes* is all the more striking, and would in itself justify the full examination of the plates which has not previously been attempted, and to which the second section of this study is devoted.[8] But the plates are not the only unusual feature of the edition. It is notable too because it was paid for and published by the Compagnie des Fermiers généraux, the body which collected taxes on behalf of the royal treasury, and which earned itself an enduring reputation for the harshness and inflexibility with which its members set about their task.

The origins of the edition have attracted comment over many years, though not all of it is particularly helpful or well informed. Vera Salomons writes: 'The edition is known as that of the "fermiers généraux," as they defrayed all the expenses [...]. It is supposed that to obtain the favour of the court to continue the [Fermiers'] monopoly, handsome presents had to be given. Whatever else may have been presented, this edition was produced for the purpose.'[9] An alternative view is put forward by Boissais and Deleplanque who wrote in 1948 that the edition, which they claim had a print run of 1000 copies, 'ne fut pas mise en vente et fut réservée aux F. G. et à leurs amis'.[10] While the information given by these commentators differs in some respects, both claim that the edition was set aside for a specific audience, composed either of courtiers or of the Fermiers and their friends. As we shall see, neither of these statements is entirely satisfactory, for a variety of reasons, not least because they do not indicate the complexity of the questions which they raise. After all, it would have been very odd to produce so large an edition wholly intended for distribution to influential members of the court, as Salomons alleges. There are, moreover, good reasons for doubting that its circulation was restricted in this way, among them the fact that, despite the many criticisms made of them at that time, the Fermiers' monopoly was not under threat in 1762. What is more, a number of specific indicators run counter to the view of Boissais and Deleplanque that the edition was intended

7. See Boissais and Deleplanque, *Les Livres à gravures*, p.20, and Griffiths, *Prints for books*, p.27.

8. A very useful pioneering study is Robert N. Nicolich, 'Seventeenth and eighteenth-century illustrations for La Fontaine's *Contes et nouvelles en vers*: engraving designs by Romeyn de Hooghe and Charles Eisen', *Papers on French seventeenth-century literature* 13:24 (1986), p.221-82.

9. Vera Salomons, 'Charles Eisen', *XVIIIth century French book-illustrators* (London, 1914 [but 1921]), p.116-17.

10. Boissais and Deleplanque, *Les Livres à gravures*, p.101.

solely for the Fermiers and their friends. In reality, the bibliographical evidence of copies in bindings of the period shows that the range of owners or recipients was wider than these two groups. Yet such copies account for only a very small proportion of those which were printed, many of which still survive today, so that neither of the hypotheses outlined above provides reliable information on which to assess the purpose or the nature of the edition.

What is more puzzling than the identity of the allegedly intended recipients of the edition, however, is the fact that most sets of the engravings prepared for it were not used in 1762, but were bound into a reprint of 1792: we have the statement from Plassan, the printer of this latter edition, that while the print-run was 800 copies (rather than 1000, as Boissais and Deleplanque claimed), 2000 sets of the plates were printed.[11] Nonetheless, most of the edition was unobtainable for many years, not because it was censored, but because copies were deliberately withheld from the market. Ordinary buyers were able to secure the work only for a very short time after its publication, and when it was briefly made available again some years later.

These considerations confront us with two important problems which need investigation. First, the accounts which have hitherto been offered of the intended audience for the book are demonstrably inaccurate in one way or another; it is therefore essential to set the record as straight as the evidence allows. In addition, the importance widely accorded to the edition means that it is of more than passing interest to determine as clearly as possible the history of its publication, not least because that story bears directly upon the development of the copperplates themselves. In turn, the circumstances in which the edition was planned and executed provide a better understanding of the Fermiers' seemingly odd behaviour as sponsors over many years of an edition which then hardly saw the light of day. The complex circumstances in which they took their decision not to make it widely available will, then, be our second concern.

The events underlying the publication and marketing of the 1762 *Contes* offer few parallels even in the convoluted and semi-clandestine world of French eighteenth-century publishing. There are indications that the Fermiers started planning the edition some years before it actually appeared. The drawings on which the engravings are based may well have been prepared from the early 1750s,[12] and a number of the engravings are dated '1759', some three years before the *Contes* appeared in print.[13]

---

11. The information which Plassan provides on the 1762 edition is discussed in detail below, in section v, 'The fate of the *Contes*', p.29.

12. See P. L. Lacroix, 'Les *Contes* de La Fontaine. Recherches sur l'édition des Fermiers généraux', *L'Artiste* 44:2 (1874), p.255-56. Lacroix's article contains much information on the edition, though it is often less reliable than the documented testimony of Baron Roger Portalis, who states that Eisen exhibited some drawings for the *Contes* in 1753 (*Les Dessinateurs d'illustrations au dix-huitième siècle*, 2 vols, Paris, 1877, vol.1, p.195).

13. See Cohen, *Guide de l'amateur de livres*, col.564-65.

The changing circumstances in which the Fermiers found themselves embroiled during these years meant that the enterprise of publishing the *Contes* took on a different significance with the passage of time. But whatever date we choose as representing its *terminus a quo*, the story of the work's publication is very closely bound up with the political and social circumstances of the time. Something needs therefore to be said, as a preliminary, about the historical context of its genesis, before we look at its publishing history.

## ii. The Compagnie des Fermiers généraux

The Compagnie's origins go far back in French history, but in its more modern form, its foundations had been laid by Colbert in 1681; despite some early vicissitudes, it grew significantly in size and importance in the course of the eighteenth century.[14] To put the matter briefly: the power of the Fermiers became ever greater as the French treasury depended to an increasing extent on the revenue which they brought in, and indeed on the loans which they made to it, often at usurious rates of interest. In a country supposedly governed by a monarch who ruled by divine right, the immense influence of the Fermiers in all aspects of the nation's finances was a constant reminder of where much of the king's power really lay.[15]

Despite their official position the Fermiers généraux, like tax-gatherers through the ages, had a consistently bad press. Antagonism towards them manifested itself early on, perhaps most famously in La Bruyère's *Les Caractères* (1688), where he refers to financiers as 'des âmes sales, pétries de boue et d'ordure, éprises du gain et de l'intérêt'.[16] This unbridled hostility continued unabated throughout the eighteenth century. To take only one early example: in 1707, there appeared a curious work, customarily ascribed to one Blanchard (of whom nothing else is known), and entitled *Les Partisans demasquez, nouvelle plus que galante*. This is an unusual blend of love-story and diatribe, in which the author can scarcely hide his detestation of the Fermiers:

Ce qui leur attire cette haine générale des hommes, ne provient que de la manière orgueilleuse & sans miséricorde, dont ils se servent pour lever les impôts que le Roy est forcé d'exiger de ses Sujets, pour soutenir sa Gloire & les intérêts de sa Couronne [...]. L'abus qu'ils font de la suprême autorité qui leur est déposée entre les mains par l'argent qu'ils financent, en persécutant sans aucun égard tous ceux qui se trouvent sous leur main; cette manière, dis-je, est [...] barbare & contre les loix naturelles.[17]

14. The best study of the Compagnie remains Yves Durand, *Les Fermiers généraux au XVIIIᵉ siècle* (Paris, 1971).

15. See Pierre Goubert and Daniel Roche, *Les Français et l'Ancien régime*, 2 vols (Paris, 1984), vol.1, p.341, and Durand, *Les Fermiers généraux*, p.57-60.

16. Jean de La Bruyère, *Les Caractères* (1688), 2 vols (Paris, 1768), vol.1, p.247.

17. Blanchard, *Les Partisans demasquez, nouvelle plus que galante* (Cologne, Adrien L'Enclume, 1707), p.15-16. The original spelling and punctuation are retained throughout this study.

In Lesage's comedy *Turcaret* (1709), which was one of the great successes of the contemporary stage, the eponymous central character is a Fermier,[18] who comes to grief through his own stupidity, greed and duplicity. Although they suffered a temporary eclipse during the Regency, when John Law outbid them for the right to farm taxes,[19] the collapse of his system in October 1720 led to their reinstatement as the royal tax-gatherers. In 1726 the Compagnie's functions were restored in full, and it continued to enjoy this position, with some modifications, until the Revolution. Despite the reversal of their fortunes under Law, there was little sympathy for the Fermiers, and on their return to office, they continued to be the object of criticism in many quarters. In *Manon Lescaut* (1731), one of the young Manon's first clients is M. de B., whom Des Grieux describes as a 'célèbre fermier général'.[20] In *De l'esprit des lois* in 1748, Montesquieu had referred scathingly to 'les profits immenses des Fermiers' and to their 'avarice importune' (Livre XIII, article 19). In 1755 Ange Goudar's *Testament politique de Louis Mandrin* found a ready audience when he glorified the exploits of the famous bandit, who had recently been executed. Mandrin is presented as an adversary of the Compagnie, which Goudar accuses of being inimical to monarchical government, and of draining away the financial life-blood of the country.[21] There were more general signs of discontent, too. Jean-Jacques Rousseau, for his part, was fervent in his criticisms of luxury and, without specifically naming the Fermiers, he was clearly hostile, on ideological grounds, to what they stood for. The impact of his *Discours sur les sciences et les arts* (1750) and his *Discours sur l'origine de l'inégalité* (1755) was considerable, and prompted much of the debate on the material inequalities of the sort which the Fermiers both embodied and caused.[22] Throughout the first half of the eighteenth century (as indeed during the second, with which we are not primarily concerned), there is evidence of a strong and widespread current of hostility against the Fermiers généraux. Time and again, they were pilloried for their cruelty, their greed, their immorality, and their indifference to the suffering they caused.

18. Turcaret is called a 'traitant' in the text, but the *Dictionnaire de Trévoux* (1762) defines this term as 'nom qu'on donne aux Gens qui prennent les Fermes du Roi', and the Fermiers tried to have the play banned. As Durand comments (*Les Fermiers généraux*, p.403): 'A travers [Turcaret], c'est toute la gent financière qui se trouve ridiculisée.'

19. See A. Cobban, *A History of modern France*, 3 vols (Harmondsworth, 1963), vol.1, p.23-27.

20. Antoine-François Prévost d'Exiles, *Histoire du chevalier Des Grieux et de Manon Lescaut*, ed. Jean Sgard (Paris, 1995), p.64.

21. See Durand, *Les Fermiers généraux*, p.441. For a similar reaction by Voltaire, see his letter of 14 January 1755 to the duchesse de Saxe-Gotha (*Correspondence and related documents*, ed. Th. Besterman, in *Œuvres complètes de Voltaire*, henceforward *OCV*, vol.85-135, Geneva, Banbury, Oxford, 1968-1977, D6083).

22. Durand, *Les Fermiers généraux*, p.491-92. Others, such as Mably, also railed against luxury (see Durand, *Les Fermiers généraux*, p.198-200).

Even though many of the comments about the Fermiers made at the time are typified by dislike of them, it is only fair to point out that some of the most influential and controversial works of the day do not openly adopt such a view, and the reasons for their silence are in themselves revealing. Despite being a prominent *philosophe*, Helvétius was reluctant to criticise the Fermiers, though his disinclination may be partly explained by the fact that, for some twelve years between 1739 and 1751, he had been one of the Compagnie's wealthiest members.[23] It is true also that, at least until the late 1750s, even the *Encyclopédie* was not overtly critical of the Fermiers. At first, as so often, such mild criticisms as we do find are expressed indirectly, or hidden in the midst of apparently innocuous articles. In the article 'Encyclopédie' (1755), for example, Diderot refers to the problems he had encountered in getting artisans to discuss the techniques of their trade, particularly in Paris, 'où la crainte des impôts les tient perpétuellement en méfiance, & où ils regardent tout homme qui les interroge avec quelque curiosité comme un émissaire des fermiers généraux, ou comme un ouvrier qui veut ouvrir boutique.'[24] More striking than this oblique hint at the Fermiers' methods and their effects is the fact that some articles in the *Encyclopédie* were conspicuously flattering to them. Pesselier, who was himself a Fermier, repeatedly comes to their defence in volume 6 (1756), with four signed articles, 'Ferme', 'Fermier', 'Finances' and 'Financier'. At the end of the first of these is an editorial note. While it is impossible to say whether it is by Diderot or D'Alembert, it is worth reproducing in full because it is one of only two such statements in the whole *Encyclopédie*:

*L'impartialité dont nous faisons profession, & le desir que nous avons d'occasionner la discussion & l'éclaircissement d'une question importante, nous a engagés à insérer ici cet article. L'Encyclopédie ayant pour but principal l'utilité & l'instruction publiques, nous insérerons à l'article* REGIE, *sans prendre aucun parti, toutes les raisons pour & contre qu'on voudra nous faire parvenir sur l'objet de cet article, pourvû qu'elles soient exposées avec la sagesse & la modération convenables.*[25]

In 'Financier', Pesselier writes:

Si l'on examine philosophiquement ces différentes subdivisions d'une profession devenue fort importante & très-considérable dans l'état, on demeurera convaincu qu'il n'en est aucune qui n'exige, pour être dignement remplie, le concours des plus grandes qualités de l'esprit & du cœur; les lumieres de l'homme d'état, les intentions du bon citoyen, & la plus scrupuleuse exactitude de l'honnête homme vraiment tel, car ce titre respectable est quelquefois legerement prodigué [...]. C'est ainsi que tous les *financiers*, chacun dans leur genre, & dans l'ordre des proportions de lumieres, de fonctions, de facultés, qui leur est propre & particulier,

23. See also Durand, *Les Fermiers généraux*, p.490-91.
24. *Encyclopédie ou Dictionnaire raisonné des sciences, des arts et des metiers*, 35 vols (Paris, Le Breton *et al.*, and Neuchâtel, no pub., 1751-1780), vol.5, p.647.
25. *Encyclopédie*, vol.6, p.515. 'Régie' (1765) is a short article, and contains no comments of the sort solicited here. Italics in the original.

peuvent être estimés, considérés, chéris de la nation, écoutés, consultés, suivis par le gouvernement.

Ce portrait du *financier* blessera peut-être une partie des idées reçues: mais l'ont-elles été en connoissance de cause? & quand elles seroient justifiées par quelques exemples, doivent-ils tirer à conséquence pour l'universalité?[26]

This article is in turn followed by the second example of an editorial comment:

*Nous donnons cet article par les raisons déjà dites au mot* FERMIER *(Finance). Bien éloignés de vouloir faire aucun reproche odieux & injuste à ceux de nos financiers qui font un usage respectable de leur opulence, & de les priver du tribut d'estime personnelle qui leur est dû, nous desirons seulement présenter aux personnes intelligentes en ces matieres, l'occasion de discuter l'importante question de l'utilité de la finance considérée en elle-même: l'illustre auteur de l'Esprit des lois étoit incapable de penser là-dessus autrement; en écrivant contre la finance en général (article sur lequel nous ne prétendons point décider), il savoit rendre justice aux particuliers éclairés & vertueux qui se trouvent dans ce corps.*[27]

The presence of two editorial glosses appended to articles dealing with the Fermiers indicates that the editors judged it better not to give offence to the Compagnie at this time, and were willing to allow a heavily biased view of them to be presented without challenge. Predictably, this attempt to ward off hostility offended those who did not have the task of managing the fortunes of the *Encyclopédie*. In the *Correspondance littéraire* of 15 May 1761, Grimm did not disguise his contempt for this procedure which, he alleged, had been widely condemned:

Autrefois, M. Pesselier faisait des fables et des dialogues des morts dont il n'est point resté de souvenirs; employé depuis par les fermiers généraux, il a consacré sa plume et ses talents à la défense de leur cause. C'est lui qui a fourni à l'*Encyclopédie* les articles 'Fermes' et 'Financier', et à qui les éditeurs de ce grand ouvrage sont redevables des justes reproches qu'ils ont essuyés à cet égard. On est étonné avec raison de trouver dans l'*Encyclopédie* une réfutation en forme des principes de l'immortel Montesquieu sur l'administration des finances, et quelle réfutation encore![28]

Even without Pesselier's craven attempt to mask the harshness of the Fermiers' conduct and methods as tax-gatherers, historical circumstances made it almost inevitable that, as the 1750s wore on, criticisms of the Compagnie would once more intensify. In the first place, the virtually unlimited powers which it already enjoyed in enforcing the collection of taxes were increased still further, as the Seven Years War (1756-1763) created the urgent need to raise more revenue. Resistance to the Fermiers' fiscal demands was construed as rebellion, and those who resisted could be imprisoned without trial, or even without appearing before a court.[29]

26. *Encyclopédie*, vol.6, p.815. Italics in the original.

27. *Encyclopédie*, vol.6, p.815. Italics in the original.

28. Frédéric-Melchior Grimm *et al.*, *Correspondance littéraire, philosophique et critique*, ed. Maurice Tourneux, 16 vols (Paris, 1877-1882), vol.4, p.404 (hereafter *CL*).

29. Durand, *Les Fermiers généraux*, p.49-50.

With the renewal of their *bail*, or right to farm taxes, in 1756, they took steps to streamline their organisation, and set about their task with more efficiency and rigour than ever.[30]

In the second place, the war brought about, for a time at least, a considerable drop in the income of the Compagnie, and hence of individual members, as shipments of tobacco from America were significantly interrupted for some time. Contemporary records show that the annual profit per Fermier fell from 261,000 livres in 1757-1758 to only 12,705 livres in 1758-1759, though it rose again to 134,529 livres in 1759-1760.[31] With a more efficient organisation and very wide powers at their disposal, and with less certainty of a secure income, the Fermiers took whatever steps they judged appropriate to protect their interests. Twenty new Fermiers were created during the war, to exact the taxes to pay for it. In this context, it is hardly surprising that complaints about their conduct become more frequent from the late 1750s onwards, or that their behaviour was now observed with resentment even by some of their own colleagues. In 1757 there appeared *Le Financier citoyen* by Jean-Baptiste Naveau,[32] a Fermier with responsibilities in Brittany, who argued that royal expenditure should be based on economy, not on extravagance. In setting out his case, Naveau found much to criticise in the personal and professional conduct of the Fermiers (vol.2, p.226-27):

les conséquences fâcheuses des fortunes si multipliées & si excessives en Finances, sont si dangéreuses qu'insensiblement les Financiers prennent le dessus dans la direction des affaires. Ils donnent en quelque sorte le ton & portent une influence très-grande dans le gouvernement intérieur; influence d'autant plus à craindre qu'elle empêche les progrès des Arts, des Manufactures, du Commerce, de l'Agriculture, de la population & de la consommation, & par conséquent met obstacle à l'accroissement du royaume, dans les objets qui en constituent la force & la richesse.

He concluded that their ambition was so unbounded that if they continued to expand their interests 'il leur faudra le Royaume & les Iles, dans cinquante ans d'ici'.[33]

This was a chance for the *philosophes* to join in the criticism of the Compagnie, and they seized the opportunity. Grimm, reviewing Naveau's work in 1757, did not dissent from his view that the finances of France

30. Durand, *Les Fermiers généraux*, p.54-55.
31. The figures are given in a table of income and expenditure preserved in the Archives nationales (G1 54[B] Bail d'Henriet, Etat de produits bruts, apointements et frais de régie). It is reproduced in Eugene N. White, *France's slow transition from privatised to government-administered tax collection: tax farming in the eighteenth century*, available as Rutgers University Department of Economics working papers, online at: http://netec.mcc.ac.uk/WoPEc/data/Papers/rutrutres200116.html.
32. The work, in two volumes, bears only the date 'M. DCC. LVII.' but is undoubtedly of Parisian origin.
33. Jean-Baptiste Naveau, *Le Financier citoyen*, 2 vols (Paris, no pub., 1757), vol.2, p.228. Compare Durand, *Les Fermiers généraux*, p.422.

needed to be better administered. He reminded his readers that what was good in the book had been borrowed from Sully, the prudent and successful finance minister of Henri IV, and he regretted that subsequent generations had failed to observe the same cautious attitude towards public expenditure:

Tout est perdu quand la dissipation se met dans les affaires. Le sort du roi en cela n'est pas différent de celui d'un particulier: a-t-on jamais vu arranger une maison sans un ordre extrême? Voilà une vérité dont nos contrôleurs généraux des finances devraient se pénétrer. Ils verraient que depuis le grand Sully on n'a pas fait une opération de finance en France qui ne tendît à la ruine du roi et de ses sujets.[34]

In the *Encyclopédie*, too, attitudes towards the Fermiers gradually hardened into hostility. By 1757 contributors had forsaken the emollient tone of Pesselier and were inveighing against what they perceived to be the scandalous luxury enjoyed by members of the Compagnie at a time when other citizens were condemned to the direst poverty. Jaucourt's article 'Fortune' leaves little doubt of his dislike of the Fermiers:

il est contre le droit naturel & contre l'humanité que des millions d'hommes soient privés du nécessaire comme ils le sont dans certains pays, pour nourrir le luxe scandaleux d'un petit nombre de citoyens oisifs. Une injustice si criante & si cruelle ne peut être autorisée par le motif de fournir des ressources à l'état dans des tems difficiles.[35]

The hostility to gross inequalities expressed in this article echoed not only the general condemnation of such a situation contained in the writings of Rousseau, but a more specific opposition, based on different considerations, which was beginning to emerge in the writings of the group known subsequently as the Physiocrats. The leading light of the coterie, François Quesnay, was later to make his reputation with his treatise *La Physiocratie, ou Constitution naturelle du gouvernement le plus avantageux au genre humain* in 1767. Early intimations of the view he was to express in that work can however be found in two articles which he contributed a decade earlier to the *Encyclopédie*, 'Fermiers (économie politique)' in 1756 and 'Grains' in 1757. In the first of these, Quesnay paints a distressing picture of the impoverished state of French agriculture, which he attributes to three causes (*Encyclopédie*, vol.6, p.532):

1° à la desertion des enfans des laboureurs qui sont forcés à se réfugier dans les grandes villes, où ils portent les richesses que leurs peres employent à la culture des terres: 2° aux impositions arbitraires, qui ne laissent aucune sûreté dans

---

34. *CL*, vol.3, p.411, 1 September 1757. Durand (*Les Fermiers généraux*, p.434) claims that Naveau's work earned 'l'estime de Grimm', but this conclusion hardly accords with the tone of the comments in the *CL*.

35. *CL*, vol.7, p.206. On the relationship between the *Encyclopédie* and the Fermiers, see John Lough, *The 'Encyclopédie'* (London, 1971), p.371-80.

l'emploi des fonds nécessaires pour les dépenses de l'agriculture: 3° à la gêne, à laquelle on s'est trouvé assujetti dans le commerce des grains.

Although he hints in this passage at the iniquitous system of taxation which, he alleged, was ruining agriculture, the true extent of his hostility to the Fermiers emerges only in 'Grains'. Here, he rejects the very notion that there should be massive inequalities in wealth and the idea that

si les uns deviennent riches aux dépens des autres, la richesse existe également dans le royaume. Cette idée est fausse & absurde; car les richesses d'un état ne se soûtiennent pas par elles-mêmes, elle ne se conservent & s'augmentent qu'autant qu'elles se renouvellent par leur emploi dirigé avec intelligence [...] les richesses renfermées dans les coffres du financier, sont infructueuses, ou si elles sont placées à intérêt, elles surchargent l'état. Il faut donc que le gouvernement soit très attentif à conserver à toutes les professions productrices, les richesses qui leur sont nécessaires pour la production & l'accroissement des richesses du royaume.[36]

In the same year, 1757, the marquis de Mirabeau published *L'Ami des hommes*, which both echoed and developed the ideas of Quesnay. Mirabeau provided an eloquent picture of what rural life could be – simple, honest, prosperous – if populations could be induced to return to the land, and could be free of unjust taxation disproportionate to their income. He goes on to paint a supposedly hypothetical (but actually realistic) picture of what might happen if nothing were done to protect and revive agriculture:

Mais si au-lieu de tout cela il se trouvoit que dans les campagnes, par l'absence de leurs seigneurs, ils ne pussent jamais espérer aucune grace ni protection; que traînés languissants aux corvées les plus dures et les plus répétées, décimés pour les milices, voyant arracher leurs haillons de dessus les buissons par les collecteurs s'ils tardent à payer les impôts; doublés à la taille l'année d'après s'ils payent, pour leur apprendre à ne pas endurer la contrainte, utile récolte des receveurs: si toutes les fois qu'ils ont manqué, il étoit question de les punir par la bourse; si le procureur, l'avocat, le juge, l'agent du seigneur, les gens du fisc, si tout cela, dis-je, les regardant en tout et par-tout comme victimes ne leur laissoit la peau sur les os, que supposé qu'elle ne fût pas bonne à faire un tambour, faudroit-il en ce cas s'étonner s'ils périssent par milliers dans l'enfance, et si dans l'adolescence ils cherchent à se placer par-tout ailleurs qu'où ils devroient être.[37]

Mirabeau returned to the attack in his *Théorie de l'impôt* (1760), in which he castigated the Fermiers for regarding trade only as a further opportunity for imposing taxes:

toutes Fermes & tous Fermiers d'imposition sur le travail, sur la subsistance, sur le commerce, sur l'industrie & sur la rétribution quelconque, sont contre le droit public & contre l'ordre naturel [...]. S'ils découvrent un filet de commerce, ils ne tendent qu'à asseoir dessus un droit de péage, qu'à l'arrêter par cent formalités

36. *Encyclopédie*, vol.7, p.830. Jaucourt was to express similar views in the article 'Impôts' (1765).
37. Victor Riqueti, marquis de Mirabeau, *L'Ami des hommes*, 6 vols (Avignon, no pub., 1756-1761), vol.1, p.227, 229.

insidieuses. Toute la vivification donc qu'ils apportent sur le territoire de l'Etat, est celle que la vue d'un oiseau de proye donne à une basse cour.[38]

Animal images are applied elsewhere to describe the Fermiers, whom Mirabeau variously pillories as 'l'hydre immortelle' (p.144), and as 'ces Wampires' (p.152); he warns the king against the 'conséquences fatales & inévitables de l'erreur énorme d'interposer une autorité, ou une agence quelconque, entre la contribution des sujets & la recette du Souverain' (p.151). This diatribe led to his being imprisoned in Vincennes for a few days before being exiled to his estates at Bignon, but it was clear that he and those who shared his views were intellectually in the ascendant. To take only one other example: in his *Testament politique du maréchal duc de Belle-Isle* (1761), Chevrier attacks the Fermiers as 'quarante hommes engraissés des besoins de l'Etat'; the government, from whose weakness they profit, he asserts, should restrain their excesses.[39] In a similar vein, the essayist and playwright Saint-Foix presented a wholly unflattering picture of a Fermier in his (admittedly somewhat laboured) comedy *Le Financier* produced at the Comédie-Française in August 1761.[40] In these and other works, the Fermiers were now becoming the object of persistent and unwelcome attention from writers of various hues, and their status in the eyes of intellectuals was as low as it had ever been, and perhaps lower.

In addition to such polemical attacks, attempts were being made at the height of the war to remove some of the generous financial advantages which the Fermiers had long enjoyed. In 1759 the newly appointed Contrôleur général des Finances, Etienne de Silhouette, introduced measures which included a requirement that the Compagnie should share equally with the crown the profits from its operations, a proposal which aroused particular resentment amongst the Fermiers.[41] Although this stipulation was subsequently abandoned when Silhouette fell from grace later that year, it indicated quite clearly that powerful forces of various kinds might again be arrayed against them.

A few voices were raised in their defence, as when Fréron declared in 1761 that they 'méritent l'estime et les éloges par l'intégrité de leur conduite et la noblesse de leurs sentiments et de leurs manières'.[42] Even so, by the early 1760s, critics of the Fermiers (including the *philosophes* as such, and others who shared their views without being closely identified with the group) were becoming ever more hostile to the Compagnie.

38. Victor Riqueti, marquis de Mirabeau, *Théorie de l'impôt* ([Paris], no pub., 1760), p.131.

39. François-Antoine Chevrier, *Testament politique du maréchal duc de Belle-Isle*, new edition (Amsterdam, Libraires associés, 1762), p.111-12.

40. See *CL*, vol.5, p.446-48, 1 August 1761.

41. See Durand, *Les Fermiers généraux*, p.82, 166. As Silhouette was in charge of finance only from March to November 1759, it cannot have been this threat to their position which inspired the Fermiers to use the *Contes* as a means of protecting their interests, as Vera Salomons claimed (*Eisen*, p.117; see above, note 9).

42. See Durand, *Les Fermiers généraux*, p.412-13.

Of course, enemies for whom the *Encyclopédie* was an object of particular loathing constantly assailed the *philosophes* themselves on all sides. Yet it did not follow that the adversaries of the *philosophes* were necessarily well disposed towards the Compagnie des Fermiers généraux, or that its members could count on the support of those who were inimical to the new ideas preached by the *encyclopédistes*, as we shall now see.

## iii. The Fermiers and the authorities

It is in the convoluted political and intellectual allegiances of mid-eighteenth-century France that we see the practical difficulties which the Fermiers faced in obtaining support for their cause. The common enemies whom they and the *encyclopédistes* had, and who might be expected to play off one against the other, included, of course, the various factions within the Catholic Church.

The Church had been suspicious of the *Encyclopédie* from its very inception, believing that it would be a focus for free-thinking, materialist atheism; such fears were understandable, for the faith had been increasingly subject to this threat since the publication of the work of Spinoza in the late seventeenth century.[43] At the same time, the Church did not fundamentally object to the Compagnie's activities in raising taxes on behalf of the king.[44] Even so, many of its members were averse in principle to the usury which underlay the operations of the Fermiers, on the doctrinal grounds that it was condemned in the Bible. This view was central to the more austerely doctrinaire tendency of the Church represented by the Jansenists, who were strongly entrenched in the *parlement* of Paris.

The theological standing of the Sorbonne had largely evaporated by the middle of the eighteenth century, and indeed for over 100 years it had not been permitted to censure books on its own authority.[45] The *parlement* consequently felt free to pursue its unvarying aim of enhancing its own position by seeking whenever it could to extend its control over censorship. It was never slow to condemn books, especially those which were of a Jesuit persuasion, or which were tinged with the new 'philosophic' spirit.[46] The persistent conflict thus engendered reached one of its highest points in 1758-1759, with the suppression of two works which became commingled in minds of their adversaries, the *Encyclopédie* and Helvétius's *De l'esprit*.

---

43. On the Church's suspicions of the *Encyclopédie*, see Jonathan I. Israel, *Radical Enlightenment: philosophy and the making of modernity 1650-1750* (Oxford, 2001), p.711-13.

44. See Durand, *Les Fermiers généraux*, p.387-97.

45. See Nicole Herrmann-Mascard, *La Censure des livres à Paris à la fin de l'Ancien régime (1750-1789)*, Travaux et recherches de la Faculté de droit et des sciences économiques de Paris, 13 (Paris, 1968), p.54-58.

46. See below, the text from Barbier quoted at note 62.

In August 1758, the *parlement* sought on its own initiative, and with no legal authority, to condemn *De l'esprit*.[47] The Archbishop of Paris, Christophe de Beaumont, delivered in November 1758 a thundering fulmination against the work. In a *mandement*, he roundly denounced it as 'propre à renverser la loi naturelle, et à détruire les fondements de la religion chrétienne', as well as being a threat to the State, the monarchy, and right-thinking people of all kinds.[48] The hostility between the Jansenists and their chief theological enemies the Jesuits (who were expelled from France in 1762) was long standing and ran deep. In some respects however they did see eye to eye, and the two groups were not averse to making common cause when they felt threatened, either doctrinally or politically. One such threat came unmistakably from the *philosophes*, whose activities now offered the rival groups a rare opportunity for a display of theological unity.[49] Hence, there was no dissent from the Archbishop's diatribe, which produced its desired effect: on 23 January 1759, *De l'esprit*, the *Encyclopédie*, and a clutch of other 'philosophical' works were denounced by the *parlement* and banned. On 8 March that year, following its examination by a group of specialists appointed by the *parlement*, an *arrêt du Conseil* was issued by the king, withdrawing the *privilège* of the *Encyclopédie*. These signs of official disapproval appeared to concede the demands of those who had been trying for years to ensure the destruction of 'philosophical' works.[50]

The *parlement*'s actions in censoring the *Encyclopédie* were prompted essentially by a concern at what its members regarded as the work's theological errors, rather than by its attacks on more secular targets such as the Compagnie des Fermiers généraux.[51] In fact, it had shown itself to be consistently hostile to the excessive profits made by financiers; it said so openly in September 1759, when it condemned the 'gains immodérés faits jusqu'à présent dans les fermes, traites et entreprises', and its views remained unchanged in the years that followed.[52] Hence, the Fermiers could not realistically count on the *parlement* to support their cause in the longer term, particularly once the *Encyclopédie*, a principal source of their grievances, had apparently been silenced by the withdrawal of its *privilège*.

47. See Grimm's account in *CL* vol.4, p.90-92; Jacques Proust, *L'Encyclopédie* (Paris, 1965), p.59-65; D. W. Smith, *Helvétius, a study in persecution* (Oxford, 1965), p.29-31; and his *Bibliography of the writings of Helvétius* (Ferney-Voltaire, 2001), p.105-15.

48. See Smith, *Helvétius, a study in persecution*, p.40, for the text of the *mandement*.

49. According to Grimm, writing on 1 September 1761, 'molinistes et jansénistes, les jésuites et le Parlement [...] et maître Joly de Fleury, avocat général du roi au Parlement, sont tous d'accord sur les ravages occasionnés de nos jours parmi nous par le fléau de la philosophie' (*CL*, vol.4, p.500).

50. See Proust, *L'Encyclopédie*, p.64-65, and Lough, *The 'Encyclopédie'*, p.24-25.

51. The *arrêt* specifically accuses the *encyclopédistes* of abusing the indulgence shown to them by the authorities, and refers to the 'tort irréparable qui en résulte pour les mœurs et la religion' (quoted by Lough, *The 'Encyclopédie'*, p.25). It makes no reference to any other negative aspect of the work.

52. See Lough, *The 'Encyclopédie'*, p.436-37, 598.

While the Fermiers benefited therefore from the actions taken by the authorities against the work, they were not instrumental in securing its suppression, and their interests were not a significant factor in determining the measures to be taken against it.

And although religious conservatives and others welcomed the silencing of the *Encyclopédie*, there was no guarantee that the authorities would always act decisively against all those who criticised the existing administration. In fact, the Fermiers had fewer friends in judicial circles than they might have supposed. If, as we noted earlier, the marquis de Mirabeau, one of the chief tormentors of the Compagnie, was briefly imprisoned in Vincennes in 1760 and released only on condition that he accepted exile to his estates,[53] the Fermiers achieved few such successes against their critics at this time. To their discomfort, the authorities were not automatically inclined to suppress works which attacked powerful vested interests, or indeed the institutions of the Ancien régime in general. This tolerance was due in large part to the officials responsible for the censorship of books.

Contrary to what is often believed, there was a tradition of informed, balanced assessment by the censors of the majority of books submitted for their scrutiny, and it would be wrong to assume that they automatically stood in opposition to any innovative ideas or attitudes. It is true that works which were judged to be overtly dangerous to the faith or to the good of society, such as Voltaire's *Lettres philosophiques* (1734) or Diderot's *Pensées philosophiques* (1746), were condemned, and their publication was officially forbidden. But even books like these were often able to circulate widely within a short time of their condemnation, and the authorities were not always unrelenting in pursuing allegedly dangerous works. As Robert Darnton puts it: 'The very notion of legality in literature remained fuzzy, because the authorities in charge of the book trade constantly fudged the line that separated the licit from the illicit.'[54] The principal official responsible for the book trade was the Directeur de la Librairie. From 1750 to 1763, this post was occupied by Chrétien-Guillaume Lamoignon de Malesherbes (1721-1794). Despite the fact that he was himself the son of the Chancellor of France, and the son-in-law of Grimod de La Reynière, one of the leading members of the Compagnie, Malesherbes was anything but an establishment lackey ready to do the Fermiers' bidding. During his time as Premier Président de la Cour des Aides, he frequently attacked the corruption and malfeasance which they practised. In September 1756 he denounced 'les taxes irrégulières et injustes qui se perçoivent depuis soixante années'; he reiterated this view

---

53. On Mirabeau's attitude towards the Fermiers, see Durand, *Les Fermiers généraux*, p.190-92.

54. Robert Darnton, *The Forbidden best-sellers of pre-Revolutionary France* (London, 1996), p.3-4.

in June 1761, and his hostility towards the Compagnie remained undiminished in the years that followed.[55]

As Directeur de la Librairie, Malesherbes's policy was to be as indulgent to the *philosophes* as circumstances allowed, and to adopt an even-handed approach towards their critics. He had tolerated the appearance of writings hostile to them, such as Jacob-Nicolas Moreau's *Nouveau Mémoire pour servir à l'histoire des Cacouacs* (1757).[56] Nonetheless, he was equally willing, in 1758, to sanction the publication of works such as La Harpe's *L'Aléthophile* and Billardon de Sauvigny's *Poëme sur la cabale anti-encyclopédique*, which retaliated against these attacks and defended the *Encyclopédie*.[57] The same broadly neutral attitude explains why he permitted the publication of works critical of the Fermiers themselves, such as those of Naveau and Mirabeau, while doing nothing to prevent the publication of their edition of the *Contes*. Like many of the censors working under his control, Malesherbes inveighed against works which he judged to be without redeeming literary or intellectual merit.[58] But he showed few signs of wishing actually to repress the tide of legitimate criticism, including that which, particularly from the 1750s onwards, constantly lapped at the gates of Church and State.[59] In the third of his five *Mémoires sur la librairie* (written in 1758-1759), he made quite clear his views on censorship in general:

Il n'est pas possible que la loi punisse ni défende tout ce qui est mal; et ceux qui gouvernent, ne doivent ni ne peuvent empêcher tout ce qu'ils désapprouvent. Si on voulait entrer dans ce détail, les censeurs acquerraient sur les auteurs une autorité illimitée. Il est temps d'affranchir les gens de lettres de la tyrannie de ces espèces d'inspecteurs qu'on a voulu mettre à leurs pensées [...]. Il ne faut donc les gêner, ni sur la forme, ni sur le ton de leurs ouvrages, et on peut leur laisser commettre un genre de fautes qui sera toujours suffisamment puni par le mépris public.[60]

55. See P. Grosclaude, *Malesherbes, témoin et interprète de son temps* (Paris, 1961), p.212, 216. Grosclaude's conclusion is that 'Ce gendre et ce beau-frère de fermiers généraux est conduit à dénoncer implacablement les excès et les injustices des grands financiers' (p.755).

56. According to d'Hémery, the police official who supervised the workings of the Paris book trade at this time, and who reported the matter in his *Journal* on 22 December 1757 (see John Lough, *Essays on the 'Encyclopédie' of Diderot and D'Alembert*, London, 1968, p.275).

57. See Grosclaude, *Malesherbes, témoin et interprète*, p.283-85. Herrmann-Mascard also concludes that Malesherbes 'a parfaitement su concilier ses idées libérales avec son devoir d'agent chargé de l'exécution de règlements qu'il désapprouve pourtant en grande partie' (*La Censure des livres*, p.30).

58. See Anne Goldgar, 'The absolutism of taste: journalists as censors in eighteenth-century Paris', in *Censorship and the control of print in England and France 1600-1910*, ed. Robin Myers and Michael Harris (Winchester, 1992), p.87-110.

59. Compare Darnton, *The Forbidden best-sellers*, p.88.

60. Chrétien-Guillaume Lamoignon de Malesherbes, *Mémoires sur la librairie et sur la liberté de la presse*, ed. Graham Rodmell, *North Carolina studies in the Romance languages and literatures* 213 (Chapel Hill, NC, 1979), p.117. The five *Mémoires* were not published until 1809.

Malesherbes's tolerant attitude brought him inevitably into conflict with the vigilant severity which typified the activities of the *parlement*. Yet such was his power and influence that he was able to mitigate the worst effects of its interference in the intellectual life of the times. Although the *arrêt* against the *Encyclopédie* was issued in the name of the king, it was in reality a way of permitting the enterprise to continue clandestinely, away from prying eyes, with the tacit approval of Malesherbes and his father the Chancellor.[61] This was an unusual, and even extraordinary, procedure, which attracted adverse comment. In his *Chronique de la régence*, Edmond-Jean-François Barbier, who was himself a member of the *parlement*, wrote that in seeking to censor the *Encyclopédie*, 'M. le chancelier a fait même une nouveauté, par rapport aux censeurs royaux. Il en a envoyé une liste au bureau de la librairie pour y être enregistrée, apparemment pour que les libraires ne reconnoissent point d'autres censeurs que ceux nommés par le chancelier, c'est-à-dire par le Roi.'[62] The appreciation shown by the *philosophe* camp for the indulgence which the Malesherbes *père et fils* displayed towards them can be seen in the *Encyclopédie* article 'Librairie' (which was written while the work was still banned, and not published until 1765). Diderot (who is here writing anonymously)[63] can find nothing but praise for the conduct of the two men in their respective posts:

Le chancelier de France est le protecteur né de la *Librairie*. Lorsque M. de Lamoignon succéda dans cette place à M. d'Aguesseau, d'heureuse mémoire, sachant combien les Lettres importent à l'état, & combien tient aux Lettres la *Librairie*, ses premiers soins furent de lui choisir pour chef un magistrat amateur des Savans & des Sciences, savant lui-même. Sous les nouveaux auspices de M. de Malesherbes, la *Librairie* changea de face, prit une nouvelle forme & une nouvelle vigueur; son commerce s'aggrandit, se multiplia; de sorte que depuis peu d'années, & presque à la fois, l'on vit éclorre & se consommer les entreprises les plus considérables [...]. Nous avouerons ici avec reconnoissance ce que nous devons à sa bienveillance. C'est à ce magistrat, qui aime les Sciences, & qui se récrée par l'étude de ses pénibles fonctions, que la France doit cette émulation qu'il a allumée, & qu'il entretient tous les jours parmi les Savans; émulation qui a enfanté tant de livres excellens & profonds.[64]

Taken together with Malesherbes's own statement of his guiding principles as a censor, this declaration makes it clear that, under his regime, the Fermiers could not readily count on the censor's office to act on their behalf in suppressing works critical of their conduct. Hence, banned works such as the *Encyclopédie* might be revived at any time under Malesherbes's

---

61. See Proust, *L'Encyclopédie*, p.66-67.

62. Edmond-Jean-François Barbier, *Chronique de la régence et du règne de Louis XV (1718-1763), ou Journal de Barbier, avocat au parlement de Paris*, septième série (1758-1761) (Paris, 1885), p.126.

63. See R. N. Schwab, W. E. Rex and J. Lough, *Inventory of Diderot's 'Encyclopédie'*, SVEC 85 (1972), p.588.

64. 'Librairie', *Encyclopédie*, vol.9, p.479.

benevolent eye, to continue the campaign of hostility to the Compagnie and other pillars of the State.

The Fermiers' view of their own position at this time is described by Grimm in the *Correspondance littéraire* for 17 January 1761, where he neatly summarises the reaction of those in power to a number of more outspoken recent publications:

Le monde ira-t-il moins son train parce qu'Helvétius a soutenu quelques para-doxes, et refusera-t-on de payer les impôts parce que M. de Mirabeau prétend que les fermiers généraux ne sont pas les piliers, mais bien les pilleurs de l'Etat? Oui, si j'en crois les dévots, tout est perdu depuis que le livre *de l'Esprit* a paru, et à moins de brûler l'auteur, on ne peut espérer de réparer le mal. Les gens de finance soutiennent que la *Théorie de l'impôt* culbutera le royaume, d'autres disent que c'est l'*Encyclopédie* qui aura cet honneur-là.[65]

So, the Fermiers, under sustained assault from the *philosophes*, could muster no significant support from the ecclesiastical or judicial authorities, who were strongly opposed to their aims and methods. In this context, the significance of their edition of the *Contes* undoubtedly changed over the years. So far as is known, they had originally commissioned the drawings in the 1750s as a purely commercial enterprise: the print-run of 800 copies argues that this was so.[66] In addition, they had already financed the publication of La Fontaine's *Fables*, which had appeared to great acclaim in four folio volumes between 1755 and 1759,[67] and to which the *Contes* would have been the natural accompaniment. There is some evidence that they were also to have been published in this august format, though this intention was never put into effect.[68] By the early 1760s, however, the embattled position in which the Fermiers found themselves was to give the endeavour a somewhat different aspect, which would make it advi-sable to modify their original intentions quite considerably. It is at this point that the publication of the *Contes* becomes entangled with the quarrels and attacks in which the Fermiers found themselves embroiled.

## iv. The publication of the *Contes et nouvelles en vers*

Very little official information on the publication of the edition is forth-coming from the archives of the book trade. There is no record of any permission having been sought or granted for it in the registers of the Directeur de la Librairie covering the years 1750-1763;[69] it is therefore

---

65. *CL*, vol.4, p.339.

66. See below, the passage quoted at note 121.

67. See for example, the review by Guillaume-François Berthier in the *Journal de Trévoux*, quoted by René Lacroix de Vineux, comte de Rochambeau, *Bibliographie des œuvres de La Fontaine* (Paris, 1911; reprinted New York, 1970), p.33.

68. See Lacroix, 'Les *Contes* de La Fontaine', p.256.

69. See Paris, BNF n.a.f. 21998-99, *Registres des privilèges et permissions simples de la librairie*, 1750-1763.

possible that the Compagnie did not formally seek official authority to publish its edition. However, this documentary silence is not especially significant: tacit permission to reprint established works of literature (even those of equivocal reputation) was often granted with only a minimum of formality. As Raymond Birn points out, during the Malesherbes regime there was a good chance that a request for a *permission tacite* would be successful: on average, in the years 1751-1763, 135 such requests were submitted annually, and seventy-nine granted.[70] It was customary, too, to extend tolerance to books of equivocal reputation and to give them a *permission tacite*, on condition that their place of publication was disguised.[71] The use of 'Amsterdam' on the title-page of the *Contes*, a manifestly Parisian book,[72] was therefore typical. In addition, a number of editions of the *Contes* had already been published in Paris (albeit with a false 'Amsterdam' imprint); a refusal to allow a new edition to appear (especially one promoted by the Fermiers généraux) would therefore have been unusual.[73] It would, of course, have been more unusual still to maintain the ban on the original edition in 1762, while allowing two counterfeit versions a year or so later; their existence is a sufficient indication that the Fermiers' work was not withdrawn because of any official prohibition on its circulation. This latter point leads us to ask what intrinsic qualities the book itself may have possessed which might explain its curious destiny.

It is quite evident that the Fermiers went to great trouble to ensure that theirs would be a sumptuous production, at least in regard to its illustrations.[74] In the *Correspondance littéraire* of 15 June 1762, Grimm praised it in fulsome terms:

On vient de faire une superbe édition des contes de La Fontaine, à la tête desquels on lit le précis de la vie de cet illustre poète par M. Diderot. Cette édition est ornée d'un grand nombre de très jolies estampes qui ont encore

70. Raymond Birn, 'The profits of ideas: *privilèges en librairie* in eighteenth-century France', *Eighteenth-century studies* 4:2 (1970-1971), p.131-68 (p.148).

71. Compare Griffiths, *Prints for books*, p.61.

72. The watermark is French, the catchwords are positioned at the start of each quire; the gatherings are signed to half, in lower-case roman, and the signatures are positioned on the right of the lower margin. All these features, found together, make a wholly convincing case for the Parisian origins of the book. See R. A. Sayce, *Compositorial practices and the localization of printed books 1530-1800*, Oxford Bibliographical Society occasional publications 13 (Oxford, 1979).

73. In *La Statistique bibliographique de la France sous la monarchie au XVIII^e siècle* (The Hague, Paris, 1965), Robert Estivals concludes apropos of book censorship that 'Les permissions tacites sont donc la production tolérée, et leur évolution, du même coup, est celle de la pensée libérale [qui] croît à travers le XVIII^e siècle [avec un] retour à la tolérance à partir de [1752]' (p.279). See also Robert L. Dawson, *Confiscations at customs: banned books and the French booktrade during the last years of the Ancien régime*, SVEC 2006:07.

74. Strangely, the paper used for the text of the 1762 edition was of mediocre quality, though that used for the plates was good. A very small number of unillustrated copies have survived, but are not mentioned separately in contemporary documents. See Cohen, *Guide de l'amateur de livres*, col.578, and A. Hédé-Haüy, *Les Illustrations des Contes de La Fontaine: bibliographie, iconographie* (Paris, 1893), p.27-29.

l'avantage d'être honnêtes quand le poète ne l'est guère. C'est ce que j'ai vu de plus joli en fait d'estampes dont on enrichit les livres. Elles sont ordinairement si mal faites qu'un homme de goût les possède à contrecœur. La plupart des estampes dont je parle sont de l'invention de M. Eisen, artiste allemand, et ce ne sont pas les plus mauvaises. Cette édition est fort belle; mais l'exemplaire coûtera au moins trois louis.[75]

This last sentence is intriguing: Grimm's use of the future tense suggests that the book was not yet on sale, and its price was consequently still uncertain at this stage. Nor does Elie Fréron make matters clearer in his comments on the edition. In the *Année littéraire* in November 1762, he remarks that 'on en trouve quelques exemplaires chez *Panckoucke* Libraire, qui vient de prendre la place de *Lambert*, rue & à côté de la comédie Françoise';[76] this detail is of more than passing interest.

Fréron was well placed to know the facts of the matter, since Michel Lambert was the publisher of *L'Année littéraire*: this same name and address appear on the title-page of the volume in which the *Contes* are reviewed. Charles-Joseph Panckoucke (1736-1798) was the scion of a well-known family of booksellers from Lille, and he was to have a spectacular career in later years as the publisher of reprints of the *Encyclopédie*.[77] In the 1760s however, he was still a young, albeit ambitious, bookseller, who could not afford to get on the wrong side of the authorities. In February 1763 the police who were searching for forbidden or contraband works raided his premises. They found, *inter alia*, nine copies of the *Contes de La Fontaine*, containing 'figures' and allegedly printed in Amsterdam. In the light of Fréron's reference to the 'quelques exemplaires' available from Panckoucke, the seizure quite probably included – or comprised – copies of the 1762 edition.[78] Panckoucke claimed that he was selling them on behalf of another (unnamed) bookseller, rather than on his own account. Whether or not this was so, the confiscated items were returned to him in May 1763, and no more was heard of the matter.[79]

This information throws a good deal of light on the marketing of the *Contes*, and on the status of the edition. The seizure of the work by the police is less significant than it might seem, since the copies in question were later returned, and this would not have happened had the book been regarded officially as dangerous. Indeed, while an exceptionally

75. *CL*, vol.5, p.108.
76. Elie-Catherine Fréron, *Année littéraire*, 292 vols (Amsterdam & Paris, Lambert *et al.*, 1754-1790), vol.8, p.66.
77. See Lough, *Essays on the 'Encyclopédie'*, p.52-110; Panckoucke's career as a whole is analysed by Suzanne Tucoo-Chala, *Charles-Joseph Panckoucke et la librairie française 1736-1798* (Pau, 1977).
78. They could in theory have been copies of the 1743/1745 edition with illustrations by Cochin, or an anonymous 'Amsterdam' reprint of 1755. Both of these (which are discussed later in this study) were however uncommon, and even if Panckoucke had copies of them, he is known from Fréron's account to have had the 1762 edition in stock.
79. Details are given in manuscript police files (BNF n.a.f., 3.348, f.83-84), and Tucoo-Chala, *Charles-Joseph Panckoucke*, p.103-104.

large number of books deemed to be either morally or doctrinally offensive were banned in 1762 (the year, let us remember, which saw the publication of two notorious works by Rousseau, *Emile* and the *Contrat social*), the *Contes* were not among them.[80] In this feverish atmosphere, the police were evidently none too careful about what they took into custody, even if they later changed their minds.

But even if Panckoucke was now free to sell his copies, an atmosphere of secrecy surrounded the edition from the outset. Remarkably, neither Fréron nor Grimm makes any mention whatever of the part played by the Compagnie in commissioning the plates which drew such high praise from them. The same air of semi-secrecy pervades the comments of the anonymous reviewer in the *Mercure de France* in January 1763.[81] While he praises a number of the plates for their 'goût', their 'force', their 'correction' or their 'sentiment', most of his comments are reserved for an eulogistic account of the fleurons and culs-de-lampe. Yet he makes no mention of the Fermiers, and concludes his review with the intriguing observation '*Lambert* & *Duchesne*, rue de la Comédie Françoise & rue S. Jacques, & plusieurs autres Libraires, ont reçu quelques exemplaires de cette belle édition' (p.145). If Panckoucke had nine copies for sale, and a handful of other booksellers a similar number, that could scarcely account for more than a fraction of the 800 copies printed. Whatever value the Fermiers placed on their edition, they were decidedly hesitant in making it available to the public even from the outset.

In an attempt to account for this curious publishing procedure, Vera Salomons and others have argued, as was noted above, that the Fermiers distributed the book to only a small number of courtiers, in order to buy influence at a time when their monopoly of tax-gathering was threatened.[82] While the book was not, to all intents and purposes, widely available, the fact that a small number of booksellers did have some copies in stock invalidates the idea that it was not available to the general public at all. What is more, there is no evidence that the Fermiers' monopoly was under threat in 1762. Even so, it is possible to change the scenario slightly, and to suppose that copies could have been presented to

80. The works concerned are listed by Félix Rocquain, *L'Esprit révolutionnaire avant la Révolution 1715-1789* (Paris, 1878), p.514-25. Most were obscure theological tracts, which in many cases had been published years previously. They were condemned mainly by the Paris *parlement*, and account for about a quarter of the total of condemnations during the whole of this period. While *Emile* was severely proscribed, the *Contrat social* was never officially condemned; it was, however, frequently seized by the police. For details of these two cases, see R. A. Leigh, 'Rousseau, his publishers and the *Contrat social*', *Bulletin of the John Rylands university library of Manchester* 66:2 (1984), p.204-27. See Dawson, *Confiscations at customs*.

81. *Mercure de France*, January 1763, 2 vols (Paris, no pub., 1763), vol.1, p.138-45. Although it regularly announces the appearance of new books of all kinds, the *Mercure* makes no other reference to the edition in 1762-1763.

82. See above, note 9, and Griffiths, *Prints for books*, p.21.

figures at court, to encourage them to bear down on the enemies of the Compagnie and make them desist in their attacks. This is a more credible hypothesis, in view of the travails the Fermiers were experiencing at the time. On this reading, at some point between the printing of the work in the first half of 1762 and the appearance of the first review in June, they would have concluded that the legal and ecclesiastical authorities were unlikely to take significant measures to stifle criticism of their activities. Since they could not rely on help from the organs of State to suppress such works effectively, so long as Malesherbes remained in charge of the book trade, they could have had recourse to less direct ways of persuading those in power to act against their adversaries. This hypothesis could explain why the remaining copies of the *Contes* were withheld for many years, because to do so would ensure that they remained rare and desirable. It therefore deserves to be considered in detail.

It is true that the Fermiers had numerous connections at Versailles, so that they could at least be sure of a hearing when they brought their grievances into the open. We know from surviving documents from the 1750s that they were in the habit of making expensive gifts to the intimates of the king in order to protect their monopoly of tax-gathering.[83] By the early 1760s they had close ties to the French establishment, of a personal and monetary kind. We know that one of the principal Fermiers, Jean-Joseph de Laborde, gave costly presents both to the duchesse de Choiseul (whose husband was successively Minister for War and Minister for the Navy in 1761-1762) and to Mme de Pompadour.[84] He was close enough, moreover, to the Contrôleur général Bertin to receive a letter of congratulation from him on the birth of his son in June 1761.[85] But as well as having friends in high places, the Fermiers were in a position to exert some influence themselves as suppliers of credit and loans. As Yves Durand concludes:

De ce gouvernement toujours à court de crédit, les fermiers peuvent infléchir les décisions en refusant ou en consentant les avances extraordinaires et les prêts qu'on est toujours tenté de leur demander. Leur carrière antérieure et les intérêts qu'ils conservent dans d'autres activités professionnelles sont des moyens d'étendre leur action, leurs possibilités, de trouver les appuis, les renseignements et le crédit [...] bon nombre de fermiers sont créanciers des grands.[86]

The evidence does show, then, that the Fermiers were well connected in the early 1760s and that, in various ways, they made it a practice to ingratiate themselves with those who were at the centre of power in the government of Louis XV, by giving and receiving presents and favours. When, in this context, we look at the bibliographical evidence provided

83. See James C. Riley, *The Seven Years War and the Old Regime in France* (Princeton, NJ, 1986), p.62-63.
84. See Durand, *Les Fermiers généraux*, p.536.
85. Durand, *Les Fermiers généraux*, p.537-38.
86. Durand, *Les Fermiers généraux*, p.95.

by the bindings on copies of the *Contes*, some potentially significant findings can be cited. In addition to the handful of copies reserved for members of the Compagnie,[87] and a dozen or so others in presentation bindings, whose owners cannot be established with any certainty,[88] at least two copies have survived in bindings bearing the arms of influential figures at court.[89] The marquis de Coislin, whose wife was a favourite of Louis XV, owned one copy. However, his arms, according to Cohen, may have been added to the binding at a later date, so it is not possible to say with certainty that he received his copy directly from the Compagnie in 1762.[90] The same author mentions (col.562) another copy, with the arms of the marquise de Pompadour, and this reference needs detailed consideration, because of her connections with the Fermiers at this time.

Until her death in 1764, the marquise remained *maîtresse en titre* to Louis XV; even if relations between the monarch and his mistress had by that time become less intimate, she continued to be an influential and significant figure at the court of Versailles.[91] She had long had close links with the Compagnie, and was thought to be the daughter of a Fermier, Le Normant de Tournehem. Whether or not this rumour was true, she was married in 1741 to his nephew Le Normant d'Etiolles, who himself became a Fermier in 1751. She is known to have helped individual members of the Compagnie on several occasions, and to have received its help in return. As Durand puts it, at the conclusion of a detailed study of the relationship between the marquise and the Fermiers:

Si Mme de Pompadour recevait l'aide de la finance, si, en cas de difficulté pour le gouvernement, elle sollicitait le crédit des financiers pour venir au secours du contrôle général, elle leur rendait également des services de recommandation et de protection. Elle possédait un réseau d'amis et de protégés, dont elle introduisait certains dans le cercle du Roi. Il n'est indifférent, ni pour l'histoire politique, ni pour l'histoire sociale, de savoir que parmi les convives du Roi dans les petits appartements ou dans les jardins aménagés par la marquise près de Trianon, il se trouvait des financiers au milieu de la noblesse de Cour traditionnelle.[92]

87. Cohen (*Guide de l'amateur de livres*, col.560-61) lists copies belonging to Seroux d'Agincourt and to M. de Beaujon; a third which belonged to Deschamps de Saint-Amand was offered by the Librairie Laurent Coulet, Paris, in September 1990 (Catalogue 8). The rarity of such identifiable copies weakens the assertion by Boissais and Deleplanque that the whole issue was intended for members of the Compagnie (*Les Livres à gravures*, p.101).

88. See Lacroix, 'Les *Contes* de La Fontaine', p.264.

89. All these groups may have been larger than the bibliographical evidence indicates.

90. Cohen, *Guide de l'amateur de livres*, col.563. On the marquis de Coislin, see the *Dictionnaire de biographie française*, ed. Jean-Charles Roman d'Amat *et al.* (Paris, 1929-), vol.9, p.166.

91. When Voltaire wanted to secure help for the widow of the Protestant Jean Calas, who had been unjustly done to death, he constantly referred to the need to involve Mme de Pompadour in the case. See his letters for 1762 in his correspondence (D10482-D10972, *passim*).

92. Durand, *Les Fermiers généraux*, p.76-77.

If the Fermiers did indeed offer copies of the *Contes* to a small number of influential figures at court, this would not have been a particularly odd procedure at that time. As Robert Darnton points out, it was a common practice for writers to offer printed copies of their works to powerful figures, in the hope of securing their patronage and protection.[93] Given the troubled history of the Compagnie at this period, it would have made sense to try to secure help against its enemies by flattering sympathetic and powerful figures in the king's entourage. This strategy might have appeared even more advantageous at a time when the authorities in charge of government and the book trade were unwilling to intervene on their behalf.

One could of course imagine a scenario in which the book's rarity and desirability could be enhanced in the eyes of its very select owners by ensuring that it could not readily fall into the hands of the *hoi polloi*. Nonetheless, this would have been to place an extraordinarily high value on the supposed influence of Mme de Pompadour. The Fermiers must have known that, if she was not unfriendly towards them, she was by no means hostile to the *philosophes* and to other groups with whom they were at odds.[94] It would also have meant that they were accepting that their heavy investment in what was to have been a commercial publication could not be realised, for fear of offending the marquise and (perhaps) a handful of other courtiers.

Despite the persistence of this view, outlined by Salomons and others, the crucial written evidence to confirm their belief has never turned up. One can hardly be surprised at this dearth of corroborative documentation: the Compagnie was unlikely to put its intentions on paper, or to leave incriminating proof of them. Yet, even in purely bibliographical terms, we have no evidence that the Fermiers presented a copy of the *Contes* to the marquise. Although the sale catalogue of her library, which was published in 1765, mentions three editions of La Fontaine's *Fables* (including the folio printing with the illustrations by Oudry),[95] it gives no indication that she owned *any* edition of his *Contes*. Hence, we cannot assert with confidence that she ever possessed a copy of the 1762 edition, let alone that one was presented to her.[96] It is unlikely that any editions of the *Contes* she might have possessed were made to disappear, or were

93. See 'A police inspector sorts his files', in Robert Darnton, *The Great cat massacre and other episodes in French cultural history* (Harmondsworth, 1984), p.163.

94. Pierre Gaxotte calls her 'l'Egérie des philosophes. Elle les pensionne, les loge, leur épargne les rigueurs du pouvoir, les pousse dans le monde et dans l'Etat' (*Le Siècle de Louis XV*, Paris, 1974, p.185).

95. *Catalogue des livres de la bibliothèque de feue Mme la marquise de Pompadour, dame du palais de la reine* (Paris, Hérissant, 1765). The three editions of the *Fables* (lots 685-87) are dated 1743, 1745 and 1755.

96. Two editions of the *Œuvres diverses* (1729 and 1744) are also mentioned in the catalogue (lots 683, 684), but they do not contain the *Contes* (see Rochambeau, *Bibliographie des œuvres de La Fontaine*, p.618-19).

discreetly withheld from sale to avoid causing embarrassment. The copy of her sale catalogue in the John Rylands University Library of Manchester contains in contemporary manuscript the prices of all the books auctioned from her library, as well as comments on those which were missing or which were withdrawn from sale. This latter category, comprising books marked 'retiré', includes Crébillon's *Tanzaï et Néadarné* (lot 1961), his *La Nuit et le moment* (lot 1972) and Diderot's *Les Bijoux indiscrets* (lot no. 2147). All of these works fell into the same 'risqué' category as the *Contes*, so that the need for discretion in respect of this one book is not apparent.

The copy bearing the arms of the marquise certainly existed, since its various owners can be traced through sales covering most of the nineteenth century. And yet, despite the fame which would naturally accrue to a copy of the *Contes* with such an illustrious provenance, its first recorded appearance, according to Cohen, is at a sale in 1829, some sixty-five years after her death.[97]. This long gap, as well as its absence from her sale catalogue, leads one to suspect that the Pompadour's arms, like those on the Coislin copy, may have been added later; at any rate, there is no proof of her direct ownership. There is thus no clear reason to suppose that the Fermiers withdrew or withheld the book from circulation in order to maintain its special status in the eyes of courtly recipients, because none can be identified with any certainty.

Even if we make the improbable assumption that this really was why the 1762 edition was withdrawn, it is hard to see why it should still have been withheld after the death of Pompadour in April 1764. Indeed, it remained unavailable, almost without a break, for some thirty years, until after the Compagnie des Fermiers généraux itself had ceased to exist. Ordinarily, it would have been quite contrary to the acute commercial instincts of the Fermiers to ignore the increasing demand for the work. But, beyond its initial distribution to a few booksellers in Paris, only a few copies were released on the market in the late 1760s, at a time when purchasers were clamouring (and paying high prices) even for the counterfeit editions, as we shall see. What is more, even assuming that the Fermiers' aim was to protect their interests in offering copies to favoured recipients, it would be hard to argue that they succeeded to any significant extent, in view of subsequent events.

The most significant of these arose from the controversy engendered in the early 1760s by the suggestion, from a variety of sources, that a single rate of tax paid directly to the crown should be levied throughout the

97. Cohen, *Guide de l'amateur de livres*, col.562. The copy was sold in 1934 at the dispersal of the collection of Henri Béraldi, and is the frontispiece to volume 6 of the sale catalogue. However, the Pompadour arms overlap with part of the elaborate dentelle decoration; as the armorial stamp used for her books existed in several versions and in several sizes, there would have been no reason for this carelessness to occur had the volume been decorated with her arms by the original binder.

kingdom of France. Vauban had vainly advocated such a system in his
*Dîme royale* in 1707, and while later attempts to revive the idea met with
no greater success, they did at least spark a lively debate. Among the
contributors to it was Antoine-Léonard Thomas, a man of letters and a
highly placed official at the foreign ministry. According to the *Mémoires
secrets*, Thomas's *Eloge de Sully*, which was crowned by the Académie
française in August 1763, was 'une satyre amère de l'Administration
actuelle' and the same source observes a few days later 'on n'a pas voulu
la laisser imprimer'.[98] The fact that the *Eloge* was published shortly
afterwards, with a genuine Parisian imprint, reveals that the Fermiers
were no more able in reality to suppress criticism at that time than before
the appearance of the *Contes* in 1762.

More damaging still to their interests was the financial controversy
which broke out in May 1763 with the appearance of Pierre-Philippe
Roussel de La Tour's *Richesse de l'Etat*,[99] which proposed a flat rate of
taxation on all those with sufficient means to pay. According to the
*Mémoires secrets* of 31 May, 'C'est une feuille in-4° qui se distribue gratis
[et qui] semble réunir tous ces avantages &, dans une forme si simple
qu'on ne peut assez s'étonner si le ministre ne l'adopte pas.'[100] As might
be expected, it sparked off a host of rejoinders, refutations and brochures.
Grimm reported on 15 July that: 'Il paraît tous les jours une feuille pour
ou contre ce projet.' He goes on:

C'est sans doute un grand inconvénient que tant de gens désœuvrés et fainéants se
mêlent d'écrire à tort et à travers, et de nous donner leurs rêves sur des choses
dont ils ne connaissent pas les premiers éléments. L'honnête et estimable avocat
Moreau [...] a le premier attaqué le système de M. Roussel, par des *Doutes
modestes*,[101] où il insiste principalement sur le danger de cette liberté avec laquelle
tout le monde imprime ses rêveries sur le bien public [...]. Il ne redoute ce danger
que pour les gens en place, qu'il trouve beaucoup trop doux de laisser examiner
leurs opérations par des écrivains sans vocation, et je conviens que les imbéciles et
les sots ont tout à craindre de la liberté de la presse; mais l'homme d'Etat qui
aura la conscience de ses talents et de ses forces la favorisera toujours; et, faisant
des criailleries des frondeurs le cas qu'elles méritent, il cherchera la récompense
de ses travaux dans l'hommage libre de quelques sages, qui devient tôt ou tard
l'arrêt du public et de la postérité.[102]

Grimm's ironic stance is notable not only for his hostility to Moreau, who
was then historiographer royal, and an old enemy of the *philosophes*, but

---

98. Louis-Petit de Bachaumont, *Mémoires secrets pour servir à l'histoire des lettres en France,
depuis MDCCLXII jusqu'à nos jours* [...], 36 vols (London, John Adamson, 1777-1789), 25
and 30 August 1763, vol.1, p.312, 324.

99. The work was reviewed at length in the *CL* of 1 July 1763.

100. *Mémoires secrets*, 31 May 1763, vol.1, p.259-60.

101. *Doutes modestes sur la richesse de l'Etat, ou Lettre écrite à l'auteur de ce système par un de ses
confrères*. This was an eight-page pamphlet, dated '13 juin 1763', and allegedly published
by 'B. Ruinart'.

102. *CL*, vol.5, p.332-33.

also because it underlines the danger to the administration represented by the unfettered discussion of France's fiscal structures at that time. The fact that Roussel's work could give rise to such heated and prolonged controversy was in itself an indication of widespread dissatisfaction with the tax regime administered by the Compagnie des Fermiers généraux. In the light of the *parlement*'s previous hostility to the Fermiers, it was not unimportant that Roussel himself was a member of it. Coming as it did at a time when, to pay for the war, a third *vingtième* was being imposed on the population,[103] and the capitation had been doubled for two years, this pamphlet summarised much of the current resentment against the inequities of the tax system. As one modern commentator observes:

*La richesse* affirmed the opinion of the Parlements that the tax system was excessively complicated and subject to the abuse of financiers. [...] Simple, concise, and initially circulated free of charge, the pamphlet became a sensation in the spring and summer of 1763 as newspapers and critics hailed its patriotism and clarity.[104]

The most prominent of the writings to which the proposal for a single rate of tax gave rise, later that year, was *L'Anti-financier, ou Relevé de quelques-unes des malversations dont se rendent journellement coupables les fermiers généraux* (1763), by the lawyer Edmé-François Darigrand. In arguing the case for a single tax, Darigrand was unsparing in his attacks on the greed and nefarious influence of the Compagnie. The following comments are typical of his approach:

Puisse l'heureuse révolution qui purgera la France du fléau des Financiers, être des glorieuses époques du règne de Louis le Bien-aimé! [...] Puisse le Dieu qui tient dans sa main le cœur des Rois, inspirer à notre Auguste Monarque le dessein de bannir de son Royaume le fléau des Financiers! Que par une déclaration de sa suprême volonté, il ordonne que l'on répartisse par chaque Corps & Communauté de son Royaume une somme totale d'imposition dont la collecte se fera sans frais, par ces même Corps & Communautés, qui en verseront le produit directement dans ses caisses.[105]

Though the Fermiers were able to secure Darigrand's detention in the Bastille, he gained much support, and his book in turn gave rise to a series of polemical tracts which further undermined the Compagnie's cause.[106]

---

103. As its name suggests, this was, at least theoretically, a tax of one-twentieth levied on income. In practice, it often became a tenth, and even a quarter. See Cobban, *A History of modern France*, vol.1, p.61-62.

104. Michael Kwass, *Privilege and the politics of taxation in eighteenth-century France: liberté, égalité, fiscalité* (Cambridge, 2000), p.220.

105. Edmé-François Darigrand, *L'Anti-financier, ou Relevé de quelques-unes des malversations dont se rendent journellement coupables les fermiers généraux* ('Amsterdam' [Paris], no pub., 1763), p.2, 93. Compare Riley, *The Seven Years War and the Old Regime*, p.217-18.

106. See also Durand, *Les Fermiers généraux*, p.432-34. The *Anti-financier* was widely read, and was reprinted at least twice in 1763-1764.

From this summary of events in 1763, it will be clear the Fermiers were now battling against a growing belief that the tax system of the country needed to be radically reformed, in a way which would put an end to the exploitation of the people, which they were accused of undertaking with almost indecent enthusiasm. Whether or not the changes to that system came about, it was evident that the system which they administered was now being criticised openly on a scale not previously seen, and might even be replaced by a more equitable form of taxation. It would therefore have been unwise to proclaim their own importance and their own values at a time when popular opinion was running strongly in favour of reform. Certainly, the continued marketing of the *Contes*, which had been at best a tentative operation even in 1762, could not now be regarded as prudent. Given the changes in public attitudes towards taxation which were widely manifest in 1763, the Fermiers had little choice but to act with caution. They therefore withdrew the edition from sale and, for greater security, ensured that it remained unobtainable, except for a short time and for reasons shrouded in mystery, for years afterwards.

These events mostly took place while Malesherbes was still Directeur de la Librairie. When he was succeeded in October 1763 by Antoine-Gabriel de Sartine, a police inspector who had a long history of acting against the authors and publishers of what he judged to be subversive works,[107] the Fermiers were able – belatedly – to exert greater influence in suppressing attacks against them. They had, after all, had a hand in securing his appointment to the post, a fact which in itself suggests that they saw the opportunity to strengthen the administrative hold over the publication of works to which they objected.[108] In January 1764 a play by Antoine Bret entitled *La Confiance trahie* was officially suspended at the Comédie-Française because several of its characters were suspected of being satirical portraits of well-known Fermiers. According to Grimm, 'On devait jouer ces jours-ci, sur le théâtre de la Comédie-Française, une comédie nouvelle intitulée la *Confiance trahie*, en vers et en cinq actes, par M. Bret; mais la police en a fait suspendre la représentation à cause de plusieurs personnalités satiriques dont elle est remplie contre les fermiers généraux.'[109]

Once Malesherbes had been replaced by Sartine, the Fermiers lost no time in getting the authorities to act; in 1762 and early in 1763, such an attempt would have had much less chance of bearing fruit, and none was reported. Yet, in March 1764, a royal decree forbade the publication of any work dealing with financial matters,[110] a step which in itself argues

107. See François Ravaisson, *Archives de la Bastille*, 17 vols (Paris, 1868-1881), especially vol.12.
108. See Durand, *Les Fermiers généraux*, p.96.
109. *CL*, vol.5, p.431; see also Durand, *Les Fermiers généraux*, p.415.
110. This was the *Déclaration du Roi, qui fait défenses d'imprimer, débiter, ou colporter aucuns écrits, ouvrages ou projets concernant la réforme de l'administration des finances*. See Durand, *Les*

that the administration and the Compagnie still had much to fear from their critics. Whatever temporary successes the Fermiers may have had in suppressing unwelcome comment, Caraccioli was able to write in 1768 that 'la mode est d'écrire contre les financiers, et cela ne sert qu'à entretenir des murmures et du mécontentement'.[111]

In the longer term, there was little likelihood that attacks on them would cease as a result of their endeavours. Such was the hatred of their methods that they had no realistic prospect of achieving their aim of preventing assaults on their reputation, even if they had gone to the trouble of distributing copies of the *Contes* to a few select recipients who had the royal ear. The attempt to control the spread of unwelcome publications was vigorous, but could only be at best partially successful, as the quantities of such writings increased. The tactics of the Fermiers in causing Sartine to act on their behalf, however useful for a short time, could not become a successful strategy. Their reputation was too tarnished, and their enemies too numerous, for their iniquities to be ignored, and the criticisms of them persisted, with growing force, until the Compagnie was dissolved in March 1791.[112]

To sum up what we have so far shown: if Mme de Pompadour and other courtiers did indeed possess copies of the *Contes* (and there is no direct evidence that they did), that fact did not noticeably help the Fermiers to achieve their ends. In fact, they were demonstrably unable to exert any significant influence against their enemies until Sartine took charge of the book trade. Even then, the Compagnie did not venture to market the work again, for fear of arousing hostility. Any attempt to explain the withdrawal of the edition on the basis that its enforced rarity would flatter its illustrious courtly recipients therefore looks unfounded. What is more, it is difficult to reconcile with what is known of the book's history, and particularly with the fact that it remained unavailable for many years.

If this explanation (and by extension, that of Vera Salomons) of why the *Contes* were withdrawn from sale is rejected, then other reasons must be found to account for the Fermiers' decision not to market it. When we look at the historical facts, the most cogent explanation lies in the widespread hostility to the tax system, and the growing clamour for a uniform rate of taxation, which surfaced in 1763. At some point, in the early months of 1763 in all probability, the Fermiers took the decision to suppress their edition. In the following pages, we shall examine its subsequent history in the light of the available evidence.

---

*Fermiers généraux*, p.434, and Keith Michael Baker, *Inventing the French Revolution* (Cambridge, 1990), p.170-71.

111. *Dictionnaire critique, pittoresque et sentencieux*, quoted by Durand, *Les Fermiers généraux*, p.432.

112. Durand, *Les Fermiers généraux*, p.622.

## v. The fate of the *Contes*

Once the 1762 edition ceased to be obtainable, anyone who wished to see what it contained had to make do with two pirated editions, issued respectively in 1764 and 1767,[113] and printed in Paris with reversed impressions of the plates.[114] Although we cannot say exactly when the 1762 edition was taken off the market, the fact that a counterfeit version was on sale as early as 1764 suggests that demand for the work was keen almost from the outset. In view of the time necessary to produce eighty new engravings, preparations for this latter edition must have begun rather earlier, probably in 1763. It is strange that the Fermiers continued to withhold the book from circulation when counterfeit editions (over which they had no control) were in demand. One can only suppose that their fear of public scorn remained so strong for some years that they would not risk making the work in its original form available at that time to please the rich bibliophiles who could afford it.

There are some signs that attempts were eventually made to put the work before the public, though here again matters are far from clear. The 1762 edition was made available again to the general public in 1767, when there appeared a very curious circular signed only by 'les éditeurs'; it is from this document that we can glean most of what we know about the early history of the edition. The circular offered provincial booksellers a large number of copies of the 1762 edition bound in calf, which could be supplied immediately from stock. The authors of the circular claimed that, as the edition had been issued without any bookseller's name on the title-page, and with an Amsterdam imprint, 'la Province n'a pas su à qui s'adresser pour en avoir'.[115]

This mysterious and very rare circular is puzzling. It is improbable (to say the least) that provincial booksellers would not have known whom to approach in order to obtain copies of books such as the *Contes*, which had been published in Paris only a few years before. The book trade in the Ancien régime was well used to dealing with subversive, clandestine or otherwise problematic works of all kinds (including many which were far more dangerous than a celebrated classic such as the *Contes*), and such publications were readily obtainable by those who knew where to find

113. See Cohen, *Guide de l'amateur de livres*, col.571, who calls the 1764 edition 'assez jolie'. In November 1767 Grimm referred to the new counterfeit edition in the *Correspondance littéraire*: 'On vient de faire une nouvelle édition des *Contes de La Fontaine*. Deux volumes petit in-12, avec grand nombre de figures, la plupart indécentes, et toutes mauvaises' (vol.7, p.490). Curiously, he makes no comment on the reasons why the 1762 edition had become unavailable, despite the obvious demand for it. There is no evidence that the Fermiers were involved in either of these editions.

114. The fact that they are reversed indicates that these editions were counterfeited, because the new engravings would have been traced directly on the originals, reversing the image when it was printed.

115. See [Maurice Pereire], 'Une circulaire du temps concernant l'édition des *Contes* de La Fontaine dite des Fermiers généraux', *Bulletin du bibliophile* (1922), p.272-75.

them.[116] Thus, if copies had been available before 1767, booksellers, who could obviously sell such a prestigious book for a high price, would certainly have traded them. The publication of two counterfeit editions within a few years is a more persuasive argument for the difficulty in obtaining copies of the 1762 *Contes* at this time than the alleged ignorance of provincial booksellers. While the circular gives some indication of how the edition was marketed, the truth behind this operation remains somewhat clouded, and we hear no more of the matter for another twenty-five years, until 1792.

In that year the Parisian bookseller Plassan published a prospectus for a new edition of the *Contes*. He made some use of the 1767 prospectus, and repeated the statement that provincial dealers had had great difficulty in obtaining the *Contes* prior to that year. More surprising is the assertion he then makes that the edition had again disappeared from the market at about that time, since he describes it as 'manquant absolument à la librairie depuis 1767' and 'séquestré depuis 1767 par des circonstances particulières'. He claims, indeed, that purchasers were deceived by the 1764 counterfeit edition, believing it to be the original, while others who wished to buy the true version 'ont été rebutés par les prix exhorbitants qu'on les payoit, même dans les ventes'.[117]

The implication of this extraordinary document is that the 1762 edition was very difficult to find not only before 1767, but afterwards as well, and indeed for most of the thirty years between its publication and the appearance of the prospectus in 1792. If what Plassan says is true, there could have been only a brief period in 1762-1763, and during 1767 (other than at auctions), when copies could be bought, before being withdrawn from the market again.

The point cannot be proved conclusively, yet there are good historical reasons for accepting Plassan's statement as reliable. First, there is the evidence of the nine copies seized at Panckoucke's shop, and the fact that few other booksellers had any copies. Second, in 1767 the market for high-quality illustrated books was buoyant. The appearance that year of a second counterfeit edition of the *Contes* showed that demand exceeded supply. What is more, the *Mémoires secrets* recorded on 10 October 1767 that Luneau de Boisjermain had recently announced the forthcoming publication of his edition of the works of Racine, which was to appear in 1768.[118] This edition was to be 'en série' with the *Contes*, so that it could sit alongside them on a bookshelf, and was to be richly illustrated by

---

116. See Darnton, *The Forbidden best-sellers, passim.*

117. Quoted by Cohen, *Guide de l'amateur de livres*, col.569-70, where the 1792 prospectus is reproduced in full. Lacroix ('Les *Contes* de La Fontaine', p.265-66) believes that Plassan was in error in stating that copies ceased to be available in 1767, and gives circumstantial reasons for believing that the correct date was 1777. However, the publication (subsequent to his article) of the 1767 circular undermines his argument.

118. *Mémoires secrets*, vol.3, p.275.

Gravelot, who also designed special decorative tools for use on the presentation bindings in which it (like the *Contes*) is sometimes found.[119] In 1767 too, the first of four quarto volumes of a translation of Ovid's *Metamorphoses* was issued, with splendid engravings by a number of celebrated artists, including Charles Eisen. This edition, which was not completed until 1771, was likewise intended to appeal to bibliophiles; it is often found richly bound in contemporary morocco, and a special pressing of only twelve copies was issued on large paper. Such was the demand for it that a second edition, using the same (by now rather worn) plates, was published at much the same time.[120] Circumstances were clearly favourable therefore to allow alert collectors of fine illustrated books a brief opportunity to acquire what had by then become a great prize, the Fermiers généraux edition of La Fontaine's *Contes et nouvelles en vers*.

Plassan's prospectus contains further, and very pertinent, revelations on the history of the *Contes* after their initial appearance in 1762. He states that 2000 sets of engravings had been printed for the edition, of which 1200 still remained unused some thirty years later: 'ayant trouvé douze cents de chaque figure de tirés, on a reconnu par la recherche et vérification des registres et papiers de comptabilité, trouvés dans le marché lors de l'acquisition, qu'il n'en avoit été vendus que huit cent exemplaires, et que les deux mille de figures ont été tirés de suite, et employés indistinctement, sans choix'.[121] This figure of 800 (which is crucial, as we have seen, to an understanding of the history of the edition) presumably includes an unknown number of the calf-bound copies referred to in the circular of 1767, though not all the copies made available at that time were bound in calf. Furthermore, some at least of those which were could not have retained their calf bindings for very long, since many have survived in expensive morocco bindings, in a style which is strictly of the period. Hence, some purchasers who were fortunate enough to acquire copies of the *Contes* during their brief availability in 1767 had them sumptuously bound or rebound to their taste, as a sign of their rarity and desirability.[122] What is more, even the counterfeit editions of 1764 and 1767 are not infrequently found in morocco bindings of the period, a fact which again shows the importance their owners attached to them.

The existence of a significant number of copies in costly contemporary bindings therefore supports the idea that the *Contes* were still much sought

119. See Cohen, *Guide de l'amateur de livres*, col.847-49, and Griffiths, *Prints for books*, p.53, note 41. Although both works are in octavo format, the volumes of the *Œuvres de Racine* are an inch or so taller than those of the *Contes* so that, in this respect at least, they are not 'en série'.

120. See Cohen, *Guide de l'amateur de livres*, col.769-72. The second printing, dated 1767-1770, is of poorer quality than the first.

121. Cohen, *Guide de l'amateur de livres*, col.570.

122. Copies of the *Contes* are also known with a 'dos maroquiné'; that is, the original calf spines have been covered in morocco while the remainder of the binding has been left untouched; this is the case with the Saint-Amand copy referred to above in note 87.

after in the late 1760s, and that they had lost none of their appeal. This contention is strengthened by the fact that a third counterfeit edition (again with the plates in reversed impressions) appeared in 1777, some copies of which were produced on large paper in quarto format.[123] Hence, even ten years later, there was still a demand for the work which could not be satisfied by the 800 or so copies of the original then in circulation.[124]

Against this background, Plassan's ambition to cater for collectors wishing to acquire copies of the *Contes* becomes understandable. His 1792 edition consisted of a page-by-page reprint of the 1762 text, into which were inserted copies of the original engravings left over from that time.[125] Although all the plates had been printed in one sequence, the edition of 1762 had, he asserted, chiefly used those from the second thousand. As they would necessarily be less sharp than the impressions pulled from plates at the beginning of the print-run, the clear implication was that purchasers of his edition could obtain the illustrations in proofs superior in many cases to those of the original edition.

It is impossible to verify every detail of Plassan's prospectus, and in particular to offer any more exact information than is set out above on the 'circonstances particulières' to which he refers in order to explain the rarity of the 1762 edition. However, his claim that the engravings used for his 1792 reprint are from the same stock as those of the original is demonstrably true, and comparisons between copies of the two editions fully support his contention that they are in no way inferior in quality.[126] Insofar as his story can be checked, therefore, Plassan was telling the truth. His statement raises another question too. If 2000 copies of the plates, and only 800 copies of the text, had been printed, the Fermiers presumably intended to use only the best of the plates for the copies of the work which they wished to offer. The fact that so many high-quality copies of the engravings remained unused until Plassan acquired them suggests that further complications arose in the publication of the edition, to the nature of which there is regrettably no clue.[127]

123. For a description, see Cohen, *Guide de l'amateur de livres*, col.571-72.

124. In 1795 yet another illustrated version of the *Contes* appeared, with plates by Fragonard. It was not a success, the number of buyers for such works having been much diminished by the Terror; again, the taste of the times was more focused on sober neo-classical designs. See Cohen, *Guide de l'amateur de livres*, col.574-82.

125. Plassan also acquired some of the unillustrated copies of the 1762 edition referred to above in note 74; into them he inserted the plates, together with reprints of the culs-de-lampe (see Rochambeau, *Bibliographie des œuvres de La Fontaine*, p.524, no. 78, and Hédé-Haüy, *Les Illustrations des Contes de La Fontaine*, p.28).

126. 'Les figures [en 1792] peuvent être aussi bonnes que dans les exemplaires de 1762' (Cohen, *Guide de l'amateur de livres*, col.573). The plates in both editions are on identical unwatermarked paper with vertical chain-lines.

127. Several other editions which appeared in the 1790s and at the start of the nineteenth century also used the (increasingly worn) 1762 plates. For the details, see Hédé-Haüy, *Les Illustrations des Contes de La Fontaine*, p.58-62.

The political climate in which the Fermiers pursued their activities was distinctly hostile to them in the years before the appearance of the *Contes*, and became more adverse still in the years which followed. Even though, for much of the 1760s and beyond, they still had to endure a tide of criticism, their edition rapidly became a desirable and sought-after book in the eyes of collectors. Thus it was that some members of that same public which roundly condemned the Fermiers for the callous brutality with which they enforced their will as tax-gatherers, rushed to acquire copies of their edition of the *Contes* on the rare occasions when they were given the opportunity to do so. To help us understand why this edition was so much in demand, something needs to be said about the earlier editions of the work, to provide a context for that of the Fermiers.

## vi. Editions of the *Contes* before 1762

The first work by La Fontaine to contain texts which appear in the later editions of the *Contes* was the *Nouvelles en vers tirées de Bocace et de l'Arioste. Par M. de L. F.*, which appeared early in 1665. Published in Paris by Claude Barbin with an *achevé d'imprimer* of 10 December 1664, it contained only three works, 'Le cocu battu et content', 'Joconde ou l'infidélité des femmes' and 'La matrone d'Ephèse'. This first printing of a few *Contes* is extremely hard to find,[128] and the earliest version now obtainable in practice is the *Contes et nouvelles en vers de M. de La Fontaine*, which, like the first, was published by Barbin, with an *achevé d'imprimer* of 10 January 1665. This was not a mere reprint of the first edition, since it contained twelve *contes* in all, as well as a *Ballade* and an *Envoy*. Even at this early stage in their history, the growing reputation and commercial success of the *Contes* is indicated by the appearance of a (poorly printed) counterfeit edition of the same year.[129] Clearly encouraged, La Fontaine published another thirteen *contes* in 1666,[130] in the *Deuxiesme partie des Contes et nouvelles en vers*; like its predecessors, this volume was printed by Barbin, with an *achevé d'imprimer* dated 30 October 1665. The first two parts of the *Contes et nouvelles en vers* were reprinted in 1669, with four new *contes*,[131] and a *Troisième partie* was issued in 1671 with thirteen new additions. In 1674 there appeared a volume entitled *Nouveaux Contes de Monsieur de La Fontaine*, containing seventeen new pieces. Unlike the three previous parts, it was published without a royal *privilège*, and bore the fictitious im-

---

128. See Rochambeau, *Bibliographie des œuvres de La Fontaine*, p.503.
129. See Rochambeau, *Bibliographie des œuvres de La Fontaine*, p.503-504, no.2.
130. The title-page is erroneously dated 'M. DC. XLVI.'
131. Two pirated editions printed in the Netherlands had already appeared in 1668 and 1669, containing *inter alia* a fragment of 'La coupe enchantée'; their appearance led La Fontaine, as he tells us in the preface, to publish the 1669 edition before it was properly finished.

print 'A Mons, chez Gaspar Migeon Imprimeur'. The *Nouveaux Contes* were refused a *privilège* in 1674 on the grounds that the work contained, in the words of the police inspector La Reynie (who was writing in 1675), 'des termes indiscrets et malhonnêtes' which might 'corrompre les bonnes mœurs et [...] inspirer le libertinage'. Copies were to be seized and confiscated by the police; anyone selling the work was threatened with 'les peines portées par les ordonnances'.[132]

So great and immediate was the impact of the attitudes expressed in the *Contes* that, as early as the *Préface* to the 1665 edition, La Fontaine felt it necessary to defend himself against accusations of misogyny: 'on aurait raison, si je parlais sérieusement; mais qui ne voit que ceci est jeu, et par conséquent ne peut porter coup?' He then responds to the accusation that he paints an untrue picture of life:

On me peut encore objecter que ces contes ne sont pas fondés, ou qu'ils ont partout un fondement aisé à détruire, enfin qu'il y a des absurdités, et pas la moindre teinture de vraisemblance. Je réponds en peu de mots que j'ai mes garants; et puis ce n'est ni le vrai ni le vraisemblable qui font la beauté et la grâce de ces choses-ci; c'est seulement la manière de les conter.[133]

There is an inconsistency here in arguing both that the presentation of women is not intended to be taken seriously, and that the reader is indeed offered a true picture of life ('j'ai mes garants'). La Fontaine's readiness to maintain both positions simultaneously may be evidence of negligence on his part, but since the wording remained unchanged in later editions, it suggests that he did wish to rebut the accusations which he mentions. Certainly, they sum up much of what was held to be objectionable in the *Contes* both in his own time and later. It is hard to see why these criticisms should have been aired so frequently if readers, whether hostile or otherwise, did not feel that there was more than a grain of truth in the picture of life which they presented. That picture is largely cynical, and allows little place for human virtue. Rather like La Rochefoucauld in his *Maximes* (1665), which are exactly contemporary with the earliest of the *Contes*, La Fontaine revealed the hidden motivations and secret conduct of human beings.[134] Even so, while he was never officially punished for publishing the *Contes*, towards the end of his life La Fontaine is reported to have expressed regret for having written them.[135]

132. See the *Œuvres complètes de La Fontaine*, ed. Jean-Pierre Collinet (Paris, 1991), p.1333-34, for further details. This edition is hereafter designated *OCLF*.

133. *OCLF*, p.557.

134. The two authors were well acquainted, and moved in the same social and intellectual circles. La Fontaine dedicated to La Rochefoucauld Fable XIV of Book X, claiming that the dedicatee had given him the subject of the narrative. See *OCLF*, p.418-20.

135. Charles Perrault, who knew La Fontaine, said that he was ashamed of the *Contes*, and 'le repentir qu'il en a fait paroistre pendant les deux ou trois dernieres années de sa vie a esté trop sincere pour n'en rien dire' (*La Vie des hommes illustres qui ont paru en France pendant ce siècle*, 2 vols, Paris, Dezallier, 1696, vol.1, p.84).

Yet despite their questionable view of human conduct, the *Contes* as a whole continued to be in demand; the first collected edition, with vignettes by Romeyn de Hooghe, was published in 1685. It was in many respects the most important of the editions to have appeared up to that time. A comparison of the editions published before it with those which appeared afterwards shows that the order of the individual *contes* was changed considerably for the edition, and this new arrangement persisted subsequently. Virtually all the editions published in the eighteenth century follow that of 1685 which, according to Rochambeau, was 'mal imprimée, et incomplète, faite sans la participation de l'auteur'.[136] For the sake of balance, the publisher, Henri Desbordes of Amsterdam, indicated in the preface that he had taken it upon himself to divide the two volumes equally, to give twenty-nine *contes* in each, inaugurating a radical departure from previous practice. The result was that several texts included in earlier editions disappeared altogether, and that the order of the *contes* in subsequent editions (including that of 1762) is quite different from that of their first appearance in separate volumes.[137]

To take only a few examples: although the three *contes* making up the *editio princeps* of 1665 were included in the first volume of most eighteenth-century editions, the first two are placed in reverse order, while the third is placed nineteenth in the thirty works which comprise that volume. In the *Troisième partie* of 1671, 'Les oies de frère Philippe' is followed by 'La mandragore' and by 'Les Rémois'. In the eighteenth-century editions, it is placed at the start of volume 2, but the other two poems are separated from it by eight other works which originally appeared in one or other of the first two parts. Variations occurred from time to time in one edition or another,[138] but the tone for eighteenth-century printings was set by the Desbordes edition published in Amsterdam in 1718. This added at the end of the second volume an epitaph for La Fontaine, and seven *contes* by other hands, namely 'Le contrat', 'Les quiproquo', 'La couturière', 'Le Gascon', 'La cruche', 'Promettre est un, et tenir est un autre' and 'Le rossignol'.[139] These additions were retained in virtually all eighteenth-century reprints of the work, including the 1762 edition.

Any specific structural coherence which La Fontaine may have intended the *Contes* to convey was undercut by these changes, which were retained in many reprints until the nineteenth century. While these alterations to the order of the *Contes* may not have bothered readers

---

136. Rochambeau, *Bibliographie des œuvres de La Fontaine* p.511, no.28.

137. Notably *Le Différend de beaux yeux et de belle bouche, imitation d'un livre intitulé 'Les Arrêts d'amours'* and *Les Amours de Mars et de Vénus*.

138. An edition of 1709 (Rochambeau, *Bibliographie des œuvres de La Fontaine*, no. 47) contains five *contes* which were not included in later editions. The edition of 1731 used in the present study (Rochambeau, *Bibliographie des œuvres de La Fontaine*, p.519, no.59) contains 'Le coup de corne', which was apparently not reprinted.

139. See Rochambeau, *Bibliographie des œuvres de La Fontaine*, p.516-17, no. 50.

unduly, the marketing of the work was undoubtedly influenced by its somewhat equivocal reputation. The reproofs which La Reynie had expressed long before continued to echo with critics in the following century, when it was not widely regarded in any way exemplary or admirable. Thus, the author of the anonymous *Vie de La Fontaine* prefixed to the 1745 edition of the *Contes* asserts 'Jamais homme n'écrivit avec plus de graces, plus de douceur, plus de naturel, plus de finesse & plus de facilité' (vol.1, p.xi). He goes on to add: 'On est cependant obligé de dire qu'il ne met pas toujours la dernière main à un Ouvrage, qu'il est quelquefois négligé, & qu'il se trouve dans cet excellent Auteur des vices de construction & quelques défauts de langage' (vol.1, p.xii). In his *Siècle de Louis XIV* (1751), Voltaire came to a similar conclusion, calling the poet 'admirable dans son genre quoique négligé et inégal'.[140] Writing in the *Correspondance littéraire* in 1755, Grimm is more indulgent, but still somewhat ambivalent: 'La Fontaine, tout libertin qu'il est, est toujours délicat, et ne blesse jamais l'imagination par des peintures trop choquantes.'[141] Even the *Vie de La Fontaine* by Diderot which prefaces the Fermiers généraux edition scarcely makes more than a passing reference to his 'génie', and is largely a recital of the bare facts of his life (vol.1, p.iii-vi). Overall, it is not easy to find any more detailed analysis of La Fontaine's work at this time, and the comments on it relate mostly to the *Fables*, rather than to the *Contes*.[142]

Their equivocal standing is reflected in material terms too. In his bibliography of La Fontaine, Rochambeau lists nearly forty editions of the *Contes* published between 1700 and 1762; in the same period there appeared some fifty-six editions of the *Fables*.[143] Many in this latter group carried a Paris imprint, and stated that they were published with official blessing in the form of a *privilège* and sometimes an approbation as well. Indeed, the great four-volume folio edition of the *Fables* (1755-1759), with their 275 plates based on designs by Jean-Baptiste Oudry, was largely financed by the Fermiers, and its publisher Montenault obtained a *privilège* for the work.[144] However, this is not the case for *any* of the editions of the *Contes* published during this period, although a number (including that of 1762) are demonstrably of Parisian origin. The work continued therefore to be regarded as somewhat controversial, at least as far as its content was concerned, even though it was not officially condemned at

---

140. Voltaire, *Le Siècle de Louis XIV*, 2 vols (Berlin, 1751), vol.2, p.376.

141. *CL*, vol.3, p.199.

142. Notably, Rousseau's disparaging comments on some of the *Fables* in Book II of *Emile* (1762).

143. See also Rochambeau, *Bibliographie des œuvres de La Fontaine*, p.514-24 for the editions of the *Contes*, and p.19-36 for the editions of the *Fables*.

144. His letter to Malesherbes is dated 15 March 1752 (BNF n.a.f. 3345, f.402-403). The *privilège* was granted on 5 June 1759, when the last of the four volumes appeared.

any point during the century.[145] That reputation has continued to our own day, and the *Contes* are still much less often reprinted or studied than the *Fables*.[146]

This bibliographical history contrasts however with the obvious enthusiasm for the 1762 edition which was manifest as soon as it appeared, and which has remained undimmed to the present time. It would have been perfectly possible for the Fermiers to market an unillustrated edition; as we noted earlier, copies without the plates did exist, though they were uncommon, and were not remarked on either at the time or afterwards. The only feature of their edition which distinguished it significantly from its predecessors was its illustrations, and it is the illustrations which explain its success. To understand why the Fermiers' edition was so much in demand, we need to consider not only the engravings themselves (as we shall do in the second and third chapters of this study), but the nature of the illustrated editions of the *Contes* prior to that of 1762. An analysis of these editions will enable us to see both the traditions within which the Fermiers were operating in commissioning the engravings from Eisen, and the distinctive nature of his work.

## vii. Illustrated editions of the *Contes* before 1762

When we consider the ways in which the *Contes* had been illustrated before 1762, the interpretations offered by artists seem to have provoked little controversy; such observations as we do find are technical rather than moral.[147] Rochambeau lists seventy-seven editions, reprints or reissues of the work published between 1665 and 1757.[148] Of these, sixteen contain some or all of the engravings by Romeyn de Hooghe which appeared in the very first illustrated edition in 1685, and which, with some alterations, continued to be used until 1737.[149] These engravings were conceived

---

145. It does not occur in the list of the books condemned by the secular authorities between 1715 and 1789 given in Rocquain, *L'Esprit révolutionnaire*, p.514-25.

146. Reactions to the *Contes* in the nineteenth century are discussed by Catherine Grisé, 'Le jeu de l'imitation: un aspect de la réception des *Contes* de La Fontaine', *Papers on French seventeenth-century literature* 10:18 (1983), p.249-62. Surveying reactions to the work up to the mid-twentieth century, John Lapp concludes that the *Contes* 'have fared ill at the hands of critics' (*The Esthetics of negligence: La Fontaine's Contes*, Cambridge, 1971, p.vii). Lapp himself concludes (p.33) 'there is no gainsaying that they are scabrous'. Less censorious is Gilles E. de La Fontaine, *La Fontaine dans ses Contes* (Sherbrooke, 1978), p.10-15.

147. Full details of all the previous illustrated editions of the *Contes* are given by Hédé-Haüy, *Les Illustrations des Contes de La Fontaine*, p.11-26.

148. Rochambeau, *Bibliographie des œuvres de La Fontaine*, p.503-24.

149. In the edition of 1737 listed by Rochambeau (*Bibliographie des œuvres de La Fontaine*, p.521, no. 66), only the frontispiece is by De Hooghe; the illustrations are of unknown provenance, a fact which may indicate that the publishers no longer believed that his work would enhance the edition. The edition used for reference to De Hooghe's work in this study is the two-volume 'Amsterdam' reprint of 1732, bearing the address 'Chez N. Etienne Lucas' (see Rochambeau, *Bibliographie des œuvres de La Fontaine*, p.520, no. 62).

primarily as embellishments to the text, so that many of the editions in which they were used proclaim on their title-pages that they are 'enrichie de Tailles-Douces dessinées par M. Romain de Hooge'. It was De Hooghe's prestige, with its implications of high artistic quality, which mattered more than the actual subject matter of the engravings.[150] While his work was long admired for its skill, it remained firmly in the sober baroque tradition of Dutch engraving of the seventeenth century. Indeed, in virtually every case, his illustrations occlude the erotic or 'improper' aspects of the stories, and present a largely innocuous, unexceptionable rendering of scenes from the text. Consequently, there was little in them to reflect the Gallic *joie de vivre* for which the *Contes* themselves were celebrated, and of which La Reynie and others had long complained. With the passage of time, De Hooghe's work came gradually to seem rather antiquated, and to underplay the qualities which made the *Contes* so much the subject of controversy. In addition, by the 1750s, his personal and professional reputation no longer stood as high as it once had. In the article 'Graveur' (1757) in the *Encyclopédie*, Jaucourt observes (vol.7, p.870): '*Romain de Hooge*, hollandois, a terni ses talens par la corruption de son cœur; on lui reproche encore l'incorrection du Dessein, & le goût des sujets allégoriques ou d'une satyre triviale.'[151]

The first significant departure from the De Hooghe tradition came in 1743, with the publication (in Paris, despite its 'Amsterdam' imprint) of an edition with headpieces by Charles-Nicolas Cochin (known as 'Cochin fils' to distinguish him from his father).[152] Comments made at the time suggest that Cochin was primarily noted for his elegance as an engraver, rather than for the daring with which he approached his task. In 1749 the abbé Raynal declared in the *Nouvelles littéraires*: 'Le sieur Cochin est très supérieur en ce genre à tous les autres par l'esprit qu'il met dans tous ses ouvrages, par l'élégance et la gentillesse de ses inventions, par les savants effets du clair-obscur qu'il entend parfaitement, enfin par

150. Gordon Ray's comment, apropos the characters in De Hooghe's illustrations for the *Cent Nouvelles nouvelles* of 1701, that 'If there is nothing subtle about their behavior, neither is there anything feeble' (*The Art of the French illustrated book*, p.4) would apply equally well to his work for the *Contes*.

151. The critical disdain for the baroque was to continue until relatively recent times. In 1951 Philip Hofer described the period as 'nearly wholly neglected', a fate which he attributes to its being 'varied and baffling' (*Baroque book illustration: a short survey from the collection in the Department of graphic arts Harvard College library*, Cambridge, MA, 1951, p.3).

152. See Cohen, *Guide de l'amateur de livres*, col.555-56, Rochambeau, *Bibliographie des œuvres de La Fontaine*, p.522, no. 71, and Hédé-Haüy, *Les Illustrations des Contes de La Fontaine*, p.22-23. The 1743 edition was reissued in 1745 with a re-dated title-page; it is to this latter issue that reference is made throughout this study. It differs slightly from the 1743 edition, in that three of Cochin's headpieces were replaced by designs provided by the artist Lancret and engraved by Larmessin. See Rochambeau, *Bibliographie des œuvres de La Fontaine*, p.522, no.71, and Christian Michel, *Charles-Nicolas Cochin et le livre illustré au XVIIIᵉ siècle, avec un catalogue raisonné des livres illustrés par Cochin, 1735-1790* (Geneva, 1987). In his standard critical study of the artist, *Charles-Nicolas Cochin et l'art des Lumières* (Rome, 1993), Michel makes no mention of his work on the *Contes*.

l'agrément inexprimable de tout ce qui sort de ses mains.'[153] The elegance and finish of Cochin's designs which Raynal singles out for praise are evident in his headpieces for the *Contes*, which must have seemed much more in tune with the taste of the times than the (by then somewhat old-fashioned) engravings of Romeyn de Hooghe. However, while this version was reissued in 1745 with a new title-page and minor changes, Cochin's engravings did not prove as successful as those of De Hooghe. Its life was extended only by the publication in 1755 of a badly printed 'Amsterdam' edition with anonymous full-page engravings based loosely on Cochin's designs.[154] Like those of De Hooghe, Cochin's illustrations are largely innocuous, eschewing bawdiness or excess, and concentrating on the human or the dramatic as sources of interest for the viewer.

These previous attempts to illustrate the *Contes* certainly influenced Eisen, if only negatively, in the work which he carried out for the Fermiers, though some parallels between his engravings and those of De Hooghe and Cochin can sometimes be discerned. In the latter case, the 1755 edition, which has little intrinsic merit, was demonstrably the source for some of his (rejected) initial attempts at illustrating the *Contes*.[155] The editions of 1745 and 1755 will be used throughout this study to situate the 1762 *Contes* in relation to previous interpretations of the stories.[156] Although the culs-de-lampe designed by Choffard for this edition are sometimes very ornate, their importance in a study of this kind is marginal, and they do not reflect the same tendencies or preoccupations as the plates. As a contemporary critic noted, their function is essentially emblematic, in that they use standard symbols to reinforce the moral of the *conte*,[157] without adding anything to the interpretation of the text.

This early bibliographical history of the *Contes et nouvelles en vers* shows, then, that there was something of a gap in the market in the 1750s. No edition was available with full-page plates of a quality likely to appeal to connoisseurs at that time; this consideration was not lost on the Fermiers. Hence, they now had the opportunity to stamp a distinctive identity on

153. The text is reproduced in the *CL* (vol.1, p.363).

154. Three volumes, in-8° (Rochambeau, *Bibliographie des œuvres de La Fontaine*, p.523, no. 75). Although neither Rochambeau nor Hédé-Haüy (*Les Illustrations des Contes de La Fontaine*, p.25) contests the 'Amsterdam' imprint, its typographical ornaments and conventions suggest Lyon as the most likely place of origin for the edition. It is extremely rare, and seems to have passed unnoticed. It was reissued, with a new title-page, in 1762. The third volume contains a number of texts not by La Fontaine.

155. It is obvious from the suppressed versions of plates contained in the Grenville copy of the 1762 *Contes* in the BL that the 1755 edition was the direct source of some of Eisen's illustrations when he first set about his task (see chapters 2 and 3 below).

156. There are useful comments on the subject in Lapp, *The Esthetics of negligence*; in *OCLF*, vol.1; and in Nicolich, 'Seventeenth and eighteenth-century illustrations for La Fontaine's *Contes et nouvelles en vers*'.

157. For example, 'Les ornemens de ce volume [1] sont terminés par le cul-de-lampe de la dissertation sur la *Joconde*, où l'on voit des grenouilles croassant après les attributs de la Poësie, vrai symbole des mauvais critiques' (*Mercure de France*, January 1763, vol.1, p.142).

their edition because the cultural climate of the time encouraged the production of fine books. In addition to those mentioned earlier, it is particularly noteworthy that in 1757, a luxuriously illustrated edition of Boccaccio's *Il Decamerone* in five volumes had been published in Paris, a French translation of which, using the same engravings, had been issued between 1757 and 1761.[158] Charles Eisen had contributed eleven of the 110 engravings with which it was embellished. No fewer than twelve of the *Contes* were acknowledged by La Fontaine as borrowings from Boccaccio,[159] though none of the episodes which he had used was illustrated by Eisen for the *Decamerone*. In the rare instances where there is some similarity of approach in subject matter (as in 'Richard Minutolo' and 'Mazet de Lamporechio'), the Fermiers took care to ensure that their engraving for the story was no mere copy of the corresponding plate in the *Decamerone*, but had its own distinctive features. It was obviously important to them to show that their edition had its own identity, and that its illustrations should not be thought of simply as approximate copies of previous engravings, whether by De Hooghe or Cochin, Gravelot, or Eisen himself. From the Fermiers' point of view, then, the way was open for them to provide recognisably distinct engravings for their edition, and they took full advantage of the opportunity.

In whatever format they were to appear, the *Contes* would be seen as an accompaniment to the edition of the *Fables* which the Fermiers had financed, and the existence of the two editions is evidence that they were undoubtedly alert to the contemporary taste for fine printing. As Montenault, the publisher of the *Fables*, explained in his *Avertissement*, the letterpress and the engravings had been printed separately 'afin que l'une & l'autre conservassent, à part & entr'elles, cette uniformité & cette bonne harmonie qu'on doit toujours rechercher dans les ouvrages de goût'.[160]

In addition, Mme de Pompadour was sufficiently interested in fine books to arrange, in 1760, for a small number of copies of Corneille's *Rodogune* to be printed at Versailles. For this edition, she herself etched the frontispiece, from a design by Boucher which was retouched by Cochin.[161] In 1761 she provided another engraving for the *Voyage de Mme et de Mme Victoire*, which was likewise printed in only a few copies.[162] Hence, at a time when the Compagnie wanted to assert its belief in its values and

158. For details of these two editions, see Cohen, *Guide de l'amateur de livres*, col.158-60, and Ray, *The Art of the French illustrated book*, p.39-41. The book was chiefly illustrated by Gravelot.

159. 'Le cocu battu et content', 'Le muletier', 'La gageure des trois commères', 'Le calendrier des vieillards', 'A femme avare galant escroc', 'Le faucon', 'Les oies de frère Philippe', 'Richard Minutolo', 'Le berceau', 'L'hermite', 'Mazet de Lamporechio', 'Le faiseur d'oreilles et le raccommodeur de moules'.

160. *Fables de La Fontaine*, 4 vols (Paris, Desaint & Saillant, Durand, 1755-1759), vol.1, p.vii.

161. For the details of *Rodogune*, which bears the imprint 'Au Nord', see Ray, *The Art of the French illustrated book*, p.24, and Cohen, *Guide de l'amateur de livres*, col.257-58.

162. See Cohen, *Guide de l'amateur de livres*, col.151.

activities, the cultural climate was extraordinarily propitious for the publication of finely illustrated books. It was no part of the Fermiers' plan to produce a scholarly version of the work, and their edition, which had no footnotes or other learned apparatus, adopted the common practice of following the text of 1685, with the additions of 1718. Instead of revising them, they sought to present the *Contes* in a form which was intended above all as a luxurious example of book production, embellished with engravings which would surpass anything seen in previous editions of the work.

While these considerations are important for the circumstantial evidence which they offer as a background to the publication of the 1762 *Contes*, there is another consideration too, and it lies in the values and attitudes for which the work had long been famous (or notorious, according to taste). Their *esprit gaulois*, which was noted from their first appearance, and which manifested itself particularly in their sceptical attitude towards the virtue of women and the honesty of men, was central to their reputation, and took many forms.[163] La Fontaine rejects the notion that monks and nuns are necessarily more spiritual than men and women who do not claim to lead pure lives; adultery is accepted as almost inseparable from marriage; social outcasts such as prostitutes are redeemed, and ordinary human vices and misdemeanours are usually committed with impunity.[164] In addition, the *Contes* repeatedly demonstrate that the clever triumph over the stupid in all walks of life, that greed is a common human failing, and that principles must often be sacrificed to expediency in the interests of self-preservation.

La Fontaine's insistence, in the 'Préface' of 1665, that such views represented a true reflection of human failings provided a comforting prospect for the Fermiers, who were often criticised by contemporaries as though they alone exhibited moral shortcomings, or were more given to vice and sin than others. The realism (or cynicism) of the *Contes* exerted a strong appeal on a corporation which believed in its own importance and its own values. Nor did the Fermiers take kindly to being criticised for their conduct by agencies such as the *parlement*, and particularly the *philosophes*, whose hostility was based on an assumption of moral superiority which their actions, it was often alleged, did little to justify.[165]

163. In the *Discours aux Welches* (1764), Voltaire writes: 'Le grand défaut peut-être des contes de La Fontaine est qu'ils roulent presque tous sur le même sujet: c'est toujours une fille ou une femme dont on vient à bout' (*Œuvres complètes de Voltaire*, ed. Louis Moland, 52 vols, Paris, 1877-1885, vol.25, p.259).

164. Ran E. Hong notes Tzvetan Todorov's observation, apropos the *Decamerone*, that misdeeds are rarely punished, and remarks that the same is true of the *Contes* ('La réécriture de deux *contes* de La Fontaine', *Papers on French seventeenth-century literature* 27:53, 2000, p.473-87, p.474).

165. By quoting selectively, the enemies of the *philosophes* could easily depict them collectively as immoral. Thus, in his *Catéchisme des Cacouacs* ('A Cacopolis', 1758), the abbé de Saint-Cyr was able to allege (p.63) that they regarded morality as a 'science frivole' by

While the *Contes* therefore embodied attitudes and beliefs which the Fermiers could use to retaliate against their attackers, the most distinctive way of doing so was through the engravings which they decided to commission for the edition. As we shall argue in the later sections of this study, the illustrations are the most important feature of the 1762 edition not only because of their technical quality, but because they embody the *Weltanschauung* of the Fermiers. Their world-view, in fact, coincided in many essentials with the view of the world and of human behaviour embodied in the *Contes*. But before we embark on an analysis of the engravings, it is appropriate to set the scene at this point by considering how and why they came to be as they are.

## viii. The genesis of the illustrations

While our knowledge of the origins of the 1762 edition is by no means complete, we do know a little at least of the circumstances in which it was published. As was often the case, the 'Amsterdam' imprint concealed the identity of a Parisian publisher, in this instance Joseph-Gérard Barbou, a member of one of the most respected book-selling families in Paris.[166] Barbou enjoyed a solid reputation as the publisher of, among other things, the series of Latin classics initiated by his uncle Jean-Joseph, and he took good care to keep on the right side of the authorities overseeing the book trade by bringing out works to which nobody could reasonably take exception. In August 1759, for example, he had obtained a *privilège* to publish an edition of Quintus-Curtius translated by Vaugelas, and in 1762 he had secured the right to publish an edition of Cicero and a French grammar book.[167] In that same year he had also published, with official approval, an edition of Ovid in Latin, which the (often censorious) *Journal de Trévoux* had reviewed in strikingly fulsome terms: 'Chaque Volume est orné d'une Estampe & d'une vignette gravées sur les dessins de M. Eisen. Cette production Typographique [...] fera recueillir de nouveau au sieur Barbou les applaudissemens de la République des Lettres.'[168] This comment is all the more significant in providing evidence that, at much the same time as La Fontaine's *Contes* appeared, Barbou and Eisen were jointly involved in another prestigious and successful publishing venture. It is not possible to say whether the link between the two works goes any deeper than this. Even so, it does at least seem that

citing a single passage from *De l'esprit*. On the 'Cacouac' pamphlets, see Gerhardt Stenger, *L'Affaire des Cacouacs* (Saint-Etienne, 2003).

166. See Paul Ducourtieux, *Comment on devenait libraire à Paris au XVIIIe siècle: les Barbou de Paris* (Paris, 1897).

167. See d'Hémery's *Journal* for 14 August 1759 and 16 August 1762 (BNF mss. fr. 24416, f.83).

168. *Journal de Trévoux*, 265 vols (Lyon, Paris, Trévoux, 1701-1767), July 1762, p.1887.

the Fermiers took great care to select for the *Contes* a publisher and an artist whose work had recently found favour even with the traditionally caustic reviewers of the *Journal de Trévoux*.

In its way, the choice of Charles Eisen to produce the drawings on which the engravings for the edition would be based was as inspired as that of Barbou.[169] By the 1750s, Eisen (1720-1778) had long since established a reputation as a fine artist, capable of producing drawings to embellish works of an impeccably serious kind. As well as enhancing the prestige of the Latin classics published by Barbou, he had, for example, illustrated a 1751 edition of the *Eloge de la folie* of Erasmus to which not even the most fastidious could object. The elegant 1757 edition of the *Decamerone* to which he had contributed had also employed the talents of artists of the calibre of Boucher, Gravelot and Cochin, and his presence in the group was an eloquent indication of the high regard in which his skills were held by his contemporaries.

The Fermiers took full advantage of the opportunity to vaunt Eisen's skill as an artist. While an engraved portrait of La Fontaine by Ficquet adorns volume 1 of the *Contes*, an equally elegant portrait of Eisen, also by Ficquet, serves as the frontispiece to volume 2.[170] It bears the legend: 'Charles Eisen, Peintre, Dessinateur du Roy, Professeur de l'Académie de St Luc, et associé de celle des Sciences, Belles-Lettres, et Arts de Rouen.' In this way, the Fermiers intended to proclaim unambiguously the fact that Eisen's contribution to the *Contes* was as important as that of La Fontaine himself.

The list of his titles and posts was doubtless designed to impress on readers his qualities as an artist, and was perhaps intended also to mask the less salubrious aspects of his life and work. The fact is that Eisen's personal reputation for sobriety and cleanliness was by no means unblemished, and in addition to uncontroversial illustrations, his output comprised drawings of a less edifying kind, to which the adjective 'galant' is usually applied.[171] In 1754, for example, he had designed the engraved titles and vignettes for a rather licentious Italian translation of the *De rerum natura* of Lucretius which was published in Paris; a copy of this work was in the possession of a Fermier général, Savalette de Buchelay.[172]

Thus, when the Fermiers needed the services of an artist of the highest technical accomplishment, who was also able to furnish drawings of a somewhat risqué kind, it was not surprising that their choice should fall

169. For an assessment of Eisen's work, see Portalis, *Les Dessinateurs d'illustrations*, vol.1, p.190-213, and Salomons, 'Charles Eisen'.
170. The portrait, which is dated 1761, was reused for an edition of Ariosto's *Orlando furioso* published by Baskerville in Birmingham in 1773 (see Cohen, *Guide de l'amateur de livres*, col.95). It is based on a painting by Vispré. The engraving of La Fontaine is based on the painting by Hyacinthe Rigault.
171. See Ray, *The Art of the French illustrated book*, p.51.
172. Cohen, *Guide de l'amateur de livres*, col.666.

upon Charles Eisen.[173] They had cause to regret their decision, however, when he was involved in a series of legal wranglings with other illustrators, which ended in the police being called to sort matters out.[174] For the vignettes and the culs-de-lampe, they called on the services of Choffard, a man with long experience in producing such embellishments. He was also asked to engrave some of the plates based on Eisen's drawings, a task in which he worked alongside men of the calibre of Baquoy, Lemire and Flipart, whose skill in such operations was well attested.[175]

The preparation of the edition, and especially of the engravings, was entrusted, probably for reasons of security as well as of convenience, to a committee made up of members of the Compagnie, under the chairmanship of Jean-Baptiste Seroux d'Agincourt (1730-1814). He was not yet a fully fledged Fermier (he was to reach that position only in 1764) but he had, since 1760, been Directeur de la Correspondance des Cinq Grosses Fermes,[176] an administrative position in which he clearly enjoyed the confidence of his superiors. He also had good connections in the world of the arts; he was himself an artist,[177] a man of taste and wide culture, as well as a collector of antiquities, whose substantial *Histoire de l'art par les monuments* (1810-1823) became a standard work of reference.

The publication of the *Contes* was evidently planned over some years. As was pointed out earlier, several of the plates are dated as early as 1759, and Eisen seems to have begun work on the pencil drawings for them in the early 1750s.[178] The available evidence indicates that most of the drawings which he submitted for the approval of the committee set up by the Compagnie were initially accepted without alteration. However, at one stage or another in the process of turning them into finished copperplates, a number were retouched to change minor details. More significantly, no fewer than twenty of his designs were subsequently judged to be unsuitable for various reasons, even though the plates based on them had already been engraved. In consequence, the gestation of the work was long and complex, and the scrutiny to which his designs were subjected explains why the illustrations bear a variety of dates. Certainly, when one looks at the complete series of approved plates, they have a family

173. Griffiths (*Prints for books*, p.21) contends that the choice of Eisen may well have been determined by the fact that he was Mme de Pompadour's drawing-master. Even if this were the reason why he was selected by the Fermiers (and Griffiths calls it only a 'plausible' suggestion), it need not have been their only motive. In any case, Eisen did not long retain her indulgence; according to Roger Portalis, 'il dégoûta bientôt la favorite par son sans-gêne et son manque d'éducation' (*Les Dessinateurs d'illustrations*, vol.1, p.197).

174. The details are given in Portalis (*Les Dessinateurs d'illustrations*, vol.1, p.193), and in Griffiths, *Prints for books*, p.18-21.

175. See Cohen, *Guide de l'amateur de livres*, *passim*, for details of the work of these artists.

176. Durand, *Les Fermiers généraux*, p.518.

177. A pen-and-ink portrait by him, probably of the abbé de Saint-Non, is in the Cabinet des Estampes of the BNF (see Pierre Rosenberg, *Fragonard*, Paris, 1987, p.278, fig. 3).

178. See above, note 12.

resemblance of tone, harmony and size[179] which betoken the considerable care that was taken to ensure that each played its part in creating a uniform whole.

Much valuable information on this process can be gleaned from two wholly exceptional copies of the *Contes* described by Cohen.[180] The first was assembled by the scholar-publisher Antoine-Augustin Renouard, and subsequently found its way into the collection of Baron James de Rothschild; it contains sixteen of Eisen's original twenty drawings for engravings which were rejected, together with many etchings and proofs, though no plates in an unrecorded state are present. The second is the celebrated 'Pixérécourt' copy, which contains nearly 200 additional proofs and etchings of the plates, though the only illustration which is not found elsewhere is a rejected version of 'Le bât'.[181] A third copy, not included in the Cohen census, can be found in the Thomas Grenville collection now in the British Library.[182] It contains several dozen etchings and proofs and fifteen rejected plates, as well as early versions of seven engravings, enabling us to follow to a certain extent the stages through which they passed before reaching their final incarnation.[183] Collectively, the existence of so many experimental or rejected versions of the illustrations, assembled in these three invaluable copies, is clear proof of the care the Fermiers took to ensure that the plates met the very specific and stringent requirements which they imposed on Eisen and his engravers. It may also be true, as has been suggested by one commentator, that the artists themselves wished to replace engravings which they judged to be unsatisfactory.[184] This can only be conjecture, since no documentation on the matter has come to light. In any event, the committee set up by the Fermiers would have had to approve the drawings and the engravings before publication, and much can be deduced as to the reasons why

179. Most plates are approximately 108 mm × 70 mm, though the dimensions vary slightly in some cases.

180. *Guide de l'amateur de livres*, col.559-61, where it is stated that a third (the 'La Bédoyère' copy) was destroyed in a fire during the Paris Commune of 1871.

181. The 'Pixérécourt' copy is so called because it was assembled by the dramatist Guilbert de Pixérécourt (1773-1844). My warm thanks are due to the antiquarian bookdealer Herr Heribert Tenschert, who purchased it at the sale of Sir David Salomons's collection in London in May 1986, and who kindly supplied me with a very detailed list of the illustrations that it contains.

182. It bears the shelf-mark G.11293-94. This copy is mentioned in a footnote by Owen Holloway, *French rococo book illustration* (London, 1969), p.21, but its importance is not apparent from his study. See also Griffiths, *Prints for books*, p.52, note 32. It is in a late eighteenth-century (English?) 'reliure doublée' of citron morocco. There is no indication in the book of the source of the extra illustrations. The collection formed by Grenville (1755-1846) was bequeathed in its entirety to the British Museum.

183. These states are discussed below in the study of the plates, chapters 2 and 3.

184. A suggestion made by Candace Clements and quoted in Philip Stewart, *Engraven desire: eros, image and text in the French eighteenth century* (Durham, NC and London, 1992), p.316.

some plates were rejected by comparing the original versions with their replacements.

Of course, terms such as 'original' and 'replacement' are open to the charge that quality is in the eye of the beholder, and that what one viewer judges to be better may not in fact have appeared so to the Fermiers or their illustrators. This objection is answered by pointing to the fact that some engravings are found in very few copies, not because they are offensive or objectionable, but because they are unarguably not very good. Thus, in a number of cases, one version is manifestly inferior in technical quality, with poor outlines and with little contrast of light and shade. In other instances the initial engraving failed to capture the intrinsic interest of the *conte*, or departed to a significant extent from the letter or the spirit of the text, and was replaced by a more faithful interpretation. Again, certain designs were evidently modified because they were felt to display too much naked flesh, or because they depicted characters in postures which some readers might regard as exceeding the bounds of decency.

Six illustrations in particular fell into this latter category: those for 'La servante justifiée', 'Le cas de conscience', 'Le diable de Papefiguière', 'Les lunettes', 'Le bât' and 'Le rossignol'.[185] The more revealing versions of the plates (that is, in their 'découvert' state) were either re-engraved to produce different scenes, or modified by the strategic placing of fig-leaves, pieces of clothing and so on, and it is in this modified (or 'couvert') state that they are often encountered.[186] To complicate matters further, impressions struck using the copperplates prepared from the original designs were sometimes bound in, so that both states of one or more plates were included in some copies. Hence, these more explicit versions were not rejected instantly (unlike the otherwise unrecorded versions of engravings in the Grenville copy); propriety need not therefore have been the first, or only, criterion invoked to decide what should be altered. Philip Stewart has suggested that copies containing these 'galant' engravings were available for those who wanted them, or who had the right connections in the bookselling world.[187] As this is one of the few attempts by commentators to discuss the variations between copies of the *Contes*, it is worth pausing to assess its validity.

The first point to emphasise is that, unlike many suites of illustrations for French books of the period,[188] those for the 1762 *Contes* are not known

185. The last of these belongs to the group of seven *contes* not by La Fontaine which were customarily inserted at the end of the work in eighteenth-century editions (see above, note 139); they were illustrated by Eisen in the same way as the *contes* written by La Fontaine himself.

186. For an analysis of the plates from an aesthetic point of view, see Holloway, *French rococo book illustration*, p.25-55. Their subject matter is described in detail by Hédé-Haüy (*Les Illustrations des Contes de La Fontaine*), p.27-63.

187. Stewart, *Engraven desire*, p.316.

188. For example, the *Œuvres de Molière* (Paris, [Prault], 1734), illustrated by Boucher, and the *Collection complète des œuvres de Jean-Jacques Rousseau* ('Londres' [Brussels, Boubers],

to have been available separately from the text.[189] At least, Cohen lists no examples, and if they had been readily obtainable, there would have been little need for the two early counterfeit versions. The existence, attested by Plassan's edition, of numerous complete sets of the plates in 1792 does not suggest that some illustrations, but not others, were issued in this way. The Fermiers therefore wanted them either to be incorporated *in toto* into their edition, or not to be used at all.

Second, the alleged practice of selecting the more alluring plates for special customers is not attested by the copies which have come down to us.[190] Two of the most celebrated 1762 engravings, those for 'Le cas de conscience' and 'Le diable de Papefiguière', are more commonly found in the 'découvert' state,[191] a fact which does not suggest that there was a concerted effort to make the more titillating versions available only to selected purchasers. Indeed, Cohen lists only *one* copy containing a large number of engravings in the 'découvert' state, and that belonged to M. de Beaujon, who was himself a Fermier général.[192] In addition, other plates with no obvious erotic content were re-engraved with only minor differences, but one state is far more common than the other.[193] Finally, a small number of illustrations which were rejected for technical reasons, but which were not offensive in any way, are scarcely ever found in copies of the 1762 edition.[194]

Hence, it is difficult to adduce any single reason for the availability or otherwise of particular plates, irrespective of their content; this is why we can draw no very positive conclusions about contemporary public taste, or the marketing of the *Contes*, on the basis of the engravings themselves. It is legitimate, however, to conclude that the plates as we now have them

1774-1783) illustrated by Moreau le jeune (see Cohen, *Guide de l'amateur de livres*, col.713, 908).

189. The noted bibliophile Louis-Jean Gaignat possessed a sumptuously illustrated manuscript of the *Contes*, though the illustrations owed nothing to Eisen's drawings (see Guillaume-François de Bure, *Bibliographie instructive, ou Traité de la connoissance des livres rares et singuliers*, 7 vols, Paris, 1763-1768, vol.4, 'Belles Lettres', no. 3161*). In the *CL* of July 1768, Grimm described these drawings as 'très-lascifs' (vol.8, p.121): Griffiths (*Prints for books*, p.170, note 28) wrongly situates this passage in the *CL* of January 1775.

190. See also Griffiths, *Prints for books*, p.22.

191. See Cohen, *Guide de l'amateur de livres*, col.561.

192. Cohen, *Guide de l'amateur de livres*, col.561. Rochambeau (*Bibliographie des œuvres de La Fontaine* p.526) claims that Seroux d'Agincourt possessed a unique copy of the *Contes* containing the different states of each of the plates. This seems to be an error: d'Agincourt assembled the eighty drawings which Eisen produced for the work, and these were later bound in four volumes with plates designed by Fragonard for an edition of 1795. This copy is now in the musée Condé at Chantilly (see Cohen, *Guide de l'amateur de livres*, col.559-60).

193. Cohen (*Guide de l'amateur de livres*, col.567) indicates that 'Le cocu battu et content' and 'Les cordeliers de Catalogne' were re-engraved 'sans différences notables'. The first version of 'Le cocu', engraved by Longueil, is more common than the inferior version engraved by Leveau and Baquoy; with 'Les cordeliers', the opposite is true.

194. For example, 'Le petit chien qui secoue de l'argent et des pierreries', 'La coupe enchantée' and 'Le contrat'.

went through a process of careful scrutiny before they were issued, and that they reflect overall the intentions and preferences of the Fermiers insofar as these can be gauged from the surviving copies. In the case of many of the more erotic engravings, detailed modifications were made to ensure that they would be less explicit. Had the process happened the other way round, it would have been more difficult to erase completely from the copperplate the traces of the features which had been removed. In other instances (such as 'A femme avare, galant escroc', 'La coupe enchantée' and 'Sœur Jeanne'), the second version of the engraving is so manifestly superior in technical terms to the earlier one that the order of the process can be determined even without external documentary evidence.

Despite the authority of tradition and of reference works such as that of Cohen, in a small number of cases it is not possible to say with certainty that one version of a plate is superior to another. In this situation, one has to make a reasoned judgement as to which is more likely to be the rejected version. While some rejected engravings are smaller in their overall dimensions than those which replaced them, this is not always true. It is, however, demonstrably the case that in virtually every *rejected* (as opposed to modified) plate, irrespective of the reason for its rejection, the characters are further away from the viewer than in the replacement version. This is a helpful guide, since the plates which were accepted without notable modifications also place the characters quite close to the viewer. This yardstick has therefore been used in the present study as a basic principle for assessing the priority of the versions considered.

It will be apparent from what has been said that the Fermiers went to a great deal of trouble to ensure that the plates for the 1762 *Contes* reflected a view of the work which gave prominence to its more controversial aspects. This was something which previous illustrations for it had not attempted to do. The illustrations were the only really distinctive feature of their edition, its raison d'être, and it would stand or fall by the public's judgement of Eisen's work. Both Grimm and Fréron praised the engravings very highly in their reviews, as did de Bure in his *Bibliographie instructive* in 1765;[195] the Fermiers therefore had every reason to suppose that their solicitude for the quality of the illustrations had borne fruit.

Yet in spite of the quality of a work with which they could not but be associated, the Fermiers recognised belatedly that the views to which they gave expression through the engravings would not be welcomed by a public which saw them as rapacious, cruel and sybaritic. If they could have got away with expressing their disdain for convention in the 1750s, they were unlikely to be so fortunate in the following decade. It was for this reason that they precipitately, and no doubt reluctantly, took the

---

195. He describes the edition as having 'de très jolies figures en taille-douce, gravées d'après les dessins de *M. Eisen*' (de Bure, *Bibliographie instructive*, vol.4, no. 3161).

edition off the market almost as soon as it had been launched. The evidence to support this view will be discussed in the final part of this study.

While the discussion of the illustrations themselves will occupy later sections of this study, it is essential at this point to outline some preliminary considerations involved in the analysis of engravings generally, and of those in the 1762 edition in particular. These theoretical and methodological questions are by no means matters of universal agreement, and some defence of the approach adopted here may help to dispel possible misunderstandings.

## ix. Questions of interpretation

Any analysis of the engravings is, of course, in itself an interpretation of an interpretation. We are looking at how an artist has transformed the verbal into the visual, a process which can only take place by his choosing to see the text in a particular fashion. Some of its given elements are thereby emphasised at the expense of others, adding to, or subtracting from, the original in an infinite number of ways. As with any illustration, the sense is 'over-determined', in that any one plate represents a distillation of many elements of the text which cannot all be shown in equal detail, nor given equal prominence. To this necessary and unavoidable process must be added the fact that any artist reads a text in relation to his own time, with his own views, his own (implicit or explicit) tastes and preferences, and on the basis of particular aesthetic and technological conventions.

The same holds true if those who commission the illustrations require the artist to reflect their reading of the text, rather than his own. In view of the particular circumstances which led to the publication of the *Contes*, it would be misleading to think of Eisen as the sole 'author' of the engravings. The enterprise was a collaborative one, involving the designer, the engravers and the vetting committee, so that we have a collective authorship, rather than an individual one. Roland Barthes and others have long questioned the notion of 'authorship' in any literary text, largely on the basis that no text can be wholly original, but must derive from earlier works. In the case of the *Contes*, it is clear that the notion can be challenged on other grounds as well.

While these factors therefore play a part in our interpretation of the plates, they do not answer the question of how we are to interpret them, and on what criteria. Philip Stewart has argued that a picture 'is never viewed without verbal context, and the more that context is complete, the more it "means" [...]. Art is afloat on a sea of words.'[196] A similar view is expressed by Martine Joly, who has drawn attention to the fundamental difficulties involved in iconographic interpretation by stating that 'l'image par elle-même, sans recours au langage verbal, n'affirme ni ne

196. Stewart, *Engraven desire*, p.37-38.

dénie rien'.[197] In one sense, both these statements are true, since the 'meaning' of an image which illustrates a pre-existing narrative is a sort of 'meta-diagesis' created *post factum* for that specific purpose. Even so, how the 'completeness' of a context is to be judged is unclear; this statement also contains an assumption (which is by no means always borne out in practice) that the artist will wish to render as much of the (con)text as possible in the illustration which accompanies it. The corollary of this view is that the artist's own inventiveness and freedom are effectively limited by the text. While he must obviously base himself on the text, he is able to see it in his own terms, and to add, subtract, emphasise or underplay any of the elements which the text provides. In other words, the illustration is to be judged in relation to the text, as an interpretation of it; it can never hope to be an *exact* rendering.[198]

It is also true, as Christopher Norris argues in discussing the inability of structuralism to account for the polysemy of a work, that 'meaning is always necessarily inscribed in a pre-existent economy of sense which it can never fully control'.[199] At the same time, while meaning can never be fully under the control of the creators of a text, by presenting the narrated events in a way which can only be the result of a multitude of specific choices, the illustration does affirm a view of the events it depicts. That view could have been utterly different in other hands, as an examination of the innumerable ways in which well-known texts have been illustrated over the years will show.

Clearly, such a view need not be unambiguous, and in all except the most elementary illustrations, it cannot be. Contemporary values, cultural associations, intertextual references and so on may all play a part in creating a complex, multivalent image. As a result, the reader, no less than the creator, will inevitably privilege some elements at the expense of others, or interpret some features in relation to pre-existent theories, such as Freudian psychology, deconstruction, Marxism, and so on. Belief systems of this kind can offer defensible insights into the significance of the illustration, though the danger of anachronistic misunderstanding, or of bending the facts to fit the theory, is a constant trap. Not the least significant objection to an over-reliance on specific theories is that they require the prior acceptance of basic postulates which are themselves not demonstrable beyond question (and which indeed those who find them untenable have often questioned).

The artist, of course, creates for readers of his own time, who judge and relate to his work as contemporaries. We cannot hope to recapture their

197. Martine Joly, *Introduction à l'analyse de l'image* (Paris, 1993), p.83.
198. In fairness to Stewart, his observations earlier in the same chapter (p.24-30) seem to me to be much more flexible and comprehensive in their recognition of the complexities of text–image relationships.
199. Christopher Norris, *Deconstruction*, new edition (London, 2002), p.52.

outlook and mentality, nor is there any point in trying to do so; yet we can, and we must, attempt to understand the iconography and the pre-suppositions of the illustrations if we are to judge them as interpretations of the text. The choice of any methodology will necessarily determine the kind of results which will be obtained. There is no value-free illustration and no value-free interpretation, and no interpretation can ever hope to take account of the innumerable valid ways in which an illustration can be read. At the same time, to reject any set of interpretative guides, and to lapse into pure empirical subjectivism, would be to ignore the values, attitudes and beliefs which, to a greater or lesser degree, underlie them. Fortunately, we are not wholly bereft of guidance in attempting to analyse the plates.

In the first place, by offering his own interpretation of a story, the artist may contrive to inflect our view of how we should read it. Such devices occur frequently in Eisen's engravings for the *Contes*, and are instrumental in guiding, if not necessarily in determining, our interpretation of them. Again, in a few cases (surprisingly few, given the close relationship between the text and the engravings), Choffard's tailpieces underscore the theme of the *conte*, complementing Eisen's interpretation. Hence, at the end of 'Joconde' the cul-de-lampe includes a crown from which two cuckold's horns emerge. That for 'Le juge de Mesle' shows a blindfolded bust of justice, at the foot of which is a pair of scales with one pan weighing more than the other because it contains a feather. Generally, however, Choffard is content simply to depict objects which occur in the story, or to use conventional symbols such as birds to designate lovers, and offers no specific interpretative comment on the text.[200]

This reliance upon stock devices as a shorthand way of communicating meaning has the curious effect of juxtaposing two sets of aesthetic prac-tices in the one work: the mimetic and the symbolic, the denotative and the connotative. In the case of the *Contes*, what is denoted is more complex, because it represents the artist's subjective (and therefore necessarily biased) attempt to render the data of the text. In contrast, what is con-noted, through the use of stock symbols, merely represents a translation of elements or themes of the text into an equivalent symbolic register owing little or nothing to the specificity of the story as recounted by La Fontaine. Two lovebirds, for example, would designate a pair of lovers irrespective of the author's approach to the *conte*. Their relationship to the story can only be determined by a reading of the text, which may confirm, or contradict, the suggestion that they are deeply in love.

Second, Eisen was as aware as other artists of his time of the icono-graphic significance attaching to particular motifs such as people, objects or scenes, of the sort detailed in Gravelot and Cochin's *Almanach iconologique*,

200. Griffiths (*Prints for books*, p.23) speaks of the 'witty appropriateness' of the culs-de-lampe. See the review in the *Mercure de France*, January 1763, vol.1, p.138-45.

published in seventeen volumes between 1765 and 1781.[201] Educated readers of the time were familiar with the conventional associations used in literature to depict, for example, deities or abstract qualities. As the anonymous *Encyclopédie* article 'Iconologie' (1758) put the matter (vol.8, p.488): 'Comme les Payens avoient multiplié leurs divinités à l'infini, les Poëtes & les Peintres après eux se sont exercés à revêtir d'une figure apparente des êtres purement chimériques, ou à donner une espece de corps aux attributs divins, aux saisons, aux fleuves, aux provinces, aux sciences, aux arts, aux vertus, aux vices, aux passions, aux maladies, &c.'

Even when no such coded representation is used in the illustration, other associations were to hand for the eighteenth-century artist, particularly in the specific and precise depiction of faces and bodily postures to convey a wide range of emotions. Interest in the representation of emotions in the theatre and in the plastic arts was strong, for the work of Charles Le Brun had a widespread and significant influence throughout the period. According to Norman Bryson, Le Brun's interest in the courtly glance in particular, and in physiognomy in general, produced 'the most prolonged meditation in European art on the meaning of the human face'.[202] He certainly played a key role in fostering the (essentially Cartesian) idea that facial expressions accurately reflected the state of the soul, and could be represented as such in painting.[203] What is more, the question of how emotions were to be rendered in art had received a new emphasis in 1759 thanks to the comte de Caylus, who instituted a prize at the Académie royale de peinture et de sculpture for the best achievement in this area of aesthetics.[204] Hence, contemporary readers of the *Contes* might have expected that an artist such as Eisen would render emotions through facial and bodily expressions in the illustrations he created for the work.[205]

They could scarcely be disappointed in such expectations, since characters invariably display some reaction to the (often highly charged) circumstances in which they find themselves. It does not follow, however, that their reactions are to be read as a simple table of equivalences. Several factors complicate the process, and render it less mechanical than might be expected from a close adherence to Le Brun's theories, however widely accepted they might have been.

201. See Cohen, *Guide de l'amateur de livres*, col.454-57.

202. Norman Bryson, *Word and image: French painting of the Ancien régime* (Cambridge, 1983), p.43.

203. The main Cartesian text used by Le Brun was the *Traité sur les passions* (1649). See Jennifer Montagu, *The Expression of the passions: the origin and influence of Charles Le Brun's 'Conférence sur l'expression générale et particulière'* (New Haven, CT and London, 1994), esp. p.7, 156-62. His lecture, given in 1668, was not published until 1698.

204. See Angelica Goodden, *Diderot and the body* (Oxford, 2001), p.98.

205. I have not found any specific reference to this topic in contemporary comments on the edition.

In the first place, the scale of the illustrations in the *Contes* was small, and afforded only limited space for the depiction of fine detail if other important elements in the story were not to be excluded. Consequently, there were few opportunities for the artist and engraver to go beyond the indication of general feelings. The almost identical facial expressions which Le Brun assigns, for example, to fear and to acute bodily pain[206] would have been almost impossible to differentiate when working in so restricted a space as that offered by the engravings for the *Contes*. In the second place, Eisen was free, like any artist, to interpret characters as he saw fit, and to present a view of their behaviour and attitudes which was not necessarily as described directly by La Fontaine. As Philip Stewart aptly observes: 'In illustration engraving, where the dimensions of the medium prevent encoding of much detail in a facial expression, emotions are not generally the focus, or if so, they must be coded primarily in gesture.'[207] The process of rendering emotion through facial expression is not, therefore, a straightforward one when we come to examine Eisen's practice in the *Contes*.

For this reason, we shall need to ask (even if we cannot always answer with any certainty) whether the expressions on the faces of the figures shown can be related in any way to these considerations. It is no less pertinent to ask whether their significance can be better understood in the context of such a discussion. It is possible to ascribe certain intentions to the creators of the engraving, whether or not those intentions are un-ambiguously expressed (as for example when evil characters are depicted as good, or the poor are made to seem ridiculous or threatening when the text makes no such assertion). When such features are repeatedly included with no specific warrant from the text, then clearly a persistent tendency is at work which cannot be ignored if we are to grasp the referential significance of the illustrations.

This view has been strengthened by a number of modern critical approaches. First, the study of illustrations has in recent years taken on a new complexity, as a result of the influence of semiotics, so that illus-trations are seen to function in accordance with a system of signs, and to be linked with more general linguistic methodologies.[208] Second, the techniques developed under the general heading of 'narratology' offer a number of perspectives which can sometimes be of use in the analysis of illustrations,[209] though not as readily might be thought. It is true that

206. See the illustrations reproduced by Montagu, *The Expression of the passions*, p.134, 137.

207. Stewart, *Engraven desire*, p.16.

208. All the studies produced from this perspective derive ultimately, of course, from the work of Ferdinand de Saussure, and, more immediately, from the pioneering *Mythologies* of Roland Barthes (1953). See Andrew Leak, *Barthes: Mythologies* (London, 1994).

209. See, for example, Mieke Bal, *Narratologie* (Utrecht, 1984); Gérard Genette, *Figures III* (Paris, 1972); Shlomith Rimmon-Kenan, *Narrative fiction: contemporary poetics* (London, 1983).

terms such as 'internal focalisation', 'external focalisation', 'zero focalisation' and the distinction between 'story', 'text' and 'narration' and so on, are now part of the common critical vocabulary, and are directly pertinent to the written text. Yet it is by no means clear that this typology, valuable as it is, can be transferred directly to the investigation of engravings based on texts.[210]

Because the image is dependent on the text, it is in a sense reductive of it, since the nuances of language available to the narrator are not at the disposal of the illustrator. These limitations are compounded by the fact that, as Barthes and others have noted, a single image cannot convey the temporal succession of events inherent in a story;[211] images therefore cannot always differentiate precisely between, for example, single events and those which are recounted once but happen many times.[212]

But even if irreducible differences remain between the two forms of expression, some visual parallel to the narratological analysis of texts can be devised. A full visual equivalent of 'internal focalisation', for example, would require us to see an illustration from the perspective of a character who can be identified in the text. While such a procedure might be possible, it is not to be found, in the *Contes* at least. There, the image based on a text is usually seen from the standpoint of an unknown, unnamed viewer who is the intermediary between the text and the reader, and of whose presence the figures in the illustrations remain ignorant. Typically, they are aware only of their relationship to one another, and not of what lies outside the frame; without being absorbed in their activities to the exclusion of others, they are framed within their own self-contained world.[213] The scene customarily offered to us is that which we would have as (presumably invisible) spectators if the 'fourth wall' of the room in which the action occurs were to be removed.[214] Hence, we see what s/he sees without knowing who s/he is. And because we see only what the unknown viewer can see, this form of representation might be regarded as approximately equivalent to 'external focalisation'.

However, such perspectives may not always place us in the same position as the characters shown in the engraving, and we may 'know' more

210. 'The "double register" whereby a first-person homodiegetic narrator plays two roles (past and present) while seeming to speak with one voice cannot be projected visually by any conventional device' (Stewart, *Engraven desire*, p.12).

211. See Joly, *Introduction à l'analyse de l'image*, p.104. Joly argues that causality likewise cannot be represented by images, but this point seems to me to be less easily demonstrable, since immediate causation, at least, can be shown (for instance, a man can display the signs of fear because he sees a lion).

212. See Stewart, *Engraven desire*, p.12-13.

213. See also Stewart, *Engraven desire*, p.101-102. The standard work on the theme of absorption in eighteenth-century French painting is Michael Fried, *Absorption and theatricality: painting and the beholder in the age of Diderot* (Berkeley, CA, 1980).

214. See Fried, *Absorption and theatricality*, p.39-72, for an analysis of dramatic gestures in illustrations to works written for the theatre.

or less than they do. We may know less because the illustrator depicts, for example, a figure whose face is hidden from us, although other persons shown in the scene can see it; we have then to decide for ourselves the appearance of the unseen face. In such cases, we must assess the hidden face on the basis of the body language of other characters (their gestures, their demeanour, their position, etc.). But we may also know more than the characters: we can tell from the text what is being transacted in the illustration and, by referring to what the omniscient narrator tells us, we may be privy to unspoken thoughts and feelings, so that we are privileged spectators. We may also know more than the characters because we can see from our perspective what they cannot. Hence, the spectator in these engravings does not have a simply passive role, but is placed in a varying and sometimes complex set of relationships with the characters presented for our inspection. Narratological approaches can therefore be of some use in alerting us to the lines of demarcation between the reader and the illustrator, and in suggesting how the information which we have to work with is encoded in the plates. However, the intrinsic differences between words and images preclude any direct methodological transfer of these procedures from the textual to the visual.

Whatever methodology is employed, the raw material of the study remains the same. What we are looking at is a group of illustrations created at a certain time and place in response to a complex set of political, social, economic and other circumstances, and executed in one of the styles typical of the period. Although this style reflects external circumstances, it also bears the mark of the realities of the time as understood by those involved in creating the engravings. Factors such as the clothes of the figures depicted, and the surroundings in which they are shown, could all have been other than as they are. They are as they are because Eisen and his engravers, working under the direction of the Fermiers, decided to make them as they are. Such details had a significance for contemporaries which we can hardly ignore if we wish to understand the semiotics of the illustrations as they were originally conceived, but we cannot study these questions in isolation from technical considerations.

In addition, the renewed interest in the function of rhetoric has led to an understanding of the ways in which the image can operate as a vector of social, political and other values. The relationship between the 'denotative' (what is shown) and the 'connotative' (what may be understood or implied) has, from this perspective, been explored to considerable effect in modern and eighteenth-century texts.[215] But even here, there is cause for caution. Alain-Marie Bassy (who has done much valuable work on book illustration) takes the view that 'c'est à travers la série que l'image

215. In addition to Stewart, *Engraven desire*, see Roger Bautier, *De la rhétorique à la communication* (Paris, 1993). For a conspectus of approaches currently adopted in the study of text–image relationships, see the *Bulletin of the John Rylands Library* 81:3 (1999), special issue *Text and image: studies in the French illustrated book*, ed. David Adams and Adrian Armstrong.

signifie. Elle n'est qu'un segment, une séquence d'un système que le lecteur devra, pièce à pièce, comme au jeu des dominos, reconstituer en totalité.'[216] Leaving aside the somewhat idealistic aspiration of reconstructing 'the totality' of any signifying system, it needs to be recognised that a multiplicity of systems can be embedded in any series of illustrations. The text–image relationship can be both intratextual, in that the image is based directly on the text, and intertextual, in that one image may refer to another. This latter relationship can manifest itself at several levels: thematic, iconographic or interpretative, and indeed in a combination of all three.[217] For this reason if for no other, to refer to illustrations as constituting a *single* 'system' is both limiting in its scope and over-prescriptive in its ambition. The image signifies, first and foremost, in its relationship to the text on which it is based. Only secondarily does it signify as part of a series, and the coherence of the series of which it forms part has to be demonstrated, not assumed in advance. Yet even if the heterogeneous 'segments' cannot be reduced to a single system, the same attitudes and preoccupations and iconographic practices may be apparent in *contes* which deal with similar subjects, but which are widely separated in the text. Such recurrences mean that the indispensable analysis of individual *contes* must be complemented by a synoptic treatment encompassing the engravings as a whole, to analyse the basis of their coherence.

Coherence is a quality which emerges not only at the level of iconography, or even of theme, but also in figurative terms. The discontinuities of the illustrations can be bridged at the thematic and iconographic level, but here again the limitations of the enterprise which the *Contes* represent need to be borne in mind. Though the illustrations may have a symbolic function, they are not easily reconciled with any attempt to interpret the *Contes* as a whole in an allegorical sense. For the abbé Mallet, writing in the *Encyclopédie* in 1751, allegory is a 'figure de Rhétorique, par laquelle on employe des termes qui, pris à la lettre, signifient toute autre chose que ce qu'on veut leur faire signifier. L'*allégorie* n'est proprement autre chose qu'une métaphore continuée, qui sert de comparaison pour faire entendre un sens qu'on n'exprime point, mais qu'on a en vûe' (vol.1, p.280).[218]

Precisely because the characters depicted are those described in the *conte* itself, and are not introduced from outside the story, and because the illustrations reflect, to varying degrees, the 'facts' of the text, they are distinct from allegory in this sense. Of course, insofar as the illustration is the product of the artist's imagination, and could have been otherwise than it is, there is an element of invention, but it is invention which

216. Alain-Marie Bassy, 'Le texte et l'image', in *Histoire de l'édition française*, 4 vols (Paris, 1983-1986), vol.2, p.155-56, quoted in Stewart, *Engraven desire*, p.xiii.

217. See also Stewart, *Engraven desire*, p.34-35.

218. Erwin Panofsky echoes this definition in calling allegories 'combinations of personifications and/or symbols' (*Studies in iconology*, New York and London, 1972, p.6, note 1).

respects the text as its starting point, and does not venture into a different level of representation. The difference between the symbolic and the allegorical is that while the symbol may be generalised metonymically to represent a more general truth as embodied in the story, the allegorical illustration offers the artist's evaluation of the characters *in other terms*. Although various 'props' are used to comment on the action shown in the illustration (candles often have a phallic significance when two lovers are shown; a hat may represent the female sex-organ), Eisen eschews the use of conventional or recognisable symbols to signify moral qualities, in the way that, for example, Monnet used a serpent to represent evil in the frontispiece to volume 1 of the 1796 edition of Laclos's *Les Liaisons dangereuses*.[219]

In looking at other texts of the period, it is legitimate to describe the text–image relationship as 'a sort of global dialogue'.[220] The engravings which Rousseau commissioned from Gravelot for *Julie ou la Nouvelle Héloïse* (1761), for example, illuminate the text and are illuminated by it, since the two were intended to be closely connected. In the case of the *Contes*, however, no such correspondence of text and image, of style and content, was possible, since the engravings and the original text were created quite separately and nearly a century apart. Their significance therefore lies less in their being contemporary with the *Contes*, like the Gravelot plates for *La Nouvelle Héloïse*, than in what they tell us about the values, ideas and perspectives of the time at which they were created.

This is especially the case in that the 1762 edition was conceived and executed in the specific, and very fraught, political and social context outlined earlier. The work was brought into being at a particular time and place, for particular reasons and in particular circumstances. These considerations distinguish it significantly from previous illustrated editions of the *Contes* published in French, giving it a social and political context not usually found in illustrated literary works of the period.[221]

We shall not be concerned to any great extent with the literary techniques, the poetry or the sources of inspiration of the *Contes*. These matters have been dealt with by previous commentators; they are not of primary concern in a study of this kind, except insofar as La Fontaine's treatment of a story used by other writers has a bearing on the illustration for a *conte*. Since modern editions do not contain all the *contes* to be found in the 1762 version, it has unavoidably been used as the base text, and page-references are given to it; the (sometimes eccentric) original spelling has been retained throughout. However, the edition itself contains no notes, and many obscure linguistic or cultural points are explicated only in more

219. See Stewart, *Engraven desire*, p.21-22.
220. Stewart, *Engraven desire*, p.xiii.
221. It is striking that Stewart's (in many ways excellent) *Engraven desire* has no index entries for 'society', 'social background' or '*philosophes*', and makes only passing reference to the Fermiers as a body.

recent editions. For supplementary information, the Pléiade edition of the *Contes et nouvelles en vers*, which forms volume 1 of the *Œuvres complètes de La Fontaine* (*OCLF*), has been used.

Essentially, then, we shall try to explain and understand Eisen's illustrations for the 1762 edition of the *Contes* in relation to the text on which they are based, and to the circumstances in which they were created. We shall therefore ask whether the work can be seen not simply as an exquisite example of the pre-Revolutionary French illustrated book, but also as a document offering a significant view of its age.

## x. Some historical conclusions

The publishing history of the *Contes* tells us more than is sometimes realised about the cultural mentality of France (or at least of Paris and Versailles) in the 1750s and early 1760s. In the first place, the fault-lines separating the literary, religious and intellectual establishment from its adversaries were malleable, and shifted with each new crisis, depending on how those concerned saw the matter. This is why Grimm's attitude towards the Compagnie changed so markedly in the space of a few years. It is also the reason why the *parlement* could be hostile both to the *Encyclopédie* and to the Compagnie des Fermiers généraux, and why Malesherbes could order that the work be withdrawn at the behest of the king, while ensuring that it continued in secret to be prepared for publication. It may also explain why Diderot could write the *Vie de La Fontaine* which is prefixed to the *Contes*, even though he was the editor of a work which had repeatedly attacked the Fermiers.

Second, the episode reveals how relatively powerless even the Fermiers were in the early 1760s against the rising tide of criticism directed against them. As tax-gatherers, they were feared, and were not to be taken lightly. As the butt of works written by pamphleteers, and even by members (or former members) of the Compagnie itself, such as Naveau and Darigrand, they floundered helplessly as they attempted to redress the balance in their favour. Despite some initial success in suppressing the attacks on them once Sartine had been placed in charge of the book trade, this perceived weakness on their part was to lead to further attacks until the Revolution put an end to the Compagnie once and for all.

Third, we can see how important the printed word was in the campaigns waged by various parties in these events. No doubt manuscripts were in circulation which belittled the Fermiers, but one is struck by the fact that many of the most trenchant attacks made on them appeared in printed books. Such works were in a number of cases published with the connivance of the censor's office, and with false places of publication, and were often reprinted several times in rapid succession. This does not argue for a strict, repressive regime of censorship directed against any and every allegedly dangerous work, but rather for a remarkably tolerant – if often inconsistent – view of books which were held to have some merit, however unwelcome their publication might be in some exalted quarters.[222]

To that extent, the publication of the *Contes* bears on much that has been written in recent years on the emergence of 'the public sphere' in eighteenth-century France. In the wake of the pioneering work of Jürgen Habermas,[223] scholars have argued that the period witnessed the development of a culture, both oral and printed, in which current concerns were debated more openly. It is often asserted that the gap between the private man and the citizen was bridged through the medium of newspapers and journals, as well as through clubs, debating societies, salons and so forth. This 'public sphere' was a new departure, in that ordinary citizens could begin to shape public opinion and influence society directly. Despite the popularity of this interpretation of the interplay between social factors and intellectual drives, it sometimes assumes too easily that discussion in pre-Revolutionary France was productive and unfettered.[224] Patently, it often was not, as the official condemnation of many 'philosophical' works amply demonstrates. It is also difficult to assess with accuracy what effect discussions, public or private, had on the course of political or social events.[225] At the very least, the circulation of ideas was often more complex than this model allows, and a simple belief in cause and effect is unlikely to take us far in understanding the clash of ideas, ideologies and interests in France at this time.

In the case of the Fermiers, there was certainly a great deal of hostile discussion concerning their conduct, their place in society, and the functions they performed. It is also true that much of that discussion took place in brochures, books and *Encyclopédie* articles, which were widely read and discussed. Yet in responding to these criticisms, the Fermiers published not a denunciation of their enemies in a diatribe of the sort which had become quite commonplace in criticisms of the *philosophes*, but a luxuriously illustrated book. If the illustrations for it were indeed begun in the early 1750s, as the evidence strongly suggests, they date from a time when the Fermiers' power was still in the ascendant, and when they were

222. See Darnton, *The Forbidden best-sellers*, ch.3.

223. See especially Habermas's *Theorie des kommunikativen Handelns*, 2 vols (Frankfurt am Main, 1981).

224. Some commentators, especially in France, have regarded Habermas's basic assumptions as historically naive; Jean-François Lyotard (1924-1998) in particular took him vigorously to task for his unremitting, Enlightenment-based defence of moral absolutes, universal rationalism, individual freedom, and intellectual independence. See Richard Rorty, 'Habermas and Lyotard on postmodernity', in *Habermas and modernity*, ed. Richard J. Bernstein (Cambridge, MA, 1985), p.159-75.

225. For further consideration of these points, see *Habermas and the public sphere*, ed. Craig Calhoun (Cambridge, MA, 1992). Alternative interpretation of the ways in which ideas circulated at this time have, of course, been canvassed very thoroughly by Robert Darnton in *The Forbidden best-sellers* and elsewhere. For his more recent reflections on the subject, see his *George Washington's false teeth: an unconventional guide to the eighteenth century* (London and New York, 2003).

not yet the object of a sustained campaign of hostility. Consequently, their intentions would not have been coloured by political considerations of the sort which obtained later. It therefore seems likely that they initially intended the work simply as an affirmation of their values, their belief in luxury, and their tolerance of the human failings of which their adversaries accused them. At a late stage, they resolved that most copies would be sequestrated for years. This decision can most convincingly be explained, on the existing evidence, by their fear that the values and attitudes expressed in the illustrations would no longer be tolerated in a work published by the Compagnie, and that it would lead to further hostility towards the Fermiers and all they were perceived to stand for.

Judged by the Habermasian yardstick, the publication of the *Contes* in 1762 belongs partly in the public sphere, in that the debates occasioned by the Compagnie took place in public forums such as the *parlement*, or in journals and books to which the public had access. It also belongs partly in a more private sphere, in that the edition was in the hands of the very small number of readers who were able to obtain copies before it was withdrawn. The fact that the book continued to be popular at a time when the reputation of the Fermiers themselves was in ceaseless decline underscores the difficulty of passing judgements on the cultural and political values of the period. We do not really know to what extent, or in what ways, the appearance of the *Contes* affected the perception of the Compagnie, at least on the part of those fortunate enough to acquire copies. The question of reconciling the theoretical model and the actual facts of the matter is a useful reminder of the dangers of over-prescription in historical interpretation.

In addition, the cultural climate of the time was propitious for the production of books intended for wealthy collectors. It is this climate which, as much as any other factor, accounted for the Fermiers' initial decision to underwrite the publication of the edition, and for its continued high reputation. These factors will need to be borne in mind when we examine the illustrations themselves, as we shall now do.

# 2. The illustrations to La Fontaine's *Contes et nouvelles en vers*, volume I

WE have looked at the historical factors which helped to shape the 1762 edition of the *Contes et nouvelles en vers*, and at the curious history of the work. We come now to the task of analysing the illustrations on which its fame rests.

## i. 'Joconde'

This was one of the very first of the *contes*, having been published in the *Nouvelles en vers tirées de Bocace et de l'Arioste* of 1665, where it was called 'Joconde, ou l'infidélité des femmes, nouvelle par M. de L. F.'. Although La Fontaine signals his debt to Ariosto, and its immediate inspiration is the *Roland furieux* (Canto XVIII, stanzas i-lxxiv), its origins can be traced back at least as far as a collection of ancient Buddhist texts (*OCLF*, 1346). The story was placed at the beginning of the first part of the *Contes et nouvelles* in 1665, and remained there in subsequent editions. It inspired Boileau's *Dissertation sur la Joconde*, which was first included in an edition of the *Contes* in 1686 and reprinted in many later editions of the work.[1]

In dealing with the proverbial infidelity of women, of which the two central male characters find many examples, it announces one of the recurrent themes of the *Contes*.[2] Yet its satirical scope is in fact much wider than this rather hackneyed theme, even without the benefit of the illustrations. La Fontaine's opens the *conte* in these terms (vol.I, p.1):

> Jadis régnoit en Lombardie
> Un Prince aussi beau que le jour.
> Et tel que, des beautés qui régnoient à sa Cour,
> La moitié lui portoit envie,
> L'autre moitié brûloit pour lui d'amour.
> Un jour, en se mirant: Je fais, dit-il, gageure,
> Qu'il n'est mortel dans la nature
> Qui me soit égal en appas.

As we can infer from the strong position of 'Jadis', both prince Astolphe and the beauties who reign at court will lose their looks, and indeed their power. La Fontaine further implies that, if the prince and the 'beautés'

1. See Rochambeau, *Bibliographie des œuvres de La Fontaine*, p.512, no. 31.
2. John Lapp (*The Esthetics of negligence*, p.117-45), argues that La Fontaine is both smilingly indulgent to the foibles of women and appreciative of their beauty, and absolves him of any charge of misogyny.

both reign, both owe their power to their looks, rather than to any intrinsic merit or authority. As Marc Fumaroli puts it: 'Seul le mode plaisant du *conte* interdit qu'un tel degré de vanité, digne d'une coquette, ne soit pas chez un roi le principe de tragédies autres que privées.'[3]

The theme of vanity, and of the fleeting nature of beauty, is taken up again with the description of Joconde recalling the moment when he discovered his wife in bed with her lover (vol.1, p.6):

> Le souvenir fâcheux d'un si perfide tour
> Altéroit fort la beauté de Joconde:
> Ce n'étoit plus ce miracle d'amour
> Qui devoit charmer tout le monde.
> Les Dames le voyant arriver à la Cour,
> Dirent d'abord: Est-ce là ce Narcisse
> Qui prétendoit tous nos cœurs enchaîner?
> Quoi! Le pauvre homme a la jaunisse!

Again, when the prince, warned by Joconde, discovers his own wife's infidelity with her ugly dwarf, his own reaction, despite the long list of unfaithful women mentioned by Joconde, is one of confusion and disbelief that such a fate should befall him (vol.1, p.11):

> L'énormité du fait le rendit si confus
> Que d'abord tous ses sens demeurèrent perclus.

Tricked again by a serving-girl at an inn, they console themselves with the thought that many women behave as their wives have done. They decide that their only sensible course of action is to return home, whereupon each of them lives 'le plus content du monde' (vol.1, p.22).

### Caption: '*Le Roi Astolphe se mire environné de sa cour; le frere de Joconde s'incline et lui parle.*'[4]

The theme of unmanliness, of vanity and of self-deception at court, is taken up in the first of Eisen's illustrations (Eisen 1), in which he at once indicates his independence of his predecessor Cochin. In the 1745 edition, Cochin portrays two men, one of whom has his back to us, in conversation at court (?). The room is furnished simply with a chair, a curtain, and with what looks like a mirror. No courtiers are present. The mirror is presented at an angle, to suggest that it distorts. In the Fermiers généraux edition, king Astolphe is presented as a rather preening, foolish figure,[5] whose hat seems to bisect his hair horizontally. He alone wears a sword,

---

3. Marc Fumaroli, *Le Poète et le roi: La Fontaine en son siècle* (Paris, 1997), p.382.
4. The individual plates' captions reproduced here are taken from the *Avis au relieur*. These provide information for the reader, though their function is more complex than that, as we shall see.
5. Compare Holloway, *French rococo book illustration*, p.36.

Eisen 1. 'Joconde', vol. 1, p. 1

but his appearance is scarcely military in comparison with the figures depicted in the background holding pikes. Astolphe is shown admiring himself in mirror; no women are to be seen, even though they are mentioned in text as envying him, or being in love with him. A bust of a woman on the fireplace to the left is shown looking away from Astolphe, as if to suggest that his attractiveness to women is not as absolute as he imagines. His hunting dog is there as a reminder of what he should do, not of what he does; as dogs are customarily used in the iconography of western art to symbolise faithfulness, its presence suggests an ironic contrast with the behaviour displayed by the king and indeed others in the *conte*. The engraving therefore suggests strongly Astolphe's foppishness, and a rather unmasculine preoccupation with himself in a world where phallic weapons are never far away, even inside his palace, as though he has need of many soldiers to guard him. This is a masculine world, in which he does not belong. The man standing to his left (the 'gentilhomme d'auprès de Rome', Joconde's brother) would be taller if he were not bowing, and the soldiers visible in the background are all at least as tall as the prince himself.

Neither the pikestaffs, nor the dog, nor the assembled mass of courtiers is mentioned in the text. Eisen's interpretation sets up masculine criteria for the conduct of the prince (or 'roi' as La Fontaine also calls him, vol.2, p.2), which he manifestly fails to satisfy. Hence, although according to the text the court ladies fawn on him, the figure seen by Eisen is a preening fop, a figure of ridicule, whatever his prowess as a lover.

*Caption: 'Joconde rentre dans l'appartement de sa femme, trouve un valet couché & endormi à côté d'elle; il l'abandonne à son remords.'*

Joconde (Eisen 2) is dressed in fashionable costume of the seventeenth century,[6] though this is not specified by the text. He is wearing a sword, just visible on the extreme right, but he shows no sign of wanting to use it to 'les envoyer dormir dans l'autre monde' (vol.1, p.5).

The bracelet and portrait of wife for which Joconde had returned to the house are on a table by the bed; the bed-sheets are rumpled, and the bed-curtains drawn back to show us clearly what is happening. His wife is half-naked, her lover completely so. Although the wife is beautiful, as La Fontaine says, the handsome lover is not wholly what one would expect from the description, twice repeated, of him as 'un lourdaut de valet' (vol.1, p.5-6). He has curly hair and seems to have dark skin, a feature accentuated by his being slightly in shadow. While we know that the servant is not a 'blondin', the word 'lourdaut' does not of itself suggest a

6. See Albert Racinet, *The Historical encyclopedia of costume* (London, 1998), p.203, and James Laver, *A Concise history of costume* (London, 1972), p.104-105.

Eisen 2. 'Joconde', vol.1, p.6

dark-skinned man.[7] Although Eisen frequently depicts peasants or the lower classes as swarthy, he may simply have intended to show that they spent much time out of doors, and were therefore markedly different from the delicately tinted upper classes. Even so, the use of curly hair in the depiction of such figures does tend to make one think that they are of at least mixed race. While authors such as Buffon had argued at this time, on physiological grounds, that all humans were essentially members of the same species,[8] the sexual association of white and black would nonetheless have been shocking to contemporary readers.[9] What is more, Eisen's tendency in the *Contes* to give gross features to lower-class men (though not to women) is not characteristic of other artists of the time, such as Cochin and Moreau whose peasants are roughly dressed, but not otherwise distinctive.[10]

Hence, the wife is not only an adulteress, but may be guilty, in Eisen's rendering of the scene, of associating with a man of mixed race, who in the perspective of the time would have been widely regarded as a 'lesser being' than Joconde. The woman (?) in the portrait in frame above door looks suitably shocked. Since the whole theme of the *conte* is that infidelity is commonplace, this reaction is provoked not so much by the act itself as by the circumstances attending it, that is, either by the origins of the lover, or by Joconde's reaction to the scene.

His anger is apparent from his darkened face (creating an ironic parallel with the lover, whose skin, presumably, is naturally dark), with his cloak billowing to suggest movement. Yet the text tells us that his anger surfaced only afterwards at the recollection of his wife's infidelity (vol.1, p.6). Because he initially refuses to tell anyone of her conduct, we have the privilege of knowing what others do not yet know. What we do know is that a handsome servant, who may be of mixed race, has cuckolded him, and that while Joconde may feel some emotion, there is no sign on the part of his wife of the 'remords' to which he abandons her. Indeed, the couple are not even aware of his presence in the room. When Joconde tells the king of his misadventures (vol.1, p.10), we learn only

---

7. The *Dictionnaire de Trévoux* (1762) defines the word as 'maladroit, stupide'.

8. See Claude Blanckaert, 'Of monstrous métis? Hybridity, fear of miscegenation, and patriotism from Buffon to Paul Broca', in *The Color of liberty: histories of race in France*, ed. Sue Peabody and Tyler Stovall (Durham, NC, and London, 2003), p.42-70.

9. In the *Encyclopédie*, both d'Aumont in his article 'Grossesse' (1757), and Diderot in his article 'Homme' (1765), mention an episode recounted by Buffon in his *Histoire naturelle* in which a white woman had given birth to twins, one of which was black, the other white. Diderot merely reports the story, but d'Aumont comments: 'Ce témoignage évident de l'infidélité de cette femme à l'égard de son mari, la força d'avouer qu'un negre qui la servoit étoit entré dans sa chambre un jour que son mari venoit de la laisser dans son lit; & elle ajoûta pour s'excuser, que ce negre l'avoit menacée de la tuer, & qu'elle avoit été contrainte de le satisfaire' (vol.7, p.958).

10. See also, for example, Moreau's illustration for Rousseau's *Œuvres*, 12 vols (Brussels, 1774-1783), vol.3, p.98, reproduced in Holloway, *French rococo book illustration*, engraving 77.

that he told his story 'sans rien oublier', so that we have no knowledge of the terms in which he recounts the episode.

In his study of the *Contes*, John Lapp argues that Joconde's immediate reaction to discovering his wife's adultery is 'in accord with the aristocratic morality which considered marital jealousy or possessiveness as essentially a bourgeois trait, a manifestation of middle-class rapacity and acquisitiveness'.[11] This is debatable. It is true that in his *Dissertation sur la Joconde* (1686), Boileau writes: 'La peinture d'un mari qui se résout à souffrir discrètement les plaisirs de sa femme, comme l'a dépeint Monsieur de La Fontaine, n'a rien que de plaisant et d'agréable' (*Contes*, vol.1, p.249). Even so, this depiction of the complacent husband is not, in Boileau's view, wholly believable: 'Voilà, sans mentir, un amant bien parfait [...]. Si je ne me trompe, c'étoit bien plutôt là une raison, non seulement pour obliger Joconde à éclater, mais c'en étoit assez pour lui faire poignarder dans la rage sa femme, son valet et soi-même' (*Contes*, vol.1, p.247).

To a classical writer, therefore, Joconde's conduct appears perplexing. Nor is his restrained conduct made any more comprehensible by the report in the text (vol.1, p.6) of the 'chagrin' which he subsequently experiences, to such an extent indeed that it alters his features almost out of recognition, and gives others the impression that he is suffering from jaundice. Eisen's concern is not, of course, with what happens subsequently, but with the rendering of Joconde's turbulent emotional state at the moment of discovery. The man whom we see in Eisen 2 is cuckolded through his wife's association with someone who is his social and perhaps racial inferior, but whose beauty, according to Eisen, is at least equal to his own. Hence, even if the reason for the wife's adultery is comprehensible from the illustration, Joconde's anger as depicted here is based as much on these social considerations as on the infidelity itself. By advancing chronologically the expression of Joconde's anger, and in interpreting as he does the features of the wife's lover, Eisen is simultaneously increasing the drama of the story and offering a social, and even racist, interpretation of the text. While the first of these considerations needs little explanation, one can see in the second, especially when it is linked to Eisen's practice in subsequent illustrations, a tendency to assimilate the servant classes and the peasantry to 'inferior' racial types.

### Caption: '*La Reine dans les bras de son nain.*'

In De Hooghe's version (De Hooghe 1)[12] the dwarf is standing dominantly over the queen, whose hand is under his chin. In the 1755 edition,

11. Lapp, *The Esthetics of negligence*, p.99
12. The headpieces by De Hooghe are reproduced for purposes of comparison. It has not been possible to obtain reproductions of all the Cochin vignettes, and only a selection is reproduced here.

De Hooghe 1. 'Joconde', vol. 1, p. 1

he is shown bending over her, and seems taller: the queen's breast is bare, and the dwarf's hand is under *her* chin. The Grenville copy of the 1762 *Contes* in the BL contains an early (and apparently suppressed) version of the illustration, designed by Eisen and engraved by Le Mire, which is a reversed copy of this 1755 plate.[13] In these three versions, Joconde and Astolphe are shown distantly peering at the couple from the rear of the room, in accordance with the terms of the text (vol.1, p.11).

However, in his second version of the engraving (Eisen 3), Eisen shows only a dimly lit face peering through the crack in the panelling at the rear of the room. By reducing the small, remote figures of Astolphe and Joconde to a single, unidentified, almost occluded spectator in the later version, Eisen concentrates our attention on the dwarf and the queen. He thus makes us see them for ourselves; in this way, the disparity between the beauty of the queen and the monstrous ugliness of the dwarf appears all the more striking, and may be intended as a contrast with the servant shown in Eisen 2. The queen is dressed in ermine, in the style of the 1660s.[14] Her dwarf in fantasy costume, with the turban and full sleeves befitting his state. Eisen makes him discard the symbols of his office, and he has thrown his jester's bauble to the ground, just in front of the step, so that his nominally inferior status is relinquished. He is, moreover, shown as being larger than the queen, with a copious turban, and a strong left leg; the effect is to make him appear both physically powerful and lustful. The queen's robes are open, her hands offer no defence; she is sitting on a raised chair which resembles a throne, suggesting that the king is betrayed through the symbol of his authority. The fact that Eisen puts the dwarf and the queen on the same level, so that their faces are side by side, further hints at the loss of respect for royal authority in the same way as the presentation of the king and courtiers in Eisen 1. This point is reinforced in another way too: although the meeting is said to take place in a 'galerie' ('lieu solitaire et tenu fort secret', vol.1, p.7), the setting looks well appointed, and a throne would not be appropriate to such a place except as a symbol of royalty. The strong masculinity of the dwarf contrasts with the foppishness of Prince Astolphe as he appears in an earlier illustration, and makes the queen's adultery perhaps more comprehensible. As Robert Nicolich aptly observes, the shock of seeing the queen disporting herself with the powerful, misshapen dwarf is not that of Astolphe alone. The engraving is placed with the printed verso facing p.11, so that the reader has to turn it over to see the scene depicted,

13. Cohen (*Guide de l'amateur de livres*, col.564) mentions an etching of this engraving which shows 'deux personnages supprimés sur les autres états', but does not indicate that an engraving was created of this version. The etching is amongst the additional illustrations found in the Pixérécourt copy.
14. See Jules Quicherat, *Histoire du costume en France depuis les temps les plus reculés jusqu'à la fin du XVIII⁴ siècle* (Paris, 1877), p.520.

Eisen 3. 'Joconde', vol. 1, p. 11

instead of being faced with the engraving as the eye travels down the text on p.10.[15]

*Caption: 'La fille de l'hôtellerie confesse à genoux le mystère; Astolphe & Joconde lui donnent l'anneau & l'argent promis.'*

The two men are dressed as before (Eisen 4); the servant-girl is in eighteenth-century domestic costume of the type familiar from the paintings of Chardin and others. She is shown half-kneeling (the text says she is 'à genoux', vol.1, p.20), begging forgiveness of the two men she has deceived. She is speaking, while they are smiling. Since the transaction was done for gain (they have promised her a ring), she is as self-interested as the two men, and has used them as much as they have used her. Each is offering her money; Joconde is pouring it from a bag (a detail not mentioned in the text), while an open money-chest can be seen on the table to the right. The men are disarmed, metaphorically as well as literally (their pistols are on the floor at the left). Joconde has come physically to resemble the king; this should not surprise us, since the king himself has decided that Joconde need not defer to him in any way (vol.1, p.11). In showing the girl on bended knee asking for forgiveness, Eisen is ironically recalling the king's status, which would normally require signs of deference on her part, and showing how far from kingly behaviour he has departed. These details are of course in the text, but it is the way in which they are selected and presented which gives a clue to the artist's intentions.

Although the sexual prowess of Astolphe and Joconde is repeatedly stressed in the *conte* itself, the image given of the two men is not entirely a masculine one. The foppish Astolphe is cuckolded by a dwarf; Joconde is betrayed by his wife's affair not merely with a servant, but with one who bears distinct traces of being of non-European origin. The king's sword offers a poor contrast with the pikes of his soldiers. Joconde's sword is scarcely visible, and the (notably small) pistols of the two men are laid aside on the floor in the final engraving, while they forgive the servant whose innocent look is in contrast with the fact that she has deceived them repeatedly. All these details are added by Eisen to undermine the masculinity of the two men and to make them seem not merely cuckolds, but ridiculous as well. Although the point will become fully apparent only later, it should be noted that this is one of the few *contes* in which the principal male characters are shown other than in eighteenth-century dress. The very fact that Eisen took pains to dress Astolphe in costume of

15. Nicolich, 'Seventeenth and eighteenth-century illustrations for La Fontaine's *Contes et nouvelles en vers*', p.235. The same commentator draws attention (p.233) to the added intimacy of the scene by our being able to see the couple in close-up, without 'sharing' the view with Astolphe and Joconde.

Eisen 4. 'Joconde', vol.1, p.20

an earlier period may mean that he wished to preclude any possibility that the king would be identified with Louis XV.[16]

Overall, the plates emphasise the foolishness of the king and the nobleman around whom the story turns. If certain elements (such as the king's self-regard, the adultery of the queen with the dwarf, the feigned innocence of the serving-girl) are to be found in the *conte* itself, they are collectively emphasised by Eisen to the detriment of Astolphe and Joconde. They also undermine any claim to innate superiority, intelligence or moral worth that the king might have. It is scarcely possible to imagine him ruling by divine right, and not at all easy to see in what respect he is superior to Joconde, or how either man is wilier than the servant-girl. The emphasis here, in contrast to the editions of 1745 and 1755, is thus on the singular ineptitude of the two men.

Lapp contends that 'by other realistic details, absent in Ariosto, La Fontaine emphasises rank and hierarchy'.[17] An examination of the plates shows that this statement is not borne out in Eisen's treatment of the main characters. The presentation of Astolphe and Joconde, the depiction of the queen's adultery, and the encounter at the inn with the servant, tend to undermine their credibility and rank, and turn them into intrinsically comic figures. This point is reinforced by Choffard's tailpiece, showing a cuckoo sitting inside a frame of branches and flowers which is surmounted by Astolphe's crown and Joconde's coronet threaded on a pair of cuckold's horns. Astolphe's sceptre ironically draws attention to his lack of authority, while the medallion containing the portrait of Joconde's wife reminds us of the reason why he discovered her infidelity. The overall effect is to mock the two men for their inability to assert their authority over their respective spouses.[18] As Lapp also remarks, La Fontaine, in his treatment of Ariosto's story, 'establishes the contrast [...] between court and countryside' (p.98). Yet Eisen chooses to depict scenes which are all concerned with events taking place indoors, whether in a palace, a house or an inn. The preference for the domestic over the natural is characteristic of his illustrations for the *Contes*, most of which have an indoor setting.

The first engraving for 'Joconde' shows a semi-public scene, while the last three are concerned with what would normally be private events. In every case, what is depicted is a particular moment or event in the story. While the indications of the text are respected with regard to specific details, rather than to generalities, the subjects treated in the engravings have a general import. The *conte* is built around the idea of marital infidelity, the power of the passions, and the view that no one is exempt

16. This was not as improbable as might be thought. Holloway (*French rococo book illustration*, p.25) points out that the couple shown in 'La chose impossible' closely resemble Louis XV and Mme de Pompadour (see below, ch.3, p.312).

17. Lapp, *The Esthetics of negligence*, p.99.

18. Nicolich, 'Seventeenth and eighteenth-century illustrations for La Fontaine's *Contes et nouvelles en vers*', p.235.

from their influence. It is of course true that women readily become the lovers of both men, however foolish their appearance. This behaviour is typical of the female sex as depicted in the *Contes*, and their willingness to be seduced is not a subject on which Eisen was free to depart from the text. At the same time, the less than respectful depiction of the king and of Joconde invites the reader to reflect on how the class structure of contemporary France is handled in the *Contes*, so that this first text offers pointers towards further investigation which need to be borne in mind in reading the remainder of the work.

## ii. 'Le cocu battu et content'

*Caption: Le cocu battu et content 'est vêtu en femme; il rentre avec précipitation dans sa maison; l'amant le poursuit'.*

The plate (Eisen 5) depicts an innocent-looking young man, and a stoutly built 'wife', who does not attempt to defend 'herself' with the stick s/he is carrying. Since La Fontaine tells us that the young man 'jusqu'au logis ainsi le convoya' (vol.1, p.28) and we see them just outside the house, this scene represents the conclusion of the beating which the husband M. Bon receives. We do not see the effects of the blows in any actual harm done to him, for he can still run, is depicted as physically strong, with obviously powerful arms, and does not look especially old. Hence, the fact that he has only 'quatre cheveux gris' (vol.1, p.24) is not apparent, any more than his age is written in his face. The cruelty of the young man is thereby attenuated, and his offence seems less heinous than might be thought from the circumstances of the text. If his misbehaviour in seducing the wife of his employer remains reprehensible, he is no longer simply an adulterous lover, an 'experienced roué'[19] cuckolding a wispy-haired and feeble old man. He has become, rather, the participant in a game of equals, in which the husband fails to defend himself, though apparently able to do so. The fact that the husband is supposedly elderly is more obvious from the tailpiece, adding to the impression that the aim of the engraving is to diminish the emphasis on his age. Eisen presents him as a man who does not seek to defend himself, rather than as an old man cruelly cuckolded by a younger rival.

De Hooghe depicts the situation much as Eisen does (De Hooghe 2), except that we see the husband's face only in profile, and the figure is not distinctively masculine. In the 1745 edition, Cochin shows the husband, who is wearing breeches, rushing headlong towards an open gate set in railings, though there is no sign of the 'logis' mentioned by La Fontaine (Cochin 1). The same scene is depicted in 1755, and a rejected version of

19. Lapp, *The Esthetics of negligence*, p.54.

74

Eisen 5. 'Le cocu battu et content', vol. 1, p. 23

De Hooghe 2. 'Le cocu battu et content', vol.1, p.21

Cochin 1. 'Le cocu battu et content', vol.1, p.21

the Eisen illustration contained in the Grenville copy of the *Contes* is merely a reversed copy of that engraving. In Eisen's final version, however, M. Bon is shown close to the house, but there is no indication that a door is open to allow him to evade the blows delivered by the lover. He therefore has no apparent means of escape, but rather than defend himself he flees in panic, to some unspecified place. He should be shown acquiescing in his ill treatment, since we are told that, in his joy at learning of his valet's concern for his wife's honour, 'Le bon hommeau des coups se consola' (vol.1, p.28). Yet the terror evident on his face does not denote acceptance of his beating so much as his cowardice.

Although the two works are only distantly related by the theme of female infidelity, the plate for 'Le cocu battu et content' recalls those which Eisen designed for 'Joconde' in that both offer representations of unmanly conduct. In the latter work, La Fontaine merely hints at the king's unmanliness, and it is in Eisen's illustration that the theme is developed. In 'Le cocu battu et content', La Fontaine clearly states (both in the title and the text of the work) that the husband puts up no resistance to attack. Eisen accentuates his complicity by making him seem both younger and more muscular than the text warrants, and by closing off any obvious escape route which could serve as an excuse for the husband's failure to defend himself. In this connection, we should recall that, although the lover's use of a stick is specified by the text, to a contemporary audience, it was a particularly humiliating weapon. In the *Encyclopédie* article 'Bâton' (1752), we find this: 'Les Maîtres-d'armes & les gens susceptibles du point d'honneur, croyent qu'il est bien plus honteux de recevoir un coup de *bâton* qu'un coup d'épée, à cause que l'épée est un instrument de guerre, & le *bâton* un instrument d'outrage' (vol.2, p.143). As in 'Joconde', the sufferings brought about by marital infidelity are glossed over or made palatable by the artist, no less than by the text. This effect is achieved in a way which undercuts received notions of manliness, and shifts the moral perspective of the *conte*, to a degree which betokens a conscious intention to present La Fontaine in a novel manner.

## iii. 'Le mari confesseur'

*Caption: Le mari confesseur 'est assis, dans un confessional, & sa femme qui l'a reconnu, lui explique l'énigme de sa confession'.*

If we look at this engraving (Eisen 6) in relation to the text, it appears anomalous. Although the *conte* is set at the time of François I$^{er}$ and the Italian wars of the early sixteenth century, the clothes worn by the couple are those of the mid-eighteenth century. The wife is fashionably dressed, while the 'priest' wears the 'perruque d'abbé' shown in plate 7 which accompanies the article 'Perruquier' (1765) in the *Encyclopédie*. At the

Eisen 6. 'Le mari confesseur', vol.1, p.31

same time, the use of the open confessional shown in this illustration (as in those designed by De Hooghe and Cochin) had long since been abandoned by the Church; the abbé Mallet's article 'Confession' which appeared in the *Encyclopédie* in 1753 states that the practice 'étoit autrefois publique; mais l'Eglise pour de très-fortes raisons, ne l'exige plus depuis un grand nombre de siecles, & n'a retenu que la *confession* auriculaire qui est de toute ancienneté' (vol.3, p.848).

The unsigned article 'Confessionnal' describes clearly the structure of confessionals (vol.3, p.849):

CONFESSIONNAL, s. m. (*Hist. ecclésiast.*) est une espece de niche en boiserie, fermée d'une porte à jour ou grillée, & placée dans une église ou une chapelle, où le confesseur est assis pour entendre les pénitens, qui se placent à genoux dans deux autres niches en prie-dieu, ouverts, & pratiqués aux côtés de la niche du confesseur, qui les entend par une petite fenêtre grillée.

Eisen, like his predecessors, makes no attempt at historical authenticity, and all three set the story squarely in the present through the use of contemporary clothing. One reason, at least, for the ahistorical representation of the confessional is that, according to the *conte*, in making her confession the wife of Messire Artus 'vient à ses pieds se placer' (vol.1, p.32); the illustration has therefore to show them face to face, irrespective of the historical facts. In addition, La Fontaine observes that the encounter takes place 'un jour de Confrairie' (vol.1, p.31), that is, on a day set aside for a gathering of the faithful devoted to a saint or other object of veneration (*OCLF*, p.1359). This detail explains the presence of other worshippers who are sketchily shown in the background.

According to the description, the illustration shows the point at which the wife is 'explaining' her infidelity to the priest/husband whom she has recognised. Since she knows who he is (while giving no outward sign that this is so), she is tacitly in command of the encounter, and his role, both as priest and as husband, is to be duped by his wife whose infidelities he strongly suspects (vol.1, p.31).[20]

De Hooghe's (very literal) illustration for this *conte* (De Hooghe 3) shows the couple during the wife's confession; no other worshippers are in evidence, and the dramatic confrontation between husband and wife is still to come. The difference between the Eisen engraving and the vignette which Cochin designed for the 1745 edition is no less marked. In Cochin's version, we see the 'priest' rising to his feet in anger (though the text does not specifically state that he does so), while the wife seems cowed into silence. Owing to the proximity of other worshippers, the wife's confession could easily have been overheard, so that the husband's obvious anger is comprehensible in the context. It should be noted that while Eisen's final

---

20. See also Nicolich, 'Seventeenth and eighteenth-century illustrations for La Fontaine's *Contes et nouvelles en vers*', p.261-63.

De Hooghe 3. 'Le mari confesseur', vol.1, p.27

version differs substantially from it, an early, suppressed engraving in the Grenville copy of the *Contes* closely follows Cochin's design.

In the Eisen version which the Fermiers finally used, the husband is silent, the wife animated. He is taken aback, while she is smiling. She has her bonnet for outdoor wear, but also a décolletage which might not be suitable for church or confession, though it would presumably please the husband whom she seeks both to tease and to placate. These indications not only contrast with the more animated (if less textually accurate) interpretation offered by Cochin; the husband's more passive role also accords with the unimpressive presentation of men offered in the illustrations to the two previous *contes*, 'Joconde' and 'Le cocu battu et content'. Even at this early stage in the work, then, a pattern of male and female behaviour is emerging which will need to be explored in the subsequent illustrations.

## iv. 'Le savetier'[21]

*Caption: Le savetier 'leve un rideau en s'avançant & prend le billet que sa femme a reçu du marchand; l'étonnement de celui-ci est marqué par son attitude.'*

This is one of the *contes* for which the illustration in the 1762 edition exists in two forms, both of which are readily found in copies. Such are the differences between the original, rejected version (Eisen 7a) and the later engraving (Eisen 7b) that the description applies only to the second, and it does not translate the actions depicted in the first. In the text, nothing is said of the actual encounter of the husband and the would-be seducer. It simply states that the arrangements outlined earlier in the *conte* were adhered to; the husband has agreed a stratagem with his wife in these terms (vol.1, p.33-34):

> Je veux me cacher tout à point.
> Avant le coup demandez la cédule.
> De la donner je ne crois qu'il recule:
> Puis tousserez afin de m'avertir
> Mais haut et clair, et plutôt deux fois qu'une.
> Lors de mon coin vous me verrez sortir
> Incontinent, de crainte de fortune.
> Ainsi fut fait, ainsi s'exécuta.

The actual circumstances of the encounter have therefore to be imagined by the artist, and a number of incidental resemblances can be traced between the two versions of the illustration. For example: in both, the beams of the ceiling are prominent, as are such household items as

21. Entitled 'Conte d'une chose arrivée à Château-Thierry' in *OCLF*, p.584-85.

Eisen 7a. 'Le savetier', first version, vol.1, between p.32-33

Eisen 7b. 'Le savetier', second version, vol.1, between p.32-33

an ewer, a basket and a small ladder, and in both the lender is shown seated in a very prominent chair. Even so, there is more emphasis on the poverty of the couple in the second version than in the first. The cupboard has changed from a solid piece of panelled furniture to a broken-down affair of wooden planks with many splits. In the revised state, the cobbler has fewer shoes to mend, showing that trade is less good, and that he is therefore more in need of a loan and less able to pay it back. The bowl of fruit shown on the cupboard in the earlier state is replaced by an empty basket; the hat and clothing hanging at the back of the room (of which there was no sign in the earlier engraving) are ragged and poor.

The relationship between the three figures shown is also different in each case. At one level, the change of emphasis is signalled by the removal of the cat which in the earlier state stares impotently at a canary in a cage; in the second version, the cage is only partly visible, and the cat has vanished without trace. This change removes the ambiguity of the symbolism, which left the reader to wonder which of the characters was to be seen as the stalker, and which as the prey. In the earlier engraving, the wife is leaning towards the merchant, who has an arm around her waist; her expression seems distracted, and perhaps even indifferent to her husband's arrival. In the revised state, the husband and wife are shown closer together; their eyes meet, and they are physically linked by the receipt from the merchant; the wife's face is shaded, as if she is blushing, though whether her blushes – if that is what they are – are due to modesty or to embarrassment at thus tricking the merchant is not clear. In the rejected engraving, the ladder leads to a bed, or perhaps to a loft; in the second version it leans against a wall, so that the wife's virtue is emphasised more than in the first version.

We are also closer to the three people involved in the second version than in the first, and can read the complicit expressions of the husband and wife more easily. In the later engraving, the husband is shown more emphatically; in the first, he creeps out from under the blanket dividing the room; in the later version, he emerges dramatically from behind the curtain. Other than that the merchant is 'peu rusé', we know little about him. His face is not shown fully in the original engraving; in the second version, it is mostly hidden from us, and his surprise is shown rather by his posture and his outstretched hands. Whereas in the rejected engraving, his hat is on the ground, there is no sign of it in the second version, perhaps because the near proximity of the scene precluded the possibility of including it.

The changes introduced in this second version place more emphasis on the circumstantial coherence of the couple's situation (their now-manifest poverty has driven them to borrow money which they can ill afford to repay, and so they have to devise a way of tricking their creditor). It also accentuates their emotional closeness, shown by their proximity and by the fact that each has a hand on the creditor's receipt. The husband is also more assertive; since the creditor has attempted to deceive him, and he is merely taking his revenge, there is no reason to depict him as creeping almost apologetically into the room, as the rejected engraving does.

Of the three major illustrators of the *Contes*, only De Hooghe makes the would-be seducer unaware of the presence of the husband (De Hooghe 4). We see him standing at a window next to the cobbler's wife, while the husband, shoe in hand, looks on. As so often, De Hooghe's images are static, and depict the scene prior to any dramatic confrontation: they are pictural and fixed, rather than mobile and fluid. In the Cochin version of 1745 (of which the 1755 plate is merely a reversed copy), the cobbler has his back to us, but spreads his hands in apparent surprise at the scene; his wife is seated beside her would-be seducer, whose face shows his utter astonishment at being discovered. The essential difference between the 1745 version and the second engraving of 1762 lies not so much in the circumstantial detail as in the role allotted to the husband. In Cochin's interpretation of the story, and in the earlier version by Eisen, he is scarcely assertive, whereas in the revised illustration he is. This self-confidence, as he defends his wife's honour, contrasts with the depiction of unmanliness in the earlier *contes*, and provides a further, complicating pointer to the examination of those which follow.

## v. 'Le paysan qui avoit offensé son seigneur'

*Caption: Le paysan qui avoit offensé son seigneur 'est à genoux;*
*il compte les cent écus à son Seigneur;*
*deux valets sont dans l'enfoncement'.*

La Fontaine presents the situation in these terms (vol.1, p.36):

> Un Paysan son Seigneur offensa.
> L'histoire dit que c'étoit bagatelle.
> Et toutefois ce Seigneur le tança
> Fort rudement: ce n'est chose nouvelle.
> Coquin, dit-il, tu mérites la hard.
> Fais ton calcul d'y venir tôt ou tard;
> C'est une fin à tes pareils commune.
> Mais je suis bon, et de trois peines l'une
> Tu peux choisir[22]

Had the peasant's offence been of a major kind, one might agree that the fine of 100 écus was proper. Since it was merely a 'bagatelle', one can see why he might balk at paying it, and prefer to accept less expensive penalties instead. It is true that he regards the financial punishment as the worst of all ('Les cent écus, c'est le pire de tous', vol.1, p.35), but we

---

22. On the *conte* itself, see Jürgen Grimm, ' "On ne vit onc si cruelle aventure": à propos du *Conte d'un paysan qui avait offensé son Seigneur*', in *Car demeure l'amitié: mélanges offerts à Claude Abraham*, ed. Francis Assaf and Andrew H. Wallis (Paris, 1997), p.25-37.

De Hooghe 4. 'Le savetier', vol.1, p.30

are not told whether this is because he is mean, or because he is simply too poor to afford such a sum. That is to say, we know nothing to the detriment of the peasant, and quite a lot which casts the Seigneur in a bad light. As La Fontaine puts it (vol. 1, p.35):

> Ce Seigneur le tança
> Fort rudement: ce n'est chose nouvelle

From the engraving which accompanies the *conte*, however, the relationship between the text and the image turns out to be less than straightforward. The scene depicts the peasant as he is at the end of the story. He is shown defeated, half-kneeling as he is in front of his lord, weighed down by the blows he has received from the two men on the left holding sticks. No doubt he also reeks of garlic as he hands over the 100 écus which he finally has little choice but to pay. The master (Eisen 8) is elegantly dressed in the latest fashions, and carries a sword, whereas the peasant is in nondescript clothes as a metaphor both of his poverty and of his lack of sophistication. He is the only figure not wearing a wig, to put him outside the circle of the master and his cronies. His submissiveness can be inferred from the text, as can the Seigneur's imperious gesture, with his right hand pointing at the money, and no doubt at the peasant too. Yet the obvious differences in physical appearance between the two men cannot be deduced from what La Fontaine tells us. With his half-open, apparently toothless mouth, the peasant makes a physically unattractive figure. In contrast, the Seigneur, who is placed in an advantageous, superior position, is young, handsome and well dressed (something we are not told by La Fontaine). The stone columns, the urn and the chair on which he is sitting are all iconographic indications of wealth added by Eisen, and may indeed allude to the Fermiers' view of themselves as pillars of the state.[23] La Fontaine describes the two figures on the left who administer the beating as 'deux forts paillards', but this description hardly assorts with the well-dressed, apparently restrained young men whom Eisen depicts. They are presumably in the employ of the Seigneur, but the way in which they are shown identifies them with his class, and further isolates the peasant. For all these reasons, it is clear that the difference between the peasant and the other characters is not merely one of social rank, but of physical appeal and wealth, which are strongly contrasted with unattractiveness and self-abasement.

Eisen's version of this story owes quite a lot to De Hooghe (De Hooghe 5); in both cases, the peasant kneels before the Seigneur, and the two 'paillards' are depicted as gentlemen onlookers, rather than as ruffians ready

23. Hyacinthe Rigault had used a similar device in his portrait of Louis XIV (1700), and Louis-Michel van Loo was to employ it again in his portrait of Louis XV (1765). See the reproductions of these paintings in Philip Conisbee, *Painting in eighteenth-century France* (Oxford, 1980), figs 89 and 90.

Eisen 8. 'Le paysan qui avoit offensé son seigneur', vol.1, p.35

De Hooghe 5. 'Le paysan qui avoit offensé son seigneur', vol.1, p.33

to do their master's bidding. But De Hooghe shows the cowed peasant in the act of handing over money, rather than as a man suffering the indignities of his punishment, while the master stretches out his hand as if to bless him. The whole scene is thus at some remove from the harshness described by La Fontaine.

Whereas De Hooghe scarcely suggests that the beating has occurred at all, Cochin shows the peasant being assaulted with sticks while the master looks on; the men beating him look as poor as he is himself. In Eisen's case, however, it is the subjugation of the peasant which is emphasised; he stares open-mouthed as the Seigneur insists on payment, while the two 'paillards' stand ready to inflict further punishment if necessary. Eisen is content to hint at what has occurred, to suggest both the force and the firmness with which the Seigneur operates, but leaving us in no doubt where his sympathies lie.

Since the Fermiers généraux published this edition of the *Contes* in order, among other things, to assert their belief in their position and their own practices, it is not surprising that Eisen should transform La Fontaine's story. He alters it in a way which conflicts noticeably with the text; his rendering of the *conte* accepts the idea that those in power have the right to punish their inferiors as they wish, though for obvious reasons the true extent of that punishment is not shown openly. A corporation which had so often been criticised for its heartless treatment of impoverished taxpayers was not averse to transforming a story so that the aesthetic values of the illustration confirmed both its own flattering view of itself and the rightness of that view.

Some support for this interpretation is to be found in Choffard's tail-piece (p.39) which shows a plate laden with cloves of garlic supported on two crossed sticks, beneath which is a bag overflowing with coins. The sticks are held together by a noose, as if to suggest the still more dire punishment awaiting those who attempt to evade paying their debts by adopting the stratagem of the peasant in this story. As in the illustrations by Eisen to earlier *contes* ('Joconde', 'Le cocu battu et content') the cruelty is understated, and it is the peasant's financial and personal humiliation which matter most here.

## vi. 'Le muletier'

*Caption: 'Les Muletiers du Roi paraissent devant lui, tête nue.'*

The thematic core of this *conte* is the duplicity practised by the muleteer on the queen, the king and his fellow servants. King Agiluf, reportedly a 'prince sage et prudent' (vol.1, p.45), is utterly deceived by the muleteer who has bedded the queen. Since, at the end of the *conte*, he is unable to decide which of the numerous servants with newly cropped hair has cuckolded him, the matter is to be kept quiet (vol.1, p.46). As John Lapp observes (*The Esthetics of negligence*, p.52-53), Agiluf is also under the misapprehension that his wife has helped to undermine his stratagem, and does not realise that she is innocent of deception, having herself been duped by the muleteer. His weakness as a king leads him simply to crop the hair of the man he suspects of cuckolding him, rather than confronting him directly as an outraged husband and ruler. His reluctance to behave regally and with authority must presumably have been known beforehand to the muleteer, who could scarcely have dared to seduce the queen if he had thought that condign punishment would be forthcoming. This point is made indirectly in the *conte*, to draw attention by implication to the king's lack of authority (vol.1, p.44):

> En ses présens le Ciel est toujours juste:
> Il ne départ à gens de tous états
> Mêmes talens. Un Empereur Auguste
> A les vertus propres pour commander;
> Un Avocat sçait les points décider;
> Au jeu d'Amour le Muletier fait rage.

Eisen's illustration (Eisen 9) shows the king in his perplexity, faced by the stable-hands who have had their forelocks cut off by the muleteer. They in turn, unaware of the identity of the culprit, or of the reasons for his action, are puzzled to know why the king should summon them. His elegant attire and pose contrast with the rough clothes and weather-beaten faces of the servants, all of whom are bareheaded out of respect, but who in the process reveal their involuntary tonsures. He may be taller than they, and better dressed, but he is no wiser. A servant, who has implicated everyone else in order to save himself, deceives all of them, including the king.

This interpretation of the story differs markedly from that of Eisen's predecessors. Both De Hooghe (De Hooghe 6) and Cochin choose to illustrate the arrival of the muleteer at the queen's bedchamber; De Hooghe shows him entering, holding a candle, as the door is held open by a servant; the queen lies in bed, her face scarcely visible amidst the drapes. In Cochin's version, the illicit visitor is shown hiding his face as he is admitted to the bedchamber.[24] But in both cases, it is the daring of the muleteer which lies at the heart of the illustration. With the Eisen engraving, however, it is the intrinsic superiority of the (unseen) muleteer which triumphs. The implications of this depiction of royal bafflement would not have been lost on readers at that period.

24. Other earlier versions had illustrated the same episode, or else had shown the king in the process of cutting off the hair of the man he suspected of cuckolding him. See Nicolich, 'Seventeenth and eighteenth-century illustrations for La Fontaine's *Contes et nouvelles en vers*', p.247-52.

Eisen 9. 'Le muletier', vol.1, p.41

De Hooghe 6. 'Le muletier', vol. i, p.37

## vii. 'La servante justifiée'

*Caption: La Servante justifiée 'est à demi renversée sur l'herbe;
son maître incliné l'embrasse; la voisine les regarde par sa fenêtre'.*

This is another *conte* for which Eisen prepared two engravings which have some similarities, but which also differ significantly from each other. In both cases, we share with the observing neighbour the sight of the couple about to make love; even if our perspective (and attitudes) are not hers, we witness the scene with her, and become complicit with her in spying on them.[25]

In the original, rejected version (Eisen 10a), the husband has his hand between the girl's legs and is almost falling upon her, pushing her downwards. It would be difficult for her to maintain the position in which she is shown, with her left knee just above the ground, and resting her whole weight on one arm. What is more, the urn behind them (which seems almost to be growing out of the husband's head) could have prevented the neighbour from having a clear line of vision to the seduction of the servant.

In the second version (Eisen 10b), the neighbour (who is a considerable distance from the couple in the earlier plate) is now so close that it would be difficult for her (unless she is short-sighted) to mistake the servant for the wife. Although the same event occurs twice, we are not told that the neighbour witnessed the scene with the wife; indeed, she cannot have done, otherwise she would have recognised the wife and known that the two women were at different times engaged in sexual acts with the husband.[26]

A fountain has been introduced on the left, and is more obviously phallic than the urn shown in the previous engraving. In the rejected version, the flowers thrown down by the servant are scattered over the ground, but in the second they appear merely to be lying there, suggesting less surprise or alarm on her part. In the earlier engraving, the husband appears to be wearing contemporary dress, but in the second he is elaborately clothed in the cloak and ruff of an earlier period. Now, too, he seems more like a crouched animal about to devour its (albeit willing) prey. In neither plate is the couple aware of having been seen by the neighbour. According to the text, the incident occurred 'de très grand matin' (vol.1, p.48); in the rejected engraving, the sky is sunny, in the second it is sombre, perhaps reflecting the emotions involved.

25. See also Stewart, *Engraven desire*, p.166-68.
26. Some useful comments on the complementary perceptions of the wife and the neighbour can be found in Ran E. Hong, 'La réécriture de deux *contes* de La Fontaine', *Papers on French seventeenth-century literature* 27:53 (2000), p.473-87.

Eisen 10a. 'La servante justifiée', first version, vol. 1, between p.46-47

Eisen 10b. 'La servante justifiée', second version, vol.1, between p.46-47

The differences between the two versions are more striking than their similarities. By revising the plate, Eisen can show the servant as a more willing participant than in the original engraving; by depicting the husband in more flowing clothes, he can show him as a (literally) much rounder figure than in the original, and the couple as two halves of one whole. This point is indicated in another way, too: in the earlier engraving, the servant's gaze does not meet that of her seducer, and her eyes appear to be closed. In the second version she looks directly at him, with no sign of shame, a presentation which underlines her equal participation in the encounter. In the earlier version, Eisen to some extent follows both the De Hooghe engraving (De Hooghe 7) and that of Cochin (which is copied in reverse in the edition of 1755). The pose in both cases is equally awkward, and the husband appears to be using physical force to keep hold of the servant or to push her to the ground, creating a suggestion of rape which is quite foreign to the text of the *conte*.

Eisen's second version shows both a greater concern for propriety and a greater emphasis on the servant's willingness to be seduced by the master. Probability is sacrificed to graphic impact by placing the neighbour much closer to the scene than in the first version. As so often in his illustrations for the *Contes*, Eisen stresses the complicity of women in their seduction, sometimes changing the engraving, as in this case, to make the point more forcefully.

## viii. 'La gageure des trois commères'

*Caption: 'Les trois Commeres font leur gageure à table.'*

All three women (Eisen 11) are dressed in very similar fashionable clothes, as if to draw attention to the resemblances between them as women. The two seated on the left and right of the table are shown being reconciled by the central member of the group in their dispute over the qualities of their husbands (vol.1, p.54). Although light comes through the tall window behind them, it does not illuminate them directly, and they are shown in semi-shadow. La Fontaine tells us that the scene takes place 'après bon vin' (vol.1, p.53), and on the floor to the left is an empty, overturned wine-bottle, with another upright beside it. The woman on the left (who is not wearing, or has lost, her bonnet) has a somewhat inebriated look as she holds out her glass for more wine from the bottle held by the woman on the right. This second figure also has a glass of wine beside her, but does not appear to be drunk. The third woman, placed in the middle to act as a peacemaker between them, has no glass, and does not look as if she has been drinking. It is difficult to see that much importance should be attached to the details of this depiction of the three women, beyond the fact that it contextualises their bibulous con-

De Hooghe 7. 'La servante justifiée', vol.1, p.43

Eisen 11. 'La gageure des trois commères', vol.1, p.53

versation. The significance of the engraving lies, rather, in the fact that it illustrates the prosperous, indolent lives which they lead, and their indifference to social conventions which require fidelity from women and frown on those who show the effects of drinking.

It is clear from the *conte* that each of these women is concerned with sexual intrigue, and not with fidelity to their husbands. The women on the right and in the centre are directly in line with the arrows depicted in the painting of Cupid hanging on the wall behind them, as if to underline the power of desire over propriety. What is more, the sense of 'commère', the term used in the description of the plate, was often not so much 'gossip' as 'femme forte et rusée'.[27] Hence, what Eisen is offering is not the sight of three chattering, ineffectual ladies but three unconventional, sexually active women who are determined to prove their superiority over men, an ambition which will be tested in the remainder of the *conte*.

De Hooghe's headpiece for this *conte* (De Hooghe 8) shows, oddly, not three but four women seated at a table, in front of paintings depicting the three episodes recounted in the tale. Two of the women are shaking hands on their wager. A cat, a traditional symbol of undisciplined freedom, appears to be smiling as it looks out at the viewer, and one of the women is seated on a stool the base of which is decorated with a carved comic mask. The emphasis is therefore, as in many Dutch emblem books of the period,[28] on the artist's complicity with the reader/viewer in mocking human foibles, and in warning either of the dangers of unfettered freedom for women, or of the futility of trying to curb their wish to act freely. Eisen offers, in contrast, a modern depiction of the scene, based on the information in the *conte*, to suggest the insouciance of the women's conduct, without drawing any larger conclusion as to human fallibility.

*Caption: '[P]remier tour. Le mari monté est dans son lit; sa femme debout en écarte avec un dépit simulé la fausse chambriere.'[29]*

This engraving (Eisen 12) is based on trickery and deception by all the parties involved. The wife pretends to be angry at her husband's infidelity (even though she has arranged it); the 'chambermaid' is her lover in disguise. The husband, scolded for his infidelity, in which his wife claims to see 'le scandale et la honte' (vol.1, p.57), is in fact no more or less guilty than they are. Yet the wife and the lover are faking emotion, while the husband is genuinely relieved to have extricated himself from the situation with no greater punishment than a scolding, being (vol.1, p.57)

27. This is the sense given by the *Dictionnaire de Trévoux* (1762).
28. See John Landwehr, *Dutch emblem books: a bibliography* (Utrecht, 1962).
29. According to Cohen (col.567), this engraving also exists in a rejected version, which is a mirror image of the one actually used, and in which the chambermaid is wearing shoes.

De Hooghe 8. 'La gageure des trois commères', vol. I, p.48

Eisen 12. 'La gageure des trois commères', vol.1, p.57

tout heureux
Qu'à si bon compte il en ait été quitte.

In accordance with the text, the 'servant' has a womanly face which is described as 'frais, délicat, le poil au menton' (vol.1, p.55).

Although Cochin used the same scene in 1745 (Cochin 2), Eisen renders it with much more attention to details of the furnishings than in the earlier edition. It would not be going too far to see in Eisen's version a luxurious setting for the episode, and a relatively poor one in Cochin's. The 'chambermaid' is now more obviously feminine than in Cochin's version, but the main difference is that the husband there throws up his hands in astonishment at being discovered, while in Eisen's version he looks impassive, in keeping with La Fontaine's text.

*Caption: '[S]econd tour. Le mari monte sur le poirier; à mesure*
*qu'il monte, son valet se déshabille, & sa femme s'arrange.'*

The text (vol.1, p.60) says only 'le Valet embrasse la Maîtresse'. We are told in the *Avis au relieur* that the husband is climbing the tree (Eisen 13), but he could equally well be coming down. Guillot the valet may be taking his trousers off, or putting them on (although this detail is not specifically stated in the text), while the wife could be undressing or getting dressed. The engraving therefore represents a series of indeterminable moments, for which only the description provides a specific interpretation. For the viewer, the problem is that the tree seems scarcely tall enough to allow the husband to be deceived by the distance between him and the couple, especially as he is able to get down 'en grand'hâte aussi-tôt' (vol.1, p.60). Eisen's reasons for depicting the tree in this way are presumably technical, and dictated by the need to respect the overall size of the frame and by his (or the Fermiers's) reiterated preference for placing the characters close to the viewer. Hence, the formal constraints of the medium, and the use of the description to clarify what might otherwise have remained ambiguous, indicate the extra-diegetic considerations which have to be weighed up in assessing the engravings.

Whatever the formal constraints at work here, the plate is, of course, the product of a series of deliberate choices on the part of the 'author', and these choices must guide our interpretation of it. The husband is dressed in the long coat and full wig typical of older men depicted in the engravings for this edition (compare 'Alix malade' and 'Le contrat'). We see only his face, and not that of the valet, or the full face of the wife. While faces in profile commonly occur in the engravings to other *contes*, it is unusual in the 1762 edition for a character's face to be wholly hidden from the viewer. Such a practice, indeed, seems to be uncommon in French illustrated books of the eighteenth century as a whole, and prompts one to ask why it should be used here. One obvious reason is that

Cochin 2. 'La gageure des trois commères', vol.1, p.46

Eisen 13. 'La gageure des trois commères', vol.1, p.62

we have seen the women in question in the first plate, and do not need to see them again. Even so, that is only a partial explanation, since we cannot tell which wife is which in that instance; it seems more likely therefore that we are not shown her face because it does not matter which of them is the wife in question. In support of this view is the fact that, to judge from the illustrations reproduced in Holloway and in Stewart, faces are hidden for two principal reasons. The first is that the characters concerned, or their reactions, play no significant role in the episode depicted, and can be ignored. The second is that their facial expressions can be inferred from the gestures which they make: the astonishment of the lender depicted in the revised engraving for 'Le savetier' is a case in point. Guillot's lack of embarrassment at pulling up (or down) his britches, and his effrontery in facing the husband he is deceiving is matched by that of the wife, whose face betrays no shame at her conduct. In fact, for different reasons, the faces of the husband and wife betray no apparent emotion, and we can reasonably infer that Guillot is similarly unmoved.

The vast parkland behind the couple is a gratuitous (though perfectly plausible) addition to what is said in the text. But far more significant for understanding the procedures underlying the creation of the engravings for the edition are the proximity of the characters, their position in relation to the viewer, and the description provided in the *Avis au relieur*.

*Caption: '[T]roisiéme tour. L'amant est aux genoux du mari armé de sabres, hallebarde & batonnette; deux femmes & un homme sont dans l'enfoncement.'*

The wife and the servant-girl are similarly dressed (Eisen 14), to show they are in league with each other. Like the previous engraving, this illustration depicts a trick played on a husband whose authority over his wife is insufficient to deter her from cuckolding him; his power is therefore illusory, as the plate demonstrates in several ways. Berlinguier the husband cuts a ludicrous figure with the contrast between his nightcap and his weapons, while the candle placed between the two women is both a reminder of the lover and a further mockery of the inadequacies of the husband. Were he to stand up, the valet on his knees would be taller than the husband. Berlinguier's wife is addressing the chambermaid 'en colère' (vol.1, p.66), pretending to order her out of the house, but this is merely a charade, a deception played on the husband for no reason other than to prove that his wife can outwit him. When he is later induced to provide a dowry for the treacherous maidservant, the trick is complete. As Lapp observes (*Esthetics of negligence*, p.55), the wife and her lover 'quite literally "pull the strings" that once again make him do their bidding, like a marionette'.

All three engravings provided for this *conte* are directed at undermining the authority of husbands, through the concerted efforts of wives and servants, which is the central theme of the text itself. To the extent that

Eisen 14. 'La gageure des trois commères', vol. 1, p.66

they represent a challenge to 'lawful' authority, and a failure on the part of the husband to behave in a conventionally 'manly' fashion, they echo the subversive and critical themes of other illustrations for the *Contes*. The article 'Mari' by Boucher d'Argis, published in the *Encyclopédie* in 1765, provides an instructive comparison with the view of a husband's authority taken by the law (vol.10, p.101):

Parmi les chrétiens, un *mari* est celui qui est uni à une femme par un contrat civil, & avec les cérémonies de l'église. Le *mari* est considéré comme le chef de sa femme, c'est-à-dire comme le maître de la société conjugale. Cette puissance du *mari* sur la femme est la plus ancienne de toutes, puisqu'elle a nécessairement précédé la puissance paternelle, celle des maîtres sur leurs serviteurs, & celle des princes sur leurs sujets. Elle est fondée sur le droit divin; car on lit dans la Genese, *chap. iij.* que Dieu dit à la femme qu'elle seroit sous la puissance de son mari: *sub viri potestate eris, & ipse dominabitur tui.*

## ix. 'Le calendrier des vieillards'

*Caption: 'Le vieillard & sa femme s'entretiennent dans le vaisseau; le corsaire les observe par une embrasure.'*

This is one of the *contes* for which Eisen radically revised his original illustration, although the description applies equally well to both. In the first version (Eisen 15a), the husband Richard is dressed in the frock coat and breeches typically used for older men in Eisen's illustrations. He is shown as an old hunchback (a point not made in the text), and is shorter than his wife. The engraving therefore makes explicit, through Eisen's own choice, Richard's inability to satisfy his wife, a point made only vaguely by La Fontaine who says that he did not have (vol.1, p.70)

de quoi servir
Un tel oiseau qu'étoit Bartholomée.

In this first version, we are, as usual, further away from the figures than in the second.

This latter plate (Eisen 15b) owes a good deal to De Hooghe in the relative positions of the three figures and the nautical accoutrements. However, De Hooghe's Richard is a well-dressed, upright and manly presence, in no sense decrepit or deferential. In Eisen's interpretation, as in De Hooghe's, he carries at his waist a money box containing the ransom for his wife (vol.1, p.74), but he is now much more aged, and coarsely dressed, with leggings and skull-cap. Since there is no indication in the text that Richard is himself poor (indeed, the opposite is suggested by the references to his high social position, his having more than one house, etc.), these changes externalise the poverty of their relationship at an emotional level. His prominent moneybox shows both that he is devoted to his wife, and that he is mistaken in supposing that happiness

Eisen 15a. 'Le calendrier des vieillards', first version, vol.1,
between p.68-69

Eisen 15b. 'Le calendrier des vieillards', second version, vol.1,
between p.68-69

can be measured in terms of financial generosity.[30] Since in the second Eisen version he is much older, his wife's disinclination to return to him, and his inability to satisfy her, become still more comprehensible than in the original engraving; his appearance also suggests, following the text, that he is a man not far from death (vol.1, p.79).

Whereas in the first version, Bartholomée is dressed in the smart fashions of the early 1760s (Quicherat, *Histoire du costume*, p.571), in the second, her dress is less ornate. This change reminds us that, in her words, 'les habits rien n'y font' (vol.1, p.78), and that her need is for love, not for ornate fashions. The contrast between the couple at a physical level is thus accentuated; Bartholomée's expression is harsher than in the first version, as she holds open the door for Richard to leave, refusing now to meet his gaze as she had in the earlier version. There is a cruelty in her indifference (as in the story), and the presence of the hammock above their heads (a detail copied from De Hooghe) adds to the sexual implications of her conduct in a way that the original does not.

The anchor-rope and rigging in both versions of the plate remind us that the scene is on a ship, but the internal setting is more obviously nautical in the original engraving than in the second, where only these elements draw attention to the location. In this respect, Eisen is closer to the text here than in the first version, since La Fontaine does not specifically state that the meeting occurred on board ship. However, Eisen departs entirely from the text in placing the corsair Pagamin in proximity to the couple. Although La Fontaine tells us that the room was closed (vol.1, p.76), and that they are 'sans témoins' (vol.1, p.78), both De Hooghe (De Hooghe 9) and Eisen depict Pagamin, unobserved, as a silent witness to the conversation of the couple. In Eisen's original engraving, he is placed at some distance from them, out of earshot, but in the second version he is close enough to see and to hear what is said. Although, in De Hooghe's engraving, Pagamin is only dimly visible outside the door,[31] in Eisen's his exotic presence offers a visual contrast with Richard, thereby diminishing further the latter's manly status. In the second version, Pagamin is shown with his finger placed on his lips (a point not made in the text), to indicate that he is reflecting on the lesson to be learned from the experience of the couple. His function now is to represent the reader as much as to be an alternative to Richard. The light is much brighter here than in the first engraving, no doubt to hint at the clarification of relationships and feelings which the scene entails. As Lapp puts it

30. According to Catherine Grisé, his arguments for concentrating on material happiness as a substitute for performing his conjugal duties are based on casuistic reasoning derived from Jesuit sources ('La casuistique dans les *Contes* de La Fontaine', *Studi francesi* 97, 1989, p.411-21, p.414).

31. Compare Nicolich, 'Seventeenth and eighteenth-century illustrations for La Fontaine's *Contes et nouvelles en vers*', p.254-57.

De Hooghe 9. 'Le calendrier des vieillards', vol. 1, p. 61

(*Esthetics of negligence*, p.72), in this *conte* 'La Fontaine transforms the Gallic tradition [of male impotence] into a plea for the rights of nature.'

Yet even this latter version by Eisen is more faithful to the text than Cochin, who shows the husband, the wife and the pirate on an elevated part of the ship, with other pirates looking on. Bartholomée seems displeased, as Richard places an (erect, phallic) bag of money into the pirate's cloak as he offers in order to ransom his wife. The shape of the bag which he proffers serves only to emphasise the sexual potency of Pagamin in a gesture from which Bartholomée turns away with distaste. Eisen prefers to remain discreet in suggesting the inadequacy of the husband as a lover, and to stress that the contempt which Bartholomée feels for him is expressed in private, as the text requires.

The distinction between Eisen's first and second engravings for this *conte* does not rest on technical grounds alone. There is more emotional and psychological complexity in the later version, and a greater emphasis on the human tragedy at the heart of the story, as well as on the sexuality of women. These are, of course, recurrent themes of the stories and of Eisen's interpretations of them.

## x. 'A femme avare galant escroc'

*Caption: 'Le mari assis devant une table feuillette un registre; l'amant est debout à côté de lui; la femme est derrière.'*

The description is equally applicable to both versions of the engraving, the earlier of which is very slightly smaller than the later. In both, the 'galant' is smartly dressed in the fashion of the 1760s and carries a sword to affirm his status as a gentleman (an ironic precision in view of his conduct towards the wife). Both versions show three figures, at the point in the story where the 'galant' Gulphar, telling the husband Gasparin that he has returned the money to his wife, asks him to delete the debt from his account-book. The books in the background are an addition by Eisen, but argue that the husband is a scholar or man of commerce.

In the rejected engraving (Eisen 16a, which has much in common with the Cochin design found in the 1743 edition),[32] Gasparin is in shadow. His features are scarcely discernible, and his back is towards the viewer; his age is indicated by his wearing the nightcap and dressing gown habitually worn by older men in Eisen's illustrations. There is nothing in the text to justify this presentation, unless we specifically interpret 'sire Gasparin' (vol.1, p.81) as a hint that he is elderly, and not

---

32. In 1745, the headpieces designed by Cochin in 1743 for this and two other *contes*, 'On ne s'avise jamais de tout' and 'Les Rémois', were replaced with designs by Lancret, engraved by Larmessin.

Eisen 16a. 'A femme avare, galant escroc', first version, vol. I,
between p.80-81

merely older than Gulphar.[33] If we read the hat as a symbol of the female sex-organ (as it often is in the Eisen's illustrations for the *Contes*), it serves as a reminder of the illicit love affair, and as a means of mocking Gasparin's sexual prowess.

While Eisen's depiction of Gasparin as an elderly man may hint that he is unable to satisfy his wife, it does not account for her wanting money for her favours. Her greed is indicated sufficiently in the title of the *conte* and in the statement that 'elle étoit avare' (vol.1, p.82). She is unsmiling, and seems to be moving away from the 'galant', offended at being tricked (she is, according to the text, 'aussi froide que glace', vol.1, p.83).

In the second version (Eisen 16b), the husband, who is now in full view, still wears a nightcap and dressing gown, but is not obviously an old man. His gaze is directed towards Gulphar's hat, perhaps suspecting its sexual significance, whereas in the earlier version he seemed almost asleep over his books. The wife's hand is on her lips as a gesture of surprise, but there is no sign of her coldness towards Gulphar: contradicting the text, she manages to smile. Her controlled reaction is more in keeping with the trick she has played on her husband in selling her favours, and is therefore more a metonymic indication of her duplicity than a direct reflection of the text. Both the wife and the 'galant' (who are equal in height to show that they are equally guilty) are now more overtly complicit in deceiving the (possibly suspicious) husband, whose physical appearance does not suggest that he is too old to satisfy his wife. Gulphar will inflict further humiliation on the (unnamed) wife by recounting publicly how he has deceived her (vol.1, p.83). The partial concealment of his hat and sword in the second version may be read not only as a way of mocking his status as a gentleman (since he does not behave like one), but also as an outward sign of his duplicity.

The placing of the figures in Eisen's two illustrations differs from that of his predecessors. De Hooghe (De Hooghe 10) shows the lover and the husband together on the left; the husband gaze is directed towards his books, while the wife looks in silent rage at the smiling Gulphar. The contrast between the two men in terms of age, clothing and so on is less marked than in Eisen, though the tall presence of the 'galant' marks him out as the superior figure, a distinction which is absent from the 1762 plates. In Cochin's vignette, the 'galant' is placed (symbolically) between the standing wife and the seated husband, at whom his gaze is directed. All three are ornately dressed, though the diminutive scale of the engraving impedes any clear correlative of emotions through facial expression. Eisen is alone in using the wide angle of the arms of the wife and the 'galant' as a counterpart to the coldness between them, and in

33. In the *Dictionnaire de Trévoux* (1762), 'Sire' is defined as a term of respect, but not specifically as one denoting age; in 'Le Gascon puni', it is used of an evidently young man (vol.1, p.88).

Eisen 16b. 'A femme avare, galant escroc', second version, vol.1,
between p.80-81

De Hooghe 10. 'A femme avare, galant escroc', vol.1, p.71

placing the three people involved in a triangle. Indeed, the description explains only their positions relative to one another, without suggesting any direct link between them; by means of these devices, Eisen indicates the emotional distance between them perhaps more subtly than either De Hooghe or Cochin.

## xi. 'On ne s'avise jamais de tout'

*Caption: 'Une suivante jette par une fenêtre une corbeille d'ordures sur la Dame, qui entre au logis aidée de deux autres femmes, & commande à sa douëgne d'aller lui chercher des habits.'*

Eisen designed two different versions of the illustration for this *conte*. In the first (Eisen 17a), which was rejected, the adulterous wife's dress is more elaborate and expensive, and thus less fitting for the premeditated plan she has in mind; the whole purpose of her ruse is to ensure that the dress is stained by what the maid throws over it. In this earlier version, as usual, the characters are further away from us; the wife also is further away from the (quite low) window from which the rubbish has been thrown on to her dress; she is not looking at the stain, and carries only a fan. Her 'galant' is visible inside the house, and the servant who threw the rubbish is distant enough from the incident to appear uninvolved. Though none is mentioned in the text, another servant from the house is shown, but her role in the event is unclear. The chaperone who accompanies the wife on behalf of the husband is shown in shadow (reminding one of the etymo-logical link between the senses of *ombrage* as both 'shade' and 'suspicion'). In pointing to the right to tell her to fetch another dress, the wife takes the chaperone's gaze away from the waiting lover. In the background can be seen the spire of the church from which the wife is returning, as a reminder that its values are of little use in preventing the sins it condemns.

In the second version (Eisen 17b), the servant is placed at a greater height above the wife, but closer to her, and the rubbish is actually falling from the basket she is holding. There is no sign of the waiting lover. Two servants from the house are shown, adding to the effect of fuss; by acting in concert with the servant at the window in accordance with the plan, they disconcert the chaperone. In her left hand the wife carries a fly-whisk(?), which replaces the fan of the earlier version, and which reveals her intention to protect herself against at least some of the less pleasant consequences of the stratagem which she has arranged. Her imperious gesture to the chaperone (who is again in shadow) is more pronounced than in the rejected version, suggesting the social gap between them rather than a ruse to deflect her attention from the waiting lover. This gesture is made at the very moment when rubbish is still falling on the

Eisen 17a. 'On ne s'avise jamais de tout', first version, vol. 1,
between p.84-85

Eisen 17b. 'On ne s'avise jamais de tout', second version, vol. 1,
between p. 84-85

De Hooghe 11. 'On ne s'avise jamais de tout', vol.1, p.75

wife's dress (or more precisely, on the back of her dress, rather than at the front, as in the first version). What is more, the two servants are attending to her while she is still standing under it. In this later version, the wife's gaze meets directly that of the servant to her left, to suggest their complicity. We therefore have several indications that this is a staged scene, in which the wife is immediately ready to send for another dress, and in no hurry to place herself beyond the range of the falling rubbish. The presence of the two servants leads one to conclude, much more than with the first version of the engraving, that this is a concerted action, that the chaperone is not part of the cabal to which the wife and the other servants belong.

The chaperone may perhaps suspect her mistress's intentions, but she cannot refuse to obey. The guard shown on the column in the background is as ineffectual as the chaperone herself in preventing what should not happen. In the distance we see the dome of a building which recalls in part both the façade of the Vatican and the Collège des Quatre Nations. The conjunction of these two embodiments of masculine wisdom and authority is proof that all men's moral strictures and learning are of little avail against the cunning of women ('nous avons beau sur le sexe avoir l'œil', vol.1, p.86). This point is particularised in the attempts by the husband to prevent his wife's infidelity (vol.1, p.85):

> [Il] avoit fait un fort ample recueil
> De tous les tours que le sexe sçait faire.
> Pauvre ignorant! Comme si cette affaire
> N'étoit une hidre, à parler franchement.

In both engravings, the contrast between the ugliness of the chaperone and the other women puts her (literally) in a bad light. We are not explicitly asked to judge the wife's conduct, but by placing in shadow the chaperone whose task it is to prevent her being unfaithful, the plate implicitly rejects her viewpoint and functions. The text does not specifically state the wife is young and attractive, but the reasons for making her appear so are self-evident. As with many of the *contes* for which two versions of the engraving exist, the second version gives a much greater emphasis to light then the first. The scene takes place more obviously in the open, near a public square. La Fontaine does not tell us that the wife had arranged for the soiling of her dress to take place, though his statement that it occurs 'Fort à propos' (vol.1, p.85) suggests strongly that some such plan has been concocted in advance.[34] The readiness with which the chaperone departs to find a clean dress suggests that she suspects nothing of the ruse, and it is left to the husband to realise that his plans have been thwarted by feminine cunning (vol.1, p.86).

34. See also Lapp, *The Esthetics of negligence*, p.118.

There are marked contrasts, therefore, between the rejected engraving and its replacement, but the differences between both versions and those provided by earlier illustrators are no less apparent. De Hooghe (De Hooghe 11) depicts not the actual incident with the maids, but the chaperone on her way to fetch a clean dress. If she is an unattractive figure in the Eisen engravings, she is now an object of derision as she makes her way through the streets, wrapped in the soiled dress as the bystanders watch her retreat. She thereby becomes the central figure in the tale, while the adulterous wife and the servants are reduced to small background presences. Some unidentified liquid continues to pour from a jug on the first floor of the house, though it falls on none of those below. The focus of the central event is thus very different in De Hooghe's version, and at the centre of his interpretation we have not drama but mockery.

In Cochin's vignette, the husband (with his 'recueil' in his hand) listens as the chaperone recounts the duplicity of his wife, who can be seen in the distance entering a house with another man. Two dogs forage in the foreground (perhaps for the 'ordures' which have stained her dress). There is no clear indication of complicity here, and little attempt on the part of the wife to conceal her adultery. Indeed, the husband needs only to turn around to see her entering the house with her lover; the fact that her conduct is so brazen, and that he fails to notice it, is in itself a comment on his foolishness. As Holloway observes (*French rococo book illustration*, p.32): 'It must seem impossible, after one sight of Eisen, that the combination of these varied elements could ever have been otherwise than as it is, and yet in the similarly telescoped presentation by Cochin it is as static as could be.'

In both the De Hooghe and the Cochin illustrations, the emphasis is placed not on the wife, but on other characters. Eisen shows the drama of the occasion, the contrast between the wife and the chaperone and, by means of the architectural allusions added to the second version, makes a wider point about the relationship of the sexes and about human behaviour in general.

## xii. 'Le Gascon puni'

*Caption: 'Il est sur son séant dans un lit; une jolie femme en sort
à demi nue, & se jette dans les bras d'une autre femme;
un jeune homme éclaire l'intérieur du lit.'*

The engraving (Eisen 18) shows a scene from the very end of the *conte*. The boastful Dorilas, whose ambition is to seduce Philis, is awakened by the arrival of Cloris and Damon. He then discovers that he has in fact spent the night (innocently) with her, under the impression that he was sharing the bed with Eurilas, whom his friends wished to deceive. His

Eisen 18. 'Le Gascon puni', vol.1, p.87

realisation of the trick played on him, following a night fearing discovery by 'Eurilas', has removed all traces of his boastfulness, and makes him an object of ridicule. We know nothing of the physical attributes of Dorilas, other than his name and that he is a Gascon. For La Fontaine, there is no need to specify further (vol.1, p.88): 'Il étoit Gascon; c'est tout dire.' Of Philis, we know that she is 'libre, gaie, sincère', that she is twenty years old and recently widowed, that she has

> des attraits par-dessus les yeux,
> je ne sçais quel air de pucelle

(despite being married – but to an old man, it is true). Of the other couple, Cloris and Damon, we know nothing except that they love each other.

It is customary for the descriptions to these engravings to identify the figures shown, and one is struck by the anonymity of the description here: it is as though the Fermiers wish to draw attention to the typical nature of the scene, rather than to highlight its distinctive qualities. Yet what is missing in the description is any indication of the emotions felt by those involved in the episode. In the closing lines of the *conte*, La Fontaine refers to '[l]a peine et la frayeur extrême' of Dorilas (vol.1, p.91). These feelings are not immediately apparent from the face of the figure sitting up in bed, who might be thought to display, at most, a degree of surprise as he holds his arms open. The feelings of the other three figures are scarcely more apparent: Damon, who holds the candle, is amused, as is Cloris on the right; Philis, with whom Dorilas has just spent the night, looks impassive.[35]

Nonetheless, Eisen has found other ways to convey how we should react to Dorilas; his clothed body contrasts with the semi-nakedness of Philis, and he is set apart from the group, suggesting clearly his isolation and his rejection by them. His boastfulness and vanity have earned his disgrace, whereas Philis is beautiful and has friends. Dorilas is set at a lower level than the other three to stress his inferiority, and Damon's open arms as he holds up the (phallic) candle mock his gesture of astonishment. Philis's legs are slightly apart, showing him 'ce qu'il avoit perdu' (vol.1, p.91), and the point is emphasised by the scarcely veiled legs of Cloris. As ever in these illustrations, the bed-curtains are opened to display a scene which would customarily be hidden, but the truth about Dorilas is revealed by visual means which require the viewer to consider not so much the depiction of individual characters as the overall coherence of the illustration.

The punishment of the vainglorious boaster is an old theme; but it is noticeable that the features of the *conte* which Eisen illustrates make apparent the Gascon's absence of attractive qualities, through the use of physical separation, a lower position and ironic iconography.

35. See Lapp, *The Esthetics of negligence*, p.134.

De Hooghe's headpiece for the *conte* (De Hooghe 12) recalls Eisen's illustration in that it depicts the moment when Dorilas, amidst the opened curtains of the bed, is discovered by the plotters. Yet he is not shown at a lower level than his companions, nor is he isolated from them. Philis likewise displays surprise through her expression and gesture, which are more striking than those of Dorilas and, owing to her proximity to the viewer, more apparent than his own. They are also difficult to account for, since she was part of the 'plot' against him. Nor does De Hooghe allow so great a display of alluring femininity as that which figures in Eisen's interpretation; though Philis does have one breast discreetly bared, she is otherwise swathed in clothing, as is Cloris. Some of the same elements are to be found in the headpiece by Cochin for the 1745 edition, though there are differences (Cochin 3). Philis's physical beauty is less apparent; Damon's gestures do not echo mockingly those of Dorilas, and the position of the three characters (the two women to the left, Damon to the right) does not isolate Dorilas literally and metaphorically as Eisen's illustration does. Hence, the difference of emphasis between Eisen and his predecessors lies in the presentation of the female figures and in the mockery of Dorilas, both of which are more apparent in the Fermiers' edition than in the earlier illustrations for this *conte*. The care which Eisen takes to interpret coherently and in his own way the information given in the *conte* is as apparent here as in his other illustrations for the work.

## xiii. 'La fiancée du roi de Garbe'

*Caption: 'Hispal nage avec l'Infante sur son dos, & gagne le rocher sur lequel il saisit une branche d'arbre.'*

This is one of the longest and most complex of La Fontaine's tales, and the text has attracted a good deal of critical comment, much of it directed at underlining the depiction of contemporary French mores in an apparently exotic story.[36] The illustrations which Eisen provided for it echo these features, distant though they might initially seem to be from the life of eighteenth-century France. The first engraving (Eisen 19) shows Hispal and Alaciel reaching the rocks after their shipwreck. Hispal still wears his hat, while Alaciel still has her royal robes and what appears to be her tiara. Her dark skin, like Hispal's turban, recalls their North African origins. But Eisen departs from the text in several significant respects. First, far from consisting only of rocks, the outcrop on which the couple are able to save themselves displays trees and bushes, the presence of which is at odds with La Fontaine's statement 'Point de quoi manger sur ces roches' (vol.1, p.98). Second, Alaciel's 'cassette' of jewels is firmly

36. See the references given in Catherine Grisé, 'Erotic dimensions of space in La Fontaine's "La fiancée du roi de Garbe"', *Modern language review* 82 (1987), p.587-98.

De Hooghe 12. 'Le Gascon puni', vol. i, p.77

Cochin 3. 'Le Gascon puni', vol.1, p.74

Eisen 19. 'La fiancée du roi de Garbe', vol.1, p.93

attached to Hispal's waist, whereas the text says 'La belle après soi la tira' (vol.1, p.97). If Hispal, who is merely a 'jeune Seigneur de la cour' (vol.1, p.95) is made to carry the box, it is not only because so large an attachment could well have hampered the progress of a young princess already encumbered by heavy robes. It is also because Eisen wishes to stress Alaciel's dependence on him. Indeed, the artificiality of social divisions is hinted at by La Fontaine, who observes that princesses 'sont de chair, ainsi que les bergères'.[37] One can also, of course, interpret 'la cassette' as connoting Alaciel's imperilled virtue, since it allows her to buy her way out of many difficult situations.[38]

Eisen follows De Hooghe quite closely, except that the shore depicted by the earlier artist is much rockier, with little foliage (De Hooghe 13). While Alaciel is shown pulling the 'cassette' behind her, there is no indication of her royal status, and her dependence on Hispal is thus represented as entirely circumstantial, with no explicit class distinction. This is also the case with Cochin's vignette, which shows a shoreline even barer than that of De Hooghe. Thus, while both previous illustrators stress the vulnerability of the two characters, Eisen has preserved the drama of their situation, emphasising their respective social rank and Alaciel's utter dependence on Hispal, reminding readers perhaps of the court's financial dependence on the Fermiers...

*Caption: 'Hispal et l'Infante sont assis au fond d'une grotte;*
*Hispal explique ses désirs à l'Infante qui l'écoute incertaine,*
*tremblante et à demi-vaincue.'*

This engraving (Eisen 20) continues the theme of Alaciel's reliance on Hispal, in the 'antre' (vol.1, p.101) where Hispal declares his love, and where (vol.1, p.103) 'L'Infante à ces raisons se [rend] à demi.' There is no sign of the rain mentioned by La Fontaine (vol.1, p.103), and while, according to the text, the couple are walking there 'un jour' (vol.1, p.101), Eisen depicts a scene only partly illuminated, to stress the secrecy and seclusion of the grotto. There is a slight problem however, in that the couple are clearly not 'au fond d'une grotte' as the description would have it, but seated outside it, surrounded by trees. Whether this discrepancy indicates that the description was prepared for a discarded plate, or is merely a sign of inadvertence on the part of the editors, it is not possible to say.

Hispal's left hand moves towards Alaciel's sex; although her gesture might be seen in itself as one of disinclination to comply with his advances, the description (and the text) make it clear that any resistance on her part is slight. Alaciel has her jewels (which are not mentioned specifically in text), and although the couple are in the woods, they are

37. Vol.1, p.95. See Lapp, *The Esthetics of negligence*, p.63.
38. This interpretation is discussed by Grisé, 'Erotic dimensions of space', p.595.

De Hooghe 13. 'La fiancée du roi de Garbe', vol.1, p.82

Eisen 20. 'La fiancée du roi de Garbe', vol.1, p.103

dressed as for court; indeed, their cloaks are so long that they drag on the ground. Their elegant attire is a reminder of their social rank, but also of the ostensible difference between them. Alaciel yields (vol.1, p.104) because natural impulses are strong enough to overcome social divisions, and hence the choice of this episode as a subject for illustrations is laden with social as well as sexual significance. Here as elsewhere, Eisen has subtly altered the indications given in the text in order to emphasise the ascendancy of the natural over the social.

La Fontaine does not mention the clothes worn by the couple, and therefore the contrast between court and country is made here for the first time. This contrast is especially apparent in the difference between the elegance of the clothing and the wild, almost Romantic, grotto which serves as a setting.[39] Something of the sort can also be seen in Cochin's illustration of the Grotto of Pozzuoli in the *Observations sur les antiquités d'Herculanum* (1754), a work which had drawn attention to the wildness of the Italian landscape. Such wildness was, of course, not unknown to seventeenth-century French painters such as Gaspard Poussin, but it was to be an increasingly prominent feature of landscape painting in France and elsewhere in the decades to come. One finds it, for example, in the work of artists such as de Loutherbourg, who painted pastorals scenes set against rocky landscapes, and in the paintings of ruins made popular by Hubert Robert and others.[40] As in other illustrations for the *Contes*, Eisen and the Fermiers show themselves attuned to developing tastes in art, no doubt as a way of increasing the work's appeal to contemporary connoisseurs.

*Caption: 'La scène est dans un pavillon. L'Infante échue par le sort au gentilhomme fait signe à sa suivante de se retirer.'*

Whereas the previous engraving depicts a seduction, this third illustration (Eisen 21) is concerned with the 'galant' to whom Alaciel offers herself in place of the 'suivante' whom he proposed to ravish. Neither woman's face betrays fear or other negative emotions, even though the 'galant' has threatened them with violence (vol.1, p.116). From her stance, the 'suivante' is torn between wanting to leave and not wanting to abandon Alaciel, who is already half-embracing the 'gentilhomme' (a point not stated in the text). Alaciel wears her royal robes, to distinguish herself from the 'suivante', and to underline the determination of the 'galant' who, despite his inferior social status, is undeterred.

---

39. Anne L. Birberick refers to the 'pastoral' setting of this part of the *conte*: 'From world to text: the figure of the nun in La Fontaine's *Contes*', in *Refiguring La Fontaine: tercentenary essays*, ed. Anne L. Birberick (Charlottesville, VA, 1999), p.95.

40. See Conisbee, *Painting in eighteenth-century France*, p.171-200.

Eisen 21. 'La fiancée du roi de Garbe', vol. 1, p. 117

This engraving therefore has echoes of the previous illustration, in that a man of lower rank succeeds in bending Alaciel to his will. The differences however are equally significant: the scene takes place not in a shady, secluded grotto, but in an open *pavillon* in the presence of the 'suivante' (though the text does not state that she witnesses the scene), and Alaciel's motives are not sentimental but self-sacrificing. The illustration represents a further stage in her acceptance of her role as a sexual partner. Whereas in the earlier plate she had to some degree resisted seduction by Hispal whom she loved, she now accepts without further ado the attentions of a man whom she does not know, and whose motives are unmixed with any sentimental attachment to her.

In the course of these three engravings, therefore, Alaciel changes from being a woman utterly dependent on a man to save her and her jewels, to being one who gives herself willingly to a potential rapist without apparently being any the worse for the experience. The text informs us from the outset that she is perhaps less innocent than she pretends, in proleptically announcing the conclusion of the story. By the time she eventually meets her fiancé, she is (vol.1, p.94)

> Veuve de huit Galans, il la prit pour pucelle;
> Et dans son erreur par la Belle
> Apparemment il fut laissé

La Fontaine does not condemn her for her conduct, seeking always to excuse it on the grounds of 'bonne intention, gratitude ou compassion' (vol.1, p.94). Yet the episodes which are highlighted in the illustrations, by altering the information given in the *conte* itself, present Alaciel's story as one of gradual self-affirmation in the face of male sexuality.[41]

There is an important distinction to be made here between the significance of Alaciel in the text and the way she is presented in the engravings. As Catherine Grisé points out, at the time he wrote most of the *Contes*, La Fontaine was, however surprising it might seem, closely linked to the Jansenists of Port-Royal. The arguments Alaciel uses to justify giving herself to her various lovers read like a parody of Jesuit casuistry, which placed emphasis on the intentions behind an action, rather than on the action itself.[42] Grisé also argues that Alaciel is treated like a commodity, to be passed from one man to another, in a perpetual 'male fantasy' (p.594). This parodic, phallocratic element is not however apparent from the illustrations, which cumulatively show Alaciel as a self-assertive, even independent woman, typical of those presented in the *Contes et nouvelles*.[43] A comparison of the engravings with the indications

41. Lapp, *The Esthetics of negligence*, p.65.
42. Grisé, 'Erotic dimensions of space', p.592-93, and Grisé, 'La casuistique dans les *Contes*', p.415-21.
43. With no sense of inconsistency, Grisé also claims that 'Alaciel's "cassette" [...] ultimately confers on her a determining power in the action' ('Erotic dimensions', p.595).

provided in the *conte* therefore shows both the significance of the interpretation in relation to the original, and the danger of seeing the engravings merely as a 'representation' of the story on which they are based. The plates are intimate, depicting amorous, or at least sexual, encounters, rather than the large-scale set-pieces such as the assault by the Corsairs (vol.1, p.95-96) or the attack on the château (vol.1, p.109-11). At the same time, the plates do echo the text in one significant respect in that both omit any reference to the violence which typifies Boccaccio's treatment of the story.[44] Similarly, the elaborate tailpiece by Choffard shows two shields bearing the initials of Mamolin and Alaciel, surrounded by garlands and flowers, with medallions hanging beneath them as reminders that Alaciel's previous lovers need be no obstacle to her wedding.

## xiv. 'La coupe enchantée'

*Caption: 'Regnault à table, dans une salle de château, avec nombreuse compagnie, refuse de boire dans la coupe.'*

There exists a rejected version of the plate for this *conte* (Eisen 22a) which is rarely found; it shows Damon spilling the contents of the cup given to him by the sorceress Nérie (vol.1, p.140-41), indicating the effect of his belief that he has been cuckolded.[45] The poor quality of the engraving, and its somewhat tedious subject matter, explain why it was discarded in favour of the much more animated version usually included in copies of the *Contes*.

Most of the men shown in the replacement engraving (Eisen 22b) have beards, in the fashion of soldiers of medieval times. Damon, who is holding the cup which can reveal whether Regnault's wife is faithful, is beardless as a sign of his youth (vol.2, p.133-34). The man seated on the left looks out directly at the viewer, pointing to Regnault, who refuses the cup which will tell him whether his wife is faithful. Regnault's gesture in turn directs our gaze across the image, towards the young man on the right who is himself pointing to the horns. This continuity of gesture establishes the link between Regnault's refusal of the cup and the likelihood of men in general being cuckolded.

With its direct appeal to the viewer and the visual designation of the traditional symbol of cuckoldry, this is one of the most overtly didactic engravings in the 1762 edition. The soldiers crowded into the room indicate how common cuckoldry is, since all those present have failed to drink from the cup proffered by Damon, and have been enlisted into his army. But these same men are the causes of cuckoldry (a point not made

44. See Lapp, *The Esthetics of negligence*, p.63-64, 68.
45. See also Cohen, *Guide de l'amateur de livres*, col.567; an eau-forte for it is included in the Grenville copy.

Eisen 22a. 'La coupe enchantée', first version, vol.1, between p.126-27

Eisen 22b. 'La coupe enchantée', second version, vol.1, between p.126-27

in any detail by La Fontaine, whose concern is with the infidelity of wives). This is clear from the phallic implications of the large number of lances (there are seventeen in all, one for each of the men present). The prominence in the foreground of a dog, the traditional symbol of fidelity, is doubly ironic, not only because of the contrast with human conduct, but also because it is placed close to the sword of one of the revellers.

Regnault alone is in armour, presumably to show that only he can withstand the temptation to drink, fortified as he is by his determination not to know the truth about his wife ('Je crois ma femme chaste, et cette foi suffit', vol.1, p.145). Through the use of deictic gestures, the emphasis is as much on the viewer's own chances of being cuckolded as those of Regnault. The text concludes (vol.1, p.146):

> Nul mortel, soit Roland, soit Renaud,
> Du danger de répandre exempt ne se peut croire.
> Charlemagne lui-même auroit eu tort de boire.

The illustration therefore invites the reader to conclude that, whether or not we follow Regnault's example in refusing to know the truth, that truth will be the same, namely that men may well be cuckolded. In that sense, Regnault's refusal to drink from the cup is of marginal importance. As he recognises, if he is unable to drink without spilling the contents (the alleged proof of his wife's infidelity), the explanation may lie in his carelessness, rather than in her misconduct, and in such cases ignorance is bliss.

De Hooghe depicts a superficially similar scene, with soldiers in Roman dress carousing at a table in a tent (De Hooghe 14), their antique remoteness suggesting the universality of the theme of cuckoldry. One of their number is wearing a set of horns, while another is spilling his drink from his cup. However, there is nothing overtly didactic here. For that, we need to look at the influence of Cochin. In 1745 we have another version of the scene, in which Regnault's back is to the viewer. As in 1762 the figures are clothed in a mixture of antiquated and modern costumes; in each case, the armour worn by Regnault vaguely resembles that worn in the sixteenth century, at the time of François I$^{er}$.[46]

Neither Cochin nor Eisen make any attempt to replicate accurately the armour of the time of Charlemagne, at which the Regnault episode is set. Their purpose is not to achieve antiquarian accuracy, any more than Gravelot, for example, sought to depict medieval armour correctly in his engravings for Voltaire's *La Pucelle* which likewise appeared in 1762. Both Cochin and Eisen (unlike De Hooghe) choose a setting which is not so much historical as vaguely antique, and make no attempt at technical correctness in depicting settings or architecture. In both cases, the men who witness Regnault's gesture in declining the cup express some degree of surprise. In both, too, there is the same didactic intent through a deictic

46. See Quicherat, *Histoire du costume*, p.374-75.

De Hooghe 14. 'La coupe enchantée', vol.1, p.112

reference to cuckold's horns, though the man seated on the left in Eisen's version has no equivalent in Cochin's vignette.

Through the use of deictic elements, Cochin and, to a greater degree, Eisen stress the applicability of the scene to the contemporary viewer, rather than its seeming remoteness from him. Most emphatically amongst the three illustrations, the roistering, cheerful atmosphere of the Eisen engraving reflects the indifference to cuckoldry advocated by La Fontaine (vol.1, p.128):

> Quand on l'ignore, ce n'est rien;
> Quand on le sait, c'est peu de chose.

Certainly, as Lapp points out (*The Esthetics of negligence*, p.103-10), the disdainful aristocratic ethic underlying these sentiments is typical of the attitude espoused in La Fontaine's time, further traces of which can be found in 'Joconde'. Whether or not such a view had percolated down into other classes at that period, there can be little doubt that, by the middle of the eighteenth century, the Fermiers themselves were not over-inclined to regard the sacraments of marriage as binding. As Durand puts it (*Les Fermiers généraux*, p.306): 'Il est deux attitudes chez nos financiers devant le mariage: l'idéal du mariage chrétien et son antithèse: le mariage de convenance où les deux époux restent libres de leur conduite, où il n'est plus question de fidélité conjugale et où, à l'extrême, le mariage paraît lui-même honteux, restrictif d'une liberté qui se voudrait totale.' In such a perspective, it becomes plausible to see in the gesture of the man on the right a confirmation of the inevitability of cuckoldry, and to regard the pikestaffs and sword as an intimation of male lust against which the viewer should be on guard. The jovial companionship depicted by Eisen is wholly in keeping with the acceptance of cuckoldry and adultery which runs not only through the illustrations, but through the *Contes* as well.

## xv. 'Le faucon'

*Caption: 'Fédéric donne un tournois [ sic ] à sa maitresse.'*

The engraving (Eisen 23) draws attention to an aspect of Fédéric's extravagance towards his mistress, which is mentioned only in passing: 'de maints tournois elle fut le sujet' (vol.1, p.148). It is not hard to see why: of all the items mentioned in the list of his expenses, a tournament is the most overtly costly item which can be realised as a scene, with huge crowds, and other signs of indulgence. Clitie, the object of his adoration, is placed in a raised loge at the top left, in the position of a queen or great lady. By being elevated in this way, she appears to us (metaphorically and literally) in the same exalted position as she occupies in Fédéric's mind. Two other figures in the loge with her are almost eclipsed; she is both the reason for the joust and its most prominent ornament. As she points her

Eisen 23. 'Le faucon', vol. I, p. 147

finger at some aspect of the contest, she seems unaware that other, more exposed, members of the crowd are attempting to flee in alarm. This indifference reflects her attitude to Fédéric's generosity (vol.1, p.149-50):

> la Belle ne prit rien,
> Argent ni dons, mais souffrit la dépense
> Et les cadeaux, sans croire pour cela
> Etre obligée à nulle récompense.

The soldiers at the front with pikes are attempting to protect, or to drive back, the crowd which seems terrified of the violence of the joust. At the same time, a large number of spectators are standing on the roof of the building opposite the loge, with only a low balustrade to prevent them from falling into the courtyard below. If we are to judge by the terror on the faces of those at the lower centre of the engraving, the crowd immediately behind the two riders is also too close for safety. The darkening skies, taken together with these details, hint at imminent peril, even though it is a danger in which people have placed themselves, as Fédéric has done.

This salutary warning is of course called into question by the sculpture surmounting the building opposite the loge. It shows Diana, the goddess of hunting, with her bow and arrows, and with a bird of prey perched on her shoulders. The sculpture is not mentioned in the text, although the classical parallels are evident from the statement that the musicians employed by Fédéric were (vol.1, p.148-49)

> gens du sacré vallon;
> Fédéric eut à sa table Apollon.

Even though the text does not specifically require a reference to Diana, a depiction of her is entirely appropriate to the story. She was averse to marriage, and was famed for her purity, qualities which offer parallels with the conduct of Clitie towards her aspiring lover. Again, Diana's reputation as a huntress meant that she was of stronger character than many men, as Clitie is stronger than Fédéric (vol.1, p.147-48):

> pour lui plaire il eût vendu son âme [...]
> Elle tint bon; Fédéric échoua
> Près de ce roc, et le nez s'y cassa.

The bird of prey attending her is not required by traditional association; it is shown as a proleptic reference to the falcon which will ultimately precipitate the union of Clitie and Fédéric, thus causing her to forsake the Diana-like aspects of her behaviour which have long kept them apart.

*Caption: 'On voit l'intérieur d'une chaumière. Une vieille est dans l'enfoncement auprès de la cheminée; la maîtresse de Fédéric lui présente une main qu'il arrose de ses pleurs.'*

Eisen's illustration (Eisen 24) depicts the scene in Fédéric's cottage after the meal at which he and Clitie have consumed the falcon which she had

Eisen 24. 'Le faucon', vol.1, p.157

hoped to obtain for her dying son. In contrast with the public pomp of the first plate, the bareness and domestic simplicity of the surroundings indicate all too clearly how far Fédéric has fallen from his previous luxurious life as a result of his blind devotion to Clitie.

Echoes of the previous scene persist none the less. Clitie is still opulently dressed, to underline the reason for Fédéric's downfall; his adoration of her is evident, and beyond help. The old woman (a 'vieille édentée', according to the text, vol.1, p.150) looks away, aware of what has brought him to this state, but unable to remedy the situation. To emphasise his fall, Fédéric is placed at a lower level than either woman, though the text does not state that he is seated when he kisses Clitie's hand. Her stance and expression are those of a woman who realises the depth of Fédéric's affection for her; it is the visual transcription of her words (vol.1, p.156):

> Vous ne m'avez jamais
> De votre amour donné plus grande marque.[47]

The hunting-guns refer obliquely to the statue of Diana crowning the building in the earlier engraving, but more immediately points up for us the decline of Fédéric, a hunter himself, as we are reminded (vol.1, p.151). His poverty and the more than modest lifestyle he has in the cottage are further underlined by the fact that he has been reduced to sacrificing the falcon with which he hunts partridge (vol.1, p.150, 152), in order to offer a meal to Clitie.

The killing and eating of the falcon is also, as it turns out, the act and the means by which the couple are brought together in this scene. Only when Clitie realises that Fédéric loves her enough to kill the falcon can she love him in return, abandoning her indifference and her aversion to the relationship. Ironically for Fédéric, in view of the death of the bird, she takes little pleasure in eating it, and does so only out of politeness (vol.1, p.154). The deaths of her husband and of her son provide the circumstantial basis for their union, but not the reason why the couple can now be together. As Lapp observes (*Esthetics of negligence*, p.62), if these deaths are essential to the story by Boccaccio which was La Fontaine's inspiration, they are attenuated in the *conte* to enable him to focus on the evolution of the relationship between the couple.

The illustration departs from the text by showing the fire tended by the servant, and the guns on the wall, and by placing on the floor the herbs referred to (vol.1, p.154) as being on the table. These departures are not without importance in themselves; the scattered herbs attest to the disorder of Fédéric's emotions, as does the fire, since we are told that though

---

47. On the dramatic qualities and literary grace of Clitie's speech to Fédéric, see Lapp, *The Esthetics of negligence*, p.88, 166.

the kitchen is habitually 'froide et fort peu fréquentée' (vol.1, p.150), Clitie is 'Une beauté qu'il n'en aimoit pas moins' (vol.1, p.150).

These changes are not, however, to be ascribed primarily to Eisen, or to De Hooghe, who in his headpiece graphically and unsparingly illustrates Fédéric in the act of killing the falcon (De Hooghe 15). They are due, rather, to Cochin (or to the derivation from his headpiece which provides the basis for the engraving in the 1755 edition). Eisen took over the chief elements of Cochin's one illustration for the *conte* because its significance emerges principally from its contrastive relationship to the first plate, designed by Eisen himself, and for which the editions of 1745 and 1755 provide no parallel. The contrast between the two plates serves to under-line the completeness of Fédéric's downfall, the dangers of allowing one-self to be dominated by one's emotions, and the material consequences of such imprudence. In the studied neutrality of the description for the plate, we are invited to ponder whether the sacrifice is justified by love.

## xvi. 'Le petit chien qui secoue de l'argent et des pierreries'

*Caption: 'Argie dans son lit reçoit le pèlerin; une suivante est dans l'enfoncement; une vieille à terre, près du petit chien, ramasse les pierreries qu'il secoue.'*

Eisen prepared two versions of the frontispiece illustration for this *conte*, though the earlier of them (Eisen 25a) is rarely found. According to Holloway, 'it is not easy to tell which is the better' (p.28), and he con-tends that 'the lady herself, as well as the chiaroscuro, have an appeal actually lacking in the subsequent version' (p.28). While the reader's preference must be a matter of taste, the Fermiers généraux clearly felt dissatisfied with the earlier plate, and one can see why. Both versions reflect, but not literally, the events described in some detail by La Fon-taine (vol.1, p.168-71). The opening lines of the *conte* attempt to establish a clear relationship between money and sexual favours (vol.1, p.160):

> La clef du coffre-fort et des cœurs, c'est la même.
> Que si ce n'est celle des cœurs,
> C'est du moins celle des faveurs.

The story of Argie's relationship with Atis does not in fact confirm the truth of this assertion, however. The precise details of the scene shown by Eisen are given only later in the *conte*, when the pilgrim's 'dog' (who is the fairy Manto metamorphosed) is able to create precious stones merely by shaking his coat (vol.1, p.171):

De Hooghe 15. 'Le faucon', vol.1, p.131

Eisen 25a. 'Le petit chien', first version, vol.1, between p.158-159

> Il se secoue:
>    Aussi-tôt perles de tomber,
> Nourrice de les ramasser,
> Soubrettes de les enfiler,
> Pélerin de les attacher
> A de certains bras dont il loue
> La blancheur et le reste. Enfin il fait si bien,
> Qu'avant de partir de la place,
> On traite avec lui de son Chien.
> On lui donne un baiser pour arrhes de la grace
> Qu'il demandoit; et la nuit vint.

While some of these details are condensed into both illustrations, the original is less elaborate than the revised plate, in that it has less sumptuous decoration, and the expression of the maidservant on the left is not clearly delineated. Argie and the 'pilgrim' Atis are not actually embracing, although their heads are close together. The 'Nourrice' shown on bended knee picking up the jewels shed by the 'dog' has her hands open in surprise at the riches before her, rather than grasping them out of avarice, as the description would have it. Argie is oblivious to the miraculous events taking place beside her, with the result that the relationship between her and Atis is not clearly connected with the activities of the dog, and the thematic coherence of the plate is undermined.

In Eisen's second version of the illustration (Eisen 25b), the two women attending Argie are again shown as wholly preoccupied with the pearls and precious stones which the dog has provided, yet their attitudes are not as shown in the earlier version. There, the maid on the left is certainly absorbed in looking at the jewels, though her mistress is as yet merely talking to the 'pilgrim'. The figure who takes her place in the revised version is so close to the couple that she appears deliberately to be averting her eyes from her mistress's conduct. She ignores it rather than remaining unaware of it, even though the amorous encounter has grown more intimate, and Argie now has her breasts bared as her arm entwines that of Atis (a point not made in the text). The effect is to make the maid complicit in the sexual availability of her mistress. There is, then, apparently little to choose between mistress and servant in terms of conduct and morality.

But this would be to misread the indications in the illustration. It is true that Argie herself does not reject the pearls, but she is not paying them much attention (her reaction remains unrecorded by La Fontaine), and is not looking at the dog which she allegedly covets enough to sleep with its master. She has angrily rejected the nurse's suggestion that she sleep with the 'pilgrim' in return for the diamond he offers her (vol.1, p.169). It is only when the nurse repeatedly makes light of marital infidelity (vol.1, p.170) that Argie, charmed by the 'pilgrim', agrees to grant him her favours in return for acquiring his dog (vol.1, p.171).[48] Of course, Argie

48. '[Argie] is overwhelmed by wonderment rather than avarice' (Lapp, *The Esthetics of negligence*, p.111).

Eisen 25b. 'Le petit chien', second version, vol.1, between p.158-59

may well see the dog as a source of wealth, but this is not stated at this point in the text, and only at the end of the *conte* does she extol the creature's merits (vol.1, p.178-79). In contrast, the nurse as depicted in the second version of the engraving is now literally on all fours with the 'dog', and is grasping the jewels shed from its coat. Her hooked nose is more pronounced than in the earlier version, to contrast her lack of beauty (and her greed) with the charms of her mistress. All in all, then, it is fair to infer that the image which Eisen gives us of Argie reflects her character as described in the text. She is a woman attracted to a man for his personal qualities, rather than for the wealth he may be able to offer her, in sharp contrast to the two servants.[49]

In other *contes* such as 'La servante justifiée' and 'Le faucon', Eisen readily adopts, often with few changes, the work of Cochin for the edition of 1745 (or the illustrations in the 1755 edition which derive from it). Here, however, he departs significantly from the earlier artist's interpretation. In Cochin's vignette (which is the basis for the reversed 1755 engraving), the dog is shown on the bed, barking at Argie and Atis as the two servants try to pick up the jewels it has scattered over the bedclothes. The couple are not kissing, though Argie's hand stretches out suggestively towards Atis's breeches. In this interpretation, the drama comes from the manifest hostility of the dog, and the sexual activities of the couple are anticipated rather than shown. In Eisen's version, the dog ignores them, and the interest is focused more on the couple who are already embracing. Both Cochin and Eisen concentrate on the depiction of the facts of the episode, and downplay quite deliberately the elements of metamorphosis and magic which, as Lapp observes (*The Esthetics of negligence*, p.110) are an integral part of the diegesis of the *conte* as related by La Fontaine.

*Caption: 'Dans un palais magique, Anselme se prosterne devant la fée Manto, métamorphosée en More; Argie les observe.'*

This second engraving (Eisen 26) offers a deliberate contrast with the first, though in another sense it continues the favourable presentation of Argie which was noted above. She was earlier shown embracing a handsome young man, and indifferent to material wealth. In contrast, her husband Anselme is shown now prostrating himself before a singularly ugly, deformed individual in order to gain materially. To do so, he must so far forget his previous virtuous conduct (vol.1, p.177) as to perform sexual services as a catamite; this proposition Argie finds so repugnant that she cannot bring herself to describe what is required of him (vol.1, p.177).

49. Philip Stewart (*Engraven desire*, p.225) concludes that 'this busy illustration is quite decent as bedroom scenes go; only reference to the text makes the sexual trade-off of all these associations patent'. On this reading, Argie's interest is essentially in the riches which the dog produces; this seems to me to misrepresent her.

Eisen 26. 'Le petit chien', vol.1, p.175

She has to be persuaded by the nurse (whose views are expounded at some length) that infidelity is no crime. In contrast, Anselme needs little encouragement before consenting to the Moor's sexual suggestion, a point made by the brevity of his reported reply (vol.1, p.176):

> Seigneur.... Anselme ayant examiné ce point,
> Consent à la fin au mystère.

Another way in which this second engraving is related to the first derives from the visible presence of Argie in the illustration. The text tells us that she merely overheard the conversation between the 'Moor' and Anselme, 'en certain coin cachée' (vol.1, p.177). By showing several witnesses to the scene (though the others are only dimly visible), and by directly foregrounding Argie herself, Eisen provides a contrast with the behaviour of the two servants in the earlier plate. Far from being indifferent to the conduct of her husband, Argie looks pensive and, as she makes clear by her comments on the arrangement, strongly disapproving. Whatever one may think of her initial conduct, it was motivated by sexual desire rather than by avarice. Argie has now become an elegant, thoughtful wife whose adultery with Atis is less reprehensible than the anticipated conduct of her husband, and who, at the end of the *conte*, is ready to forgive (vol.1, p.180). Anselme is shown in his nobleman's clothes, before he is transformed into a page, the better to emphasise his self-abasement before the Moor.

De Hooghe chooses to illustrate the same episode (De Hooghe 16) but while the figure of Argie is more prominent, and gazes in anger at Anselme, the Moor is a tall, stately figure who towers over his willing accomplice, with no indication of impropriety or of any dubious relationship. A comparison of the two treatments reveals yet again Eisen's attachment to the unconventional, and even the indecorous, in human relationships, as though to underline the imperfections of human beings rather than to dissimulate them, as De Hooghe so often does.

The effect of the two engravings by Eisen is to diminish any blame which might be directed at Argie, and to present her as both less venial than other women and less blameworthy than her husband, thereby taking the same stance as Ariosto in the *Orlando furioso*.[50] While the two illustrations largely echo the text, the changes which Eisen introduces cause them to be deeply interrelated in a way which itself provides a commentary on the respective behaviour of Anselme and Argie. In the engravings, we therefore have further evidence of the way in which Eisen interprets the text. His technique is to provide a series of connected comments on it, the significance of which can only be appreciated when they are seen as a group, rather than as individual, paradigmatic renderings of segments of the *conte*.

50. See also Lapp, *The Esthetics of negligence*, p.116.

De Hooghe 16. 'Le petit chien', vol.1, p.142

## xvii. 'Pâté d'anguille'

*Caption: 'Le valet dégoûté de pâtés d'anguille, se plaint à son maître
de n'avoir autre nourriture; la scène se passe dans la cuisine.'*

While the description is accurate (Eisen 27), it tells (as descriptions so
often do) only half the story, for it omits any reference to the circumstances leading up to the discussion involving the servant and his master.
The servant's complaint that he has been served eel pâté too often is
occasioned by the master's decision to this effect; that decision in turn is
motivated by the reaction of the servant to learning that he has been
cuckolded by the master. The latter is therefore on hand to point out the
moral of the tale (vol.1, p.184):

> Mon ami, dit-il, je m'étonne
>  Que d'un mets si plein de bonté
> Vous soyez si-tôt dégoûté.
> Ne vous ai-je pas oui dire
>  Que c'étoit votre grand ragout?
>  Il faut qu'en peu de temps, beau Sire,
>  Vous ayez bien changé de goût?
>  Qu'ai-je fait qui fût plus étrange?
> Vous me blâmez, lorsque je change
>  Un mets que vous croyez friand,
>  Et vous faites tout autant?

There are several sources of tension in this tale. In the first place, the
servant is, so to speak, hoist with his own petard when his advice is turned
against him. In the second, he tries to give his master a lesson in proper
behaviour. This is in itself a departure from the usual social hierarchy,
and though other contemporary examples can be found in Molière and
elsewhere, such a reversal of the customary order is practically absent
from La Fontaine's *Contes*. In the third place, the servant acts in a way
which is contrary to the views of the narrator. The structure of the *conte* up
to the point where the servant rejects the eel pâté shows him attempting
to enforce the vows of marital fidelity which the narrator has already
rejected as unrealistic, and a matter of little consequence in itself (vol.1,
p.182):

> Bien sot de faire un bruit si grand
> Pour une chose si commune.

In addition, the narrator repeatedly states 'Diversité, c'est ma devise', and
he tells us at the end of the story that the servant (vol.1, p.186)

> Devint commode
> Même on dit qu'il suivit la mode
> De son maître, et toujours depuis
> Changea d'objets en ses déduits [...]

Eisen 27. 'Pâté d'anguille', vol.1, p.181

> Nimphes, grisettes, ce qu'il put.
> Toutes étaient de bonne prise;
>     Et sur ce point, tant qu'il vécut,
> Diversité fut sa devise.[51]

Both the narrator and the master therefore adopt towards infidelity an attitude which differs from that initially expressed by the servant, and it is their view which is shown to prevail. The servant is thus put in the wrong through the narrative, through his own inconsistencies and especially through his inability to take his own advice.

His position is consequently disadvantaged not only in social terms, but also because his views are rejected and shown to be ones which he himself cannot adhere to in practice. In the illustration which Eisen provide for this story (Eisen 27), essentially the same technique is used as in 'Le paysan qui avoit offensé son seigneur' and 'On ne s'avise jamais de tout', and which will be used elsewhere: that is, the actor in the story who is in a socially inferior position is shown as less attractive (toothless and short in stature as he is) and physically subordinate to the socially superior character. The servant is, after all, the injured party, who has done nothing to deserve the master's conduct towards him in seducing his wife. In addition, the narrator questions, if only for a moment, the selfishness implicit in the master's attitude (vol.1, p.185):

> Car après tout doit-il suffire
> D'alléguer son plaisir sans plus?

Despite these fleeting doubts as to the validity of the master's views (and those of the narrator), it is clear that the servant is not placed on the same level as his master, either literally or figuratively. He is shown in a physically subordinate position, and one could reasonably argue that the female servant seen to the right of the master is inclining towards him, indicating support for his views, and by implication, those of the narrator. Indeed, this proleptically announces the subsequent attitude of the servant himself, who becomes a great seducer in his turn (vol.1, p.186).[52]

But before becoming his master's disciple, the servant's shock at seeing his own arguments used against him is palpable from his open-mouthed reaction to what he hears. Eisen's illustration has little in common with De Hooghe's (De Hooghe 17), which depicts a man (probably the master) seated at a table on which lies a pâté. He stretches out his hand to take that of a female servant, while a cat and dog quarrel over a plate of food on the floor. This is a semi-symbolic rendering of the story, from which all reference to the male servant is excised in favour of a metaphorically generalised reflection of human relationships which allows us

---

51. Similar views are expressed in previous *contes*, such as 'La coupe enchantée' and 'Le petit chien'.

52. Compare Lapp, *The Esthetics of negligence*, p.123-24.

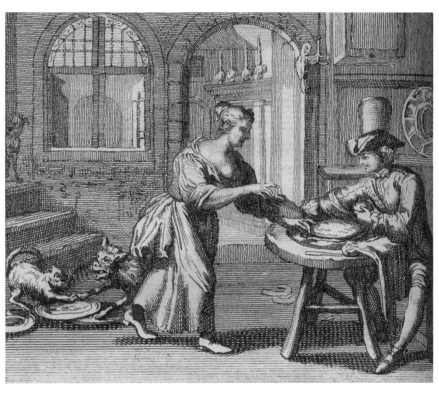

De Hooghe 17. 'Pâté d'anguille', vol.1, p.162

to infer support for the views expressed by the narrator and the master. Eisen's illustration is largely based on Cochin's vignette for the 1745 edition, with the servant seated, and the master standing, in a large kitchen. There, however, the servant's attitude is merely one of mild protest at his monotonous diet, with none of the surprise evinced by the cuckold depicted by Eisen. In that illustration also, two other servants are seated at the table, but take no part in the conversation, and offer the husband no support.

This *conte*, then, takes further than previous tales in the collection the view that cuckoldry is a matter of small importance. It also brings the cuckold and the seducer face to face (something which does not happen in *contes* such as 'La coupe enchantée' and 'Le petit chien'), and gives the better role to the seducer than to the husband. In this respect, Eisen sides entirely with the views endorsed by the master and the narrator.

# xviii. 'Le magnifique'

*Caption: 'Le Magnifique est assis près de la dame dans un sallon orné; Aldobrandin dans l'enfoncement a les yeux sur sa femme.'*

As sometimes happens in this edition, when a *conte* is set in another time or place, the tendency to show the characters in eighteenth-century costume gives way to a deliberate exoticism, with seventeenth-century clothes to convey the Florentine setting, and with characters wearing neither wigs nor swords (Eisen 28).

In the story, the role of the wife is to appear staid, and apparently unresponsive, but the fact that she does not respond overtly means that she assents to the propositions of the 'Magnifique'. As befits his sobriquet (his 'nom de guerre' as La Fontaine has it, vol.1, p.187), he is well dressed (as he is not named in the *conte*, the designation makes him the archetype of the elegant seducer). The husband Aldobrandin, who has the scowling features which Eisen habitually gives to unsympathetic characters in the *contes*, is not good-looking, and is dressed in a way which pales in comparison with the clothes of the Magnifique. This drabness, coupled with his jealousy and possessiveness (vol.1, p.188), is accentuated by his being drawn in grey, in contrast with the darker shades used for the Magnifique and for Aldobrandin's wife. The obvious charm of the Magnifique and the statuesque immobility of the wife make the contrast stronger still. Even so, this distinction is not simply a matter of the perspective created by the engraver's use of weaker lines in order to suggest the more distant part of the room and the furnishings. It is true that Eisen does sometimes use this technique simply to suggest perspective, as in the engraving for 'Le mari confesseur', or for 'On ne s'avise jamais de tout', for example. In other instances, such as the present *conte* or the second state of

Eisen 28. 'Le magnifique', vol.1, p.187

the engraving for 'A femme avare, galant escroc', however, it is used to suggest that one character is subordinate to another. At the same time, the darker tones used for the clothing of the lady and her seducer, and for the drapes in the top right of the illustration, serve to make them all part of the same unity, and to exclude the husband.

The use of such shading marks out this plate from the previous engravings for this *conte*. De Hooghe shows the couple conversing, with the husband standing on the left, dressed more strikingly than his rival (De Hooghe 18), which rather contradicts the *données* of the story. In Cochin's vignette for this *conte* (Cochin 4), the room is less ornate, and the physical appeal of the two main characters is disguised by our being placed at some distance from them. In the illustration for the 1755 edition, which largely follows Cochin, the artist has placed a clock on the wall above Aldobrandin's head, to indicate the passing of the 'quart d'heure' which the Magnifique asks to be allowed to spend in conversation. In the 1762 edition, this clock (which is not mentioned in the text) is relegated to the tailpiece of the *conte*.

Thus, the engraving externalises not only physical attractiveness, but personality as well. The fly-whisk (?) in the lady's hand is symbolic, and tells him that she is attracted, even when she cannot say so in words. In its symbolic function, it reproduces what the illustration itself tells us, that words are not the only means of communication. Indeed, the techniques used by Eisen and his engraver to offer a range of meanings and nuances which are absent from other illustrations for the story, indirectly confirm the same point.

## xix. 'La matrone d'Ephèse'

*Caption: 'On voit dans un antre sépulcral la matrone, sa suivante, & le soldat; les deux derniers transportent le corps du mari enveloppé d'un linceul. Une potence est apperçue au-dehors.'*

In the background (Eisen 29) can be seen the gallows towards which the body of the late husband is being transported from the tomb, at the suggestion of the servant. La Fontaine's text says only (vol.1, p.204) 'La Dame y consentit [to the servant's suggestion]', and Eisen shows the deception being carried out. The faces of the soldier guarding the gallows and of the servant are obscured as they carry out their task, so that we do not know their reactions to what they are doing; yet we really need to know only those of the widow. She is not looking at the body of her late husband, whose face is outlined under the shroud. Her eyes are closed, perhaps to avoid looking at his face, but equally because she may be about to kiss the soldier. Indeed, the fact that she leans towards him is wholly in keeping with the indications of the text (vol.1, p.202):

De Hooghe 18. 'Le magnifique', vol.1, p.168

Cochin 4. 'Le magnifique', vol.1, p.161

Eisen 29. 'La matrone d'Ephèse', vol. 1, p. 197

> Le Dieu qui fait aimer prit son temps; il tira
> Deux traits de son carquois; de l'un il entama
> Le soldat jusqu'au vif; l'autre effleura la Dame.

Her hands point to the gallows as if giving instructions to the soldier and the servant, and suggesting that she no longer has any objection to the body of her husband being used in this way (vol.1, p.203). While Eisen has shown all three characters as equally complicit in the deception, he allows us to infer that the widow has undergone the greatest transformation; having found love with the soldier, she is no longer tearfully obsessed with her late husband.

This representation of the relationship between the three characters differs significantly from the versions produced by De Hooghe (De Hooghe 19) and Cochin. The former depicts all three protagonists, inside the house of the widow, with whom the soldier is seemingly engaged in debate, as the servant, a smile on her face, hauls the dead man from his tomb. The soldier's hands are extended in disbelief at what is proposed, and the widow smiles at him. Cochin (whose illustration is the basis of the 1755 edition) shows the wife kneeling by the body of her husband, while the servant points to it and the soldier gestures in consternation both at the body and at the empty gallows. Cochin has seized upon the plight of the soldier as the most dramatic moment in the story. De Hooghe and Eisen, in contrast, illustrate the point at which (with notable rapidity, as La Fontaine observes) the widow's past life is abandoned for a new love; the implications of this presentation of female fickleness need no emphasis.

While some of the same elements (the three protagonists, the gallows, and the open tomb) are present in De Hooghe and in Eisen, they are not used in the same way. The outdoor setting, the prominence which is given to the gallows, the emphasis on the clothing of the figures, and the simplicity of the décor are of more than passing significance. In choosing to include them, Eisen offers almost a parody of paintings showing the 'Descent from the Cross' or the 'Lamentation' which had been a standard part of Christian iconography for centuries. If it is permissible to read the illustration in this way, it would form a further link in the chain of anti-Church propaganda which connects so many of the plates for this edition.

# xx. 'Belphégor'

*Caption: 'Le manant que le bourreau tient par les cheveux, fait battre la caisse. L'esprit immonde sort du corps de la Princesse en convulsions. La scène se passe sur une place, en présence du Prince.'*

Eisen (Eisen 30) shows the evil spirit (a tiny winged figure on the left, sitting on the old man's shoulder) being forced from the Princess's body by the sound of the drums just before the farmer is due to be hanged. As

De Hooghe 19. 'La matrone d'Ephèse', vol.1, p.176

Eisen 30. 'Belphégor', vol.1, p.205

can be seen from the buildings in the background, the scene is set in a city in modern France, not sixteenth-century Italy. Apart from the somewhat 'Italian' hat worn by the figure of the Prince on the right (Racinet, *Historical encyclopedia of costume*, p.159), the costumes are not historically precise. While the 'manant' is in seventeenth-century dress (p.481), the drummers are in archetypal, rather than accurate, clothes. This is because, as elsewhere, the Fermiers généraux are attempting to give a period flavour to the plates, rather than a historically accurate rendering of the scene. A number of details (including the appearance by the Devil) are taken directly from the *conte*: these include the gibbet with which Mathéo is threatened, and the soldiers' pikes in the right background. The parasol on the right indicates metonymically the money which he is promised, and the presence of members of fashionable society. The choice before him is a stark one, with the crowd impassive and equally ready to accept either the expulsion of the demon or Mathéo's death by hanging.

Into this worldly, even cynical, tableau Eisen introduces a scene which is reminiscent (like the plate for 'La matrone d'Ephèse') of religious art and, in this case, particularly that of the eighteenth century. The expression and the religious robes of the pious figure supporting the princess as she swoons, like the pose of the princess herself, recall directly the paintings of Restout, Drouais or Doyen.[53] They also recall a more specific work, Montgeron's *La Vérité des miracles opérés par l'intercession de M. de Pâris* (1737). This controversial publication (an augmented version of which appeared in 1741, with a further volume in 1747) describes a series of miraculous cures allegedly effected in the 1720s around the tomb of an ecclesiastic, François de Pâris, at the cemetery of Saint-Médard in Paris. These miracles were illustrated in a number of anonymous plates, several of which show characters in postures similar to those of the princess depicted here by Eisen.[54]

The commingling of the worldly and the religious in this plate can scarcely be read as a testament of belief. Mathéo has tricked the demon into leaving the princess's body; had he failed to perform the exorcism, his life would have been forfeit, and no mercy would have been shown, either by the prince or by the crowd (vol.1, p.215). The rendering of the exorcism, with its deliberate echoes of the religious art of the time, is intended to recall, in the context of a *conte*, the miracles by which the Church maintained its power over the people. La Fontaine makes no reference to the reactions of the crowd when the demon is expelled from the princess's body, so that the pressing throng, agog with credulity as it witnesses the event, is an addition of Eisen's.

53. A typical example is Restout's *The Death of St Scholastica* (Musée des beaux-arts, Tours). It is illustrated in Conisbee, *Painting in eighteenth-century France*, p.35.
54. For details of the illustrations to Montgeron's book, see Cohen, col.733.

There is nothing of these overtones in De Hooghe's headpiece for this *conte* (De Hooghe 20). His interpretation is faithful to the text, if conventional in its realism. He makes no mocking concession to the supernatural, and no allusions to the Church: there are no Devils to attest to the effectiveness of the exorcism, and the princess is being helped by her courtiers rather than by a priest. The prince (who is simply described in the text as a 'spectateur') is seated on a dais raising him above the crowd. Eisen's prince is detached and impassive as he watches, but not isolated from his subjects.

His 'demotion' here is more marked than in Cochin's engraving, in which he stands firmly apart from the throng. It is true that the general setting and arrangement of Eisen's illustration, such as the prominent presence of drummers, and details such as the parasol, are borrowed from Cochin. In his version however, as in De Hooghe's, the figures supporting the princess (who is seated rather than swooning) are not recognisably in religious dress. Rather than depicting a Devil as such, Cochin metonymically indicates his expulsion by showing smoke coming from the princess's mouth, though there is no such reference in the text. Cochin seems therefore to stand midway between the conventional realism of De Hooghe and the mocking scepticism of Eisen. Whereas La Fontaine has provided a tale of the supernatural, Eisen's illustration focuses on the public spectacle, public gullibility, socially sanctioned cruelty, and the ability of the peasant to get himself out of an awkward situation by using his wits.

## xxi. 'La clochette'

*Caption: 'Le jeune villageois approche pour embrasser une fillette attirée dans un bois.'*

The engraving for this *conte* exists in two versions; a comparison between them is instructive in understanding the larger purposes of the illustrations in this edition. In the rejected plate (Eisen 31a), both the girl and the man have expressions which denote unpleasant emotions (lust in his case, terror in hers). Again, she looks somewhat older than thirteen, the age given in the *conte* (vol.I, p.220). The clothing covering her legs magnifies their size, a point which also suggests that she is older than in the text. The brim of her hat acts almost as a halo, and she has a glow (presumably of innocence) around her; she seems about to fall to the ground, putting out her arms to save herself, and recalling perhaps the age of human innocence before the Fall. As the couple look at each other, the girl's fears are a direct reaction to the behaviour and expression of her attacker. The cow shown in the centre background is unperturbed by the girl's cries, as if to emphasise that no one can hear her (vol.I, p.221), or indeed to suggest that such events are commonplace.

De Hooghe 20. 'Belphégor', vol. I, p.184

Eisen 31a. 'La clochette', first version, vol. 1, between p. 218-19

Dissatisfaction with this earlier design evidently led Eisen to create a second version, which is more sharply delineated (Eisen 31b). Unlike the great majority of the revised engravings for the *Contes*, that for 'La clochette' does not bring us significantly nearer, in spatial terms, to the characters. None the less, there are some notable differences between the two versions. Now, the young man comes towards the milkmaid from the front; her hands are held in an attitude more indicative of confusion, and she is looking upwards, as if asking heaven to help her, rather than at her attacker. While she looks noticeably older than thirteen, the man's face wears a smile, and he is therefore not as threatening as in the first engraving. He approaches her with open arms as if greeting a long-lost friend, an interpretation supported by the description 'Le jeune villageois approche pour *embrasser* une fillette attirée dans un bois' (my italics). The wood offers less shelter to him, and is more open and sunlit. Whereas in the original plate he seems to emerge from behind a tree, he now springs forward with no obvious hiding place to act as a cover. The light surrounding the girl, and her halo-like hat, have both vanished. The hornless cow shown in the earlier state has now acquired horns, a detail which may also suggest that sexuality pervades the world, and is not specific to humans. These elements attenuate what we are told by La Fontaine (vol.1, p.220):

> Notre galant vous lorgne une fillette
> [...]
> Le malheur fut qu'elle étoit trop jeunette,
> Et d'âge encore incapable d'aimer.
> Non qu'à treize ans on y soit inhabile;
> Même les lois ont avancé ce temps;
> Les loix songeoient aux personnes de ville,
> Bien que l'amour semble né pour les champs.

A note in the Pléiade edition (p.1493) recalls that a law of 1639 had allowed girls to be married at the age of twelve, and that La Fontaine had originally written 'quinze ans', only to replace the phrase with 'treize ans'. The import of these lines is that, while girls living in a city may be sexually mature at twelve or thirteen, those living in the country are less likely to be so, even if rural life seems to fit them better for sexual activity at that age. Such is the case with the milkmaid whose misfortunes are the subject of this *conte*.

Hence, although the law did allow girls of twelve to be married when La Fontaine wrote, he obviously had misgivings on the matter. More to the point, Eisen would have been stepping outside the bounds of social (and even legal) propriety in 1762 in showing the milkmaid as old enough for a sexual relationship at thirteen. Jaucourt writes in the article 'Puberté' in the *Encyclopédie* in 1765 (vol.13, p.549): 'Dans toutes les parties méridionales de l'Europe, & dans les villes, la plûpart des filles sont *puberes* à 12 ans, & les garçons à 14; mais dans les provinces du

Eisen 31b. 'La clochette', second version, vol.1, between p.218-19

nord & dans les campagnes, à peine les filles le sont-elles à 14, & les garçons à 16.'

But of course what we have in the *conte* is something very close to a rape, and here the law was equally clear. The jurist Boucher d'Argis clearly states in the article 'Viol' (also published in 1765): 'Lorsque le crime [rape] est commis envers une vierge, il est puni de mort, & même du supplice de la roue, si cette vierge n'étoit pas nubile' (vol.17, p.310). Eisen (or the Fermiers) therefore resolved in both engravings to make the girl look older, in order to remove any suggestion of illegality, while suppressing, in the revised version, the intimations of innocence which surrounded her in the first state. In so doing, he diminishes the gravity of the offence, and seems not to dissent from the view of the girl's attacker (which La Fontaine does not contradict) that (vol.1, p.221)

> Toute chose est permise
> Pour se tirer de l'amoureux tourment.

There is, then, no condemnation of the attacker's conduct, and the closing lines of the *conte* rather suggest that the girl was imprudent to walk alone in the woods (vol.1, p.221):

> O belles, évitez
> Le fond des bois, et leur vaste silence.[55]

De Hooghe will have none of these complexities; his headpiece (De Hooghe 21) avoids any hint of violence, or even any great fidelity to the text. He offers a picture of pastoral innocence, in which a couple are seen talking in a woodland glade, watched by a cow which seems amused at their encounter. Although Cochin anticipates Eisen in making the girl older than the text warrants, no doubt for similar reasons, the attacker in his version is seen with his arms around her as she attempts to flee and is about to fall to the ground. This is to offer an interpretation of the events which is at once more violent (because it shows the attacker grappling with his victim as she tries to flee in terror) and less complex (in that it lacks any suggestion of innocence) than either of Eisen's versions. While Eisen sometimes follows Cochin in his choice of subject matter, he does not imitate him slavishly. Indeed, one could argue that Cochin is sometimes more direct, and that Eisen's tendency is, so to speak, to smooth away the rough edges of human conduct in order to achieve a more aesthetically pleasing result.

---

55. '[S]ince she courted the danger by failure to avoid (*éviter*) the dark forest, she bears some responsibility for what occurred there' (Stewart, *Engraven desire*, p.215). There may also be an echo of Pascal's assertion in the *Pensées* (1669) that 'le silence éternel de ces espaces infinis m'effraie'.

De Hooghe 21. 'La clochette', vol.1, p.196

## xxii. 'Le glouton'[56]

*Caption: Le glouton 'prêt à recevoir un remède, se fait apporter la hure de son esturgeon'.*

Eisen (Eisen 32) makes a domestic tragedy from the incurable gluttony of the man depicted by La Fontaine. There is no reference in the text to the weeping figure at the back holding a handkerchief to her eyes, and no specific indication (beyond the reference to 'mes amis') of how many people attend to the needs of the grossly fat glutton. The expressions on the faces of those around him denote concern, rather than disapproval of his destructive self-indulgence, and even his vast, naked backside does not inspire disgust in the servant who is about to insert an enema into it.

The plate thus creates a contrast between the insatiable appetite of the glutton (and the self-indulgence associated with it), and the caring, concerned attitudes of those attending him. As in so many of the engravings for these *contes*, a curtain is shown drawn back as if to reveal the truth about gluttony, but it can equally well be taken to reveal the kindness of others towards a man undeserving, in the customary view, of their solicitude. In other words, friendship and concern are as much a part of the human condition as rabid self-indulgence. As so often, one is not surprised to see the Fermiers offering an interpretation of a *conte* in which the sins of the flesh are not subject to the condemnation which usually accompanies their depiction in conventional moral judgements.

De Hooghe's rendering of the story (De Hooghe 22) offers some parallels to Eisen, in that numerous friends surround the dying glutton, including a weeping woman. There is nothing, however, of the physical frankness or even grossness which we find in the 1762 plate: all is controlled, well ordered and discreet. Cochin's vignette for 'Le glouton' presents a man who is less physically gross than in Eisen's version, and who is shown fully clothed. He is attended by only three figures, a servant holding the fish-head, another man holding an enema, and a third who appears to be trying to reason with the glutton. None shows any particular concern or disquiet at his behaviour, so that the high drama of the Eisen version becomes, in Cochin's hands, merely a domestic genre-piece.

## xxiii. 'Les deux amis'[57]

*Caption: Les deux amis 'sont sous un berceau de feuillages; la fillette est debout au milieu d'eux'.*

In this engraving (Eisen 33), Eisen's inventiveness is shown to full effect. The illustration is built on a contrast. On the one hand is the elegant,

56. Entitled 'Autre conte tiré d'Athénée' in *OCLF*, p.587.
57. Entitled 'Conte tiré d'Athénée' in *OCLF*, p.586.

Eisen 32. 'Le glouton', vol. I, p.223

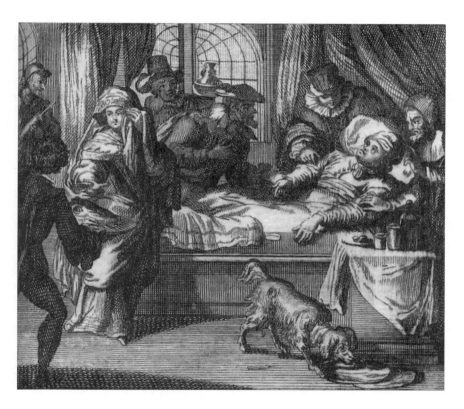

De Hooghe 22. 'Le glouton', vol.1, p.199

Eisen 33. 'Les deux amis', vol. I, p.225

formal garden in which the scene is set, and on the other the disregard of order and propriety apparent in the attitudes and behaviour of the two men and of the girl who is the object of their attentions. This contrast is entirely the work of Eisen himself, since nothing is said in the text of the background setting depicted here. In addition, the engraving shows the reactions of the 'fillette', which are nowhere reported by La Fontaine, so that Eisen makes her a more active participant in the discussion. At the same time as she points to the man on our right, she leans away from him as he tries to touch her face. The cross-pointed hands of the girl and this man indicate some conflict of view. In this context, her gestures may well mean that she prefers his rival. For her part, there is no suggestion that she is unwilling to gratify the desires of her admirers (vol.1, p.225):

> Le tems venu que cet objet charmant
> Put pratiquer les leçons de sa mère.

There is no question, then, that she will simply be the object of male lust, unlike the milkmaid in 'La clochette', though there is no hint that she is aware that either man could be her father. Her willingness to oblige is thus less reprehensible than the ambitions of the two men, each of whom, despite his fine clothes, is prepared to take the risk of committing incest with his putative daughter. For this reason, this *conte* might properly be regarded as one of the most morally bankrupt in the collection.

But there is a second point to note in Eisen's interpretation of the scene. La Fontaine gives his two male characters names borrowed from classical antiquity, Axiocus and Alcibiades. These two men were respectively uncle and nephew who, as close friends of Socrates, were condemned with him by the Athenian authorities for having profaned the divine mysteries.[58] Nothing in La Fontaine's description ('Jeunes, bien-faits, galans, et vigoureux') associates them with two such noble, persecuted figures. Indeed, as in other *contes*, Eisen's tendency is to make the scene familiar by dressing the characters in contemporary clothes even when there is no hint in the text that this is required. The fact that all three protagonists are in contemporary, expensive dress gives the interpretation an immediate point of reference for readers of the *contes*; it suggests that the behaviour of the two men is as applicable to the mid-eighteenth century as to ancient times. This aspect of the scene is emphasised further by the choice of setting, which might best be described as an elaborate 'bosquet'. Although the term does not occur anywhere in the text, what we are shown fits very well with the definition offered by d'Argenville in his *Encyclopédie* article on the subject (1752; vol.2, p.337):

---

58. See the article 'Socrates' in the *Encyclopedia Britannica*, 25 vols (Chicago, 1950), vol.20, p.917.

BOSQUET, s. m. (*Jardinage*) petit bois planté dans les jardins de propreté; c'est comme qui diroit *un bouquet de verdure, un bois paré*, au milieu duquel on trouve ordinairement une salle ornée de fontaines & de pieces de gason, avec des sieges pour se reposer.

Les *bosquets* font le relief des jardins; ils forment une de leurs principales parties, & font valoir toutes les autres: c'est par leur moyen qu'on couvre toutes les vûes desagréables.

The suggestion that 'bosquets' are intended to hide what is disagreeable is wholly in keeping with the attempts by each of the two friends to hide their motives by attributing the paternity of the girl to the other. It might also be thought that the finery in which all three are dressed likewise covers the basest kind of human conduct.

The contemporary significance of the illustration is not exhausted by Eisen's choice of clothing for his characters. In the early 1760s, 'bosquets' had taken on particular literary connotations as a result of the enormous success of Rousseau's *Julie ou la Nouvelle Héloïse*, published in 1761. To accompany the work, Gravelot had designed twelve engravings for which Rousseau himself had devised lengthy descriptions, and which were bound with the illustrations in a *Recueil d'estampes*, available separately from the novel.[59] As a result, many readers who could not afford (or who did not want) the full text could gain an idea of its contents and tone from what was in effect a condensed version of the work. The link between 'bosquets' and scarcely repressed sexual longing had been made in the description for the first engraving of the series, 'Le premier baiser de l'amour', which concludes with the words: 'Tout le tableau doit respirer une ivresse de volupté qu'une certaine modestie rende encore plus touchante.'[60] Eisen's illustration for 'Les deux amis' in some ways echoes this illustration for *Julie*. It is true that, instead of the two female friends, and one aspiring lover, we have two male friends and a girl caught between them; yet the same 'volupté' and a recognisably similar 'bosquet' are discernible in both.

De Hooghe (De Hooghe 23) has a group of decorous, classically dressed figures, representing the two men, the girl and her mother, engaged in calm debate, with a port scene in the background. In Cochin's vignette for the 1745 edition, the girl is seated inside a room as the two men, dressed in contemporary clothing, argue over her, but she remains uninvolved in their discussion, a passive spectator.[61] While Eisen certainly borrowed from De Hooghe and from Cochin in a number of instances, in this case his debt is to Gravelot, and to the Fermiers' recurrent belief that female sexuality was as potent as that of the male.

59. Details of these engravings can be found in Cohen, *Guide de l'amateur de livres*, col.904-905, and in Ray, *The Art of the French illustrated book*, p.42.

60. *Recueil d'estampes pour la Nouvelle Héloïse* (Amsterdam, Rey, 1761), p.7. See also chapter 3 of this study (p.205).

61. See Holloway, *French rococo book illustration*, p.29.

De Hooghe 23. 'Les deux amis', vol.1, p.201

## xxiv. 'Le juge de Mesle'[62]

*Caption: Le juge de Mesle 'siège; deux avocats s'approchent &*
*tirent la paille'.*

We learn from the text only that the lawyer who wins his case by drawing
the long straw held by the judge 's'en va gai comme un prince' (vol.1,
p.227). The illustration (Eisen 34) shows the two advocates at the
moment when the case is decided by these means. La Fontaine states
merely that 'La cour s'en plaint' (vol.1, p.227). However, the angry
expression worn by the advocate who has lost, and the consternation on
the faces of the members of the court ranged at the side of the steps
leading to the judge's chair to witness the proceedings, make full use of
the implications of this phrase.

Even in this apparently simple scene, Eisen intervenes to present a view
of the story which is not based entirely on the wording of the *conte* itself.
Both the 1760 edition of the *Œuvres de Racine*, with engravings designed by
Sève, and the 1768 edition of the same author's works, with engravings by
Gravelot, show judges wearing their hats as part of their official dress in
*Les Plaideurs*. Eisen shows his judge hatless, to indicate a lack of concern
for formality; the judge's attitude explains his impatience with the pet-
tifogging legal arguments of the two counsel, and his willingness to depart
from normal judicial procedures. He is also shown as being at the same
height as the two lawyers, as if to hint that he is not in any sense superior
to them in authority. This point distinguishes Eisen's illustration from
those of De Hooghe (De Hooghe 24) and Cochin, who both show the
judge in full legal panoply, towering over the two lawyers. Eisen's willingness to emphasise the informality of the proceedings, without
attempting to parody the legal process otherwise, suggests none too subtly
his sympathy for the judge, and his unwillingness to share the manifestly
censorious view of the disappointed lawyer and other members of the
court. This disabused view of the legal process could not have failed to
appeal to the Fermiers, whose disagreements with the lawyers making up
the *Parlements* dated back over decades.[63]

## xxv. 'Alix malade'[64]

*Caption: Alix malade 'est au lit; un médecin lui tâte le poulx; un autre*
*parle à un laquais auquel Alix fait signe d'aller chercher son confesseur'.*

To indicate their professional status, the two doctors attending Alix (Eisen
35) are in long wigs.[65] The man on the right who acts as the 'messager' to

62. Entitled 'Conte du juge de Mesle' in *OCLF*, p.589.
63. See the chapter 1 of this study.
64. Entitled 'Epigram' in OCLF, p.757.
65. Compare the engravings for the article 'Perruquier' (1765) in the *Encyclopédie*.

Eisen 34. 'Le juge de Mesle', vol.1, p.227

De Hooghe 24. 'Le juge de Mesle', vol. 1, p.203

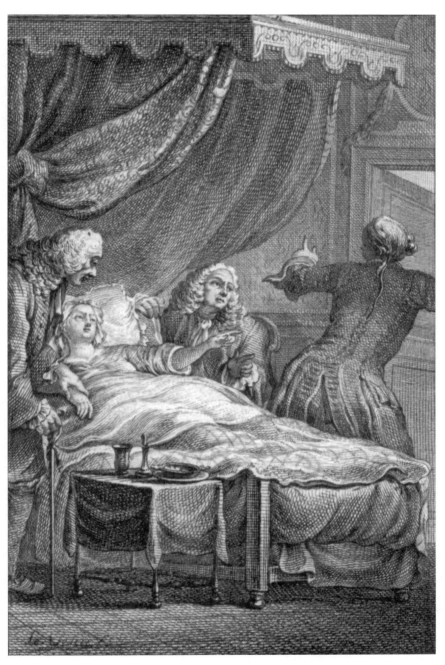

Eisen 35. 'Alix malade', vol. I, p.229

père André has his back to us, and is in a short wig, a sign that he is younger and more fashionable, since long wigs were the exception is society by 1762; he can also run fastest. His imminent departure is anticipated by showing the open door. We do not see his face, since his role is mechanical, and his status immaterial.

Alix is shown in an elaborate bed, and surrounded by doctors; both of these features allow us to infer her wealth, though nothing to this effect is said in the text. The scene is set at the point where they despatch a messenger to fetch a confessor, père André who, it turns out, 'depuis dix ans confesse en Paradis' (vol.1, p.229). The faces of the medical men reflect their concerns. On the left, an elderly doctor, with a drawn face and leaning on his stick, is clearly moving towards the close of his own life, while the other, by anxiously asking the messenger to fetch the confessor, shows that he has given up hope of helping Alix to recover. The candle on the table by the bed is out, suggesting that she too has not long to live. This is a drama of pointless urgency, since we all have to die; Alix's desire for a confessor whom she has not seen for over ten years is brought on only by her fear of death, and there is a poignant irony in the fact that the confessor himself has died since she last saw him.

In his rendering of this scene, Eisen departs from the models offered by his predecessors. De Hooghe depicts Alix bare-breasted and lying prone (De Hooghe 25). One doctor sits at her bedside, while another examines the contents of a flask; to a healthy-looking woman, the young messenger is explaining the fate of père André by pointing heavenwards. The time-frame of the scene is thus very different from Eisen's, since De Hooghe's concern is with the messenger's return, rather than with his departure. The contrast between the dying Alix and the robust, healthy woman addressed by the messenger may be read also as a *memento mori*, a warning that even someone who looks so full of life cannot escape the inevitable fate of all humans. In its own way, De Hooghe's version thus focuses as firmly as Eisen's on the inevitability of death, though the ironic role which Eisen allots to the aged doctor finds no parallel in De Hooghe. But both are more urgently concerned with this theme than Cochin, whose headpiece for the 1745 version shows the young messenger pointing towards an unseen object (presumably a door) on the left, but giving no sign of imminent departure. This lack of urgency is correlative with the depiction of the two doctors, neither of whom appears to be in poor health.[66]

The link between these three differing interpretations of the *conte* is that none of them attempts to turn it into a satire of the medical profession, or of religious belief. This is a human drama which focuses on the most profound of human issues, death. In an engraving which offers few

66. The edition of 1755 reproduces the elements of the Cochin illustration in reverse.

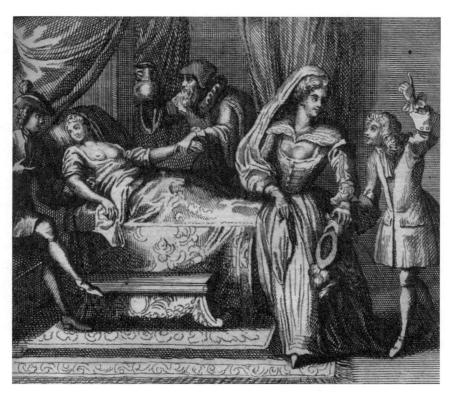

De Hooghe 25. 'Alix malade', vol.1, p.205

opportunities for satire or for sexual innuendo, Eisen remains true to the underlying theme of the *conte*, without trying to connect it to wider concerns in his interpretation of the work.

## xxvi. 'Le baiser rendu'

*Caption: 'Le paysan embrasse l'épouse du Seigneur;*
*deux laquais suivent la dame et son mari.'*

In this *conte*, Guillot allows a gentleman to kiss his wife Perronelle. Shortly afterwards, the gentleman marries, and allows Guillot in turn the privilege of kissing his wife. It is the latter episode which is illustrated by Eisen (Eisen 36), as we can see from the obvious distinction between the rough clothing of Guillot and the smart attire of the couple.

We know nothing of Guillot himself, though the name tells us that he is unlikely to be of high birth, and the story would of course lose much of its point if all the characters involved were of similar social rank. Yet Eisen accentuates the unusual nature of the incident beyond anything found in the text. This point is clear in the attention which it attracts from the public, and more especially in the reaction of the figures in the left background, one of whom appears to be holding a fan in an attitude of surprise. We know from other examples, such as the two hired bullies depicted in the plate for 'Le paysan qui avoit offensé son seigneur', that Eisen was quite capable of presenting characters of no social distinction as physically attractive. But Guillot, again with no warrant from the text, is shown as burly and coarse-featured, in order to highlight the contrast with the lady of quality whom he is permitted to kiss.

Nothing is said in the text of the reactions of either woman to being kissed in public, and in her husband's presence, by a man to whom she is not married. But it is clear from the engraving that, while her husband looks on rather like a bemused sheep, the wife is repelled by the attentions of the unprepossessing Guillot. While his (somewhat massive) right leg encroaches on her skirt, she holds her fan at the height of her sex, creating a symbolic barrier to any further advances on his part. There is every indication in the illustration, therefore, that the class barrier will not be crossed easily, even though the story as recounted by La Fontaine contains no adverse comment on the class differences between the characters.

Eisen's interpretation of the story is markedly different from De Hooghe's, in which the gentleman's wife complacently turns her face towards Guillot, offering no resistance (De Hooghe 26). Nor is there any sign here of bystanders whose reactions would allow us to gauge the social propriety or impropriety of the peasant's behaviour. While the lady's husband looks complacently on, declining to intervene, only the presence of a rather agitated dog tells us that all may not be in order. In Cochin's

Eisen 36. 'Le baiser rendu', vol.1, p.231

De Hooghe 26. 'Le baiser rendu', vol.1, p.207

vignette for the 1745 edition, the onlookers may seem shocked, but the lady's serving-men remain uninvolved, and she herself shows no dislike of the peasant. On the contrary, she seems to be smiling at him, and does not use her fan as a defence as his hand moves towards her sex. Eisen has therefore accentuated the class differences in a way which is quite foreign to the interpretation of the *conte* offered by De Hooghe and Cochin, but which echoes the Fermiers' distrust, and perhaps even dislike, of the lower classes.

## xxvii. 'Sœur Jeanne'[67]

*Caption: Sœur Jeanne 'est en prière; l'abbesse et les nones surviennent & se voyent dans l'enfoncement'.*

Two versions of Eisen's illustration for this *conte* exist. In the earlier engraving (Eisen 37a), we are close to Sœur Jeanne; we are at some distance from the abbess and the other nuns, who are standing on the steps at the entrance to the room where she kneels in prayer; she is wholly oblivious of their presence, and is not looking at the devotional text open on the lectern before her. The impression we have of her is therefore one of deep devotion to her religion, to the exclusion of all else; she is indeed the

> sainte fille,
> Toujours en oraison

described by La Fontaine (vol.1, p.233). Her function is to serve as an example of piety to the other members of the convent, which is why the abbess and another nun are pointing in her direction, in conformity with the text. This earlier plate is therefore a faithful rendering of many of the essential elements of the story. Anne L. Birberick observes that in this *conte*, the first by La Fontaine to deal with the sexual feelings of nuns,

> it is only Sister Jeanne who dwells in the ethical space; in other words, it is Sister Jeanne alone who forswears her worldliness (and her sexuality) and lives 'en sainte fille' [...] entry into the ethical space can be achieved only after one has transgressed; it can be achieved only after one has lived outside the physical space circumscribed by the grill.[68]

This interpretation is compatible with the rejected engraving, but it is wholly at variance with the second version (Eisen 37b). Here, we are closer to the scene than in the earlier design. Jeanne is not looking at the open folio (presumably a work of a religious nature) which lies on the floor, alongside a scourge, both discarded accoutrements of convent life.

---

67. Entitled 'Conte de ****' in *OCLF*, p.588.
68. Birberick, 'From world to text', p.183.

Eisen 37a. 'Sœur Jeanne', first version, vol.1, between p.232-33

Eisen 37b. 'Sœur Jeanne', second version, vol.1, between p.232-33

From her expression and posture, it is clear that she is thinking of the child to whom she gave birth before entering the convent, and whom she imagines in her arms; so great is her absorption in her thoughts that all else fades from her mind. As in the rejected engraving (but for quite different reasons), she is unaware of the presence of the other nuns and abbess, even though they are now standing much closer to her. Her utter absorption in her thoughts is accentuated by the fact that the scene is set in a more open, public part of the convent than the original illustration, where a bare room sufficed for the décor. As in the earlier engraving, we have five nuns and the abbess, but originally only two were pointing towards her, whereas now three are doing so. Their reaction to the externalisation of her thoughts is understandably more emphatic, and more poignant, than the conventional piety of the rejected version. While the abbess is perceptibly older than the other nuns, they are young and attractive enough to nurture thoughts of having children themselves, an aspiration doomed to disappointment in the convent.

In showing Jeanne in this way, Eisen has changed the illustration from a depiction of devotion after sin to a portrait of psychological loss, regret and longing on the part of Jeanne herself and of the other nuns. The extent of their devotion can be measured in the lines (vol.1, p.233):

> Nous serons aussi sages qu'elle
> Quand nous en aurons fait autant.

Jeanne is still thinking of the child she has been parted from, rather than of the spiritual consolations of religion; Eisen has changed the perspective from that of the other nuns towards her to that of Jeanne's own attitude to her past and present. She is no longer shown as a pious model for the others, but as a woman lost in her own thoughts of thwarted maternity. The curtain above the stairs is drawn back to reveal a stairway which would allow her to leave the scene, but she does not take it; her escape is into her feelings for her baby. The 'grille' mentioned by La Fontaine is no longer a physical barrier to the outside world; it is the human, maternal barrier of inconsolable loss. Both De Hooghe (De Hooghe 27) and Cochin offer much the same scene as in Eisen's rejected version, with the perspective reversed; Jeanne thus becomes a distant figure in the background, while the other nuns and the abbess are close to us. In reflecting faithfully the indications of the text, they draw attention to the exceptional piety of Sœur Jeanne in the eyes of the other nuns, but ignore the personal human drama which she embodies.

This is one of the few plates in the *Contes* to show the self-absorption of an individual which Michael Fried has identified as a major characteristic of French eighteenth-century painting.[69] Most of the plates show figures

69. Fried, *Absorption and theatricality*. Another example is the figure of Guillot in the plate for 'Le cas de conscience'.

De Hooghe 27. 'Sœur Jeanne', vol.i, p.209

who are not preoccupied with their own thoughts, but are deeply conscious of the presence of, and their relationship to, other individuals depicted in the illustration. The fact that such a plate is exceptional in the context of the *Contes* as a whole underlines Eisen's sympathy for the unspoken sufferings of nuns which Diderot was describing at the same time in composing his novel *La Religieuse*.[70] At the same time, of course, Eisen once again points to one of the the recurring themes of the *Contes*, namely that religious figures are no more exempt from sexual feelings than the most worldly of their contemporaries.

## xxviii. 'Imitation d'Anacréon'

*Caption: 'Un jeune peintre travaille au portrait d'Iris.'*

The description is only an approximation of what is shown in the illustration. It makes no mention of the visitor (the unnamed interlocutor of the *conte*) standing to the right of the easel (Eisen 38) and offering comments or guidance to the (equally anonymous) artist as he paints. The subject of the *conte* is the idealisation of women; this idea is instanced by the visitor's request that the painter depict his mistress Iris (whom the painter has not seen) by painting Venus herself, so alike in beauty are the two women.

In this apparently simple poem, La Fontaine (like Anacreon whom he takes as his inspiration)[71] raises the question of the nature of artistic creation, and the representation of the ideal in the real.[72] Iris and Venus are allegedly interchangeable, so that the painter has only to take the one as his model in order to find the other. But in reality this solution will not work: Venus can be represented as the ideal, but Iris is (presumably) a real woman, and either the portrait will reflect her true appearance or it will not. An idealised, imagined Iris may well be beautiful enough to be considered the equal of Venus, but is not necessarily a good resemblance. For the lover, of course, the distinction is immaterial, since Iris represents his ideal, and an idealised, but simultaneously true, view of her is what he seeks. The problem raised by this *conte* is an ancient one, which was discussed by Plato in the *Republic*. Art is the representation of what is not there, a copy of a particular instance of the Ideal, which we cannot know,

70. Several early editions of *La Religieuse* (published in 1796) contain engravings depicting life in a convent. They are studied in my article 'Les premières illustrations de *La Religieuse*, ou la via non dolorosa', in *La Douleur: beauté ou laideur*, ed. Angels Santa (Lleida, 2005), p.41-52.
71. He uses two of Anacreon's *Odes*, nos. XXVIII 'Sur sa maîtresse' and XXIX 'Sur Bathylle'. See also *OCLF*, p.1436.
72. Diderot reflects on the same topic in the postface to his short story 'Les deux amis de Bourbonne' (1770).

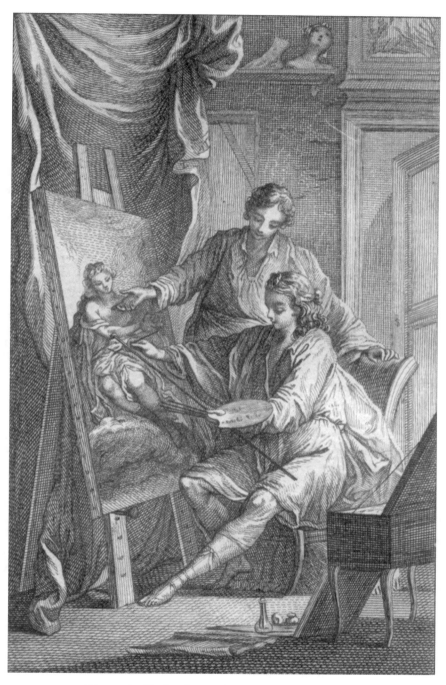

Eisen 38. 'Imitation d'Anacréon', vol.1, p.235

and is thus twice removed from true knowledge.[73] But Anacreon attempts to subvert this doctrine by allowing Venus to represent the knowable ideal of beauty, and the painter's mistress to be the 'copy' of this ideal, and vice versa.[74]

By conflating the ideal and the real, the speaker indirectly raises a problem central to the illustration of the *Contes*, and to this 1762 edition in particular. The Fermiers refused some engravings which, in their view, did not adequately convert the sense of the printed word into visual form. We know, from the evidence of the Grenville copy for example, that some of Eisen's illustrations went through several stages before reaching a state which the Fermiers found acceptable. It may be that further versions of these or other designs existed, as sketches, etchings or even as copperplate engravings, of which no trace now remains. Whatever the facts of the matter, it is clear that the Fermiers, and Eisen himself, went to much trouble to produce a set of designs which, as far as possible, embodied their final view of how the work should be illustrated.

Much of Eisen's inspiration comes from De Hooghe, who likewise shows the artist and the client before a painting of Venus/Iris (De Hooghe 28), though the setting is a purely classical one, as distinct from the contemporary décor used by Eisen. Cochin is also one of Eisen's sources, in the use of furnishings, and in the positioning of the two men, both of whom are looking at the painting of Venus. However, a second artist can also be seen on the left, bent over a canvas on which are visible the outlines of a different female nude, as if to emphasise the subjectivity of beauty and the difficulty of rendering the ideal. A study of the plates for the 1762 edition shows that this subjective element in artistic creation was not a primary consideration for Eisen and the Fermiers who sought, sometimes through the elimination of variants, a single, and perhaps even idealised, representation of the text which they wished to illustrate.

## xxix. 'Autre imitation d'Anacréon'

*Caption: 'Un homme est assis auprès du feu; l'Amour s'échappe de ses bras après lui avoir décoché une flèche.'*

La Fontaine's text gives no indication of the writer's appearance or age, but Eisen (Eisen 39) makes him a mature, bearded man dressed in ancient costume. Nor is there any hint as to the sort of house he has, but

73. See *The Republic of Plato*, translated with notes and an interpretative essay by Allan Bloom (New York and London, 1968), p.193-220.

74. The *conte* also challenges the distinction between *alethia* (that which points beyond itself) and *adequatio* (that which represents directly). This distinction, so Marian Hobson maintains, is central to the conception of art prevailing in eighteenth-century France (*The Object of art: the theory of illusion in eighteenth-century France*, Cambridge, 1982, esp. p.15-17).

De Hooghe 28. 'Imitation d'Anacréon', vol.1, p.210

Eisen 39. 'Autre imitation d'Anacréon', vol.1, p.237

De Hooghe 29. 'Autre imitation d'Anacréon', vol.1, p.212

the draperies shown here suggest a large space within the dwelling. The fire, a symbol of the love which the man feels for Climène, lights the scene. A large, symbolically empty bed can be seen behind him. Cupid is shown suspended in mid air, his lightness and ability to fly contrasted with the heaviness of the man slumped in his chair, and emphasised by the wide angle between them. On the floor, the large bundle of sticks prepared for the fire suggests that his love will long continue to burn before his passion dies down.

Much of the inspiration for Eisen's illustration comes from De Hooghe, who likewise shows the lover, seated by a fire (in the open air, with classical columns in the background) holding up his hands in futile defence against Cupid's dart (De Hooghe 29). De Hooghe's Cupid is however a large draped figure borne on clouds, not the fractious child ('le petit scélérat', vol.1, p.238) shown by Eisen. In Cochin's vignette for the 1745 edition, the man holds Cupid firmly in his arms, and is apparently the stronger of the two. In contrast, De Hooghe and Eisen represent the man with his 'couardise' (vol.1, p.238), timorous, fearful of what the future holds, overcome by the power of Cupid whose arrow has pierced his heart.

In a work in which the human triumphs over the supernatural, this plate offers a striking contrast with what we find in numerous other illustrations by Eisen. Yet it can be also linked with *contes* such as 'Le calendrier des vieillards' and 'Le faucon' which show the perennial tendency of men to enslave themselves to women (the reverse situation is less apparent in the *Contes* as a whole).

# 3. The illustrations to La Fontaine's
## *Contes et nouvelles en vers*, volume 2

THE second volume of the 1762 *Contes et nouvelles en vers*, with its 310 pages, is noticeably longer than the first, which has 270 pages. Its greater length is accounted for by the larger number of *contes* which it contains (forty-one as against twenty-nine in vol.1), although not all of them are by La Fontaine. Their source was not, however, a matter of concern to the Fermiers and their illustrators, since the plates to this second volume are as technically accomplished as those of the first, and reveal the same outlook and attitudes as those which were examined in the previous chapter.

## i. 'Les oies de frère Philippe'

*Caption: 'La scène se passe sur l'une des places de Florence; un jeune homme s'échappe des bras d'un vieil ermite pour se jetter dans ceux de deux jeunes beautés.'*

The first engraving which Eisen prepared for this *conte* (Eisen 40a) was rejected, and replaced by a second (Eisen 40b). Although Boccaccio identifies the city in question as Florence, La Fontaine's text simply says that the father took his son to 'la ville prochaine' (vol.2, p.6), without naming it. Indeed, the emphasis in the first version of the engraving is on the rural, rather than the metropolitan. The city is indicated only by a synecdochic stone column and pedestal on the extreme right, and by vaguely drawn buildings in the distant background; Eisen also includes some token trees in the scene to recall the rural origins of the two men. The stone column intersects the branches, to indicate the contrast represented by town and country, echoing the reactions of the pair, who are newly arrived in the city from their rural retreat. This distinction is paralleled by the contrast between the elegant clothing of the two women on the left, and the rough peasant costume of the son. The father's robes ('il voulut être hermite', vol.2, p.4) underscore more heavily still the fact that the son has been brought up in an environment in which he has little contact with civilisation, and consequently few opportunities to see or become acquainted with women of any sort. Eisen employs some standard devices as correlates of feeling to externalise emotion: the dark sky, the apparently agitated branches of the trees, and the umbrella/sunshade carried by one of the women all betoken an impending storm. Since one tall branch pierces its way through the surrounding branches, as does the column, the sexual

Eisen 40a. 'Les oies de frère Philippe', first version, between p.viii and p.1

Eisen 40b. 'Les oies de frère Philippe', second version,
between p.viii and p.1

connotations of the 'storm' are apparent as the young man responds with alacrity to the spectacle of these hitherto-unknown creatures.[1]

At least, this is the implication of the description for the illustration, but as it stands the plate does not justify the wording, and one can see several reasons why the Fermiers may have regarded it as unsuitable. By placing the father *between* the son and the women, Eisen does not adhere strictly to the wording of the description (one wonders, in passing, why it omits the fact that the two men are related). In turning his face away from the women, and towards his son, the father does not entirely reflect the information given by La Fontaine. The text states that, as a result of the death of his wife, 'Le monde lui fut odieux' (vol.2, p.4), yet his expression is less one of odium than of concern.[2] Nor is it clear where the two women could be going, since they seem to be heading straight towards the very solid base of the column. The perspective is also problematic: the dress of the nearer of the two women touches the father's cloak, even though he and his son are at some remove from the column. Such technical shortcomings (which are rare in the illustrations as we have them) would alone have been enough to explain the rejection of this first plate by the Fermiers.

Eisen's representation of the subject of this earlier engraving is largely his own invention, except for the presence of a tree on the left. The same device is also used by De Hooghe, who adds a prominent, and perhaps phallic, column in the background (De Hooghe 30). In this latter version, the imposing figure of the father is almost shielding his (somewhat smaller) son from the sight of the women, and there is little here on which Eisen could build. In Cochin's vignette for the 1745 edition, the use of a pillar suggests a large building, though there are no rural elements of the sort found in Eisen. However, the father, dressed in his hermit's robes, is clearly angry with the two women to whom his son is paying attention. We thus have, in Cochin's interpretation, a misogynistic old man who sees the charms of women as a trap into which his son is falling through his naiveté. Eisen, however, depicts the son attempting to free himself from his father's grip and to rush towards the two women, showing the drama of the relationship between parent and child. As so often, his concern is with the expression of natural, spontaneous feeling, and with the acceptance of human sexuality, whatever constraints society or parents may try to place upon it.

In revising the illustration (Eisen 40b), Eisen literally marginalises the father, and brings the figures of the son and the two women into greater prominence (as in the earlier version, a third woman can just be seen, this

---

1. Lapp, *The Esthetics of negligence*, p.77, and *OCLF*, p.1412.

2. The academic tradition of depicting the passions by recognised facial expressions and features dates back at least to the teachings of Charles Le Brun (1619-1690), and especially to his *Conférence sur l'expression générale et particulière* (c.1678). The old man's concern, and the 'ravissement' of his son, are depicted in accordance with Le Brun's illustrations used in engraving XXIII of Watelet's *Encyclopédie* article 'Dessin' (1754). For a study of Le Brun's influence on later French art, see Montagu, *The Expression of the passions*.

De Hooghe 30. 'Les oies de frère Philippe', vol.2, p.1

time on the extreme right of the engraving). No trees now suggest the countryside, and the roadway is paved instead of being made simply of earth. The son is still dressed like a peasant, so that the strong contrast between the two cultures is again made via the clothing of the male and female protagonists, and by the much more obvious and elaborate cityscape which serves as a background to the encounter. Here, the son seems even more out of place than in the earlier plate. In the second version, the women are clearly aware of his interest in them, even if they display somewhat disdainful expressions at his unconventional approach. The notion of his transgressing accepted social norms by his conduct is underlined by the scowling face on the shield of the statue visible at the top left of the illustration. Yet the text says nothing of any actual encounter between the son and (vol.2, p.7) the

> jeunes beautés
> Aux yeux vifs, aux traits enchantés

who fascinate him as soon as he sets eyes on them. The reaction of the women is thus an invention of Eisen's, and one which is far more emphatic in the replacement engraving than in the original. In this way, the artist echoes what La Fontaine himself says in the preamble to the *conte* in which, addressing his female readers, he defends himself against accusations of misogyny (vol.2, p.2):

> Le monde ne vous connoît gueres,
> S'il croit que les faveurs sont chez vous familieres.

This point can obviously be better made by showing the women disdainfully rejecting the approach by the son than by showing them apparently ignorant of his interest, as they are in the rejected engraving. Eisen has therefore transformed the scene not only into a series of contrasts: nature versus civilisation, poverty versus wealth, man versus woman, age versus youth, and wisdom versus impetuousness. He has also created, more emphatically than in the original version, and independently of any indications in the *conte* itself, a conflict between two classes, the peasantry and the wealthy, with the strong suggestion (found also in Cochin) that between the two there is a great gulf fixed. Choffard's tailpiece for the *conte* echoes this idea by depicting at its centre a bird which tries to fly, but which is held down by a string attached to the ground.

## ii. 'Richard Minutolo'

*Caption: Richard Minutolo 'est assis sur un sopha au fond d'une chambre; Catelle qui vient d'ouvrir les volets de la croisée, tombe à demi-pâmée en reconnoissant son amant'.*

One of the most striking aspects of this illustration (Eisen 41) is the contrast it offers with the statements contained in the text and the description.

Eisen 41. 'Richard Minutolo', vol.2, p.9

The setting is supposedly the 'chambre noire' in which Richard has deceived Mme Catelle into meeting him. Such a room is usually a place of solitary monastic retreat or penitence, a sense recalled by La Fontaine's observation that Catelle went there 'Non pour jeûner, comme vous pouvez croire' (vol.2, p.12).[3] Consequently, there is no mention in the text of the sofa, the luxurious draperies or the carpet shown in the illustration, though Eisen could have found them in De Hooghe's head-piece for the *conte*. La Fontaine states that Catelle is 'plus d'à demi-pâmée' from shock at finding herself with Richard (vol.2, p.15), and from fear of the harm which the discovery will do to her reputation. The woman shown in Eisen's illustration is however standing, not swooning; De Hooghe's Catelle, in contrast, gives every sign of wanting to flee from her seducer as he falls to his knees behind her (De Hooghe 31). Her dress is sober and her demeanour is reserved, unlike that of the bare-breasted woman imagined by Eisen.

Eisen adds two other erotic elements, of a symbolic kind: the prominent tricorn hat on the left, and the sword in its scabbard lying beneath it. It is of course the case that Richard has removed these accoutrements because he is indoors and seated; even so, in foregrounding these symbols so clearly, Eisen creates a none-too-subtle contrast with the apparent resistance of Catelle, and provides a clue to what will follow in due course when her resistance has been overcome by the force of Minutolo's eloquence (vol.2, p.17).[4] But however successful his eloquence may be, Richard's words carry echoes of the views expressed by the man who waylays the shepherdess in 'La clochette' (vol.1, p.221), since he tells Catelle (vol.2, p.15):

> Adresse, force, et ruse, et tromperie,
> Tout est permis en matiere d'amour.

In one sense, Eisen is merely using artistic licence to embellish the scene, and to make it more agreeable to the eye than it would have been if, like Cochin in the 1745 edition, he had followed literally the wording of the text at this point. Yet this is not the only reason for his choices. In contrast to Richard's bluntness, the text twice draws attention to its own reticence in describing matters of some delicacy (vol.2, p.13 and vol.2, p.17):

> Quant au surplus, je le laisse à penser:
> Chacun s'en doute assez sans qu'on le die
> [...] D'une faveur en une autre il passa;
> Eut un souris, puis autre chose encor;
> Puis un baiser, puis autre chose encore.

3. Compare *OCLF*, p.1355, n.1.
4. 'The *conte*, in La Fontaine's hands, demonstrates the power of language' (Lapp, *The Esthetics of negligence*, p.46).

De Hooghe 31. 'Richard Minutolo', vol.2, p.8

While reticence can be visual as well as verbal, Eisen chooses an approach which allows him to suggest truths which La Fontaine himself discreetly veils. Indeed, one could argue that the theme of the engraving is the revelation of hidden truths. Catelle's clothes are open, like the window and the bed-curtains; in addition, her skirt is raised to reveal her petticoats. However, she is not shown prostrate with shame or shock. This is surely because to depict her in this way would have been to produce a scene akin to rape; it would have altered the whole tone of the illustration, and would thereby have betrayed the text. Instead, she covers her eyes with her arm, a point which is not made in the *conte*. Even so, the illustration suggests both that she wishes to avoid truths which she cannot contemplate, and that she is strong enough to withstand the experience without undue harm, thus proleptically referring to the events related later in the *conte*. The function of the illustration, here as elsewhere in the 1762 edition, is therefore to reveal the truth, even when the text itself does not say what occurred.

## iii. 'Les cordeliers de Catalogne'

*Caption: 'La foule est grande à l'entrée du couvent; frère Frapart introduit l'une des payantes; frère Roc est réduit à choisir; une vieille est écartée, une jeune admise.'*

As in other *contes*, there is an element of anticlerical satire here which belongs as much to La Fontaine as to his traditional sources; it emerges most clearly in the sermons preached by the monks to seduce their female congregations. Critics have seen, in the specious arguments used by the monks, evidence both of La Fontaine's anticlericalism,[5] and of his wish to attack the casuistry of the Jesuits, under the influence of his associates at Port Royal.[6] The Eisen engraving (Eisen 42) does not show the Cordeliers in the act of preaching a sermon, but the consequences which arise from their doing so, in that the female members of their congregation obediently come to them for sex. We should note the contrast between worldly wealth, as displayed by the quality of the women's dresses, and the (apparently) self-denying simplicity of the monks' attire. The scene shown refers to the lines (vol.2, p.24)

> Les beaux Peres n'expédioient
> Que les fringantes et les belles,
> Enjoignant aux sempiternelles
> De porter en bas leur tribut.

Frère Frapart is said to be one of the most active of the monks, while 'Frère Roc à vingt se chaussoit' (vol.2, p.23). In some respects, the illustration

5. See Jürgen Grimm, ' "Comment on traite les pervers": la satire anticléricale dans les *Contes*', *Papers on French seventeenth-century literature* 23:44 (1996), p.159-72.
6. See Grisé, 'La casuistique dans les *Contes*', p.413.

Eisen 42. 'Les cordeliers de Catalogne', vol.2, p.19

reflects the terms of the text, but in others it does not. The monks as depicted by Eisen are not 'beaux', though the faces of the women make sufficiently clear the difference in the treatment meted out to those who are young and those who are less so. Nor does the 'couvent' as represented by Eisen have any specifically religious markings or signs. The effect is therefore to suggest that this is less a religious house than a place where men and women meet for sexual encounters. In this respect, Eisen differs significantly both from De Hooghe and from Cochin. De Hooghe offers a view of the street in which the 'couvent' is situated, just as one of the cuckolded husbands is about to set fire to it, watched by a couple in elegant dress (De Hooghe 32). Cochin's 1745 vignette shows a monk haranguing his female congregation (Cochin 5). While the latter headpiece depicts what would be a conventional scene of piety if we did not know the purpose of the monk's sermon, Eisen shows monks behaving in a way which flouts their vows of celibacy, though he makes the female congregation equally complicit in the disregard of those vows. He does not depart from the content of the text in this respect, though the diegesis is condensed from a general description into a specific synecdoche.

In showing the women as complicit with the monks, Eisen is more indulgent than La Fontaine. The cruel revenge inflicted on the monks by the men of the town whom they have cuckolded is recounted in the text with a glee, as Lapp remarks (*Esthetics of negligence*, p.126-27), not to be found in the *Cent Nouvelles nouvelles* from which La Fontaine took the story. Eisen's decision to make the improper encounter of the monks and the women the subject of the illustration, in preference to either a depiction of the sermon or the vengeance wreaked on the monks, is not surprising. It is to be explained by the persistent hostility towards the Church, which runs through the illustrations to the 1762 *Contes*. Without being overtly censorious, the engravings collectively depict a world of sexual intrigue, and even of debauchery, which had deep roots in French literature from the Middle Ages onwards. Yet it takes on a heightened significance in the context of the struggles for power in which the Church and the Compagnie des Fermiers généraux were engaged in pre-Revolutionary France, and which were outlined in chapter 1 of this study.

## iv. 'Le berceau'

*Caption: 'Colette assise sur la couchette avec sa mère, se chausse; le berceau de l'enfant est derrière elles; le père assis, met ses souliers.'*

This engraving sums up one of the most complex stories related by La Fontaine, in which a number of unforeseen sexual encounters ensue from the displacement of a child's cradle from its usual place beside the innkeeper's bed. Eisen is not primarily concerned with these permutations,

De Hooghe 32. 'Les cordeliers de Catalogne', vol.2, p.17

Cochin 5. 'Les cordeliers de Catalogne', vol.2, p.17

which involve the innkeeper, his wife, and two young noblemen, one called Pinuce and the other unnamed (Eisen 43). His subject is the obviously satisfied reaction, the following morning, of the innkeeper's wife and his daughter Colette, and the somewhat disgruntled attitude of the innkeeper himself to what has occurred.

The *conte* makes much of the fact that the mother and daughter are willing accomplices in their seduction. La Fontaine observes that Colette is especially attracted to Pinuce because he is a 'gentilhomme bien-fait' (vol.2, p.29), and because she has (vol.2, p.30)

> Le cœur trop haut, le goût trop délicat
> Pour s'en tenir aux amours de village

while her father tells him that his inn is too modest 'pour gens de votre état' (vol.2, p.31). As illustrated by Eisen, the scene does not correspond exactly to what the *conte* tells us, though it approximates to the closing lines (vol.2, p.36):

> On se leva; ce ne fut pas sans rire;
> Car chacun d'eux en avait sa raison.

Again, although one of the male characters puts his fingers to his lips as a sign to the mother to say nothing, this is only an approximation of La Fontaine's phrase (vol.2, p.36)

> Tout fut secret; et quiconque eut du bon
> Par devers soi le garda sans rien dire.

We are not told that any one character makes this gesture, so that its depiction stands metonymically for the silence observed by all the participants in the night's activities. It is true, as Holloway remarks (*French rococo book illustration*, p.31), that each of those involved has his or her own view of what occurred during the night. Yet the four characters other than the husband/father are all looking at one another: they share a secret from which he is excluded because he has accepted the lies which Pinuce's friend has concocted to explain what occurred during the night. What is more, the class differences to which La Fontaine draws attention are not apparent from Eisen's illustration, although they do feature in, for example, the third illustration for 'Joconde' and in the plates for 'Les oies de frère Philippe'. Eisen here suppresses such distinctions by crowding the characters together, making them a coherent group in their nightwear.

Eisen's blurring of class distinctions is all the more significant if Holloway is correct in saying (*French rococo book illustration*, p.25) that some of the characters in this illustration are recognisable as personalities who were anything but members of the lower classes. The mother, seated on the left, apparently resembles Mme d'Epinay, while the figure standing at the back is said to look like the marquis de Saint-Lambert, the lover of her cousin Mme d'Houdetot. Whether or not this is the case is difficult to say, since Eisen's characters tend to be types, rather than individuals, and

Eisen 43. 'Le berceau', vol.2, p.29

often resemble one another facially from one engraving to another. However, it is true that the future Mme d'Epinay was brought up by her aunt, who was married to a Fermier général, that she herself had married a Fermier in 1745, and that she had a liaison, in her unhappy marriage, with the son of another Fermier, Dupin de Chenonceaux.[7] The Fermiers could well have decided, therefore, that they wished to make a joking reference to members of a family who, by 1762, had gained widespread public attention as a result of their involvement with Jean-Jacques Rousseau.[8] The inclusion of such contemporary references would reinforce the impression that, by a variety of means, the Fermiers were ready to use the illustrations for the *Contes* to comment on the life of the times. Even if no more specific intention lay behind the illustration to this *conte*, readers would have been alerted to its personal resonances, and the allusions would not have been lost on the small group of readers who managed to acquire copies of the *Contes* at the time.

Class distinctions are, however, central to De Hooghe's interpretation of the story, since he depicts the two noblemen with their horses arriving at the inn, to be met by the obviously deferential innkeeper and his family (De Hooghe 33). Cochin's vignette for this *conte* takes full advantage of the breadth of the page, though it makes less of the close bond between the characters, and hints at least at the triumph of the noblemen (Cochin 6). One of the friends is shown recounting his adventures to the innkeeper, who seems understandably irate at the news, as his wife and daughter look on, smiling at the memory of the night's events.

Unlike Eisen, neither De Hooghe nor Cochin illustrates this *conte* in a way which might have the slightest personal application. At the same time, Eisen undeniably does allude to more permanent aspects of the human condition; the illustration is crowded with characters, both because of its format and because a place needed to be found for the prominent positioning of the cradle which has led to the confusion. By placing it between the two women, Eisen offers a reminder that the same behaviour is exhibited down the generations, and indeed that their behaviour the previous night may result in the birth of yet another child.[9]

## v. 'L'oraison de S. Julien'

*Caption: 'Renaud d'Ast est dépouillé dans le bois par ses honnêtes compagnons de voyage.'*

In this engraving (Eisen 44a), as so often, Eisen does not so much echo the details provided by La Fontaine as offer a specific, individual,

7. See Durand, *Les Fermiers généraux, passim*, but esp. p.258-59, 591-93.
8. See the article on Mme d'Epinay by Gustave Charlier in the *Dictionnaire des lettres françaises: XVIIIᵉ siècle*, ed. François Moureau (Paris, 1995), p.457-58.
9. For an analysis of the literary qualities of this *conte*, see Lapp, *The Esthetics of negligence*, p.51-52.

De Hooghe 33. 'Le berceau', vol.2, p.27

Cochin 6. 'Le berceau', vol.2, p.27

Eisen 44a. 'L'oraison de S. Julien', second version, p.37

interpretation of them. Renaud is dressed in the costume of the seventeenth century, as are the robbers who beset him. His clothes, stance and face all suggest a passive, and even slightly effeminate, nature. The rather phallic moneybag being removed by the robber standing to the right suggests that Renaud's manhood is called into question by his passivity, whatever his subsequent sexual prowess with the lady who shelters him. It is not hard to understand why he was so easily robbed, since the list of items taken by the thieves does not state that he was armed (vol.2, p.40):

> Ils lui prirent en somme
> Chapeau, casaque, habit, bourse et cheval;
> Bottes aussi.

Although La Fontaine says that Renaud was robbed of his boots as well, he is shown still wearing them, so that we are in the midst of the robbery. He is surrounded, and although he is obviously younger than the trio who rob him, he seems powerless against their attack, a characteristic emphasised by Eisen.

This interpretation differs wholly from that of De Hooghe (De Hooghe 34) and Cochin, who both depict Renaud with a lady in her room, in amorous conversation. Cochin adds two tall, lit candles on the table, and the 1755 edition has the same scene in a reversed impression. Eisen used one or other of these versions as the basis for a suppressed engraving for the *conte*, to be found in the Grenville and Pixérécourt copies (Eisen 44b). As Holloway observes (*French rococo book illustration*, p.7), Eisen here makes much of the luxury of the apartment and of the clothes borrowed by Renaud from his benefactress; the hint of what is to follow is provided by the prominent bed in the background, though the lady looks rather distant and uninvolved. Nonetheless, this episode of the story entails a somewhat routine encounter between the couple, and the Fermiers (or perhaps Eisen himself) presumably felt that it offered less opportunity for comment on Renaud's conduct than the version included in standard copies of the *Contes*.

In depicting him as a passive and even somewhat effeminate individual, Eisen takes up a technique which he had used in the very first engraving of the *Contes*, showing the vanity of Astolphe in 'Joconde'. Both Astolphe and Renaud are dressed in light, rather elaborate clothing of an earlier period, which tends to emphasise the femininity of their demeanour. In neither case can La Fontaine be said to suggest such an interpretation, and Eisen's predecessors do not choose to see the characters in this way. In both cases, Eisen allows us to infer that a man failing to display masculine, self-affirming qualities, is less than a man, whatever his sexual prowess. The point is perhaps all the more pertinent in 'L'oraison de S. Julien', which opens with a frank refusal by La Fontaine to believe in

De Hooghe 34. 'L'oraison de S. Julien', vol.2, p.35

Eisen 44b. 'L'oraison de S. Julien', first version (reproduced from Owen
Holloway, *French rococo book illustration*, London, 1969, plate 28)

the efficacy of 'brevets, oraisons et paroles' (vol.1, p.37). A man has to rely on his own resources, since God is unlikely to help those in need.[10]

## vi. 'Le villageois qui cherche son veau'

*Caption: 'Sous l'arbre le plus touffu de la forêt, le Jouvenceau s'extasie aux genoux de sa Dame; la tête du villageois perce l'épaisseur du feuillage.'*

The text contains no reference to 'l'arbre le plus touffu de la forêt', but only to 'l'arbre le plus beau' (vol.2, p.53). Eisen makes the foliage abundant for two reasons (Eisen 45). First, it obviously enables him to hide the man who has lost his cow, and thereby make him less conspicuous to the couple lying under the tree when he is only a few feet above them. Second, with the roughly triangular shape of the foliage, he can hint at the lush pubic hair of the woman, whose lover exclaims (vol.2, p.53)

O dieux, que vois-je, et que ne vois-je pas!

We see what the lover will no doubt see shortly after the moment depicted here, so that the tree is a proleptic visual metaphor for the sexual encounter. As Philip Stewart observes (*Engraven desire*, p.167), we are not told that the *villageois* sees what the *galant* sees; nonetheless, both Eisen and Cochin depict him enjoying a good view, though only in the 1762 edition are the sexual correlates wholly explicit. The sparse foliage of his tree does not hide De Hooghe's villager (De Hooghe 35), though the couple beneath are behaving decorously enough at this stage. Cochin depicts the woman with only her corsage open, and the *villageois* is so close to the couple that his presence is almost absurdly obtrusive (Cochin 7).

Eisen is therefore careful both to make the actual scene more credible by hiding the observer, and to suggest by artistic means what cannot be shown in a collection which is careful not to exceed the bounds of conventional decency.

## vii. 'L'anneau d'Hans Carvel'

*Caption: 'Tandis que Carvel ronfle auprès de Babeau, le Diable fait comme il est dit.'*

Despite the description, we cannot know that Carvel is snoring, though we can presume that he is asleep, since he is undisturbed by the presence

---

10. John Lapp (*The Esthetics of negligence*, p.59) argues that the rejection of these three forms of religious utterance should not be seen 'as evidence of anti-clericalism but rather as a skilful way of emphasizing the power of language, for in the game of love the scorned "paroles", "charmes" and "brevets" acquire their full value.' This reading misses the point: La Fontaine himself admits that words are of great importance in lovemaking (vol.1, p.37), but whatever their efficacy in human terms, he goes out of his way to reject them as a means of influencing the Deity.

Eisen 45. 'Le villageois qui cherche son veau', vol.2, p.53

De Hooghe 35. 'Le villageois qui cherche son veau', vol.2, p.49

Cochin 7. 'Le villageois qui cherche son veau', vol.2, p.49

of the Devil. Eisen makes his Devil come down to the bed and take Carvel's hand (Eisen 46) and, as Holloway observes (*French rococo book illustration*, p.21), he has used dark shading for the curtains, the bed-sheets and for the Devil himself. This technique creates a strong contrast between these elements of the illustration and the (natural?) light from an unseen source which falls on the sleeping couple of Carvel and Babeau. By using these sombre tones, Eisen makes his Devil blend in with the bed-clothes, so that he becomes, so to speak, a material being, instead of an ethereal element in Carvel's dream. The division between the real and the supernatural is therefore brought into question in one of the few *contes* in which the supernatural occurs. Max Milner has written of the ridicule heaped on the notion of the Devil by many eighteenth-century writers, and this reduction of the Prince of Darkness to an imaginary being accords entirely with this tendency.[11]

The contrast between Eisen's approach and that of previous illustrators is striking. De Hooghe shows us Carvel and his wife sleeping peacefully (De Hooghe 36), while the massive, cloven-footed Devil stands near the bed, his upper torso obscured by gibberish written in Hebrew lettering, and by a divine flame burning despite his presence. While such a representation of the Devil does seem to be unusual in Dutch art of the period, it was commonplace in earlier times to associate the Devil with Jews since both were heretics, and De Hooghe's depiction of him may hark back to this tradition.[12] Unlike Eisen's, De Hooghe's Devil is so real that theological weapons are needed to combat his presence. In Cochin's vignette for the 1745 edition, a (somewhat benign) Devil floats over the bed, and Carvel seems to be looking directly up at him. This version of the story stands midway between De Hooghe's traditional horror of the Devil, and Eisen's implicit mockery of the notion; the Devil can still fly, but is hardly a threat.

No less significant than these changes for an understanding of Eisen's procedures is the description for the 1762 illustration. It refers to the event as described in the text ('comme il est dit'), as if to draw attention to the obscenity of the story by refusing (out of an apparent respect for decency) to describe exactly what is occurring. But the text itself tells us only that the Devil placed Carvel's finger 'où vous sçavez' (vol.2, p.56). Hence, explicit crudity is twice avoided, once on the part of La Fontaine and once on that of the Fermiers, but the procedure is one which makes the reader complicit in the understanding of what is referred to only obliquely. This assumed complicity, as we shall see in the final part of this

11. Max Milner, *Le Diable dans la littérature française: de Cazotte à Baudelaire 1722-1861*, 2 vols (Paris, 1960), vol.1, p.65-68.

12. For some discussion of Devils in the art of the period, see Jane P. Davidson, *The Witch in northern European art 1470-1750* (Düsseldorf, 1987).

Eisen 46. 'L'anneau d'Hans Carvel', vol.2, p.55

De Hooghe 36. 'L'anneau d'Hans Carvel', vol.2, p.51

study, is integrally bound up in the thinking which underlies the Fermiers' involvement with this edition of the *Contes*.

## viii. 'L'hermite'

*Caption: 'Une mere présente humblement sa fille à l'hermite qui faisant mine de reculer, la convoite du coin de l'œil.'*

La Fontaine's story has been linked with the condemnation of religious hypocrisy which often recurs in French literature of the mid-seventeenth century.[13] Nonetheless, despite the still greater prominence of anticlericalism in the eighteenth century, it would be wrong to assume that Eisen unswervingly follows his lead in this respect, notwithstanding the initial impression which the illustration might make on the reader (Eisen 47). The plate depicts the first meeting of the mother and daughter with the hermit, since at the second the mother goes away at once, leaving the girl alone with him. Eisen conceals the hermit's face from us, inviting us to imagine his appearance for ourselves, though we can partly see his piercing gaze which transfixes the two women. His reaction to the girl is shown chiefly by his throwing out his right arm in an attitude of (feigned) surprise ('Le papelard contrefait l'étonné', vol.2, p.62), as if warding off an evil spirit. The tailpiece by Choffard (p.65) shows a figure dressed in a monk's cowl and wearing a mask, implying that even if we were to see his face, we would not be seeing his true character.

It is true that the monk's duplicity is alluded to in the illustration. The scourge with which he pretends to flagellate himself to prove his devotion is scarcely noticeable at the bottom left of the illustration, and there is no physical indication of his allegedly self-inflicted punishment. At the same time, the light from an unknown source which can be seen behind his head may also be part of his trickery, serving almost as a halo to signify his holiness. His duping of the women also relies on an apparently open and frank demeanour; this impression is strengthened by the hole he has made in the wall of his cell, so that they can glimpse his supposed self-flagellation (vol.2, p.61-62). In Eisen's interpretation, if there is no flagellation, there is no need for a hole in the wall. On the other hand, a somewhat rickety roof offers little protection from the elements, and the wooden planks supporting it give only a modicum of privacy. This visibility, and ostentatious poverty, is part of the monk's strategy of deception, the better to lead the unwary into his trap.

Yet in a number of significant respects, Eisen makes the point that the monk is not entirely to blame for the sexual initiation of the girl which follows. First, the older woman is given a harsh, unsympathetic face, more

13. See Grimm, ' "Comment on traite les pervers" ', p.166-68.

Eisen 47. 'L'hermite', vol.2, p.57

typical perhaps of an 'entremetteuse' than of a caring mother, and there is no sign in her demeanour of the trembling or blushing mentioned specifically in the text (vol.2, p.62). Second, La Fontaine himself tells us that the girl is 'Jeune, ingénue, agréable et gentille' (vol.2, p.58), and that if she is still a virgin, this is 'moins par vertu que par simplicité' (vol.2, p.58). Eisen takes her complicity further: she is shown smiling at the monk, and she holds her hat prominently by her side; while this is no doubt as a sign of respect, there is something distinctly sexual about its shape.[14] Eisen also hints at the girl's complicity by involving her directly in the conversation between her mother and the monk: she is shown standing close to them, instead of being, as the text states, '[à] six pas d'eux' (vol.2, p.62). Third, we are given to understand by these means that the girl's seduction is the result as much of the women's willingness to believe in the monk's injunctions as in his trickery. In being apparently so open to the world, he encourages the willing credulity of the mother and the sexual interest shown by the daughter. In thus changing the indications given in the text, Eisen makes the encounter between the three characters more direct. He arranges the elements of the story to give the impression that the girl's seduction is already well on the way to being accomplished, and not just because the monk has successfully deceived the two women.

In De Hooghe's interpretation (De Hooghe 37), the hermit is seen in front of a perilously placed hovel at the top of a rocky outcrop, of the sort familiar from medieval and later paintings of saints in the wilderness. The mother stands respectfully bowing to him, as the daughter, her arms folded, waits in the background. The hermit, his right arm outstretched, shows no interest in the girl and seems unaware of her presence, an interpretation which is consistent with the information given in the text (vol.2, p.62). The arrangement of the figures in De Hooghe's headpiece emphasises the significance of the monk and the mother, relegating the girl to a minor role. It is Cochin who brings the three together, in showing us the meeting of the monk with the mother and daughter in his rudimentary 'home'. Unlike Eisen, however, Cochin allows us to see the monk's deceptively pious face, and displays prominently a skull as a *memento mori*; the mother seems worried, and even fearful, while the girl herself stands mute and submissive. The relationship between the three characters, and their attitudes towards one another, are thus quite different from what we find in Eisen. Typically, he takes a more cynical view than his predecessor not only of female sexuality, but also of the motivation of those who use the Church as a cover for their sexual ambitions, and suggests that a combination of these two influences is at work here.

---

14. As Lapp points out (*The Esthetics of negligence*, p.128), La Fontaine's reference to the monk's 'chapelet [...] long d'une brasse, et gros outre mesure' also has sexual connotations.

De Hooghe 37. 'L'hermite', vol.2, p.54

## ix. 'Mazet de Lamporechio'

*Caption: 'Mazet dort dans le jardin; deux religieuses le considèrent à dessein.'*

La Fontaine recounts the discovery of the sleeping Mazet by the two nuns in these terms (vol.2, p.71-72):

> De ces deux donc, l'une approchant Mazet,
> Dit à sa sœur: Dedans ce cabinet
> Menons ce sot. Mazet étoit beau mâle,
> Et la galante à le considérer
> Avoit pris goût; pourquoi sans différer
> Amour lui fit proposer cette affaire.

For the major elements of his engraving of this episode, Eisen draws on a very old tradition (Eisen 48) which goes back as far as the 1492 edition of Boccaccio's *Decamerone* from which the story derives.[15] The 1762 illustration places the emphasis on the actions, collaboration and gestures of the two nuns, who are duly seen arranging for Mazet to be taken to the 'cabinet'. One difference between La Fontaine and Boccaccio is that the Italian writer makes his nuns hesitate as they consider how to proceed with seducing Mazet; in contrast, La Fontaine allows one of the nuns to take the initiative and to suggest a plan with which her companion agrees (vol.2, p.71). Eisen follows him in this respect, adding to the conspiratorial air by showing the nun on the right whispering her suggestions into the other's ear. In this way, there is less chance that Mazet will overhear her: he is lying close by, and may or may not be asleep (La Fontaine leaves the point undecided, vol.2, p.71). As with other engravings depicting the contrast between the theory and the practice of religious celibacy, Eisen creates an erotically charged atmosphere by adding details of his own to echo La Fontaine's remark that purity is not a necessary accompaniment to a life of devotion (vol.2, p.67-68):

> Encore un coup ne faut qu'on s'imagine
> Que d'être pure et nette de péché,
> Soit privilége à la guimpe attachée [...]
> Tentation, fille d'oisiveté,
> Ne manque pas d'agir de son côté:
> Puis le désir, enfant de la contrainte.
> Ma fille est nonne; *Ergo*, c'est une sainte:
> Mal raisonné.[16]

15. See also Nicolich, 'Seventeenth and eighteenth-century illustrations for La Fontaine's *Contes et nouvelles en vers*', p.237-38.

16. Jürgen Grimm argues, not altogether persuasively in the context of the *Contes* as a whole, that these lines are a plea by La Fontaine for a better sexual education, and more freedom, for women, and hence an attack on the clerical practices of the time, since Boccaccio makes no corresponding point (' "Comment on traite les pervers" ' p.164-65). See also Birberick, 'From world to text', p.183-86.

Eisen 48. 'Mazet de Lamporechio', vol.2, p.67

For this reason, Eisen ironically displays the whiteness of the wimples worn by the two nuns while adding other details which point to the sexual overtones of their encounter with Mazet. By enclosing within a tall hedge the garden where he is found (an interpretation not based on any textual evidence), Eisen suggests the secrecy of the convent, a feature also indicated metonymically by the nuns whispering to each other. The pointed corset of the dress of the nun on the right draws the viewer's eye to the area between her thighs, emphasising her sex, as does her bent leg which is visible beneath her dress; in addition, the arrangement of the rake and shovel by Mazet's feet proleptically hints at the sexual relationship which he will have with them. No doubt the open end of the watering-can visible in the bottom right-hand corner of the engraving is intended to serve the same symbolic purpose.[17] As so often with Eisen, a secret is being revealed by the illustration, in a way that is not true of illustrations in other editions of the *Contes*.

De Hooghe uses the same basic setting as previous artists, showing the nuns in the garden of the convent (De Hooghe 38). In his headpiece, however, they debate what to do about Mazet, rather than whispering together, so that the sense of secrecy is lost. De Hooghe shows Mazet lying beside his spade, but the sexual connotations imparted by Eisen are not in evidence. In Cochin's vignette of 1745 (and in the reversed copy of 1755) one of the nuns takes Mazet by the arm as she leads him into the recesses of the garden, while the other keeps watch in the background. Like De Hooghe, Cochin places less emphasis on the conspiratorial collaboration of the two nuns, and he makes Mazet an active participant in the enterprise. There is little sign of the sexual symbolism which Eisen uses to convey the nature of the encounter between Mazet and the nuns. As a consequence, Cochin can only vaguely hint at the contrast between the temptation of the flesh and their vows of chastity, merely suggesting a tension which is prominently central to Eisen's interpretation of the *Contes*.

## x. 'La mandragore'

*Caption: 'Lucrèce est au lit; messer Nice lui présente le prétendu Meunier les yeux bandés; Ligurio éclaire l'intérieur du lit.'*

Eisen employs the customary appurtenances of bedroom scenes used in the illustrations to this edition: the *lit à baldaquin*, the copious drapes pulled back to reveal the bed, and a candle which is just visible on the bedside table (Eisen 49). He also uses a much more prominent (phallic?) candle to illuminate the scene, as if to suggest, ironically, that the servant Ligurio and his master Callimaque are bringing enlightenment to a situation in

---

17. On the sexual allusions in the text of the *conte*, see Lapp, *The Esthetics of negligence*, p.72-74.

De Hooghe 38. 'Mazet de Lamporechio', vol.2, p.62

Eisen 49. 'La mandragore', vol.2, p.75

which they are in reality duping both Lucrèce and her aged husband Nicia. Callimaque is blindfolded, but metaphorically, it is Nicia who is unable to see what is happening, even though Callimaque is scarcely different from the man whom he has already met. The engraving reflects the differing emotions on the faces of those involved: resignation in the case of Lucrèce, stolid determination in that of Nicia, the anticipation of Callimaque, and the non-committal sense of duty on the face of Ligurio.

Despite following the text in general terms, Eisen shows neither the false beard and chin, nor the flour-covered person of the 'Miller' impersonated by Callimaque, and thus avoids making him the slightly ludicrous figure described by La Fontaine (vol.2, p.83):

> Le lendemain, notre amant se déguise,
> Et s'enfarine en vrai garçon Meûnier;
> Un faux menton, barbe d'étrange guise;
> Mieux ne pouvoit se métamorphoser.

In the Fermiers généraux version, Nicia, whom he succeeds in duping very easily, helps Callimaque towards the bed; he is therefore about to cuckold a man who is shown helping him. This is not, however, a depiction of rank ingratitude on Callimaque's part, since one could equally argue that Nicia deserves to be punished for his willingness to sacrifice the life of another man to his own purposes, and that he finally demonstrates indifference to the fate of the 'Miller.'

There are few significant differences between De Hooghe, Cochin and Eisen in their interpretations of this *conte*. Eisen draws heavily on the 1685 De Hooghe illustration for elements of his engraving, such as the open draperies of the bed and the candle. De Hooghe omits to show the servant Ligurio, so that his depiction of the scene is more intimate than that of his successors (De Hooghe 39). Nicia's position, as he stands between Callimaque and (a somewhat resigned) Lucrèce, holding the hand of each, underlines his central position in the *conte* as the 'intermediary' between the two. Yet the sense of urgency which Eisen and Cochin (Cochin 8) give to his role in the proceedings is not apparent in De Hooghe.

The editions of 1745 and 1755 do not show any candle, though light does comes from an unseen source on the left. Both also show a chamber pot which is not present in De Hooghe, or indeed in Eisen, where the emphasis is on sex, not on other bodily functions. In both the 1745 and 1755 versions, too, Callimaque is in heavy disguise, so that he looks much older than in reality. Nicia, who is anxious for the exercise to begin, appears almost to be running towards the bed (the angle at which we see him could also mean that he is sitting on it, though the position would be physically difficult to sustain, especially for an old man).[18]

---

18. The representation of weight, balance and realism in eighteenth-century art is discussed in Etienne Jollet, *Figures de la pesanteur* (Nîmes, 1998).

De Hooghe 39. 'La mandragore', vol.2, p.70

Cochin 8. 'La mandragore', vol.2, p.69

Hence, all the illustrators, from De Hooghe to Eisen, emphasise the duplicity of Callimaque, the anxiety of Lucrèce, and Nicia's gullibility. This is one of the relatively few *contes* in which there is a considerable degree of similarity between the various illustrations. The reason is no doubt that it offered few opportunities for depicting any elements of interest other than the meeting of the three main characters.

## x. 'Les Rémois'

*Caption: 'La scène est dans la chambre du peintre; les deux maris sont dans un cabinet dont la porte est entr'ouverte; le peintre conduit dame Alix à son but, tandis que l'hôtesse va à la cave avec dame Simonette.'*

Eisen provided two versions of the illustration for this *conte*. Both are based on the following segment of the text (vol.2, p.93-94):

> Le compagnon vous la tenant seulette,
> La conduisit de fleurette en fleurette
> Jusqu'au toucher, et puis un peu plus loin;
> Puis tout à coup levant la colerette,
> Prit un baiser dont l'époux fut témoin.

Only the description allows the reader properly to understand what is being represented. It is not obvious that the woman to be seduced is dame Alix, rather than Simonette, since the same events occur twice in the *conte*. This earlier interpretation (Eisen 50a) [19] differs in two important respects from the wording of the *conte*. According to the text, Alix is 'seulette' with the painter, but the two women going to the cellar are clearly visible in the doorway at the back, and one of them appears almost to be looking into the room where the painter is engaged in seduction. In addition, we are told of the two husbands that (vol.2, p.93)

> Du cabinet la porte à demi close
> Leur laissant voir le tout distinctement,
> Ils ne prenoient aucun goût à la chose.

In the engraving, they are behind a window, and if there is a door, it is not shown as half open (though such an arrangement would offer a parallel with the half-open door leading to the cellar). By this small alteration to the indications given in the text, Eisen increases the frustration of the husbands, since they can see clearly what is happening, but can only stand and watch, without being able to open the window. The illustration makes the scene a more public seduction than is suggested by the text, even though the couple involved are unaware that they are being observed. The very prominent candle used in all three illustrations serves

19. This earlier Eisen version is rare in copies of the 1762 edition, but was often included in the reprint of 1792.

Eisen 50a. 'Les Rémois', first version, between p.88-89

as a reminder of the passions at work here; and yet the posture of the apparently reluctant Alix, who recoils from the painter as she raises a warning finger to him, conflicts with what it is customarily taken to imply.

In the second version of the illustration (Eisen 50b), we are as usual closer to the scene depicted, and have a better idea of the emotions experienced by the characters whose faces are now more clearly shown. Nonetheless, this engraving is not technically superior to the first in all respects. Unusually for the *Contes*, there is a slight awkwardness in the rendering of Alix's right arm, perhaps because the painter's own arm is around her neck and over her shoulder, isolating Alix's lower arm somewhat, and seeming almost to make it independent of her body.

Whatever the technical failings of the second engraving, the two wives are again uncomfortably close to the scene of seduction, but no less oblivious of it. However, the husbands are now shown, as the text requires, behind a half-open door, able to witness the scene but unable to intervene. The major difference between the two engravings, however, is that whereas Alix was previously shown resisting the painter's advances, she is now more complicit in her seduction. It is true that she holds up a warning finger, but her body now leans towards him, rather than away from him, and he is shown kissing her, again as the text indicates. Here too, the differences between the two engravings bear out the Fermiers' contention that women are willing partners in sexual activity, as La Fontaine himself would so often have us believe. In addition, of course, the changes which Eisen introduces bring the illustration into closer alignment with the text, and this is no doubt one of the major reasons why some of the engravings were altered.

De Hooghe's interpretation of the *conte* is quite distinct from that of his successors (De Hooghe 40). He shows us only a man attempting to seduce a woman (who backs away from his embrace) inside a closed room: an easel in the background shows that the setting is a studio. No other figures are there to observe the scene, apart from a dog lying on the floor as a discreet (and erotically symbolic) witness to the proceedings. De Hooghe therefore depicts, with his customary propriety, one of the painter's many incidental amorous encounters (vol.2, p.89), rather than the episode which is central to the *conte*.

Eisen's illustrations can be validly compared only with the interpretations of the *conte* to be found in the editions of 1745 and 1755, from which a number of similarities and differences emerge. All four scenes contain reminders that this is an artist's house, with easel, frames and palette clearly shown, and in three instances a prominently placed (phallic) candle hints at what is afoot (De Hooghe makes no such allusion). All three versions show the couple being observed by the men outside the window, although their intimacy has not progressed as far as it does in the later 1762 engraving, and in the two previous versions the woman is

Eisen 50b. 'Les Rémois', second version, between p.88-89

De Hooghe 40. 'Les Rémois', vol.2, p.83

further from the artist as he tries to embrace her. However, though a knife is shown on the table in both of Eisen's versions, a wine bottle visible in the two earlier editions is not present in either of the 1762 illustrations.

This apparently small alteration shifts significantly the basis of the episode, since it suggests that what occurs is due to sexual desire alone, and that drink is not an important factor in accounting for the conduct of the pair. Indeed, in both 1762 versions, Alix's 'colerette' is lying on the floor, as an indication of abandonment, and in the second at least she makes little effort to repel the painter's advances. The effect of the extra intimacy of this engraving, showing the couple closer together, is to mock the husband even more than in the earlier versions; he has to witness his wife's obvious willingness to cuckold him, and he can do nothing to prevent her. By telescoping the action, so that it occurs when the two women are scarcely out of the room, Eisen also shows a disregard for convention, though the husband witnessing the scene can hardly command sympathy since he himself had intended to cuckold the painter.

As so often in his illustrations for the *Contes*, Eisen places more emphasis than his predecessors on the sexual willingness of women, and on their tendency to deceive their husbands with little thought for the consequences. The tailpiece by Choffard (vol.2, p.97), which shows an artist's palette pierced by several brushes, is too obvious in its implications to need comment. It also shows a fisherman's cage in which are trapped two fish and two eels, as if to suggest that men and women alike are prey to their sexual appetites, from which there is no escape.

## xi. 'La courtisane amoureuse'

*Caption: 'Constance va se placer en travers au pied du lit de Camille.'*

This description strikes one as somewhat odd. It is true that Constance (whose name would be ironic for a prostitute, if she did not display precisely that quality here) is reduced to such despair by Camille's feigned indifference that (vol.2, p.108)

> Elle va donc en travers se placer
> Aux pieds du Sire, et d'abord les lui baise.

Holloway reads the engraving (Eisen 51) in precisely this sense, seeing in it the depiction of 'the last straw of her humiliation' (*French rococo book illustration*, p.34). But the position in which Constance is shown suggests that she aspires to be Camille's equal, and is about to share his bed on that basis. What strengthens this impression is that next to the bed Eisen places a three-branch candelabrum which alludes to the erotic implications of the encounter. A discarded carnival mask lies beside the candelabrum, suggesting that pretence has been put away, and that the truth is revealed

Eisen 51. 'La courtisane amoureuse', vol.2, p.99

here. The candles of course throw (literal as well as metaphorical) light on the scene, as do the open curtains of the bed. The uncovering of the truth is suggested also by the fact that Constance, for once, will not be pretending to feel passion for a man, having abandoned her previous 'public' persona. Their relationship can proceed successfully only if she continues to forsake not only her former way of life, but also her former attitude towards men. She will then cease to play the role which her calling required her to adopt in order to deceive them. Even so, these are not simply signs that she has forsaken her former behaviour; she has forsaken her haughtiness too. La Fontaine, who remarks on her 'orgueil' and calls her 'fière' (vol.2, p.100), also observes that her way of dressing reflects her demeanour:

> De son orgueil ses habits se sentoient,
> Force brillans sur sa robe éclatoient,
> La chamarure avec la broderie.

Now, Eisen shows her without her jewels, which La Fontaine calls 'Ce que le sexe aime plus que sa vie' (vol.2, p.107). Although we cannot see them, she has discarded them along with the expensive dress which lies on the floor, enfolding the dagger with which she has undone its fastenings, and with which she had contemplated suicide in response to Camille's apparent coldness (vol.2, p.107).

If Constance's mask has been removed, another has, so to speak, taken its place. To test her fidelity, and even to humble her, Camille, whom La Fontaine describes as 'd'humeur douce, traitable, à se prendre facile' (vol.2, p.101), feigns indifference, and subsequently feigns sleep as well (vol.2, p.108). His apparently unfeeling treatment of her is further underlined in the plate by his imperious gesture commanding her to take her place at the foot of the bed (compare vol.2, p.108: 'Quelle victoire! Avoir mis à ce point / Une beauté si superbe et si fière!'). Having thrown her dress to the floor, and wearing only a simple shift as she obeys Camille's orders, she is intended to evoke the reader's sympathy, whereas Camille himself is made to look domineering and unfeeling towards her. While the eroticism of the scene is evident even if we do not relate it to the text of the *conte*, the artificiality of Camille's behaviour is apparent only when we compare the illustration to the text.

In De Hooghe's interpretation, Camille's bed is visible only in the background (De Hooghe 41). Constance kneels at his feet to remove one of his stockings as he gazes at the candle which burns brightly to his left on a stand, and is placed parallel to the quill emerging from the inkholder on his desk. If there are sexual suggestions here, they are, as with Eisen, of an appropriately repressed kind, lying under the surface of the outwardly calm encounter between Camille and Constance. In contrast, De Hooghe shows the couple looking away from each other, so that they seem distracted and uninvolved in what is happening, and there is little of

De Hooghe 41. 'La courtisane amoureuse', vol.2, p.91

the anticipated intimacy of Eisen's version. Cochin adopts this interpretation in its essentials, including two candles illuminating the scene on the right of the engraving, though he shows Camille only half turned towards Constance, so that again their eyes do not meet. In the 1755 edition, the same scene is shown in reverse.

In all these cases, the obedience of Constance to Camille is clearly in evidence. Like La Fontaine himself, the illustrators do not condemn Constance's character or behaviour, but concentrate on her beauty and her submissiveness. Yet there are distinctly erotic overtones in Eisen which are less apparent in his predecessors.[20] Again, perhaps the most significant aspect of the 1762 illustration is that, in setting out quite explicitly to win our sympathy for a woman who might not be thought to deserve it, Eisen's illustration is again subtly subversive of received social values.[21]

## xii. 'Nicaise'

*Caption: 'La jeune épousée sort du jardin; Nicaise revient
avec son tapis; mais le moment est passé.'*

In accordance with La Fontaine's statement that 'L'aurore était prochaine' (vol.2, p.118), the sky shown in Eisen's illustration (Eisen 52) is appropriately dark and, again following the text, the garden is situated near a wood (vol.2, p.118). Nicaise carries a substantial carpet, a detail which shows both his concern for the (unnamed) lady's welfare and his expertise in judging the quality of material, a point on which she compliments him ironically (vol.2, p.123). Her dress, for which he shows such unwonted (and unwanted) concern, is rich and elegant, thus accounting more convincingly for his conduct (vol.2, p.123):

> On eût dit une reine,
>  Rien ne manquoit aux vêtemens,
> Perles, joyaux et diamans.

All Eisen's predecessors adopt the same basic approach, showing the encounter between Nicaise and the lady as he returns with his carpet. But there are important differences. Most obviously De Hooghe, with no warrant from the text, adds a group in the distant background frolicking around a naked man (or statue), perhaps as a reminder of the lady's recent nuptials, and thus, ironically, of the ease with which she prepares to commit adultery (De Hooghe 42). His version shows the couple at the point where Nicaise 'joyeux de telle prouesse' (vol.2, p. 121)

---

20. For another sympathetic depiction of a 'fallen' woman, see also Gravelot's illustrations to the 1753 'Amsterdam' (i.e. Paris) edition of Prévost's *Histoire du chevalier Des Grieux et de Manon Lescaut*.

21. Cohen (*Guide de l'amateur de livres*, col.566) mentions an unfinished proof for an illustration to this *conte* found in the Béhague copy, but gives no further details.

Eisen 52. 'Nicaise', vol.2, p.113

De Hooghe 42. 'Nicaise', vol.2, p.103

returns with his carpet, to face the 'dépit' of his now-disillusioned companion; this is a less dramatic moment than that illustrated by Cochin and Eisen, which concentrates on the collapse of the relationship, rather than on the process leading to that point.

As is often the case, Eisen shows greater respect for the precise details of the text than De Hooghe, Cochin, or the unnamed artist who worked on the 1755 edition. Hence, neither the carpet carried by Nicaise nor the dress worn by the lady is rendered with as much detail as in the 1762 engraving. Again, in no previous illustration is the sky as dark, and there is little sign of a wood, so that the external correlates of emotion are missing.

The rolled-up fan which the lady points in Nicaise's direction is not mentioned in the text, and is not shown in the illustrations to the three earlier editions, despite its obvious phallic (and hence, in this instance, ironic) connotations. Although she is accompanied in all the earlier illustrations, no 'compagne' keeps watch for her mistress in the Eisen version. Nor is this necessarily a derogation from the text, which does not make it unambiguously clear that the appointed 'compagne' ever arrives on the scene, even though she is 'instruite du mystère' (vol.2, p.118).

By excising any reference to a witness, Eisen makes us the privileged spectators of an encounter which is both bizarre and comic. It takes place, after all, at dawn in an otherwise deserted park, where a newly married but potentially unfaithful wife, dressed in her best clothes and jewels, is engaged in an altercation with a young man carrying a large carpet. It is unlikely that, in such circumstances, they would wish to be observed. As interpreted by Eisen, then, this is a 'private public moment' in which characters would not behave as they do if their somewhat louche conduct were to be witnessed by others. Here, as so often in the designs which he conceived for the *Contes*, Eisen finds ways to indicate that he is revealing what might otherwise not be known, telling the truth about human behaviour with more emphasis than other artists interpreting the same material.[22]

## xiii. 'Comment l'esprit vient aux filles'

*Caption: 'Pere Bonaventure jette Lise sur le lit de sa cellule.'*

Eisen made at least two attempts to render this *conte* in visual terms. The Grenville and Pixérécourt copies contain an etching not apparently found elsewhere. It shows a bearded priest standing over the girl, and about to push her on to the bed. While there is textual authority for such a scene (vol.2, p.127), the wording of the *conte* is at odds with other aspects of this interpretation; for example, the depiction of Lise as lost in

22. In Gravelot's illustrations for Boccaccio's *Il Decamerone* (1757-1761), for example, characters emerge from behind curtains more often than they are revealed by curtains drawn back for the viewer.

contemplation, with a halo of light around her, is difficult to reconcile with La Fontaine's assertion that (vol.2, p.126-27)

> Il n'étoit nuls emplois
> Où Lise pût avoir l'âme occupée:
> Lison songeoit autant que sa poupée.

What is more, such a harsh picture of the encounter, with its emphasis on the innocence and even the holiness of the girl, contrasting with the violence of the monk, would have evoked the idea of rape, in the same way as the rejected engraving for 'La clochette'. Associations of this kind would have been inimical to the lightness of spirit with which the Fermiers wished to infuse the edition.[23]

To take the illustration usually found in copies of the work: Eisen's interpretation (Eisen 53) relies, as so often, on the idea of opening the scene to the spectator. The monk's room (it is hardly the cell mentioned in the text at vol.2, p.127) is brightly lit; a bed is shown with its curtains drawn back to offer a clear view of the proceedings. The text states that Lise was thrown on to the bed (vol.2, p.127), yet Eisen shows her seated on it, with no indication, in this instance, of violence or sudden movement. Lise is naive to a degree, at only fourteen or fifteen (vol.2, p.126), yet her face registers no alarm at her treatment; her head is tilted slightly back, as the text states, and there is no resistance on her part. There is every indication that she is willing to be seduced, and it is noticeable that the position of her left hand draws attention to her sex. As La Fontaine says 'La belle prend le tout en patience' (vol.2, p.126), and in due course 'Lise rioit du succès de la chose' (vol.2, p.128), a detail which no doubt accounts for the proleptic smile on her face.

De Hooghe shows the monk and the girl standing outside the door of a monastery, observed only by a carved angel and other sculpted figures (De Hooghe 43). While the smiles on the faces of Lise and the monk suggest clearly enough what is to happen, no impropriety is shown, and it is not clear that she is as young as the text states, or as naive. In the Cochin version of 1745, the monk is seen standing in the open air outside his room, talking to a female whose age is not clear (Cochin 9). Both De Hooghe and Cochin thus depict an earlier stage in the story, from which any overt sexual content is absent. Eisen, in contrast, shows us the reality of a seduction in which both parties are complicit, and which, so to speak, takes us behind the scenes to reveal what would normally be hidden from view. One might almost speak of a progression in seduction, moving from De Hooghe's apparently innocent meeting, through Cochin's depiction of a closer relationship, to Eisen's image of the seduction itself. Such a trajectory might be regarded as summing up the essential differences in the approach which the three artists adopt.

23. See also Lapp, *The Esthetics of negligence*, p.145.

Eisen 53. 'Comment l'esprit vient aux filles', vol.2, p.125

De Hooghe 43. 'Comment l'esprit vient aux filles', vol.2, p.113

Cochin 9. 'Comment l'esprit vient aux filles', vol.2, p.110

## xiv. 'L'abbesse malade'

*Caption: 'L'abbesse entourrée de ses religieuses & de deux médecins, raisonne avec sœur Agnès sur le remède proposé.'*

As Martha M. Houle has shown, this *conte* embodies the typical moral dilemmas which inspired the *cas de conscience* so often debated in La Fontaine's time in salons as well as in ecclesiastical circles.[24] The comparison is particularly appropriate to an understanding of the engraving (Eisen 54), in which the nuns and doctors are arranged around the abbess as they debate whether she should accept the advice to take a lover, or remain true to her vows of chastity. Now, La Fontaine does not state that any nuns, other than Sœur Agnès, are present when the abbess is seen by the 'Faculté' (vol.2, p.132), so that there is no textual basis for Eisen showing her surrounded by members of the convent. It is Sœur Agnès who is responsible for informing the other nuns of the abbess's plight (vol.2, p.133), a procedure which would scarcely be necessary had they been present at the consultation.

The Eisen version depicts no fewer than six nuns and two doctors. In the Cochin illustration, three nuns and two doctors are in attendance. Whereas in Cochin's vignette they are shown keeping a respectful distance from her, Eisen shows them crowding round her, so that her supposed status as a figure of authority becomes diminished in the midst of the crowd, and it is consequently the debate which matters most. Cochin places the doctors and the abbess in stark, brightly lit relief, and opposite them shows two nuns dressed in black. While the contrast between the two groups is strong, it is not obvious that this difference in shading has any symbolic significance, despite the description of the abbess as having 'Pâles couleurs' (vol.2, p.131). Eisen, however, shows the abbess and Agnès dressed in white, as if to emphasise their solidarity, rather than the abbess's pallor, and the doctor is dressed in black to provide a purely visual contrast in an engraving which would otherwise be (literally) monotonous.

The Cochin engraving is set entirely within a closed room, with no obvious source of light, while in the Fermiers généraux engraving a large window on the right illuminates the scene, and the abbess is lit from another unseen source. In 1745 the nuns are not obviously young, whereas, in the 1762 edition, neither they nor the abbess seem very old. Another contrast between the two engravings can be seen in the faces of the two doctors. In 1745 the abbess spreads her hands in a gesture of

24. Martha M. Houle, 'The play of *bienséances* in La Fontaine's *L'Abbesse*', *Papers in French seventeenth-century literature* 18:34 (1991), p.109-21 (p.115-21). Further consideration of manuals of *cas de conscience* can be found in Jacques Lebrun, *La Jouissance et le trouble: recherches sur la littérature chrétienne à l'âge classique* (Geneva, 2004), p.66-89.

Eisen 54. 'L'abbesse malade', vol.2, p.131

weariness; Agnès and one doctor convey their involvement in debate by their gestures, while on the left a nun raises a hand in surprise or shock. In the Eisen version, Agnès, the abbess and one of the doctors all point towards the left (perhaps towards a door leading to the outside world?). One nun at the back has her hand raised, but the gesture and her appearance do not suggest shock or surprise. In this respect, Eisen foregrounds and, in diegetic terms, anticipates the consequences of the consultation reported by La Fontaine. To spare the abbess any embarrassment, all the nuns agree to undergo the same 'cure', a decision which La Fontaine describes by alluding to Rabelais's story of the sheep which follow one another instinctively (vol.2, p.134):[25]

> De ses brebis à peine la première
> A fait le saut, qu'il suit une autre sœur;
> Une troisième entre dans la carrière:
> Nulle ne veut demeurer en arrière.

In view of their general willingness to undergo the same experience as the abbess, it is appropriate that a group of nuns should participate in the discussion, even if to show them attending the consultation does involve a departure from the text. The same process of diegetic condensation dissolves the abbess's objections to what the doctors propose. Although her reservations are expressed publicly, any scruples she may have are overcome by a general predisposition to follow their advice. On this reading, it becomes clear why the Fermiers généraux engraving is more public, and shows a larger number of people around the abbess. Typically for the *Contes*, it makes more subtle use of light and shade, and there is a notable absence of any reaction of surprise or shock on the part of the nuns at what is proposed.[26]

Unlike Eisen and Cochin, De Hooghe shows only the abbess and a doctor in conversation in an otherwise deserted corridor or cloister (De Hooghe 44). All three artists are notably restrained in illustrating this *conte*. Both Eisen and Cochin provide illustrations which could almost be based on a contemporary painting with the theme of religious devotion, so removed are they from any suggestion of sexual impropriety. Only the absence of any shock or dismay on the part of the nuns or of the doctors gives the clue to the thoughts behind the incident, a point which is apparent only if one reads the text. In that sense, both the Cochin and the Eisen engravings may serve indirectly as *exempla* of the view that nuns have sexual needs which must be satisfied like those of other women if they are to remain healthy. Certainly, there is nothing in either engraving to underpin Birberick's contention that 'La Fontaine [...] reveals the

25. Compare *OCLF*, p.1456, and Lapp, *The Esthetics of negligence*, p.124-26.
26. The *conte* is analysed by Lapp (*The Esthetics of negligence*, p.124-26), and by Birberick ('From world to text', p.186-90), who both draw attention to its mixture of eroticism and sympathy for the sexual longings of the nuns.

De Hooghe 44. 'L'abbesse malade', vol.2, p.118

irony inherent in the nuns' transgression, since as an act of cuckoldry, it is perpetrated against the one who would lead them away from temptation: their spiritual husband, Christ.'[27]

## xv. 'Les troqueurs'

*Caption: 'Sieur Oudinet à table, sous la feuillée d'un cabaret, avec les deux villageois & leurs femmes, dresse le contrat du troc.'*

Eisen emphasises the rustic aspects of the scene (Eisen 55): behind the group can be seen a rather rickety fence, with some pieces of wood stacked behind it. Both married couples are visibly intoxicated, and the pair seated on the right of the notary Oudinet are particularly the worse for drink. In contrast, Oudinet himself is sober, and better dressed than the remainder of the company. The inn sign, with its new moon, is doubtless intended to reflect the mutability of human wishes (as La Fontaine observes: 'Dieu nous créa changeans', vol.2, p.135). Whatever the moon's traditional association with the chastity of the goddess Diana, it clearly does not evoke that association here: suspended on a pole which supports a garland of flowers, the sign constitutes, rather, an obvious sexual symbol, the sense of which is apparent from the text (vol.2, p.136-37):

> Notre pasteur a bien changé de Cure:
> La femme est-elle un cas si différent?
> [...] Femmes aussi trompent assez souvent.[28]

These points serve to differentiate Eisen's interpretation in significant ways from those of De Hooghe and Cochin. De Hooghe has one couple departing somewhat drunkenly, watched by the notary and by the other (no less intoxicated) pair (De Hooghe 45). An ass grazing nearby reminds us both of the stupidity and the obstinacy of those who think to improve their lot by changing partners in this way.[29] No other symbols are apparent, and De Hooghe, as is his custom, omits any overt reference to the sexual connotations of the story.[30]

In Cochin's version, one inebriated man and two women are standing, while the other man remains seated at the table opposite Oudinet (Cochin 10). The drunken man has his arm around one of the women, who looks in triumph at her visibly downcast rival. Like De Hooghe, Cochin also

27. Birberick, 'From world to text', p.188.

28. See also Grisé, 'La casuistique dans les *Contes*', p.414.

29. Compare Lapp, *The Esthetics of negligence*, p.140-42, who comments particularly on the comparison between women and beasts on which La Fontaine lays so much emphasis, but which finds no place in Eisen's illustration.

30. Nicolich observes that, in comparison with Eisen, De Hooghe 'appears more "proper" where sexuality is concerned' ('Seventeenth and eighteenth-century illustrations for La Fontaine's *Contes et nouvelles en vers*', p.269).

Eisen 55. 'Les troqueurs', vol.2, p.135

De Hooghe 45. 'Les troqueurs', vol.2, p.123

Cochin 10. 'Les troqueurs', vol.2, p.119

includes an ass, just visible on the left in his headpiece. His interpretation of the episode depends partly on the role of drink and partly on the sexual rivalry between the two women, rather than on male sensuality. Eisen, in contrast, gives equal prominence to all four participants, and the sexual symbolism suggests that all of them are equally motivated by this consideration. His view here and elsewhere is that men and women are in some respects alike, and equally changeable in their sexual impulse: in this instance, drink merely brings out this side of their nature. This scene has none of the idealised, pastoral elements which Gravelot brought to the illustrations for Rousseau's *La Nouvelle Héloïse* (1761), and which differ so markedly from the brutal realities of rural life as depicted here.

## xvi. 'Le cas de conscience'

Caption: '*Anne derrière des saules, promène son regard sur un jeune garçon nud.*'

This is one of the most frequently reproduced examples of an engraving for the *Contes* which exists in two states, one (Eisen 56a) 'découvert' and the other (Eisen 56b) 'couvert'.[31] They are very similar, and are distinguished chiefly by the addition of some foliage to hide the sex of Guillot, whom Anne observes as he is bathing. Only her head and shoulders are visible through a gap between two pollard-willow trees; she is able to see Guillot's body, though only at an angle, so that the engraving, following the text, avoids any direct sexual confrontation between them. Whereas the sky is dark in the 'découvert' version, in the 'couvert' state it is lightened. It is tempting to believe that such a change reflects the idea that the 'découvert' engraving uses less light, in order to preserve the modesty of the two protagonists. However, a study of various copies of the edition shows that the lighter tones of the 'couvert' state are evenly distributed, and are therefore likely to be the result of wear and tear on the surface of the copperplate, or of differences in the inking between one pressing and another, rather than of any deliberate alteration.

De Hooghe likewise shows a somewhat sombre sky (De Hooghe 46), though (unusually for him) a rather phallic branch at the centre of the headpiece relieves the gloom, and replaces, so to speak, the original which Guillot's right hand conceals. It is also lightened, in his headpiece, by the obvious enjoyment which Anne, placed in the foreground, derives from spying on Guillot. Although Cochin's sky is certainly light, his Guillot looks somewhat aged as he sits to perform his ablutions. Anne thus has less reason to base her curiosity on his physical beauty, especially as he

---

31. The technical difficulty of removing a significant element from the engraving without damaging it or leaving any traces makes it more likely that the 'découvert' version came first. See Stewart, *Engraven desire*, p.316.

Eisen 56a. 'Le cas de conscience', first version, between p.142-43

Eisen 56b. 'Le cas de conscience', second version, between p.142-43

De Hooghe 46. 'Le cas de conscience', vol.2, p.130

has little in common with the man whom La Fontaine describes as (vol.2, p.145)

> au corps jeune et frais,
> Blanc, poli, bien formé, de taille haute et droite.

Again, Cochin's pollard-willows are strangely shrivelled, affording little cover for Anne as she gazes at Guillot. Her physical posture as shown in his vignette is distinctly precarious, and could not be long sustained. With so little cover from the trees, she would scarcely have time to observe the naked man at her leisure (vol.2, p.145) without being noticed or losing her balance. To that extent also, Cochin's interpretation of the scene is at variance with the text (vol.2, p.144):

> Anne ne craignoit rien, des saules la couvroient,
> Comme eût fait une jalousie.

He presumably departs from La Fontaine's indications in order to give us a better view of the scene. But this is not the only change which he introduces: the drama in Cochin's interpretation derives, in part at least, from our uncertainty whether Anne can sustain her awkward pose as she looks at the rather aged Guillot. The dénouement of the event may therefore be farcical. In both De Hooghe and Eisen, in contrast, the source of the drama lies solely in the possibility that this young, god-like figure may notice her spying on him, with unpredictable consequences. Both artists exploit the possibilities of the scene to the full, since Guillot has only to move slightly to notice that he is under observation. Their depiction of the encounter is also more overtly sexual than Cochin's, in that we are able to see expressed on Anne's face the 'désir' (vol.2, p.145) which makes her 'toute honteuse' (vol.2, p.146).

Guillot is presented in the 1762 edition as almost a marble statue, with the light falling on his perfect white torso, partly clothed in a long and typically antique sheet. Eisen is alone is placing him in the foreground of the illustration, so that we, as viewers, are able to see clearly for ourselves the almost classical beauty to which Anne responds. It could be argued, too, that there is something almost feminised in the way in which he presents Guillot, with his downcast eyes, as if to suggest that Anne's naiveté leads her to see only the idealised male, and not the somewhat effeminate reality. Indeed, La Fontaine does hint that Anne perceives Guillot in this idealised (and to that extent, unreal) way, as though he were an artist's model to be copied (vol.2, p.145):

> force gens assis comme notre bergere,
> Font un crayon conforme à cet original.
> Au fond de sa mémoire Anne en sçut fort bien faire
> Un qui ne ressembloit pas mal.

The fact that all three illustrators choose this episode tends to divert attention from the remainder of the *conte*, which develops the comparison between Anne's frustrated contemplation of Guillot and her response to her *curé* when the pike which he has asked her to cook as a penance for her 'sin' does not materialise. Her retort to him: 'Autant vaut l'avoir vu que de l'avoir mangé' (vol.2, p.148) precisely echoes the *curé*'s condemnation of her behaviour towards Guillot. If this line is to take on its full significance, we need to see Anne gazing fixedly at him, since the sense of her response can be appreciated only if we see the longing she herself has experienced in doing so. But even if Anne's interest is clear in both states of the Eisen engraving, the differences between them go further than the foliage added to preserve Guillot's modesty. With the 'découvert' version, we are placed in much the same relationship to him as Anne herself, though we can see him even more clearly; we become viewers (or voyeurs) with her, and our attitude towards her gaze cannot avoid being self-referential. La Fontaine does state that her contemplation of Guillot is both erotic and aesthetic, yet this passage should not be taken as elevating Anne's behaviour to a higher level, as she is ashamed at her own conduct.[32] In the 'couvert' state, she can still see Guillot's nakedness, but we cannot, so that the equivalence of viewpoint created in the 'découvert' state no longer applies. The 'couvert' state of the engraving might then be seen as affording us an aesthetic, rather than an erotic, experience, though it could also be argued that the concealment of Guillot's sex draws attention to it more emphatically than the wholly undraped version. In this instance at least, the state of the engraving has implications for us as active readers of the *conte*, and not merely as passive spectators.[33]

The existence of the engraving in two states also raises the moral question posed indirectly by the *curé*'s reaction to Anne's revelation that she has watched Guillot (vol.2, p.146):

> Etre dans ses regards à tel point sensuelle!
> C'est, dit-il, un très-grand péché.

His words must mean that it is not the fact of contemplating Guillot's nakedness which makes Anne culpable, but the sexual desire which she feels as she does so.[34] Consequently, the innocent gaze is not reprehensible, and we as readers cannot be criticised on moral grounds if we look at Guillot's naked form without desire. Hence, the presence or absence of the foliage is of itself less significant than the spirit in which we consider the scene. This point derives from the anti-casuistic, satirical background to La Fontaine's story, in that the line used by the *curé* and by Anne

32. Lapp (*The Esthetics of negligence*, p.155) considers that Anne triumphs over her shame, but this seems improbable from the text.

33. Many copies of the *Contes* contain the engraving in both states, but each is commonly found on its own.

34. See on this point the article 'Regards' in Jean Pontas's *Dictionnaire des cas de conscience*, 2 vols (Paris, 1715), vol.2, unpaginated.

herself is borrowed from theological debates on whether one can innocently look without lusting.[35] The *conte* makes it clear that Anne does not do so, but necessarily leaves open the viewer's reaction.

When we seek to explain why the 1762 edition is so much more direct in its representation of male (and indeed female) nudity, the answer is partly commercial, given the Fermiers' original intention to market their edition, and partly one of attitude. As we have seen, a recurring feature of the Eisen illustrations is that they open a scene to the viewer's gaze, laying bare what would normally be hidden from public view. Hence, aspects of human behaviour are revealed in a way which is not so much wilfully salacious as deliberately intended to unmask, not so much for pornographic reasons as for reasons of propaganda.

After all, Gravelot's illustrations for Boccaccio's *Il Decamerone* in 1757-1761 and for Voltaire's *La Pucelle* in 1762 (both of which contain similar illustrations of naked figures) were offered to the general public at much the same time as Eisen was preparing the illustrations for the *Contes*. The fact that Gravelot was asked to provide a 'suite libre' of pornographic engravings for the *Decamerone* is itself a clear pointer to the more tolerant, freer taste of the times.[36] The Fermiers did not however seek to cater for such tastes in the *Contes*, where sexuality never becomes overtly prurient, and where liberty never degenerates into licence for its own sake. We should not forget that they took the trouble to have this engraving altered to hide Guillot's naked form, rather than to expose it.

## xvii. 'Le diable de Papefiguière'

*Caption: 'Perrette montre au Diableteau, qui n'avoit rien vu, la balafre qu'elle lui dit avoir reçue de Philipot.'*

La Fontaine depicts the Devil as a harsh, grasping master whose treatment of his tenant farmer Philipot leaves much to be desired. Eisen, however, ignores this aspect of the story, making the Devil a repugnant creature whose ugliness is entirely supernatural, and thus contrasted with the human charms of Perrette. He illustrates (Eisen 57) the section of the *conte* in which Perrette displays her sex to the Devil, claiming that her husband (vol.2, p.156)

> m'a fait
> Cette balafre. A ces mots au folet
> Elle fait voir... Et quoi? Chose terrible.
> Le diable en eut une peur tant horrible,
> Qu'il se signa, pensa presque tomber.

35. See also Grisé, 'La casuistique dans les *Contes*', p.414-15.
36. See Ray, *The Art of the French illustrated book*, p.40 and chapter 4 of this study, below p.374.

Eisen 57. 'Le diable de Papefiguière', vol.2, p.129

The dynamic of this engraving derives not so much from the opposition between good and evil as between beauty and the beast, avoiding indecency through the placing of Perrette in profile.[37] Eisen depicts the Devil in the traditional form of a cloven-footed satyr, with wings and a repellent face made uglier still by the frightened grimace he wears at the sight of Perrette's sex.[38] While the *conte* states that Perrette is 'échevelée' (vol.2, p.155), adding to the impression that she has been assaulted, Eisen shows her as coiffured and self-possessed, displaying no fear or repugnance at the sight of the Devil, and confident of her ability to outwit him.[39] Lapp observes (*Esthetics of negligence*, p.139) that La Fontaine 'obviously satirises the arrogance and self-sufficiency of the Seigneur'. This may well be the case when one looks at the historical significance of the *conte* itself, but the mockery in which Eisen indulges in the illustration is of the Devil as devil, not as cruel *Seigneur*. He thus avoids any temptation for readers to associate this repugnant creature with the conduct of the Fermiers themselves.

Eisen follows De Hooghe and Cochin in mocking the Devil, though his predecessors adopt a very different approach to illustrating the *conte*. De Hooghe shows the ill-tempered meeting between the Devil and the 'vilain' Philipot to whose fields he lays claim, and whose reaction, as he ploughs his fields, is to raise a cattle-whip to threaten the intruder (De Hooghe 47). The Devil's face and head are obliterated by a burst of light[40] (a depiction deriving, no doubt ironically, from his sobriquet 'Lucifer', or 'the bringer of light', a name which La Fontaine mentions, vol.2, p.130); the same method is used to draw attention to his sex.[41] He thus becomes at the same time too repellent to be shown, and an object of derision, since he is outwitted both by Philipot and (later) by Perrette. In drawing attention to the Devil's sex, De Hooghe alludes to an ignorance of sexual matters which Perrette will exploit, and which is central to Eisen's interpretation.

Cochin's vignette for the 1745 edition also takes as its starting-point a much earlier stage in the story, when the Devil, trying to sell his produce at market, is mocked for his ignorance. Whereas De Hooghe emphasises his repellent character by refusing to depict him in his entirety, Cochin domesticates his Devil by limiting his diabolical characteristics, showing

37. A 'couvert' version also exists, in which her dress is longer. See Hédé-Haüy, *Les Illustrations des Contes de La Fontaine*, p.49.

38. As Lapp observes (*The Esthetics of negligence*, p.138), La Fontaine retains little of the religious satire which he found in his model Rabelais, and the Devil's naiveté in this and others matters is purely comic.

39. Lapp (*The Esthetics of negligence*, p.137) underestimates the 'naïve cunning' of the peasantry as displayed in this *conte*.

40. Such defaced images of the Devil were common even in medieval manuscripts. See Bezalel Narkiss, 'On the zoocephalic phenomenon in medieval Ashkenazi manuscripts', in *Norms and variations in art: essays in honour of Moshe Barasch* (Jerusalem, 1983), p.49-62.

41. The theological ironies created by the Christian tradition of describing Lucifer as 'prince des ténèbres' are elided in eighteenth-century theology. The *Dictionnaire de Trévoux* (1762) merely states 'Lucifer, dans le Christianisme, est un nom qu'on donne au Prince des Ténèbres, au chef des Démons.'

De Hooghe 47. 'Le diable de Papefiguière', vol.2, p.136

him as a man with claws on his hands and feet, and small horns on his head, so that he becomes only very slightly devilish.

Eisen's move away from the approach taken by earlier illustrators reflects not only a change in contemporary taste, but also a significantly different attitude towards the *Contes* themselves. His illustrations do not exemplify the alleged lack of taste to which so many commentators had drawn attention since the first publication of the *Contes*, but are a celebration of the human, and a rejection of the supernatural with its restrictive theological associations and its tacit deference to the authority and power of the Church. These elements are clearly apparent in the way in which both De Hooghe and Cochin depict the Devil in this *conte*. With the Fermiers généraux and Eisen, however, the mockery of the supernatural is only one aspect of a much broader sceptical attitude towards received values and institutions. And, as is so often the case, Eisen and the Fermiers affirm their independence of the illustrative tradition of the *Contes* in order to offer an interpretation which centres not on the theological but on the erotic and on variations of the male-female relationship.

## xviii. 'Féronde, ou le purgatoire'

*Caption: 'Féronde dans le caveau, est corrigé de sa mécréance,
à coups de verge.'*

Like 'Le diable de Papefiguière', 'Féronde' has as its protagonist someone whose cruel character and occupation (as a 'Receveur' or estate-manager) might invite unfavourable comparisons with the Fermiers themselves.[42] Whether for this reason or on aesthetic grounds, Eisen's illustration (Eisen 58) and the accompanying description give no indication that Féronde is in any sense comparable to members of the Compagnie. He is punished for his 'mécréance' (that is for his suspicious and jealous attitude towards his wife, who is indeed unfaithful), though the punishment might be thought excessive in a situation in which both parties are at fault. Féronde is depicted in the engraving as suffering the punishment ('huit ou dix coups de forte discipline') meted out by the supposed 'anges consolateurs' (vol.2, p.162). As La Fontaine puts it (vol.2, p.162):

> l'ange étoit un drole,
> Un frere Jean, novice de léans:
> Ses Compagnons jouoient chacun un role
> Pareil au sien, dessous un feint habit.

The interpretation which Eisen places on the text can be linked in several respects to his other illustrations for the *Contes*. La Fontaine does not state that the monks who administer Féronde's beating are dressed in white

42. Durand (*Les Fermiers généraux*, p.272-78) shows that for several generations, Fermiers were often the sons of 'receveurs'.

Eisen 58. 'Féronde, ou le purgatoire', vol.2, p.157

robes, though this point might be inferred from their being members of the same order as the 'abbé blanc' who has arranged his punishment. Even so, the reason for giving them so great a degree of prominence is that, along with the coffin on the floor and the austere surroundings, their ghostly appearance makes it easier to convince Féronde that he is in Purgatory (vol.2, p.162). Again, his nakedness is not stated in the text, and the 'caveau' is unusually well lit for a place which ought to be rather dark. By giving strong emphasis to whiteness and light (and indeed to Féronde's nakedness), Eisen is able to reveal what would otherwise be hidden, a feature typical of his approach to illustrating the *Contes*. At the same time, these features comment ironically on the deception and hypocrisy practised by these supposedly holy figures. By extension, the same charge can be levelled against the abbé whose trickery La Fontaine compares to that used by followers of 'le faux Mahom' such as the Old Man of the Mountains (vol.2, p.158).[43]

By showing Féronde attempting to flee from the two men administering the beating (who are in any case impostors), Eisen suggests that he has at least a chance to escape excessive punishment. Certainly, there is little here to indicate unequivocally that a cruel official is being treated with undue harshness, and if there is no attempt to evoke sympathy for Féronde, neither is there any for his assailants.

Eisen's interpretation can readily be compared with the illustrations which De Hooghe and Cochin provided for previous editions, since all three deal with the beating which he receives. However, there are notable differences in the way in which they treat the episode. De Hooghe sets the scene in a bare room with no obvious ecclesiastical features (De Hooghe 48). Féronde, in his coffin, is surrounded by 'anges' dressed in a variety of animal masks, cowls and horns, giving them the appearance of semi-human creatures of the sort familiar from the work of Hieronymus Bosch and his followers in earlier centuries.[44] De Hooghe's interpretation is therefore not overtly satirical or anticlerical, unlike Eisen's and verges on the occult, especially as there are no specifically contemporary references.

In Cochin's vignette, Féronde, seated and half-naked, is beaten by two figures in white robes, while two others look on. As in the Eisen version, the coffin is on the floor near him. The scene is lit, though less brightly than in the Fermiers généraux engraving, and Féronde is surrounded by figures who resemble ghosts rather than human beings. Perhaps most significant is the fact that, in depicting the suffering Féronde propped helplessly against a wall as he is beaten, Cochin makes him more an object of pity than the recipient of just retribution. While Eisen does not go so far, he typically avoids the depiction of physical excess or unpleasantness

43. Lapp (*The Esthetics of negligence*, p.56-57) regards the text as showing 'the idleness, gluttony and lechery' of the clergy.

44. See especially *The Garden of earthly delights* (Madrid, Prado Museum), which was painted about 1500.

284

De Hooghe 48. 'Féronde, ou le purgatoire', vol.2, p.144

in the illustrations of the *Contes* in a way which distinguishes the 1762 edition from its immediate predecessors.

## xix. 'Le psautier'

*Caption: 'En plein chapitre, Isabeau avertit l'Abbesse que son psautier est un haut-de-chausse.'*

This engraving (Eisen 59) has at least two features typical of Eisen's illustrations for the *Contes*. For once, both are borrowed from De Hooghe, and neither is to be found in Cochin. First, the canopy under which the abbess sits is not mentioned in the text, but it resembles many of the ornate furnishings to be found in other engravings in the 1762 edition. Second, Eisen reveals to our gaze a scene which would normally be private. The matter under debate is, after all, the allegation that Sœur Isabeau has entertained a *curé* in her room (vol.2, p.169). Not only is the 'chapitre' a process internal to the convent (the word is used here in the sense of a reproof given in the presence of all the members of the community);[45] in addition, the windows of the room where it is held have been covered to keep the proceedings from prying eyes.

These general features of the Eisen illustrations are especially appropriate in this instance. The posture and gestures of Sœur Isabeau show that she is intent on pointing out to the abbess the fact that she has a pair of men's breeches on her head, thereby challenging her absolute authority and making her a figure of ridicule. The truth of the abbess's conduct is thus made public within the convent, where her position matters, despite the precautions taken to keep the proceedings secret from the outside world. Cowering before the revelations made by Isabeau, the abbess's tacitly recognises her guilt; the trappings of her superior office are consequently of no avail in protecting her against the exposure of her conduct. In this instance, then, the techniques of the illustrator and the themes of the *conte* are in harmony to an unusual degree.

Despite their similarities of setting, De Hooghe and Eisen differ on significant points. De Hooghe's abbess, seated in conclave (De Hooghe 49), is not shown in the undignified accoutrements depicted by Eisen, nor is she obviously abashed at the public rebuke administered by Sœur Isabeau, to whom she makes a gesture of reproach. Hence, the crucial element of mockery is absent from the De Hooghe version, and though he has assembled a larger number of nuns to witness the proceedings, the relationship between accuser and accused is considerably different from that depicted by Eisen.

---

45. 'Réprimande publique dans une maison religieuse' (*Dictionnaire de Trévoux*, 1762).

Eisen 59. 'Le psautier', vol.2, p.167

De Hooghe 49. 'Le psautier', vol.2, p.152

In Cochin's interpretation for the 1745 edition, the room is not blacked out, and the abbess is shown, as in De Hooghe's version, arguing with Isabeau (who is clad distinctively in black) in the presence of a group of nuns, so that again there is no sign of contrition. However, by showing the abbess with the 'haut-de-chausse' on her head, Cochin offers a spectacle of pointless defiance, somewhere between the De Hooghe and the Eisen interpretations of the text.

It is of course significant, but not by this time remarkable, that Eisen should seize the opportunity to mock the institutions and hierarchies of religion in a way wholly in keeping with the attitudes expressed by La Fontaine, but greatly at variance with the practice of his predecessors. His abbess is depicted as both contrite and foolish, a combination of characteristics not to be found in De Hooghe or in Cochin.

Yet if Eisen can add visual elements which are not mentioned in the text, there is a play on words which, owing to the differences between the two media, cannot be achieved by any engraver. According to Anne L. Birberick,[46] 'psautier' was a libertine term for the male or female sex-organ, so that the ecclesiastical and vulgar uses of the word were united in the *conte* in a way which Eisen does not seek to reproduce. Ambiguity is now largely eschewed in favour of literalness.

## xx. 'Le roi Candaule et le maître en droit'

*Caption: 'La femme du roi Candaule au bain.'*

The rather unexpected canopy above the queen's head (Eisen 60) is a reminder of the 'revelatory' nature of many of Eisen's illustrations, and brings immediately to mind his design for 'Le psautier'. As so often, its presence is more decorative than symbolic, since it is scarcely large enough to conceal the queen from prying eyes. In any case, as king Candaule points her out to Gygès, it is difficult to suppose that she could remain unaware of their presence, though the text suggests that she does (vol.2, p.174-75). But the absence of any reaction on her part *in the illustration* can be read as an indication that she may be unconcerned at being observed, and not necessarily that she is unaware of it. We have noted previous examples of Eisen's technique of presenting figures in improbable proximity to one another.[47] The prominent position of king Candaule and of Gygès is clearly deliberate, rather than a response to the scale or perspective of the engraving. While Eisen's purpose is perhaps to convey the queen's real or feigned absorption in her tasks, the perspective allows us to see the expression on the faces of the two men. This is a proleptic detail, since, as we learn from La Fontaine, when the queen and

46. Birberick, 'From world to text', p.192.
47. See 'La servante justifiée' (p.95) and 'Le villageois qui cherche son veau' (p.228), for example.

Eisen 60. 'Le roi Candaule et le maître en droit', vol.2, p.173

Gygès become lovers, his pleasure consists largely in looking at her beauty, and when he admires her, it is chiefly as a spectator (vol.2, p.177):

> aux yeux de Gygès
> S'étaloient de blancs objets.[48]

The theme of the woman bathing who is apparently unaware of the men watching her had, of course, long been a favourite one with painters, who often used the biblical story of Bathsheba as the basis for their work. Philip Stewart compares the engraving with Rembrandt's painting of the subject, making the point that, in the case of the queen, 'the stark positioning of her leg across the whole front plane is much more arresting' (*Engraven desire*, p.152). It is of course notoriously difficult to trace exact sources in art, especially when a subject is one of the standard motifs of western painting. Although Stewart is surely right to draw attention to this parallel, an equally plausible derivation for the statuesque depiction of the queen can be found in Candaule's offer to allow Gygès to spy on the naked queen (vol.2, p.174):

> Proposez-vous de voir tout ce corps si charmant
> Comme un beau marbre seulement
> Je veux que vous disiez que l'art, que la pensée,
> Que même le souhait ne peut aller plus loin.

Surrounded as she is in her bath by fountains and waterspouts, the figure of the queen is indeed reminiscent of marble statuary, such as that at Versailles depicting 'Le bain de Diane' or representing various French rivers. In those well-known instances, however, the female figures are either partly clothed or else, unlike the queen, do not draw attention to their sex by placing a hand between their thighs. Nonetheless, La Fontaine displays some sympathy for the queen; he undoubtedly has a primarily male audience in mind in this instance, asking his readers to imagine her reactions on learning that she has been spied on (vol.2, p.176):

> Je voudrois pour un moment,
> Lecteur, que tu fusses femme:
> Tu ne sçaurois autrement
> Concevoir jusqu'où la Dame
> Porta son secret dépit.

Yet Eisen's construction of the engraving does not require us to adopt this view of her feelings. His reason for depicting her in this pose is obviously to enhance her sexual appeal to Gygès, and of course, as in 'Le cas de conscience', to make the reader a voyeur as well. In fact, we are in a sense more involved in the proceedings even than the king and Gygès, in that we see the queen directly, whereas, in Stewart's words, 'their angle of vision is [...] less privileged than ours' (*Engraven desire*, p.152). At the same

---

48. Lapp (*The Esthetics of negligence*, p.148) points out that the lovers' relationship is 'visual rather than physical'.

time, her seeming (but improbable) unawareness of the presence of the two men means that the viewer cannot decide whether she is a woman of loose character displaying her charms in order to please, or an illustration of innocent unconcern. In either case, Eisen's approach implicates the spectator; through the choice of subject and the disposition of the figures, he makes us complicit in the spectacle of the queen's nakedness. In this way, he is also questioning our right to make judgements on the behaviour of the characters who look at her in the engraving. We shall return to this point in considering the overall significance of his illustrations for the *Contes* in the final chapter of this study.

De Hooghe takes the same encounter as the subject of his headpiece, and may have served in some respects as Eisen's model (De Hooghe 50). We have the same Junoesque representation of the queen, with similarly elaborate fountains surrounded by draperies. Here, however, the queen turns to face the viewer, while the king and Gygès are distant figures, scarcely visible through a curtained door at the back of the room. Consequently, they do not have the same prominent status as spectators of the naked queen which Eisen gives them. That function now devolves upon an ornamental putto astride a sea-creature at the side of the bathing pool, so that Eisen's parallel with the human is removed, or is at least at one remove, for the putto has a distinctly lifelike quality. Since there are no obviously voyeuristic human spectators here, and only a surrogate statue to contemplate the queen's nakedness, the viewer's relationship to the scene is not quite the same as in the 1762 plate. We are not now made complicit with the king and Gygès; we alone are spectators, and we alone are voyeurs.[49]

This is one of the few instances where Eisen can be seen to have borrowed significantly from De Hooghe, who is typically a model of propriety in his depiction of women. Although the perspective of the two engravings is very different, the same moral questions are raised in both versions of the illustration.

Caption: '*Le maître en droit poussé en chemise dans son école.*'

This plate exemplifies the discrepancy between status and state. The professor is pushed into the room semi-naked in his night-attire (Eisen 61). Two students have their hands raised in surprise; another points in mockery, while others stare. On a panel above the door through which he is being pushed can be seen the inscription 'Ecole de droit', a further

49. As Simon Schama pertinently points out, in many seventeenth-century Dutch paintings based on mythology, 'naked exposure *is* the story. [...] In keeping with the double standard that was expected of both patrons and artists [nude women] even as they were ostensibly being ogled by figures inside the history, were lavishly displayed to the beholder' (*Rembrandt's eyes*, London, 1999, p.393; italics in the original).

De Hooghe 50. 'Le roi Candaule et le maître en droit', vol.2, p.158

Eisen 61. 'Le roi Candaule et le maître en droit', vol.2, p.178

reminder of the gap between his official position and his present undignified situation. An (apparently) classical painting to the left on the wall, and books on the right of the door, are similar reminders both of scholarly order and of his downfall. His hesitant gait, and apparent submission to the old woman, who seems stronger and more robust than he is, further undermines his dignity. An academic gown and hat lie discarded on the floor to the right, to indicate the abandonment of academic propriety by all concerned.

In Cochin's vignette for the edition of 1745, two diplomas or carvings can be seen on the wall of the room as a sign of its academic purpose. However, the old woman shown here is noticeably smaller than the professor, and is able to push him into the room only because she knows better than he does where he is going. The Fermiers généraux version owes something to Cochin's inspiration, but is more censorious in its depiction of his fall from grace, and gives more emphasis to the cruel mockery of the students as he enters the room. At the same time, in placing him directly in front of us, instead of in profile as Cochin does, Eisen asks us to assess the man's conduct for ourselves, as a person with whose behaviour we are confronted. He is a cuckolded husband who wants to prevent his wife from deceiving him further, and to his cuckoldry is added the chagrin of public ridicule. We are asked to judge (rather as though we ourselves were students in the school of life, rather than of law) whether he is to be blamed, scorned or pitied. Like the first engraving for this *conte*, it asks us to judge others, but in the process to judge ourselves. As so often in the Fermiers généraux edition, the viewer is as much the subject (or object) of the artist's concern as the scene which is depicted.

## xxi. 'Le diable en enfer'

*Caption: 'Dans la grotte de son hermitage, frere Rustic éveille Alibec, &*
*lui persuade qu'il faut commencer par emprisonner le Diable.'*

In a rejected illustration for this *conte*, to be found in the Grenville and Pixérécourt copies, the priest (who has a notably disagreeable face) is shown standing over the girl, with his hand poised to open his robe. The elements of the scene are reversed from those shown in the standard engraving for this *conte*, with the priest on the right and the young Alibech on the left. This very rare version[50] was no doubt rejected (like that for 'Comment l'esprit vient aux filles') because of the unprepossessing depiction of the monk, and the sexual crudity of his stance; both of these

50. Cohen (*Guide de l'amateur de livres*, col.566) does not refer to this engraving, so that it is almost certainly not recorded in any other known copies, even those which included many rejected versions of the illustrations.

elements would have been at variance with the way ecclesiastics of all types are usually represented in the edition.

In the version of the illustration included in most copies (Eisen 62), Rustic is rather older than is suggested by La Fontaine, who calls him 'jeune saint très-fervent' (vol.2, p.191). Eisen shows a considerable degree of intimacy between the monk and the girl, and emphasises (or exaggerates) the disparity in their ages by showing him with a bald or tonsured head so that, even as a mature man and a priest, he is prey to irresistible lust. He crouches beside Alibech, addressing her with his left hand raised to emphasise his words, as he delivers his sermon. With her eyes meeting his gaze, she lies unresistingly on his rolled mat, supported by its high headrest. Her dress is in disarray, showing her breasts and her petticoats. Her right hand moves towards him, while his right hand hovers over her stomach. The basis for this more accurate depiction of the story than in the original engraving is the passage in which La Fontaine describes the girl's seduction (vol.2, p.194):

> Moitié forcée et moitié consentante,
> Moitié voulant combattre ce désir,
> Moitié n'osant, moitié peine et plaisir,
> Elle crut faire acte de repentante.[51]

A rolled-up curtain or blanket is supported on a pole above their heads. In the background can be seen a rough ladder. Although it apparently leads nowhere, its top is next to a candle supported in an oil lamp suspended from the ceiling. As so often, the open curtains and the candle are used to tell us that something hidden is being revealed to the spectator. The light falls particularly on Alibech's upper torso and on Rustic's head. Ladders were commonly used in art to recall the ladder in Jacob's dream, by means of which men ascended to heaven (Genesis 28:12-16).[52] Its position next to the light, which illuminates the flesh, is an ironic commentary on the monk's abandonment of his religious vows. On the left, faintly visible, is his bed, at the head of which is a shelf containing some books, none of which are open, further underlining his abandonment of monkish wisdom.

In the Cochin version of 1745, a somewhat fraught-looking Alibech is lying on a rough wooden bed, fully clothed, half-turned towards Rustic as he stands over her with his almost skull-like features, apparently preaching. The setting is a simple, half-lit cell, with his bed on the other side of the room. A folio lies open, supported on a simple box-lectern behind him. There is little here to suggest that Alibech co-operates in her seduction, as Eisen would have it. His Rustic is older and more experienced than the naive (if willing) Alibech, but both, in their different ways, are responsible

51. See also Lapp, *The Esthetics of negligence*, p.71, who calls the mechanism of the *conte* 'the irony of innocence'.
52. See Sarah Carr-Gomm, *Dictionary of symbols in art* (London, 1995), p.121-22.

Eisen 62. 'Le diable en enfer', vol.2, p.189

for what occurs. Eisen fully echoes the views intimated by La Fontaine, that sexual desire will override religious vows, an idea already expressed in, for example, 'Les cordeliers de Catalogne' and 'Comment l'esprit vient aux filles'.

Neither Cochin nor Eisen follows De Hooghe in the way they choose to illustrate this *conte*. The headpiece of the 1685 edition (De Hooghe 51) is reminiscent of a biblical scene, in which a mature-looking Alibech says farewell to a robed and bearded figure leaning on a stick. Like Rustic in the 1762 edition, he bears little relation to the young, lusty hermit described by La Fontaine, though no other comparison between the illustrations for the two editions is possible. De Hooghe's engraving, which may well represent the departure of Alibech after her encounter with Rustic, is an innocent pastoral scene, wholly at variance with the subject of the *conte*. There is a difference here, not merely of subject matter, but of approach to questions of religious satire, on which De Hooghe and Eisen hold radically different views.

## xxii. 'La jument du compère Pierre'

*Caption: 'La scène est dans une étable. Compere Pierre, ses lunettes sur le nez, leve les mains au ciel pour le succes de la métamorphose dont messire Jean s'occupe, & dont Madeleine attend le résultat.'*

By setting the scent in a cowshed (Eisen 63), rather than inside the couple's house, Eisen immediately raises a problem of credibility, since such a setting is an unusual place to find the armchair over which Madeleine has draped her clothes. La Fontaine provides no such information, but Eisen's reason for choosing this location is obviously that it reflects Madeleine's role as a 'jument'. The dog in the right-hand corner may refer to the comparison with the lustful *curé*, who is described as being (vol.2, p.200):

> comme un chien qui fait fête
> aux os qu'il voit n'être pas trop chétifs.

However, nothing in the text itself suggests that a dog is present at the scene, and its inclusion here tells us something of the indirect way in which Eisen, like La Fontaine himself, proceeds to evaluate the story for the reader.[53] Dogs were commonly used to symbolise both fidelity and lust,[54] so that the presence of this detail is readily explicable, at least in

53. Lapp remarks a propos of this *conte* on La Fontaine's 'ability to veil the grossest subject with understatement and imagery' (*The Esthetics of negligence*, p.57), an approach reflected in the allusiveness of the Eisen illustration.
54. Carr-Gomm, *Dictionary of symbols in art*, p.81, and Nicolich, 'Seventeenth and eighteenth-century illustrations for La Fontaine's *Contes et nouvelles en vers*', p.266.

De Hooghe 51. 'Le diable en enfer', vol.2, p.171

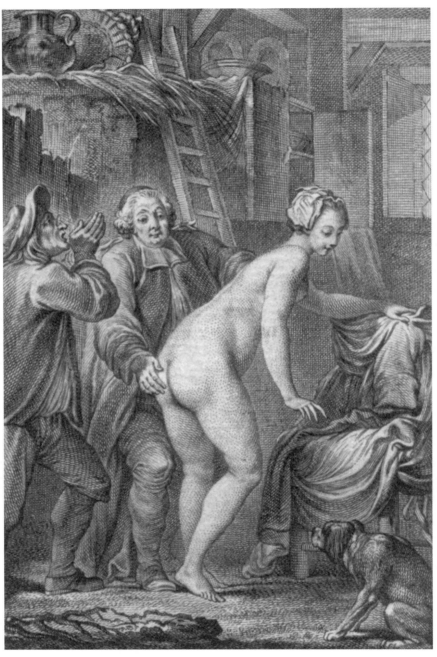

Eisen 63. 'La jument du compère Pierre', vol.2, p.199

one sense. Yet the dog is not itself obviously lustful, and seems rather woebegone, as if to suggest that the conduct of its master and mistress is a source of shame or regret. The same may be said of Messire Jean, whose behaviour becomes more reprehensible still in the light of the couple's desperation to obtain money. The prominent ladder in the background may have a symbolic significance, as it does in the previous *conte*, 'Comment l'esprit vient aux filles',[55] in that it underlines forcefully the difference between the purity of the priest's calling and his actual conduct. This point is reinforced by the depiction of Pierre saying his prayers, whilst the priest remains impassive as he sets about the seduction of the farmer's wife.

Although some elements of the illustration (including the dog) can be found in De Hooghe, the setting is less obviously impoverished (De Hooghe 52). A cow can be seen in the background, and a hen is perched on the windowsill, while a cooking-pot is steaming in the fireplace. Pierre stands contemplatively by, spade in hand, as the *curé*, showing no sign of devotion, places his hands on Madeleine's shoulders. De Hooghe's Madeleine is as yet only half-naked and is seen from the front, so that she retains some modesty. Eisen's interpretation of the *conte* therefore goes further than De Hooghe's by showing her completely naked but, as Nicolich points out (p.268-69), he chooses to depict a much more critical moment of the story, just before the *curé* attaches a 'tail' to Madeleine. In other words, Eisen takes the action as far as decency permits, but no further, a practice of which we have seen other examples in the *Contes*. His interpretation also differs markedly from Cochin's. In the 1745 edition the setting is again an appropriately bare room, but with no obvious indication that it is a cowshed; Pierre is seated, mouth agape but silent, as the priest proceeds with his task of seducing the semi-naked Madeleine. Her complete nakedness in Eisen's illustration underlines her willingness to participate in the enterprise, with no sign of the 'pudeur' which, in the text, makes her hesitate to do as the priest requires (vol.2, p.203).

Unlike the two earlier illustrations, the Fermiers généraux engraving shows the point in the *conte* at which Pierre reveals the true extent of his gullibility as he, in effect, gives thanks to God for the seduction of his wife. As so often, Eisen emphasises not only the lust of the clergy but also, and less typically for the time, women's sexuality, rather than their traditional modesty. Their availability does not, of course, lessen in any way the satirical, and even anticlerical, implications of the story. These aspects are more fully explored in 1762 than in the illustrations by De Hooghe and Cochin, as part of the critical stance adopted by the Fermiers généraux towards their enemies in the Church. For that stance, of course, the illustrations of the *Contes* are only one vehicle.

55. In the original editions of the *Contes*, these two works were widely separated; their conjunction is a feature of eighteenth-century editions.

De Hooghe 52. 'La jument du compère Pierre', vol.2, p.179

## xxiii. 'Les lunettes'

*Caption: 'Dans le chapitre du couvent, les nonettes nues entourent la prieure. Les attitudes disent le reste.'*

Although a 'découvert' version of the plate for this *conte* does exist, it was not widely available and is apparently found only in the Pixérécourt copy (Cohen, *Guide de l'amateur de livres*, col.566). With the standard version shown here (Eisen 64), we have one of the rare examples in the *Contes* of a description being used to comment directly on the illustration itself. Clearly, the latter part of the wording adds nothing to our understanding of the engraving, at least on one level, and in a diegetic sense would be largely meaningless without the text. Nonetheless, the words 'les attitudes disent le reste' imply that what is depicted is readily understandable, because it is, in the most basic sense, natural. As Martha M. Houle puts it: 'Sin, if sin there is, is excused by the natural [...] reaction of the male character at the sight of these unclothed young nuns.'[56] The section of the text to which the engraving refers runs as follows (vol.2, p.211):

> la machine [...] échappa, rompit le fil d'un coup,
> Comme un coursier qui romproit son licou,
> Et sauta droit au nez de la prieure,
> Faisant voler lunettes tout à l'heure,
> Jusqu'au plancher. Il s'en fallut bien peu
> Que l'on ne vît tomber la lunetiere.

The wording does not mention that the prioress is half-kneeling, in close proximity to the unnamed youth. In the guise of Sœur Colette, he has made one of the nuns pregnant, and now stands naked before her and before eight young, beautiful and undraped nuns. Their presence has caused him to have an erection, breaking the restraining cord seen around his waist. Even if the direct cause of the prioress's discomfiture is hidden from us (as is normal in the *Contes*), Eisen reminds us in at least two ways of what is at issue. Her pince-nez, which can be seen in mid air, has a distinctly phallic association, since it is shaped like a pair of testicles, while the erect pillars of the church recall what we cannot directly see of the youth's manhood. It is also noticeable that the curvilinear folds of the prioress' left sleeve are positioned just where the man's (rather large and curiously shaped) organ would be in a state of exceptional arousal. The shape, indeed, is less that of a penis than of a snake, creating an association whose erotic relevance for a church founded on a belief in the Fall of Man needs no stressing.[57]

Eisen also uses the austere church interior to heighten the contrast between the sexual vigour of the youth and the enclosed world of the

56. Houle, 'The play of *bienséances* in La Fontaine's *L'Abbesse*', p.112-13. Lapp (*The Esthetics of negligence*, p.131) comments that 'This is [...] the dynamism of nature itself'.
57. See Genesis 1:3.

Eisen 64. 'Les lunettes', vol.2, p.207

prioress. The nakedness of the nuns, and the pleasure which most of them feel as their eyes focus on the young man's erection, underline the futility of their pretensions to shun the temptations of the flesh. By showing the shocked reaction of the prioress, which contrasts with the pleasure displayed by the nuns, Eisen reveals his sympathy with the argument made at the start of the *conte* that (vol.2, p.207)

> Je veux que les nonains
> Fassent les tours en amour les plus fins;
> Si ne faut-il pour cela qu'on épuise
> Tout le sujet: le moyen? C'est un fait
> Par trop fréquent; je n'aurois jamais fait.

It is the nuns and the youth who are behaving in accordance with nature, and the prioress's shocked refusal to recognise the fact (like that of the Church itself, with its emphasis on clerical celibacy) is simply unrealistic. The point is made indirectly by La Fontaine himself, who takes the view that (vol.2, p.209-10)

> Notre commune mere,
> Dame Nature

gave males and females sexual organs which have essentially the same origins. In the context of the debates taking place on the function and usefulness of convents in the 1750s and 1760s,[58] this engraving makes the ethos of the convent unnatural, and excuses both the youth and his lover for their 'irreligious' conduct.

In contrast, the illustrations provided by De Hooghe (De Hooghe 53) and by Cochin have an outdoor setting. They are based on the latter part of the *conte* which makes no reference to the beauty of the nuns. It concentrates instead on the punishment inflicted by some of the more elderly sisters on an innocent miller who has replaced the real 'sinner' in the hope of enjoying the sexual favours of the young nuns. Like most of the illustrations which De Hooghe and Cochin provided for the edition, their work *represents* the scene described in the text, with its cruelty and its hints of sexual frustration. They make little attempt to comment on the action from the point of view of the spectator as Eisen's illustrations do, and their headpieces retain their primarily illustrative function.

---

58. The French government closed some 1500 convents in the 1760s (see Cobban, *A History of modern France*, vol.1, p.110). The attacks mounted on the convent system in the *Encyclopédie* and elsewhere further undermined belief in their value. See Georges May, *Diderot et 'La Religieuse'* (New Haven, CT, and Paris, 1954), especially p.170-81.

De Hooghe 53. 'Les lunettes', vol.2, p.187

## xxiv. 'Le cuvier'

*Caption: 'Tandis que le tonnelier racle l'intérieur du cuvier, sa femme &
son amant vont renouer leur entretien interrompu.'*

This engraving (Eisen 65) gives great emphasis to light, not only from the
tonnelier's candle inside the barrel, but also in bathing the two illicit
lovers in a glowing halo. In 'La clochette' (vol.1, p.219-21, p.172 in this
volume), Eisen had initially provided an illustration in which the young
girl is similarly bathed in light, perhaps to suggest her innocence. There is
therefore some basis for concluding that the illuminated lovers in Eisen's
illustration for 'Le cuvier' are likewise exempt from censure, as indeed
they are in the *conte* itself (vol.2, p.215):

> Soyez amant, vous serez inventif:
> Tour ni détour, ruse ni stratagème
> Ne vous faudront: le plus jeune apprentif
> Est vieux routier, dès le moment qu'il aime:
> On ne vit onc que cette passion
> Demeurât court, faute d'invention.

Here as elsewhere ('Les lunettes' being a case in point), Eisen takes up
La Fontaine's defence of sexual love as a natural human activity, with its
attendant infidelities, deceptions and trickery. It is true that at the end of
the *conte* there is reference to the 'tour fripon du couple' (vol.2, p.217), but
they can scarcely be blamed if they are merely exhibiting what have
already been presented as universal human tendencies. Hence Eisen's use
of the 'natural' light in which the couple are bathed functions not simply
as the counterpart of the artificial light from the candle carried by the
husband inside the barrel, but as a means of indicating the 'naturalness'
of their behaviour.

As the barrel-maker's wife points to her husband (no doubt in
mockery), the couple are so close to him that it seems impossible that he
should remain ignorant of their activities. This is a feature of other
illustrations prepared by Eisen for the *Contes*. It occurs, for example, in
'La servante justifiée' and 'Le roi Candaule et le maître en droit', in
which the sexual pleasure of the characters (and the voyeuristic pleasure
of the viewer) is likewise associated with a high risk of discovery. The
lover and the wife are more elegantly attired, to set them apart from the
husband. He is shown as a large, roughly dressed, clumsy-looking man; he
appears to be of the peasant or artisan class depicted, for example, in 'Le
paysan qui avoit offensé son seigneur' and 'Le baiser rendu'. The fact that
Eisen gives what might be called a family resemblance to characters of the
same social class in widely separated *contes* is in itself suggestive of contemporary expectations and interpretations, as well as of the Fermiers'
own view of such individuals.

Eisen 65. 'Le cuvier', vol.2, p.215

A reading of this kind would be in keeping with the tenor of the *conte*, where the wife is clearly more astute in business than her husband. A clue to the nature of the relationship between the wife and the lover is provided by the lover's hat shown on the left, which is suggestive of the female sex-organ. In addition, brightly lit, in proximity to the husband and out of doors, they gaze unashamedly into each other's eyes. All the devices used in this engraving are found elsewhere in the *Contes* in a variety of combinations which give continuity and, so to speak, a meta-language for communicating the message behind the illustrations.

De Hooghe offers a sanitised version of the scene, in which the lover, watched by the wife, emerges from the barrel to allow the husband to inspect it for flaws (De Hooghe 54). A garland hanging discreetly on a pole in the background alludes, as Eisen does in 'Les troqueurs', to the sexual nature of the relationship. However, a dog barking at the lover as he emerges from the barrel does not denote approval of his conduct on De Hooghe's part, nor is the husband the clumsy oaf depicted by Eisen; consequently, the moral perspective of the engravings is by no means similar, whatever their superficial resemblances.

Cochin uses essentially the same elements of the story as De Hooghe and Eisen. Like Eisen's, his adulterous couple consort next to the barrel containing the husband, but Cochin makes no use of light or sexually suggestive props to achieve either artistic or symbolic effects. Again, the husband's face is completely invisible, so that there is no contrast with that of the lover. As so often, Cochin's illustrations are functional, and their link with the text is purely diegetic.

## xxv. 'La chose impossible'

*Caption: 'Satan se présente au galant & à sa belle, et confesse qu'en effet la chose est impossible.'*

The setting (Eisen 66) is an elegant contemporary French drawing-room, and the clothes worn by the couple are those of the 1760s. Eisen achieves a startling effect of contrast (much as he does in 'L'anneau d'Hans Carvel' and 'Le diable de Papefiguière') by juxtaposing a character from legend or mythology with figures dressed in the fashions of the time. As a consequence, in this resolutely worldly Enlightenment setting, it is the Devil who seems out of place. The human couple are in no way made subordinate to his allegedly infinite supernatural powers, but seem rather to be relishing their victory with quiet mockery of their adversary. As the description indicates, the fragility of the Devil's power can be gauged from the one pubic hair which he holds in his left hand. By its shape, which resembles his own horns, the hair ironically underlines how easily he has been thwarted. The engraving represents the triumph

De Hooghe 54. 'Le cuvier', vol.2, p.195

Eisen 66. 'La chose impossible', vol.2, p.219

of the human over the supernatural, and of human cunning over someone thought usually to be duplicity personified.

Like many of Eisen's illustrations to the *Contes*, this example sets out to mock or satirise aspects of the Church, and suggests strongly that belief in the supernatural, or in any forces other than those which are purely human, has no place in the France of the time. This interpretation is not implied in La Fontaine's text, which is so imprecise in chronological terms that Eisen could legitimately have chosen a wholly different setting for the illustration. His reasons for not doing so are apparent. According to Holloway (*French rococo book illustration*, p.25), in this engraving Eisen 'came too near to pointing at the sovereign himself and Madame de Pompadour', and the woman depicted does indeed resemble the Pompadour as shown in portraits by Boucher and other artists of the time.[59] Whatever the truth of the assertion, his decision to include a very prominent mirror at the rear of the room is a clear hint that the engraving was intended to have a contemporary resonance, and to reflect the life of the times. If he did intend the couple to resemble the king and his mistress, the suggestion that in the France of Louis XV human cunning could outwit the supernatural forces of the Devil would certainly have appealed to philosophical tastes, if not to the king himself.

These points emerge more strongly still when we compare Eisen's illustration with De Hooghe's strikingly baroque headpiece, the setting for which is as far removed from eighteenth-century elegance as can be imagined. His Devil is a monstrous, infernal blacksmith, working furiously in the bowels of hell itself in a fruitless attempt to achieve the impossible task (De Hooghe 55). Cochin seems, as so often, to stand midway between De Hooghe and Eisen in his interpretation of the story. Like Eisen, he sets the scene in an elegant drawing-room, though his Devil, like De Hooghe's, is surrounded by clouds of smoke, and he shows the couple looking rather intimidated by his presence, despite their success in outwitting him. It is left to Eisen to bring out the superior cunning of (and to make sly reference to) the couple against whom the Devil has chosen to prove himself, and who so obviously, and calmly, enjoy their triumph.

## xxvi. 'Le tableau'

*Caption: 'Dans une cellule jonchée de fleurs, une chaise se rompt sous un lourdaut; l'action des deux nones est relative au texte.'*

In illustrating this *conte*, Eisen undertakes a comparable challenge to that which La Fontaine himself accepts in recounting the story, a task to which he draws particular attention (vol.2, p.223):

---

59. See in particular the portrait of Mme de Pompadour by Boucher (1756) in the Wallace Collection, showing her in a blue flowered dress, with an open book in her hand.

De Hooghe 55. 'La chose impossible', vol.2, p.199

> On m'engage à conter d'une maniere honnête
> Le sujet d'un de ces tableaux
> Sur lesquels on met des rideaux [...]
> Tout y sera voilé; mais de gaze, et si bien,
> Que je crois qu'on ne perdra rien.

This reference to the 'veil' (both ecclesiastical and metaphorical) has given rise to comment,[60] since it hints that some matters will be left unexplained. Indeed, there is some doubt as to the reasons for the collapse of the chair on which one of the nuns is occupied with her lover (vol.2, p.229-30):

> Ou soit par le défaut
> De la chaise un peu foible, ou soit que du pitaut
> Le corps ne fût pas fait de plume,
> Ou soit que sœur Thérèse eût chargé d'action
> Son discours véhément et plein d'émotion,
> On entendit craquer l'amoureuse tribune.

By leaving the matter undecided, La Fontaine allows the reader more freedom to interpret the *conte* at will, without inflecting our attitude towards any of the participants. Mindful of this deliberate uncertainty, Eisen similarly avoids depicting the scene in a way which explains the collapse of the chair for any one reason.

He created two different illustrations for this *conte*; the first, which was rejected, is slightly smaller than the second.[61] Both, however, are complex enough in their relationship to the text to require detailed analysis, as the second part of the description shows. According to La Fontaine, the *conte* is set in a suburb of 'la ville de Cithère' (vol.2, p.224-25). Eisen ignores any such indications (including any which might have been derived from the well-known paintings by Watteau depicting the island of Cythera).[62] He offers us instead (Eisen 67a) what is unmistakably a contemporary French setting, yet one with an obvious relevance to the depiction of the mores of the Church at that time. In this first version, the scene is set in what looks like a well-appointed drawing-room, with a painting and decorations, rather than the austere 'cellule' of a convent. A curtain at the window is drawn back to let in the light, in keeping with Eisen's usual practice. Only the clothing of the two nuns relates directly to their calling so that, with their elaborate surroundings, they are poised between the world and the cloister.[63]

The chair on which one nun and the 'lourdaut' are engaged in sexual activity is shown breaking, and the participants are caught at moment when their surprise is greatest. One strut of the chair, in the lower right

60. See Birberick, 'From world to text', p.195-98.
61. See Cohen, *Guide de l'amateur de livres*, col.568.
62. Both artists were natives of Valenciennes, and Eisen's work has sometimes been compared to that of Watteau. See E. W. Bredt, *Die drei galanten Meister von Valenciennes* (Munich, 1921).
63. Compare Anne L. Birberick's comments on the 'false division between the cloister and the salon' in the *contes* which feature nuns ('From world to text', p.198).

Eisen 67a. 'Le tableau', first version, vol.2, p.223

corner of the engraving, is set at a distinctly phallic angle, while the legs of
the man and of the nun on his lap are sufficiently exposed for the viewer
to gauge the nature of their activity. It is noticeable that, as in several
other *contes*, Eisen accentuates the debauchery of the woman in question
by pairing her with a man of distinctly gross and unappealing features, as
if to suggest that some form of miscegenation is taking place. One of the
most interesting aspects of this engraving, from a diegetic point of view, is
that it shows the two nuns at loggerheads before the chair has collapsed,
whereas the text states that they fight only after this has happened,
perhaps because (vol.2, p.230)

> sœur Thérèse [avoit] chargé d'action
> Son discours véhément et plein d'émotion.

Her expression of ecstasy (which Eisen borrows from religious painting of the
time)[64] makes her indifferent to Claude's attempts to unseat her, but the
conjunction of the two events does not correspond to the text, since the chair
has not yet collapsed. Hence, the action of the *conte* is telescoped in order to
create a dramatic engraving in which pleasure and anger are simultaneously depicted, and the immodesty of the two nuns is given full scope for
expression. Their uninhibited conduct is made more remarkable still by the
apparent decorum of the setting, with its elegant drapes and furnishings.
But however obvious the sexual debauchery depicted here, Eisen, following the same procedure as he had used in 'La clochette', avoids making
either of the nuns look as young as La Fontaine suggests (vol.2, p.225):

> La moins jeune à peine comptoit
> Un an entier par-dessus treize.[65]

Uninhibited as Eisen's nuns may be, they are not precocious adoles-
cents indulging to the full in the sins of the flesh. This point is significant
for at least two reasons. First, towards the end of the *conte*, La Fontaine
himself draws attention to the difference between describing an incident
such as this and depicting it visually (a question raised, if not answered,
by his decision to entitle the *conte* 'Le tableau'; vol.2, p.231):

> Or ai-je des nonains mis en vers l'aventure,
> Mais non avec des traits dignes de l'action;
> Et comme celle-ci déchet dans la peinture,
> La peinture déchet dans ma description
> Les mots et les couleurs ne sont choses pareilles,
> Ni les yeux ne sont les oreilles.[66]

64. See, for example, Jean Restout's *St Vincent de Paul et St François de Sales* (1732), which
is in the Eglise Sainte-Marguerite, Paris, and which is reproduced in Conisbee, *Painting in
eighteenth-century France* (p.47, fig. 31).
65. *OCLF* (p.888) gives the nun's age as 'seize', but it is given as 'treize' in the editions of
1745 and 1762.
66. Lapp (*The Esthetics of negligence*, p.36-41) analyses the *conte* in detail, though his
remarks on this passage are inconclusive.

These lines promise more than they deliver, in that the differences be-tween words and colours are left unexamined, but La Fontaine does at least indicate that some things may be said which cannot be shown, a point not lost on Eisen.

The age of the two nuns is also useful in suggesting the values enshrined in the *Contes*. Debauchery is usually tolerated in those old enough to participate knowingly in such activities. But it should not be forgotten that the eighteenth century could number among its achievements the story of the fifteen-year-old prostitute recounted in Prévost's *Manon Lescaut* (1731), and the amours of the eleven-year-old heroine of *Thérèse philosophe* (1748).[67] The fictional Manon was the same age as the real-life Louisa O'Murphy, who was already the mistress of Louis XV when she served as a model for Boucher's *Odalisque* in 1752. These examples not-withstanding, the Fermiers' reticence on this point indicates clearly the limits beyond which they were not prepared to go, even at the cost of departing from the text of the *Contes*.

In the second version of the engraving (Eisen 67b), Eisen shows the couple after the chair has broken, with the man lying on the floor. Claude is attempting to drag away Thérèse, whose face still wears an expression of satisfaction even after her fall from the chair, though neither her dress nor that of the man is in the disorder shown in the first engraving. The 'lourdaut' (vol.2, p.232) is no longer gross and heavy, but a good-looking young man, a change which may make Thérèse's pleasure more readily explicable. While the room is still elegant, the wine and fruits (which the two nuns had prepared for the lover who did not arrive) are now shown much more prominently, to underscore the unexpected nature of the encounter which does take place. As they have not been eaten, the impli-cation is that those present have been diverted by other pleasures. The source of the rather faint light coming into the room is unclear, even though a large window is visible at the rear. Claude's anger is seen in her gestures ('elle en veut venir aux coups', vol.2, p.230), while the man, for his part, looks almost in shock at what has happened (his mental heavi-ness is a correlate of his physical bulk).

This second engraving is less explicit than the first, and it follows more closely the text of the *conte*. It places more emphasis on the anger shown by Claude as she attempts to remove Thérèse, on the appropriately hand-some features of the 'rustre', and on the food and drink which is part of the orgy. Rather than the sexual indulgence shown in the original engraving, the whole impression now is one of utter disorder which overwhelms those involved; self-control and dignity are lost as a consequence of sexual

67. *Thérèse* is usually attributed (conjecturally) nowadays to the marquis d'Argens; a number of its many reprints contained engravings which Cohen (*Guide de l'amateur de livres*, col.734) discreetly calls 'très curieuses' or 'libres'.

Eisen 67b. 'Le tableau', second version, vol.2, p.229

frenzy, and following the unexpected collapse of the chair. The flowers on the floor mock the lines (vol.2, p.226)

> Sur le linge ces fleurs
> Formoient des lacs d'amour, et le chiffre des sœurs.

Eisen (or his commissioning editors) therefore wanted an illustration depicting the chaos of the scene, rather than the sexual misconduct of the two nuns with their visitor, perhaps because the first version of the engraving concentrated on the sexual at the expense of the confrontational and the comic.

In fact, Eisen takes much the same disapproving view as De Hooghe, who depicts essentially the same scene as the latter engraving (De Hooghe 56). The legs of the table on which the food is set out are those of a satyr, and De Hooghe also adds two classical busts and a statue of a naked woman; each of these is shown with its eyes averted from the debauchery on display. Yet there is little sign in De Hooghe's headpiece that the women are nuns, or that the setting is a convent. The dress of all three participants is classical (the man is wearing armour), so that nothing of the satirical import created by Eisen is to be seen in this earlier illustration. Although, *mutatis mutandis*, De Hooghe may well have served as the basis for Eisen's illustration, Cochin takes nothing from him. In his version, one of the nuns is seated at the table, while the other is standing as they agree to receive the 'lourdaut' coming through the door. While the floor is strewn with flowers, and the walls appear to be hung with tapestries or other decorations, there is no sign of any food or drink on the table, and no indication of the sexual activities which will ensue. As so often, it is Eisen who brings out both the satire and the contemporary application of the story.

## xxvii. 'Le bât'

*Caption: 'Un peintre reçoit de la femme de son confrere un baiser au moment où il lui peint un âne et son bât.'*

The engraving for this *conte* exists in two versions; in its rejected form (Eisen 68a) it is recorded only in the Pixérécourt copy, which contains a large number of additional proofs, etchings and other material not found in standard copies of the *Contes*.[68]

---

68. Cohen (*Guide de l'amateur de livres*, col.568) observes that the engraving is 'retouchée au crayon noir, de la main de l'artiste, sur l'épreuve terminée'. The Pixérécourt copy was later in the library of Sir David Salomons, whose collection was auctioned in London on 25 June 1986; the two versions of the engraving for 'Le bât' are reproduced in the Christie's catalogue of the sale (p.37).

De Hooghe 56. 'Le tableau', vol.2, p.203

Eisen 68a. 'Le bât' (reproduced from the Christie's auction catalogue of
the library of Sir David Salomons, 25 June 1986, vol.2, p.37)

In this version, the artist's studio is largely hidden by a heavy drape serving as a backdrop to the couple. The lover kneels in front of the wife, who leans back on her chair with her skirt raised above her waist as he paints the saddled donkey, the symbol of cuckoldry, on her stomach. In the background, half-hidden by the drapery, is a painting on an easel showing a semi-naked woman whose posture recalls that of a Boucher nude. On the wall to the left, and also partly obscured by the drapery, is a painting of a seated, semi-naked woman with another figure. On a high shelf at the back can be seen a bust and the lower part of a sculpture, both of which are facing away from the intimate scene taking place before them. Beside the kneeling artist is a large paint-box with its lid raised.

In the standard version of the engraving (Eisen 68b), a heavy curtain is drawn back to reveal the woman's dress in disarray, displaying her breasts, as she is about to kiss her lover, who half-kneels before her, with his brush poised. The woman in the portrait on the wall behind them seems to peer round the curtain and to look at them disapprovingly. Several small sculptures on the shelf at the right have their gaze turned away from what is happening. On the easel is a painting showing a setting recognisably similar to that of the studio, and with a man running away from a woman who stands behind him (perhaps designating proleptically the painter fleeing before the husband returns).

The reasons why the earlier engraving was rejected are not hard to fathom in the context of the *Contes* as a whole. It is poorly lit, the curtain behind the couple is excessively large, and there is no obvious emotional interaction between them. While the earlier engraving is significant for our understanding of the evolution of the illustrations in the *Contes*, all these features were changed in the second version, which is at once more complex and more alive than the rejected plate. Its technical superiority over the first is evident from even a brief comparison: the additional detail of the window, draperies and works of art, the use of light, and the obvious feelings of the couple for each other, are all better managed in the second engraving than in the first.

In both versions, nonetheless, Eisen is raising the same aesthetic point. The presence of the paintings on the easel and on the wall, and of the sculptures on the shelf, contrasts with the 'reality' of the scene of adultery depicted in the engraving, yet both are of course equally the product of artistic endeavour. In that sense, the apparent distinction between them is abolished, and they exist on the same plane, for the viewer, even if the lovers themselves are depictions of beings with an existence beyond the illustration. Although they never existed as flesh and blood individuals, they do have a fictional 'life', in that they appear in the text on which the illustration is based, whereas the decorative elements in the illustration are added by Eisen without the warrant of the text. In addition, the lover is painting yet another image on the body of his mistress. Its status is different from that of the paintings in the studio, since it is intended to

Eisen 68b. 'Le bât', vol.2, p.233

mock the lady's husband, and thus to represent yet another level of artistic endeavour, the symbolic, with a coded reference to his being made a fool of.[69] By putting together the 'real' and the 'created', Eisen turns the illustration into a meditation on what art does when it represents the 'real'.

He contrasts momentary action (the posture of the painter, the kissing couple and their feelings, the light streaming into the room) and what is permanent (the sexual impulse). One might even argue that the painted donkey represents another aspect again of the question of durability, since the sculptures, the paintings on canvas, and the artist and his mistress are likely to last unequal amounts of time. The painting of the donkey, of course, will probably be less enduring than any of the other objects shown. At the same time, the juxtaposition of sculpture, painting and humans raises the question of what art is intended to do, what purposes it can serve. If artists turn their gaze away from the reality of human conduct, as the sculpted figures seem to be doing, then they ignore life to no purpose. If art expresses disapproval of eternal human foibles, as the woman in the painting to the left of the window does, this too is futile.[70] One of the recurrent themes of the *Contes*, and of Eisen's engravings, is that humans beings are not easily dissuaded from following their penchant for vice, or at least for self-indulgence. This remains the case whatever prohibitions society or religion may place on them, and whatever the cost in human terms, of the kind hinted at in the portrayal of the angry husband in the painting behind the couple. Eisen's engravings are therefore rarely judgemental, and such ideas as we can glean of the limits which the Fermiers imposed on themselves in commissioning the plates come from a comparison of the rejected versions and those which were accepted for the edition. From one of the simplest of the *contes*, Eisen thus derives one of his most profoundly meditative engravings.[71]

There is something of this complexity also in the headpiece which De Hooghe provided for this *conte*, though it is expressed differently (De Hooghe 57). He depicts the couple quarrelling, beside an overturned chair, after the return of the husband; the wife is fully clothed, and only a nude statue of a woman between them in the background hints at any

69. In bringing together the apparently real (the lovers) and the created (the works of art), Eisen is uniting what Marian Hobson calls *adequatio* and *aletheia* (*The Object of art*, p.15-16).

70. The emphasis on art as a source of pleasure through beauty was of course commonplace in France at this time; much of the aesthetic theory of the Enlightenment is summed up in a phrase from the *Encyclopédie* article 'Tableau' (1765) by Jaucourt: 'La peinture est faite pour plaire à l'esprit par les yeux' (*Encyclopédie*, vol.15, p.804). It would be hard to find anything produced in France before the Revolution which corresponds to the realism of Hogarth in *The Rake's progress* and other works, which would have been regarded as 'low'. See Hobson, *The Object of art*, p.156-58.

71. Norman Bryson discusses a more complex example in considering Vermeer's *Young woman seated at a virginal* (*Word and image*, p.8-28).

De Hooghe 57. 'Le bât', vol.2, **p.212**

impropriety. As with the Eisen illustration, the viewer is invited to meditate on the relationship between the expression of sexual feelings in humans, with all its attendant complexities, and the calm depiction of beauty in an artistic medium.

In Cochin's vignette, the adulterous wife is seated with her back to us, while the lover is shown seated and facing the viewer. The saddled donkey is depicted not on the stomach of the wife, but in a drawing hung on the easel behind the painter. No physical contact occurs between the couple. A portrait hangs on the wall behind them, although its gaze is not directed at them. Cochin has therefore removed any sexual suggestion from his interpretation of the *conte*, partly by refraining from showing the couple engaged in illicit behaviour, and partly by depicting the donkey as a drawing on the easel, departing wholly from La Fontaine's text, and distorting utterly the meaning of the story.

## xxviii. 'Le faiseur d'oreilles et le raccommodeur de moules'

*Caption: 'Guillaume renverse la femme d'André sur un lit; le pauvre André caché dans un retranchement de l'alcove reçoit une juste restitution.'*

To illustrate this story of Guillaume's revenge for being cuckolded by André, Eisen shows his obviously phallic gun placed in parallel with Guillaume's leg, pointing directly towards the hidden figure of André (Eisen 69). There is no mention of these details in the text, although André, who is now unarmed (vol.2, p.241), is evidently close enough to witness the scene while remaining unnoticed (vol.2, p.243). By positioning the gun in this way, Eisen suggests both Guillaume's sexual prowess and his ability to take revenge on André with no fear of further retaliation, thus inflicting not merely revenge, but sexual humiliation as well. This point is reinforced by the willingness with which André's wife accedes to Guillaume's 'revenge', though the illustration has none of the violence towards her implied in the text (vol.2, p.242):[72]

> il vous prend la commere,
> Et près d'André la jetta sur le lit,
> Moitié raisin, moitié figue en jouit.
> La dame prit le tout en patience;
> Bénit le ciel de ce que la vengeance
> Tomboit sur elle, et non sur sire André.

Her passiveness is dictated by the text itself, and does not therefore constitute a departure from Eisen's usual depiction of adulterous women. Yet if there is a moral lesson to be drawn here, it is in the figure of André

---

72. Lapp (*The Esthetics of negligence*, p.69) calls Guillaume 'brutal', claiming that 'violence has become sexual'.

Eisen 69. 'Le faiseur d'oreilles et le raccommodeur de moules', vol.2, p.235

himself. His wife is unaware that he is hidden nearby, and Guillaume is 'si fort ému, tellement irrité' (vol.2, p.242) that he is in no mood to consider the niceties of social conduct as he revenges himself on the man who has cuckolded him. André's shamefaced reaction to Guillaume's behaviour with his wife is indicated by his crestfallen demeanour as he witnesses what the description calls 'une juste restitution' at the hands of the man he had previously cuckolded. In the absence of any specific guidance on the appearance of the characters in the text itself, Eisen has to resort to stock faces and postures to convey the action, and it is the position of those involved, as much as their facial expression, which conveys what is occurring. Eisen's interpretation of the scene has both a psychological and a symbolic coherence which derives from the wording of the text, without directly borrowing from it.

De Hooghe's headpiece for this story has none of the violence or sexuality of Eisen's version (De Hooghe 58). While it is difficult to be sure, his subject seems to be the meeting between André and Guillaume's pregnant wife Alix which precipitates Guillaume's revenge. It may, however, represent the meeting which Guillaume asks her to arrange, and at which he plans to take his revenge on his rival. In either interpretation, it is the politeness of the two characters which strikes one most forcefully, and the utter absence of any sexual connotation, beyond the symbolic presence of a dog watching them. Cochin's vignette for the 1745 edition uses the same episode as Eisen as its starting-point, but treats it differently. Guillaume's gun is merely propped against a chair, and is no obvious threat, either literally or metaphorically, to André. Both he and his wife looked shocked at Guillaume's approach, so that her 'patience' is not in evidence. As ever, it is Eisen who most strongly depicts the sexual tensions of the story, often owing nothing to his predecessors, or else using their inspiration to depict events more explicitly than is their custom.

## xxix. 'Le fleuve Scamandre'

*Caption: 'Cimon caché dans les roseaux en sort, &
surprend sa belle qui prenoit un demi-bain.'*

This illustration (Eisen 70) has several elements typical both of the *Contes* and of its time. Eisen follows the general rules on the depiction of mountains summarised by the artist Montdorge in the *Encyclopédie* article 'Gravure' in 1757 (vol.7, p.889):

Les montagnes & les rochers, lorsqu'ils sont sur les premiers & seconds plans, doivent être travaillés d'une maniere un peu brute, en quittant & reprenant souvent les tailles, en les variant suivant les plans des pierres & des rochers, en les entre-mêlant de plantes, d'herbages, & de terreins: pour ces objets, lorsqu'ils se trouvent dans les lointains, ils doivent participer de l'interposition de l'air; être peu décidés dans leurs inégalités & dans les accidens qui les accompagnent.

De Hooghe 58. 'Le faiseur d'oreilles et le raccommodeur de moules',
vol.2, p.214

Eisen 70. 'Le fleuve Scamandre', vol.2, p.245

The angular, rough outlines specified by Montdorge are certainly found in Eisen's illustration, together with the requisite plants and grasses. At the same time, the gloomy lighting, the rocky outcrops, waterfalls, wild nature, and solitude were all typical of the 'Romantic' scenery which would come into fashion from the 1760s onwards. Only 'solitude' is specifically mentioned in the text (vol.2, p.246), so that the general composition owes something to tradition, something to emerging fashion, and something to Eisen's own inventiveness.[73]

The girl in the engraving (who remains unidentified by La Fontaine) is similarly typical of the time. She is wearing eighteenth-century peasant dress; beside her lies a broad hat of the sort worn by Eisen's country girls, as in 'Le villageois qui cherche son veau' and 'L'hermite', and familiar from paintings by Reynolds in England and Vigée-Lebrun in France.[74] As the description states, the girl looks startled, and leans backwards at Cimon's emergence from the reeds, putting out her hand to protect herself. Although her surprise at the youth's approach is evident, Eisen has departed from the text which states that on seeing Cimon, 'elle court se cacher' (vol.2, p.247). There may well be a textual reason for this change. The Fermiers généraux text (like that of *OCLF*) states that Cimon (vol.2, p.247)

> mouille ses vêtemens
> Se couronne de joncs et d'herbe dégouttante.

In the edition of 1745 (like that of 1755, which has no engraving for this *conte*), the lesson of the text is 'dégoûtante'. This latter form of the adjective would explain the girl's stance in the Cochin engraving, in which she reacts with horror as Cimon, with his matted hair, advances towards her in an attempt to embrace her. If his hair is merely dripping ('dégouttante') with waterweeds (correctly arranged in Eisen's illustration in the form of a crown), then she has less reason to be alarmed, though she might well be startled. Cimon would scarcely wish to appear 'disgusting', but might well want to increase the deception that he is a river-god by wearing waterweeds, the better to trick and seduce her. La Fontaine does not judge his deception too harshly, observing merely (vol.2, p.249):

> En ce tems-là semblables crimes
> S'excusoient aisément: tous tems, toutes maximes.

Hence, whatever readers in his own day might think, La Fontaine apparently sees no great harm in what has been done, and a dowry will in

---

73. See Conisbee, *Painting in eighteenth-century France*, p.194-96, for examples of similar landscapes by Fragonard, Vernet and others.
74. See, for example, Reynolds' portrait *Nelly O'Brien* (painted 1762-1764) in the Wallace Collection and Vigée-Lebrun's *Self-portrait in a straw hat* (after 1782) in the National Gallery, London.

any case repair any damage to the girl's reputation (vol.2, p.249). Eisen therefore shows Cimon reaching out towards the girl, whose hands are outstretched to steady herself as she falls back in surprise, though she may equally well be attempting to defend herself from his advances. This ambiguity, which echoes the indeterminate status of the 'crime', is not unexpected in Eisen's depiction of women. It is, of course, reminiscent of the replacement illustration to 'La clochette', in which the object of a man's advances is shown with arms raised as she turns to flee, though she is without the halo of innocence which surrounds her in the rejected version of the engraving.

In both these *contes*, La Fontaine suggests that male sexuality should be accepted for what it is, without incurring excessive disapproval, and in both cases his view is echoed by Eisen. But it should be remembered that this indifference to the girl's fate was not the only attitude towards her expressed in the 1760s. In his *Encyclopédie* article 'Scamandre' of 1765, where her name is given as Callirhoé,[75] Jaucourt observes (vol.14, p.739):

On a d'abord de la peine à comprendre la simplicité de Callirhoë. Elle étoit d'une illustre famille; elle avoit eu sans-doute une éducation convenable à sa naissance. Jamais l'esprit & la science n'avoient paru avec tant d'éclat que dans le siecle de cette aimable fille, cependant les fictions des poëtes canonisées par les prêtres, lui avoient tellement gâté l'esprit, qu'elle croyoit bonnement que les rivieres étoient des divinités, qui se couronnoient de roseaux, & auxquelles on ne pouvoit refuser la fleur de la virginité.

Nothing of this blatantly anticlerical stance is apparent in La Fontaine or in the Fermiers généraux version, where Callirhoé is indeed a simple 'ingénue' (vol.2, p.246) who is led by the heat, the solitude and 'quelque dieu malin', rather than by the machinations of priests, to bathe in the Scamander.

De Hooghe takes the hint that this 'crime' need not be shown in a way which would lead to Cimon's condemnation by readers (De Hooghe 59). He chooses a setting whose chief feature is a waterfall gushing from rocks surmounted by trees, and in which mountains are a distant and un-remarkable prospect. His Cimon stands oar in hand, facing an apparently trusting girl who displays no inclination to flee as she sees the reeds which seem to be sprouting from his head. The couple stand at some dis-tance apart; if the girl looks untroubled, it is because Cimon is making no attempt to approach her. De Hooghe therefore offers a scene of pastoral innocence, with no hint of violence or revulsion. If Eisen avoids the harsher consequences of the episode in his illustration, the very ambiguity of his stance places it in a less idealised category than De Hooghe's interpretation.

75. She is identified in the letters of Eschine, the original source of the story (*OCLF*, p.1494).

De Hooghe 59. 'Le fleuve Scamandre', vol.2, p.222

## xxx. 'La confidente sans le sçavoir, ou le stratagème'

*Caption: 'Une femme laide et vieille querelle un beau garçon
debout devant elle.'*

This scene (Eisen 71) represents the second of the three encounters
between Cléon and Alis, who acts as his intermediary with Aminte. On
the table before them are the 'rubis et diamants' which Aminte falsely
claims to have received from him (vol.2, p.256). To enhance the illustration of a story which is atypical in being uneventful, Eisen has recourse
to a number of conventional, stock devices. La Fontaine says nothing of
the décor of the room in which the meeting between Cléon and Alis takes
place. The luxurious furnishings (and notably the very elaborate baroque
clock) are therefore added to enhance the visual interest of the encounter,
and to remind readers of the lifestyle which it was, in part at least, the
purpose of this edition to defend.

The posture and gestures of the characters (one with hand on hip, the
other with outstretched palms) are self-explanatory. Cléon has the in-
offensive, even passive, demeanour of the man who does not readily engage in sexual intrigue.[76] Eisen gives Alis a swarthy appearance, as if to
indicate her unprepossessing nature (she is 'sévère et prude', vol.2, p.253),
and it should be recalled that a similarly gratuitous conjunction of this
sort was found earlier in the rejected engraving for 'Le roi Candaule'. The
prominent clock shows the passage of time, and presumably hints at the
midnight rendez-vous which Aminte has indirectly given to Cléon via Alis
(vol.2, p.258). The aggressive dog is used here not so much to indicate
sensuality as to echo the harsh words of Alis, increasing his perplexity in
the face of an accusation of which he is utterly innocent. The use of a dog
to convey an attitude (a process which can be seen also in the engraving
for 'La jument') offers an example of Eisen's conflation of the generally
symbolic and the specifically functional. Dogs are traditionally associated
either with lust or with fidelity, but the dogs used in both these instances
are not so much reflecting these qualities as acting as surrogates for
attitudes expressed either by characters in the stories or else, as here, by
figures in the illustration. La Fontaine mentions neither the clock nor the
dog, and their presence indicates that, when the *conte* itself provides little
material to furnish an illustration, Eisen had recourse to conventional
elements to enhance the interest of the subject, turning them in his fashion
to serve other purposes.

The point emerges more clearly still if this engraving is compared with
the headpieces provided by De Hooghe and by Cochin. In the first
(De Hooghe 60), Aminte hands to Alis the jewels and the portrait which
she claims to have received from Cléon (vol.2, p.256). Apart from some

---

76. 'Aminte has a natural barrier of incredulity and timidity to break down' (Lapp, *The
Esthetics of negligence*, p.49).

Eisen 71. 'La confidente sans le sçavoir, ou le stratagème', vol.2, p.251

De Hooghe 60. 'La confidente sans le sçavoir, ou le stratagème', vol.2, p.227

furniture and draperies, the room is bare, and there is little of interest on which the viewer can focus. Cochin shows the same scene as Eisen, with the positions of the characters reversed, but with no clock or dog, and with a somewhat plainer setting than the Fermiers were to provide. In a story with few opportunities for the artist's invention to display itself, all three illustrators were evidently hard pressed to offer a scene interesting enough to capture the reader's attention. The fact that neither of the episodes which they chose is in any way remarkable serves only to underline the dramatic paucity of this *conte*, and to demonstrate Eisen's ability to provide a focus of interest by concentrating on the dramatic and the circumstantial.

## xxxi. 'Le remède'

*Caption: 'La gouvernante, une seringue à la main, se dispose à donner le remede; l'amant est en posture.'*

Eisen here has recourse to the customary devices used in other bedroom scenes in the *Contes* (Eisen 72). The chamber pot, with a notably phallic spout, as well as a candle, can be seen on the bedside table; the curtains are open to reveal a bed large enough to accommodate the two lovers. The gouvernante's right foot is slightly raised above the floor, as if to show her in the act of inserting the syringe with all her might into what she takes to be the girl's behind. This detail, like the chamber pot and candle, and of course the syringe itself, adds an erotic dimension to the story. At the same time, the gouvernante, even with her glasses and with light streaming into the room, cannot distinguish a male backside from its female counterpart. The sexual hints provided by Eisen therefore stand in ironic counterpoint to her age and, it is implied, her ignorance of sexual matters.

De Hooghe's interpretation of this *conte* (De Hooghe 61) is (as might be expected) less overtly erotic than that of Eisen, and even of Cochin. The gouvernante, syringe in hand, approaches the bed in which the lover's face alone is visible. Such a direct encounter emphasises the gouvernante's poor eyesight, though the text gives no warrant for supposing that the two are at any point face to face. The figure of the mistress, lying almost hidden in the bed, is only dimly visible, so that the erotic impact of the scene is again diminished.

For the edition of 1745, Cochin provided a vignette which was certainly the source for Eisen's design in 1762 (and which was closely copied in the edition of 1755). The two interpretations are alike in their general layout and in the accoutrements shown. In 1745 and 1755 large curtains are open over the bed on which the lover is lying; the gouvernante is ready to insert the syringe; a chair and a chamber pot are placed by the

Eisen 72. 'Le remède', vol.2, p.259

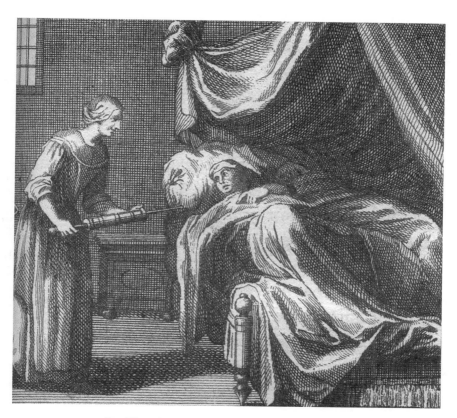

De Hooghe 61. 'Le remède', vol.2, p.235

bed. Unlike Eisen, Cochin shows nothing phallic about the pot; no candle is visible, and the gouvernante's feet remain firmly on the ground. These differences are sufficient to tell us clearly that, even when he borrowed his inspiration from an earlier source, Eisen was able to add his own individual touches. His approach leads him to accentuate certain elements of the illustration, in order to link it not only to the erotic aspects of the *conte* itself, but also to the eternal themes of youth and age, sexual naiveté and human error. This latter theme is, appropriately, what is at stake in the 'procès qui n'auroit point de fin' to which La Fontaine refers in the closing lines of the *conte*, and in which he points up the futility of responding to obtuse critics who accuse him of altering the facts of the story.

## xxxii. 'Les aveux indiscrets'

*Caption: 'On voit courir deux hommes, l'un bâté, l'autre sanglé;*
*le peuple s'assemble à leurs cris.'*

Eisen respects (Eisen 73) the statement in the text that, as the two men run about at 'maint carrefour' (vol.2, p.268), uselessly parading their emotions at discovering the past history of their wives, 'Chacun en rit' (vol.2, p.268). He adds a frightened child and two dogs which are not mentioned by La Fontaine, and which strengthen the impression that the two men are together creating a bizarre public spectacle, since their behaviour is irrational and alarming to man and beast, and to old and young alike. In accordance with La Fontaine's observation that each of the spectators witnessing the scene knows 'Qu'il a de quoi faire rire à son tour' (vol.2, p.268), the numerous visible onlookers are mainly men. A woman is pictured on the right of the illustration to point out to the two children the lesson which their generation will learn in due course. The city setting is made apparent through the variety and size of the houses in the background; Eisen also adds a weather vane on the church, to the right, as an indicator of human fickleness, to which the men and their spouses, in their different ways, testify.

The illustration is indebted to varying degrees both to De Hooghe and to Cochin. The capering dog is copied from De Hooghe's setting (De Hooghe 62), which is otherwise a rather under-populated street, in which the two men featured in the story are observed by a third, and by a woman looking out of a window. While the man wearing a strap around his waist is in semi-shadow, his saddled companion stands prominently at the centre of the engraving. There are however few signs that the two men are the object of public mockery, so that there is little of the generalised disgrace associated with their behaviour in Eisen's illustration.

In Cochin's version, the two men are again shown, with saddle and strap, running along a street, mocked by the bystanders. As in the Eisen

Eisen 73. 'Les aveux indiscrets', vol.2, p.265

De Hooghe 62. 'Les aveux indiscrets', vol.2, p.240

plate, children can be seen at some distance from them, joining in the general derision. However, as with De Hooghe, there are significant differences between the two engravings. First, Cochin shows the men running along the street in a straight line, rather than aimlessly circling as they do in the Eisen illustration; second, their behaviour is merely ridiculous, and not frightening or bizarre; finally, there is no weather-vane or church to hint at the instability of human emotions. Hence, Eisen pays greater heed than does Cochin to La Fontaine's assessment of the conduct of the two men (vol.2, p.269):

> Quelle folie! Imprudence est un terme
> Faible à mon sens pour exprimer ceci.

As so often in the illustrations to the 1762 edition, we are implicitly asked to accept human foibles such as infidelity or sexual misconduct, since to do otherwise is unrealistic, and is sure to lead to greater misery. The point emerges diagetically through the corpus of Eisen's illustrations as a whole, and interdiagetically through comparison with the previous interpretation of the *Contes* offered by De Hooghe and Cochin.

## xxxiii. 'Le contrat'

*Caption: 'Le beau-pere assis dans son cabinet, présente*
*le contrat à son gendre qui le reçoit.'*

Eisen provided two different illustrations for this *conte*, the earlier of which (Eisen 74a) is absent from most copies of the edition.[77] Nor is this surprising, since the subject conflicts with the description, in showing the two men standing rather than sitting. They are shown in an ornately decorated room; although the father-in-law is older and stooped, he is physically heavier and more imposing, not least because of his greater experience of the world. He has his hand on the shoulder of the younger man, proffering the money with which he hopes to persuade him to remain married to his daughter, who has given birth to another man's child. A wall-clock placed prominently in the background (as is often the case with Eisen's illustrations for this edition) is here used to create an implied contrast between the passage of time, which transforms youth into old age, and the eternal, recurrent features of human behaviour which are the subject of the *conte*.

The second version of the plate (Eisen 74b) corresponds more closely to the description, and the older man is seated as he hands the contract to his indignant son-in-law. Their surroundings are less ornate than in the earlier version, though a clock is again displayed prominently. The effect

---

77. See also Cohen, *Guide de l'amateur de livres*, col.568. It is recorded only in the Rothschild and Pixérécourt copies of the 1762 edition, but unused copies were often included in the Plassan reprint of 1792.

Eisen 74a. 'Le contrat', first version, between p.270-71

Eisen 74b. 'Le contrat', second version, between p.270-71

is to concentrate the viewer's attention on the transaction itself, and thus on human motivation, rather than to distract the eye with the elaborate décor surrounding the two men. However, in the later version, the younger man's three-cornered hat is prominently shown in his hand, whereas in the earlier illustration it is largely hidden under his arm. Eisen sometimes uses such hats, because of their shape, as a metaphor for the female sex-organ, and if the hat is given the increased prominence in the second version, it is precisely because it reminds us of the subject of the *conte*. In the earlier version of the engraving, the son-in-law looks expressionless, but in the later version he is smiling, reflecting more closely the very end of the *conte* (vol.2, p.275):

> A ce discours le gendre moins fâché
> Prend le contrat, et fait la révérence.

Neither De Hooghe nor Cochin seizes on this aspect of the story, since both prefer to present the two men as somewhat distant partners in the arrangement. In De Hooghe's headpiece (from the prominent furnishings in which Eisen may well have derived the clock motif), the father holds the contract in one hand while restraining the young man with the other. They do not look at each other, and appear to have little to say (De Hooghe 63).

Cochin's vignette for the edition of 1745 was probably the source of Eisen's earlier illustration for the *conte*. There too, the two men are standing up; the contract is prominently visible in the hand of the father-in-law as the younger man reaches forward almost greedily to take it, reflecting the fact that he makes 'bien du fracas' (vol.2, p.274). Both look angry, however, so that the emphasis here is quite different from that of either of the two versions created by Eisen. By showing the elder man sitting down in the later version of the plate, Eisen draws attention to his age, but also to his superior wisdom, to which the younger man is shown to defer. Instead of the standoff shown by De Hooghe, and the confrontation depicted by Cochin, Eisen's two versions are based on the theme of reconciliation, so that youth bows to the experience and wisdom of age. The clock shown in his two versions is absent from Cochin's vignette, which therefore does not emphasise the passage of time; in doing so, it ignores the moral of the story, which is that each generation has to learn to accept human foibles.

## xxxiv. 'Les quiproquo'

*Caption: 'Une femme aimable paroît sur les degrés d'une cave; devant elle est son mari, & dans l'enfoncement un jeune homme; l'étonnement des trois personages décéle le quiproquo.'*

As in other illustrations by Eisen for the *Contes*, the description indicates the subservience of the engraving (Eisen 75) to the text. The nature of the

De Hooghe 63. 'Le contrat', vol.2, p.245

triply adulterous misunderstanding between the wife, the husband and the friend is not to be deduced from the setting or from their expressions, unless we read the text beforehand. It may seem odd that Eisen has chosen to show the husband Clidamant as the possessor of a fine house with colonnade and gardens. He is, after all, in such financial straits that he has to share with his friend the cost of buying the favours of the servant Mme Alix (vol.2, p.281). Even so, the reason is clear: Eisen wishes to draw attention to the presence of nature (that is, metonymically, of human nature) in the midst of the apparently civilised. This point is made by La Fontaine in his observation that, although Clidamant should be happy with his beautiful wife (vol.2, p.279),

> Le diable est bien habile;
> Si c'est adresse et tour d'habileté
> Que de nous tendre un piège aussi facile
> Qu'est le désir d'un peu de nouveauté.

Yet the most striking feature of the illustration emerges when we compare it with the description to the plate, which claims that all three characters are surprised at the turn of events. This view of their behaviour is based on the wording of the text (vol.2, p.283):

> Mais quand l'époux vit sa femme monter,
> Et qu'elle eut vu l'ami se présenter,
> On peut juger quel soupçon, quel scrupule,
> Quelle surprise eurent les pauvres gens.
> Ni l'un ni l'autre ils n'avoient eu le tems
> De composer leur mine et leur visage.
> L'époux vit bien qu'il fallait être sage.

In fact, although the surprise of the two men is obvious (the husband's hands show as much, while the friend holds up his hat defensively), the wife's face displays no obvious reaction to their presence. Eisen in this respect reflects the text (vol.2, p.283-84):

> Mais sa moitié pensa tout découvrir.
> J'en suis surpris; femmes sçavent mentir
> La moins habile en connaît la science.

The woman shown in the illustration does display the self-possession which La Fontaine believes to be typical of her sex, rather than the surprise which she is said to feel elsewhere in the text, and in the description.[78] Eisen therefore selectively turns *some* of the textual indications into a comment on the respective abilities of men and women to conceal the truth of their behaviour. The dress which the wife wears, and behind which her legs are outlined, hints at her willing complicity in the double

---

78. According to John Lapp (*The Esthetics of negligence*, p.121), the text means that the wife '*almost* fails to maintain her composure' (italics in original), though the justification for this view is not apparent in the text.

Eisen 75. 'Les quiproquo', vol.2, p.277

'infidelity' which has taken place, so that her capacity for deceiving her husband will be tested to the full.

As so often in the *Contes*, Eisen presents women as having a greater capacity for duplicity than men, even when to do so requires a somewhat partial reading of the text.[79] At the same time, by setting the scene at least partly amid external nature, he hints at the universality, and inevitability, of such conduct. His interpretation differs significantly from those of De Hooghe (De Hooghe 64) and Cochin. Both his predecessors set the scene inside the house (thus omitting the implied comparison between human and external nature), and show all three characters abashed at the turn of events. In this, the last of the contes written by La Fontaine himself, Eisen's interpretation is a *mise en garde* against human weakness; it is also a tacit acceptance that such is the way of the world, about which we can do little except to try to avoid the pitfalls of life.

## xxxv. *Contes* not by La Fontaine

The last five contes were included in many eighteenth-century editions of the work, even though they were not universally attributed to La Fontaine.[80] They need to be considered in the present study because the Fermiers généraux commissioned illustrations from Eisen to accompany them, without distinguishing them from those which were written by La Fontaine himself. An *Avertissement* added at this point by the Fermiers attributes this group to authors other than La Fontaine, but explains that because they had been included in previous editions, 'on n'a pas osé les rejetter dans celle-ci' (vol.2, p.285).

## La Couturière
## Par M. Autereau

*Caption: 'Une none sur le lit de sa cellule, reçoit entre ses bras son amant déguisé en fille.'*

As in other contes set in religious houses, the setting here (Eisen 76) is more worldly than ascetic: the nun's cell is well appointed, with hangings, boiseries and, on the wall, a painting of a woman averting her gaze from the scene before us. To convey the ardour of the couple, Eisen leaves the

79. Lapp (*The Esthetics of negligence*, p.120) evokes La Fontaine's use here of 'the female cynicism and licentiousness of the Gallic tradition'.
80. They were first added as a group to an 'Amsterdam' edition of 1718 (see Rochambeau, *Bibliographie des œuvres de La Fontaine*, p.516-17, no. 50). This edition supplied new headpieces in the style of De Hooghe, who had died in 1708, which were used in many subsequent editions, including that of 1732 cited here. The editors of the 1745 edition assert that 'les [cinq] contes suivans n'approchent que médiocrement de ceux de Mr. de La Fontaine' (vol.2, p.249). Even so, like the Fermiers, they are unwilling to depart from established practice by excluding them.

De Hooghe 64. 'Les quiproquo', vol.2, p.250

Eisen 76. 'La couturière', vol.2, p.287

bed-curtains in the customary open position. He also uses the opportunity afforded by the text to present what seems to be an amorous encounter between two women. He arranges the nun's headdress so that it resembles long, flowing hair, while the lover's clothing is deceptive enough to create the impression that what we see are two women embracing. The significance of this illustration was probably not lost on a public which was well used, by the 1760s, to novelistic descriptions of Sapphic love affairs in convents.[81] In this regard it is, as so often, instructive to compare the 1762 illustration with the work of Cochin and the artist who provided the headpieces in the style of De Hooghe. 'De Hooghe'[82] depicts the encounter between the errant nun and the mother superior in the refectory (De Hooghe 65); their antagonism is plain, but the scene has no trace of the eroticism which Eisen brings to his interpretation of the story. Cochin's vignette shows a plain, undecorated room, in which the couple are seated at a table on which are laid some clothes or other material. Although the lover's arms are around the nun's waist, and they may be about to kiss, they are not yet doing so.

The description, like Eisen's illustration itself, extrapolates from the text, which makes no specific reference to the lovers embracing. By concentrating on this aspect of the *conte*, and adding the portrait as a comment on what occurs, Eisen maintains his practice of 'revealing' the hidden side of human life, showing us scenes which would not normally be enacted in public. The presence of the 'disapproving' portrait raises a further question. It is that of whether Eisen's illustrations, like the *Contes* themselves, can properly be regarded as having an immoral aspect, or can withstand the criticism of censorious readers who see immorality in telling the truth, even when nothing immoral is visually depicted.[83]

## Le Gascon
## Par le même Auteur

*Caption: 'Deux gascons sont à table au-dehors d'un cabaret;*
*la servant va chercher du vin, & tournant la tête,*
*elle exprime du geste le mot du conte.'*

The latter part of the description indicates the allegedly close relationship between the engraving (Eisen 77) and the text. And yet, as in 'Les quiproquo', both description and illustration depart to a significant ex-

81. 'Pour peu qu'on fréquente la littérature romanesque des années 1720-1760, on s'aperçoit que [le thème du couvent] donne assez souvent lieu à des descriptions et digressions libertines rendues encore plus émoustillantes par la grande jeunesse des personnages' (May, *Diderot et 'La Religieuse'*, p.132).

82. For simplicity, the name 'De Hooghe' is used here, in inverted commas, to designate the anonymous illustrator of these additional *contes*. There is no indication in the 1732 edition that any other artist was responsible for the engravings.

83. For a discussion of this point, see chapter 4 below (p.374).

De Hooghe 65. 'La couturière', vol.2, p.259

Eisen 77. 'Le Gascon', vol.2, p.289

tent from the wording of the *conte*. At no point does the text state that both men are Gascons, but only that a Gascon is talking 'au cabaret, avec un camarade' (vol.2, p.289). His friend, seated on the right, seems rather sheepish as he listens to the list of the other's conquests, so that he has nothing of the boastfulness which traditionally defines the Gascon. The servant as depicted by Eisen is not 'grosse' as the text states (vol.2, p.289), and seems to be listening attentively without mocking the speaker. Although, according to the description, she is about to fetch more wine, and has an empty bottle in her hand (and neither of these points is supported by the text), the paraphernalia and outward signs of drunkenness depicted in 'Les troqueurs', for example, are not shown here. Hence, Eisen is not suggesting (and the text does not suggest) that the Gascon's boasting is due to inebriation, but is merely the traditional characteristic of his birthplace.

In Eisen's interpretation, the allegedly boastful man is made into an attractive figure in comparison with his subdued companion, while the maidservant looks at him with interest. Her reason for doing so may be hinted at by the fact that his hat (whose symbolic value in the Eisen illustrations needs no further comment by this time) is prominent, while his companion has none. His boastfulness is by implication transformed into a wholly plausible recital of his conquests, to the list of which the servant-girl may be willing to be added. The indications given in the *conte* are therefore changed so that the Gascon becomes the focus of the reader's interest, rather than the figure of fun he is in the text. Eisen's decision to interpret the *conte* in this way is, then, a further example of the divergence between text and image and, indeed, between the image and the description which is intended to elucidate its meaning. That the description does not fully correspond to the text may be no more than an oversight. Even so, the presentation of the Gascon, his friend and the servant girl is clear evidence of Eisen's (and/or the Fermiers') wish to focus on the role of sexual attraction rather than on mockery.

Eisen owes much to Cochin in this instance. The attentive serving-girl, the nondescript friend and the attractive Gascon are all borrowed from the vignette of 1745. 'De Hooghe' has nothing to offer Cochin or Eisen. His rendering of the *conte* is not only very different, but also seems to be unrelated to the text in crucial ways. Whereas M. Autereau (vol.2, p.289) describes 'un Gascon l'autre jour à table, au cabaret, avec un camarade,' 'De Hooghe' shows a group of men seated at an inn-table (De Hooghe 66). One is holding forth, as two of the company listen to him, while a third pours wine from as bottle, and a fifth (half-hidden) looks on. Although the man seated on the left appears to be addressing the company, the figure pouring wine from bottle is also speaking, so that the 'Gascon' cannot readily be identified. Faced with the broken wineglass on the floor, and an evidently boisterous company, the maidservant wears an expression which denotes anger or exasperation rather than mockery;

De Hooghe 66. 'Le Gascon', vol.2, p.261

what is more, her feelings are directed at the whole group, rather than specifically at the man discussing his sexual conquests. The focus of the illustration is the four men, and only secondarily the servant. In an obvious reminiscence of Dutch genre paintings, 'De Hooghe' suggests an inn peopled by merry topers. The man pouring wine from a bottle is clearly not of the same ilk as Eisen's Gascon, and the serving girl glaring at the group is not of the same mind as Eisen's. As he and Cochin demonstrate, there is no inherent difficulty in retaining the essential elements of the story, so that 'De Hooghe''s decision to depart from the text cannot be explained by technical considerations.

Even though this illustration is not by De Hooghe himself, it resembles the headpieces which he designed. There is no obvious tendency in his work to prefer scenes of jovial sociability, even when the text allows him to do so; celebrating the joys of life is not a habitual feature of his art in the *Contes*. The only likely explanation for the artist's decision to increase the number of men included in the headpiece is that it allows the servant to express exasperation with the male tendency to indulgence in sensual pleasures, whether in drink or in sex. In this respect, 'De Hooghe' clearly sympathised with the views of Protestant Holland in the late seventeenth century, where such an attitude was not unusual,[84] though it differed markedly from that adopted by Eisen and the Fermiers the best part of a century later in (nominally) Catholic France.

## La Cruche
### Par le même auteur

*Caption: 'Jeanne renversée sur le gazon auprès de sa cruche & d'une Fontaine, accepte la mort que Jean lui propose.'*

Eisen prepared an initial version of the engraving for this *conte* which survives in only a very few copies of the work.[85] It shows a rural scene in which both figures are standing. Jean raises Jeanne's skirt, while she covers her face with her arm. On the right, from the Neptune-like face of a fountain gushes a single stream of water. Although it has some similarity

84. Many Dutch genre paintings expressed distaste for sexual and alcoholic excess, echoing the attitude in evidence here. As Bob Haak puts it: 'That smoking, drinking, card and trictrac playing, and lovemaking continued to have negative implications is clear not only from inscriptions on graphic art, but also [...] from the ceaseless warnings by seventeenth-century preachers from their pulpits' (*The Golden age: Dutch painters of the seventeenth century*, London, 1984, p.93).

85. Cohen (*Guide de l'amateur de livres*, col.568) mentions that this engraving is included in the Rothschild and Schumann copies, and suggests that it was extracted from 'une suite de Basan intitulée *Recueil de petits sujets utiles aux artistes*.' This assertion is problematic. First, no published work by Basan with this title is recorded (other *Recueils* by him are known, but they are all later than the *Contes*). Second, although Eisen occasionally collaborated with Basan, he is not known to have been involved with any of Basan's *Recueils* (Cohen, *Guide de*

to the Cochin headpiece for the *conte* (Cochin 11), it may have been rejected because it simply failed to reflect the action of the text. Before the encounter, Jeanne has stumbled and fallen, and though she presumably rises again, we are told that Jean 'Vous la jette sur le gazon' (vol.2, p.292). It would therefore have been inappropriate to show them both standing up at this point. But the engraving may also have been rejected because of the overtly sexual nature of Jean's approach, and because, like the rejected plates for 'La clochette' and 'Le diable en enfer', it could have suggested that a rape was about to take place. This avoidance of gross sexuality is characteristic of the illustrations for the 1762 edition of the *Contes*, and points to a continuing concern for propriety on the part of the Fermiers.[86]

In the engraving included in standard copies of the edition (Eisen 78), the metaphorical terms used in the text are ignored. Eisen consequently dispenses with the euphemistic 'poignard' (vol.2, p.292) which Jean uses to 'kill' Jeanne. At the same time, sexual references, both direct and indirect, are widely used here. As Philip Stewart observes (*Engraven desire*, p.80), Jean's hand is directly over Jeanne's sex; a phallic stick protrudes from the leaves at the girl's feet, while a similarly unambiguous fence-post can be seen in the centre of the illustration, above Jean's head, in parallel with the chimneys of the houses in the background. No less suggestive, but of the female sex-organ, are the open neck of the jug, the opening of the fountain and the curious fold in the middle of Jeanne's dress. This latter feature, with the material dividing the opening of the fold in two, indicates that she is a virgin, an interpretation entirely compatible with her previous ignorance of sexual matters (vol.2, p.292):

> Grand-merci Jean: je suis la plus humble des vôtres.
> Les tuez-vous comme cela?
> Vraiment j'en casserai bien d'autres.

'De Hooghe's' illustration for the *conte* is less overtly sexual than Eisen's (De Hooghe 67). Jeanne sits on the ground, her water-jug prominent but as yet unbroken (contrary to what is said in the text, but for obvious reasons); Jean, a much bigger figure, is about to embark on her seduction. His intentions are clear, and both the handles of the pump and the water-jug are adequate symbols of his alleged prowess. In the Cochin illustration, the sexual overtones are still less apparent: pointing to her broken jug, Jeanne weeps copiously as Jean brandishes a dagger before her, but this is no more than the reflection of what the text actually says, and Cochin

---

*l'amateur de livres*, col.114-17). It is more likely therefore that this plate was one of the numerous rejected designs for the *Contes* which, in one form or another, found their way into a few notable collections of the engravings.

86. Stewart's assertion (*Engraven desire*, p.79) that 'it is difficult to tell whether Jeanne's lover is beginning to lift her skirt or they are, rather, depicted after the fact' is compatible with the plate itself, but not with the description.

Cochin 11. 'La cruche', vol.2, p.254

Eisen 78. 'La cruche', vol.2, p.291

De Hooghe 67. 'La cruche', vol.2, p.263

does not seek to exploit its opportunities in the way that Eisen, and to a lesser extent 'De Hooghe', does. The artist who supplemented the De Hooghe headpieces was drawing on a long tradition of sexual symbolism in Dutch art; Eisen, for his part, could rely on the fact that in France, Jean-Baptiste Greuze among others had already popularised the use of broken jugs, dead birds and so forth to symbolise lost virginity.[87] As so often, Eisen exploits the sexual willingness of women, in accordance with the wording of the text, but in a way which is more emphatic than his predecessors, and which emphasises the instinctive, natural impulse underlying and prompting sexual behaviour.

## Promettre est un, et tenir est un autre
## Par M. Vergier

*Caption: 'Perrette est assise sur le gazon;*
*Jean, content de lui, s'en va.'*

This engraving (Eisen 79) is a good example of the ways in which Eisen uses sexual allusions and motifs directly and indirectly to comment on the story. At one level, the activities which have taken place are sufficiently indicated, in a visual analepse, by the fact that Perrette's dress is dishevelled and raised above her knee, while her legs are set apart at an angle incompatible with modesty. But Eisen is not content with these clear hints of what has transpired, and uses more subtle means as well. Jean's hat is held at the level of Perrette's sex, with the crown pointing in that direction, and at an angle which suggests how it might well appear after strenuous sexual activity. The branch above their heads is shaped and positioned to suggest a giant erect phallus, in mockery of Jean's vain pretensions. His self-satisfaction contrasts with the obvious disappointment shown on Perrette's face and with her hand-movements, which combine surprise with pensiveness. This is raw sexual nature, and a very different representation of the *conte* from that offered by either 'De Hooghe' or Cochin. 'De Hooghe' sets the scene in a bedroom, but both characters are fully clothed (De Hooghe 68). The bedclothes are undisturbed, and only Perrette's raised left leg and discarded shoe hint at recent sexual activity. Although Jean's hat is held at much the same angle as in Eisen's illustration, it is not in proximity to Perrette, and the sexual

87. His *Les Œufs cassés* (New York, Metropolitan Museum of Art) dates from 1756, and the first of several paintings entitled *Jeune fille pleurant son oiseau mort* was exhibited in 1759. Norman Bryson argues that Greuze employs the symbolism of broken jugs, lost birds and so on as a way of repressing or disavowing his desires (*Word and image*, p.150-51). This reading points up the varied senses attaching to the use of the same symbolic language in different works of art. Eisen relies on the same understanding of symbolism as Greuze, but the text supplies the preliminary information required if we are to grasp what is depicted in the engraving. He therefore does not need to conceal – or to draw attention to – his own attitude towards the symbols he employs.

Eisen 79. 'Promettre est un, et tenir est un autre', vol.2, p.293

De Hooghe 68. 'Promettre est un, et tenir est un autre', vol.2, p.266

allusion is therefore at most indirect. Although the fingers on Jean's right hand are clearly visible, the image does not suggest that he is indicating his sexual prowess; it is Perrette who, in holding up both hands, reminds us of his unfulfilled promise. In Cochin's interpretation of the story (Cochin 12), the vignette precedes any proof of Jean's prowess as a lover. The couple are sitting in the open, not far from a cottage; Jean holds up both hands in a way which seems to suggest the size of his manhood, as Perrette looks on in wonder. 'De Hooghe' offers only the vaguest of sexual hints, in keeping with the understated sexuality of all the engravings actually designed by De Hooghe, while Cochin indulges in gentle mockery of male sexual vanity. Only Eisen, whose explicitness stops just short of indecency, gives the viewer a clear idea both of the nature of what has occurred between the couple and the distance between what has been promised and what has been achieved.

## Le Rossignol
## Par M. Lamblin
## Conseiller au Parlement de Dijon
### ou
## Par M. Du Trousset de Valincourt
## De l'Académie Françoise

*Caption: 'Catherine & Richard sont sur un lit, sans drap ni couverture; la mere observe & gronde entre ses dents; Richard écoute la proposition du pere.'*

This final engraving for the *Contes* exists in two versions, one of which (Eisen 80a) is not present in most of the recorded copies of the 1762 edition; it was therefore in all probability one of the series of rejected plates.[88] It differs from the version most frequently encountered (Eisen 80b) in the layout and distribution of the figures and in its implications, rather than in its subject matter. In the rejected version, the couple lie to the left on a dishevelled bed whose immense canopy is raised to reveal the scene, and in front of which is a chair on which their clothes are spread. A chamber-pot and two pairs of shoes can be seen under the bed. Beyond the canopy are sketched classical pillars, trees and buildings. Catherine's parents are standing on the right. Her father points accusingly at Richard who, like Catherine herself, is naked. Although the details are hidden from the viewer, it can be gleaned that Catherine, in conformity with the text (vol.2, p.305), is asleep and has her hand on Richard's sex as, watched by her parents, he half-raises himself to confront them.

88. It may be based on the drawing in the Renouard copy mentioned by Cohen (*Guide de l'amateur de livres*, col.568).

Cochin 12. 'Promettre est un, et tenir est un autre', vol.2, p.257

Eisen 80a. 'Le rossignol', first version, between p.294-95

Eisen 80b. 'Le rossignol', second version, between p.294-95

In the usual version of the plate (Eisen 80b), most of these elements are retained, though in reverse. In both cases, and in keeping with his customary practice, Eisen shows the bed-curtain raised to reveal the nakedness of the couple. He again arranges the characters in two pairs, with the mother and daughter further apart than Richard and the father. In this way, he indicates, following the text, that the two men are able to agree on what should be done, while the mother is at loggerheads with her daughter, who remains asleep and uninvolved in the confrontation.

Despite these similarities, there are differences of emphasis. Most obviously, both the couple on the bed and Catherine's parents are now closer to the viewer than before. The canopy is less elaborate than in the first version; while the means by which it is held up are no longer shown, the pillars and trees are more distinctly visible in the background, and no nearby house is shown. The chamber-pot placed under the bed in the earlier engraving has now vanished, and only the two pairs of shoes remain. Catherine's discarded corsage is more prominent now than in the earlier engraving. What is more striking even than these points, however, is that the depiction of Catherine in the rejected version was presumably felt not to make sufficient use of the opportunity presented by the lines (vol.2, p.303):

> Catherine avoit dans sa main
> Ce qui servit au premier homme
> A conserver le genre humain.

This action is therefore more blatantly depicted in the second version, and in some copies of the plate at least, the head of Richard's penis can be seen.[89] In other cases (as here), this detail has been effaced by the engraver. In the earlier version, Catherine's mother is bathed in shadow to reflect her rage as reported in the text (vol.2, p.304):

> Elle voulut crier, et l'appeler mâtine,
> Chienne, effrontée, enfin tout ce qu'il vous plaira.

However, in the second version, she is more obviously overcome with shock, can scarcely believe the scene she is witnessing, and raises her hand in astonishment.[90] As a result of these changes, the scene is more precisely focused in the second version than in the first. While the absence of any local habitation may remove the danger of the family's shame becoming widely known, the mother's distress at the scene before her is more strongly depicted in the later version, transforming the event into a personal, rather than a public, disgrace. However, in showing the mother, in the later version, as overwhelmed by shock and shame, Eisen departs significantly from the text in order to contrast her responses with those of her husband.

89. Both versions are reproduced by Griffiths (*Prints for books*, p.24, 25).

90. In Eisen 80a her right arm is rendered awkwardly, providing an additional reason for replacing the plate.

The wife's reactions are caused at least as much by the realisation that her daughter is growing up as by the unexpected turn of events. Before seeing the couple together, she had referred to the girl as 'la pauvre enfant' (vol.2, p.303), and has to adjust somewhat rapidly to the idea that she is a child no longer. This double realisation is too much for her, at least as Eisen sees the matter, and the second version of the engraving brings this point out clearly. Ultimately, it is the husband who, with a more practical turn of mind, takes command of the situation, by realising that nothing is to be done except to regularise the union of the couple through marriage (vol.2, p.304-305):

> Vous m'avez fait outrage: il n'est qu'un seul moyen
>  Pour m'appaiser, et pour me satisfaire;
> C'est qu'il vous faut ici, sans délai ni refus,
>  (Sinon dites votre *In manus*)
> Epouser Catherine; elle est bien demoiselle.

Hence, the story concerns the need to accept that children grow up, and that an unmarried daughter becomes a woman, whose interests a father must safeguard as best he can. The columns in the background (which are not mentioned in the text, and which assort oddly with the contemporary dress of the parents) serve both as phallic symbols and as a reminder that it is men who keep in place the structure, the order and proportion of society. It will be remembered that kings (Louis XIV and Louis XV are cases in point) were often shown in their official portraits standing near columns, to indicate symbolically that they were the 'pillars of the state'.[91]

As ever, it is instructive to compare Eisen's interpretation of the text with that of 'De Hooghe' and Cochin. 'De Hooghe' uses pillars in much the same way as Eisen (De Hooghe 69), although he depicts a somewhat later part of the story, in that the notary is now present to regularise the couple's union (vol.2, p.305). Catherine is asleep, while Richard is presumably the figure dressed in hat and cloak standing next to the bed talking to his lover's parents. The fact that Catherine remains asleep during the proceedings is not incompatible with the text, which states simply that 'On écrivit, on signa' (vol.2, p.305). Although her consent for the marriage would obviously have been forthcoming, she is still (in the eyes of the law, if not in practice) under her parents' control, and it is primarily their permission which is needed for the matter to proceed.[92] By depicting her in this way, De Hooghe is indicating her exhaustion, and

91. Hyacinthe Rigaud's portrait of Louis XIV is in the Louvre, and Louis-Michel van Loo's painting of Louis XV is in the Wallace Collection. See Conisbee, *Painting in eighteenth-century France*, p.116-17.

92. 'Si les parties contractantes sont majeurs de 25 ans accomplis, le défaut de consentement des pere & mere n'opere pas la nullité du mariage; mais les parties, quoique majeurs de 25 ans, sont obligées de demander par écrit le consentement de leurs pere & mere, & à leur défaut de leurs ayeul & ayeule, pour se mettre à couvert de l'exhérédation' (Jaucourt, article 'Mariage', 1765, *Encyclopédie*, vol.10, p.108).

De Hooghe 69. 'Le rossignol', vol.2, p.269

her indifference to the legal formalities required by her parents. They, appropriately on this view, are visible only as a shadowy presence in the background, while Catherine, Richard (?) and the notary are highlighted as more substantial figures. In Cochin's vignette, we see a large bed, with a curtain partly drawn back to reveal in the background the upper part of Catherine's naked body. Only the top of Richard's head can be seen from the viewer's perspective. The husband and wife are arguing on the other side of the curtain, with a large window behind them to light the room. There is no suggestion that the scene takes place on a balcony exposed to the open air, as Eisen and 'De Hooghe' are careful to indicate, nor does the architecture take on a symbolic value. In contrast, both versions of the Eisen illustration, with their nudity, their affirmation of female sexuality, and the attempt to assert male authority, form a wholly appropriate ending to the *Contes et nouvelles en vers*.

# 4. The lessons of the Eisen illustrations

## i. General observations on the interpretation
of the illustrations

No study of a complex literary text, or of a set of sophisticated illustrations, can hope to exhaust their meaning or their interest. La Fontaine's *Contes et nouvelles en vers* have been closely scrutinised, and have attracted (often unfavourable) comment, for over three centuries. Eisen's illustrations for the 1762 edition have long been admired, and their genesis has been known in minute detail for a century or more, thanks to the labours of Renouard, Cohen and others. Commentators such as Owen Holloway, Philip Stewart and Antony Griffiths have likewise done much to advance our understanding of the relationship between text and illustration in French books of the eighteenth century. Nonetheless, the 1762 edition, for all its bibliographical pre-eminence, has not previously been investigated in detail from this point of view.

The general premise underlying the approach to the *Contes* adopted here was set out in the first part of this study. It is that the Fermiers withdrew the edition from the market because, in the climate of hostility towards them which prevailed in the early 1760s, the defence of their lifestyle and values embodied in the engravings would have increased public animosity towards them. Only the Eisen illustrations differentiate the 1762 edition from its predecessors, and it is the attitudes and values to which they testify which need to be understood in any examination of their content. The salient points in Eisen's rendering of the stories of La Fontaine have been set out in the previous section, and it is time now to formulate some general conclusions about what we can learn from such a study. We shall begin by describing some practical considerations impinging on the analysis of the plates, before discussing what they tell us of the Fermiers and their reasons for publishing their edition.

## ii. The presentation of the plates – themes and variations

### *The position of the plates in the edition*

In examining the plates for this edition, it is essential to remind ourselves first of all of the contrast which they offered with the existing tradition of illustrating the work. The headpiece-engravings by Romeyn de Hooghe which were first used in 1685, and which were repeatedly employed in editions published in the eighteenth century, were finally supplanted only in 1743; yet the headpieces which Cochin designed for the edition published that year were smaller than those of De Hooghe.[1] In using full-page illustrations, the Fermiers were therefore breaking decisively with a long-standing tradition, and changing significantly the ways in which the *Contes* were read.[2]

Whereas the De Hooghe and Cochin illustrations are placed above the opening lines of each *conte*, those by Eisen are placed before the text, or, in the case of *contes* with several engravings, as close as possible to the section of the text from which they derive. In virtually all cases, the engraving is placed so that the reader has the relevant text and the plate in the same opening. In a few instances, where the relevant text within a *conte* is printed on the recto of a leaf, and hence on the viewer's right-hand side, the engraving is positioned to open on the left, so that the reader does not see it until the page is turned. In such examples, the opening of the plate may have an effect of surprise, since the reader has no advance warning of the challenge to conventional values which is to come. This is especially true of the third engraving for 'Joconde', which shows the queen dallying with her dwarf. It is true also of the second engraving for 'Le petit chien qui secoue de l'argent et des pierreries' in which Anselme is shown prostrating himself before the Moor whose catamite he is to become. In other instances, however, the effect is less striking because the subject matter is in itself less unusual (for example, the second engraving for 'La gageure des trois commères'). But whether the plate is positioned before a text or within it, the reader cannot deal simultaneously with text and image. The engraving is dependent on the text, and would have little 'meaning' without it, except in the most basic sense of showing recognisable people and objects in relation to one another.

The reasons why characters behave as shown in the illustration, the relationship between them, the significance of the locations, and even the historical period at which the scene is set, are all matters closely linked to the way in which the artist sets about interpreting the text. But they are in turn wholly dependent, in either a positive or a negative sense, on what the text has to say. For this reason, readers must bring to bear two separate processes in order to grasp the significance of the engraving at any level above that of simple embellishment. They must read the text and then turn to the illustration (or vice versa) to see how the text has been interpreted visually, and how it differs from the engraving. Of course, many readers will not take so much trouble over the plates. Even so, the care with which the Fermiers and their artists approached the task of illustrating the *Contes* suggests that they intended the engravings to be

1. De Hooghe's headpieces are approximately 70 mm × 80 mm; Cochin's are 52 mm × 70 mm.

2. The plates for the edition of 1755 were full-page, but to judge from bibliographical evidence it was uncommon, and unlikely to have had much impact. The technical quality of its illustrations is also greatly inferior to that of plates for other eighteenth-century editions of the *Contes*.

examined in some detail, and not to serve merely as a decorative appendage to the text.

## *The variations between copies*

One consideration which complicates the reader's assessment of the plates in this edition, is that the experience of reading the work may not always be the same, since the engravings may vary from one copy to another. Although twenty or more plates initially designed by Eisen were rejected for various reasons, their existence made possible a considerable number of permutations. Thus, copies of the *Contes* can often be found containing either the original or the replacement version of many of these plates, with no obvious explanation to account for their apparently random selection. In some cases, the rejected version was included, but the replacement was not, and vice versa; in others, the rejected and the replacement versions were included side by side. Only a few copies contained virtually all the rejected plates and their replacements, together with proofs of those printed in very small numbers, and so on. Information on how the plates in individual copies were selected is virtually non-existent, but the wide variations between copies do suggest that, while a few were specially made up to be exceptional, most of the others were put together haphazardly.[3] This situation is wholly untypical of illustrated French books of the eighteenth century, and is one more reason why the 1762 edition of the *Contes* stands apart from other comparable works of the time.

The differences between the rejected and the replacement versions of the plates are sometimes considerable, sometimes slight. They consist often in the perspective which the artist adopts, in the closeness or otherwise of the viewer to the scene represented, or in the degree of nudity shown. In a few instances the two versions are radically distinct: the dull original designs for 'L'oraison de S. Julien' and 'La coupe enchantée' were understandably replaced by more telling engravings, and the second version of the plate for 'sœur Jeanne' is a thorough reworking of the story. These details, as we have argued, can often signify a very great discrepancy in approach, so that even (sometimes) subtle distinctions between two versions can offer clues to a very different attitude on the part of the designer or his editors. The two engravings for 'La clochette', or for 'La cruche', are cases in point. When the plates are distinct in the degree of nakedness which they depict (as with 'Le cas de conscience', or 'Le rossignol'), readers could obviously react differently to each of them, in accordance with the view they took of such matters.

Because of the variations in the plates from one copy to another, and because each tale is largely independent of the others, and can be read in

---

3. See also Griffiths, *Prints for books*, p.22-23.

whole or in part, and in any order, individual readers were free to arrive at widely differing interpretations of the *Contes*. The latitude thus given to them is a crucial factor in assessing the significance of the plates. It goes far towards explaining the distinctive importance of the edition not only in purely bibliographical terms, but also in terms of what it tells us about the Fermiers, their values and their attitudes towards their critics. In this respect, the printed descriptions accompanying the plates in the *Avis au relieur* are eloquent testimony to the wider purposes of the edition.

## The printed descriptions of the engravings[4]

If the placing of the plates is a significant factor in the *Rezeptionsästhetik* of the *Contes*, so too is the handling of the descriptions which accompany them. In French illustrated books of the eighteenth century, a variety of practices can be observed in the use of descriptions and captions. Often, no captions were used at all, and it was left to the reader to determine the relationship of the plate to the text. This practice was common in those relatively few novels which were illustrated, and in which only a page-indication on the plate showed where it was to be inserted in the volume.[5] In other cases, especially with plays, an untitled plate was placed at the start of the text to which it related, as a frontispiece; this practice was used, for example, with Gravelot's illustrations for Luneau de Boisjermain's' edition of the works of Racine (1768).[6] Sometimes, the name of the text was added as a subtitle to the engraving, as with Boucher's illustrations for the works of Molière (1734), and the Oudry/Cochin illustrations for La Fontaine's *Fables choisies* (1755-1759). Another way of captioning the engravings, which Gravelot adopted for *Le Théâtre de Pierre Corneille* (1764), was to add below the printed area the lines of text on which the scene shown was based. With historical works in particular, this technique was carried further, in that detailed information on the scene depicted was added in a cartouche at the foot of the engraving. This was the device adopted by Nicolas de Fer for his *Histoire des Rois de France depuis Pharamond* (Paris, J. F. Benard, 1722) and by Cochin in his full-page engravings for Hénault's *Abrégé chronologique de l'histoire de France*, 2 vols (Paris, Prault, 1768). Captions of this kind were, of course, a particular feature of books in larger format such as quarto or folio, which afforded the space needed for the (often copious) wording. However, it can

4. As was indicated in the second part of this study, the descriptions referred to in discussing the 1762 edition are those contained in the *Avis au relieur*.

5. Examples include *Les Caprices du destin* by Mlle L'Héritier (1718); *Le Gage touché* by Eustache Le Noble (1722); Marivaux's *La Vie de Marianne* (1731-1741), and Diderot's *Les Bijoux indiscrets* (1748). The page indications of illustrations in novels were often retained when the same engravings were reused, so that they are sometimes wrongly positioned in later reprints.

6. Cohen (*Guide de l'amateur de livres*, col.848) notes that in this edition 'les figures sont presque toujours sans légende'.

sometimes also be found in books of smaller size, such as Le Maire's *Les Traits de l'histoire universelle* (1760). In all these examples, the information which the reader was thought to need was communicated integrally with the engraving itself.[7] The Fermiers, however, chose to proceed otherwise, taking their cue from another well-established method for describing the content of illustrations, about which something must now be said.

The 1751 edition of Erasmus's *Eloge de la Folie* (Paris, no pub.) has engravings which are untitled, but which are described in a detailed *Explication des figures, qui indique en même-tems leur place*, inserted after the title-page. With Sève's engravings for the *Œuvres de Racine* (1760), only the name of the play to which the plate serves as a frontispiece is given at the foot of the engraving. An extensive *Explication des planches* (including the vignettes) is however inserted at the start of each of the three volumes. The explanatory notes for the plates are detailed, and often involve an analysis of the motivations and conduct of the characters at that point in the play. Hence, the engraving for *Mithridate* is presented in these terms: 'Le jaloux Mithridate ne voulant point après lui laisser survivre Monime, avoit chargé Arcas, un de ses Officiers, de présenter à cette Princesse la coupe empoisonnée: au moment que Monime alloit avaler le poison, arrive Arbate, qui de l'ordre de Mithridate, arrache la Coupe & jette le poison. Acte V. Scène III.'[8]

Perhaps the most striking example of this tendency, and certainly one of the most successful books in which it can be observed, was Rousseau's *Julie ou la Nouvelle Héloïse* (Amsterdam, Rey, 1761).[9] He attached considerable importance to ensuring that the twelve engravings (which were eventually designed by Gravelot) were properly placed in relation to the text, and worried endlessly about the details of the individual plates.[10] Subtitles were added to each engraving, except the last showing the death of Julie, but their main interest from our point of view lies in the extensive commentaries by Rousseau which accompany them, and which offer copious insights into the thoughts, feelings and conduct of the figures depicted. The information is in fact so detailed that, as he himself recognised,

7. Such examples Roland Barthes called 'ancrage', in that the significance of the wording is limited to informing us about the image in question ('Rhétorique de l'image', *Communications* 4, 1964, p.40-51).

8. *Œuvres de Racine*, 3 vols (Paris, [Le Breton], 1760), vol.2, p.2.

9. Though the work is usually known by this name, it was of course called *Lettres de deux amants* [...]. Rousseau had originally wanted François Boucher to carry out the work, because he would design the plates 'supérieurement [...] dans la perfection que l'entreprise éxige' (see his letter of 21 June 1759 to his publisher Marc-Michel Rey (*Correspondance complète de Rousseau*, ed. R. A. Leigh, 52 vols, Geneva, Madison, WI, Banbury, Oxford, 1965-1989, no.836). It seems likely that this plan foundered for financial reasons (see Jo-Ann E. McEachern, *Bibliography of the writings of Jean-Jacques Rousseau to 1800*, 2 vols, Oxford, 1993, vol.1, p.133-34).

10. For details, see Cohen, *Guide de l'amateur de livres*, col.904-905, and McEachern, *Bibliography of the writings of Jean-Jacques Rousseau*, p.133-41.

it was virtually impossible for any engraver to convey in such a limited space all the nuances implied by the descriptive material, which was intended primarily to clarify the sense of the illustrations.[11]

Hence, by 1762, the Fermiers had at their disposal a range of recent precedents allowing them to interpret, explain or comment on the illustrations to the *Contes*. In the event, they departed from previous practice by directing their remarks not at the reader but at the binder, in a sixteen-page *Avis au Relieur. Pour placer les Estampes des Contes de M. de La Fontaine dans l'Edition d'Amsterdam 1762.*[12] In both the *Œuvres de Racine* and *La Nouvelle Héloïse*, the explanatory material is bound integrally with the text and included in the pagination. In the *Eloge de la folie* (which was illustrated by Eisen), the *Explication* is unpaginated; it is bound and signed separately, but is obviously intended to clarify for the reader the sense of the engravings. The Fermiers' decision to separate the *Avis* from what precedes, and the essentially factual tone of the wording describing the plates, might therefore suggest that it was not intended to be seen as an integral part of the *Contes*. Yet since it is present in the great majority of copies,[13] the studied neutrality of its descriptions, and the jocular over-precision of its title, could equally be read as a game which the editors are playing with readers. And indeed, such playfulness would not be out of place in the category which the *Contes* are often said to exemplify, that of the rococo book.

## iii. The *Contes* as a rococo book

The term 'rococo' was invented in the nineteenth century to describe (often pejoratively) the art of the eighteenth. Thus the *Oxford English dictionary*, whose origins go back to the mid-nineteenth century, defines 'Rococo' as 'having the characteristics of Louis Quatorze or Louis Quinze workmanship, such as conventional shell- and scroll-work, meaningless decoration; excessively or tastelessly florid or ornate.' While 'rococo' is now perhaps less a term of abuse than it was, it is still associated with the self-consciously pleasing and pretty. Michael Levey defends it for its engagement with humanity in the paintings of Watteau, but acknowledges that it was preoccupied with a desire 'to be decorative and light-hearted' which resulted in its 'disengagement from reality.'[14] Writing in

11. 'La plupart de ces sujets sont détaillés pour les faire entendre, beaucoup plus qu'ils ne peuvent l'être dans l'exécution' (*Recueil d'estampes pour la nouvelle Héloïse*, Amsterdam, Rey, 1761, p.[3]). Duchesne published another edition of the *Recueil* in Paris. See Cohen, *Guide de l'amateur de livres*, col.904, and Ray, *The Art of the French illustrated book*, p.42. See also Stewart, *Engraven desire*, p.19-21.

12. The *Avis* was not included in the table of contents, and its position varies from copy to copy.

13. Cohen (*Guide de l'amateur de livres*, col.558) includes the *Avis* in the collation of the *Contes*, as an integral part of the work.

14. Michael Levey, *Rococo to revolution* (London, 1977), p.52.

1982, Gordon Ray did not dissent from the Goncourt brothers' judgement a century earlier that in illustrated rococo books ' "prettiness [...] became the soul of the age" '.[15] Readers of the article 'Rococo style' in the *Catholic encyclopedia online* today will learn that 'The "beautiful sensuality" is effected by masterly technique, especially in the colouring, and to a great extent by quite immoral licenses or mythological nudities as in loose or indelicate romances. [...] Rococo is indeed really empty, solely a pleasing play of the fancy.'[16]

These comments had in a sense been anticipated two centuries earlier, when the rococo was at its height, even though the term itself had not yet come into being. As Marian Hobson has argued, eighteenth-century commentators had much the same objections in mind when they attacked the *papillotage* of contemporary art. Their objection was that such an approach led to the discontinuity and interruption of the aesthetic experience, resulting in a fragmenting of the spectator's attention. As a consequence, the viewer is repeatedly made aware, as he tries to find the unity of a work of art, that what he is offered is an illusion, rather than a representation, a false, rather than a true, rendering of nature.[17]

This persistent tendency to regard rococo illustrations as designed to please, but also to mislead or even to corrupt, has led to their being under-appreciated for what they tell us about the values of those who created (or, as in the case of the *Contes*, commissioned) them. While the adjective 'rococo' describes in convenient shorthand the overall style used for illustrations at this period, it tells us nothing about their relationship to the text on which they are based, or the purposes which they served. This silence on the part of commentators has its origins in the belief that what matters is the technique of the illustrations. As their content is necessarily dependent on the text which inspired them, that content in itself can matter only insofar as it represents a visual rendering (though not necessarily an equivalent) of the text. The comments of Boissais and Deleplanque, writing in 1948, are wholly representative of this attitude. Discussing French engravers of the eighteenth century, they write: 'Tous possèdent une étourdissante virtuosité. De leurs doigts, naissent à miracle les compositions les plus variées. Ils dessinent rapidement, nettement [...]. Ce que l'emphase parfois, et la froideur aussi ne sauraient cacher, c'est une infaillible science du dessin, un bon goût, un sérieux réel, qualités non exclusives, elles-mêmes, de noblesse et de distinction.'[18] Because this attitude remains widespread even today, the illustrations in books of this period are not usually considered from the point of view of the social and political circumstances in which they were produced. The fact that this perspective is generally forsaken when examining the self-consciously

15. Ray, *The Art of the French illustrated book*, p.6.
16. The text may be consulted at http://www.newadvent.org/cathen/13106a.htm.
17. Hobson, *The Object of art*, p.52-55.
18. Boissais and Deleplanque, *Les Livres à gravures au dix-huitième siècle*, p.20-21.

'committed' illustrations produced at the time of the French Revolution only underlines the dichotomy which has developed in approaches to works published before and after 1789. Gordon Ray makes the point when he argues that in the 1790s 'The great new presence was Jacques-Louis David (1748-1825) who employed neo-classicism to depict the civic virtues of victorious Romans and a little later the noble simplicity of the primitive Greeks. His painting was stark, engaged, and linear, in contrast to that of the *galant* eighteenth century with its playful, curvilinear depiction of light and frivolous subjects.'[19]

Even if one accepted that the illustrations in rococo books deserved such censure, it would not follow that La Fontaine's *Contes* should be summarily dismissed as being tainted with the same alleged vices. It is undeniable that Eisen's illustrations are highly ornamented, that everyday objects are depicted with much attention to detail, and that the compositions are indeed pleasing to the eye. While features such as flowing draperies, billowing cloaks and so on may indeed link the engravings to what is customarily called the rococo, there are significant discrepancies which justify our examining them in a way which is not limited by this predetermined perspective. For one thing, the most characteristic appurtenances of rococo painting (clouds, putti and classical inspiration) are rarely to be found in these engravings, so that the typical rococo frame of reference is singularly diminished, and replaced by the contemporary, the everyday and the down-to-earth. It is true that what Norman Bryson calls 'body as posture'[20] can be found in the engravings, since the female body, in particular, is often presented for our admiration. We are offered a depiction of women who have aroused the desires of suitors, adulterous husbands, lecherous monks or other male participants shown in the engravings; were such women to be presented as unattractive, the engraving would lose its point. This is somewhat different, nonetheless, from the position described by Bryson, in which 'the male within the painting acts as surrogate for the male viewer, to whose sexuality the image is exclusively addressed'.[21] Rather, the reverse is true: usually, the male character in the *conte* is, first and foremost, attracted to the female, and the response of the viewer is of secondary importance; we do not need to share his reaction (and may not do so) in order to understand the story. Nor do Eisen's engravings display the 'elimination of coherent space' which Bryson also discerns as one of the characteristics of rococo painting,[22] since they are set in a recognisable world of objects, furniture, buildings, and so on which stand in perfectly normal relation to one another. It is therefore not sufficient to label the engravings as rococo and pass on. While they display some elements of

19. Ray, *The Art of the French illustrated book*, p.119.
20. Bryson, *Word and image*, p.95.
21. Bryson, *Word and image*, p.98.
22. Bryson, *Word and image*, p.96.

the rococo, and a preoccupation with human sexuality in particular, it still remains to establish how that preoccupation is transmitted to the reader or viewer, and whether the illustrations deserve the moral censure normally meted out to the *Contes* as a text.

The stories are usually derived from earlier sources, especially Rabelais, Ariosto's *Orlando furioso*, Boccaccio's *Decamerone*, the *Heptaméron* of Marguerite de Navarre, and the *Nouvelles Récréations* of Bonaventure Des Périers.[23] Very few are, so far as can be judged, La Fontaine's own invention, and even these, like the stories in the other works on which he drew for his material, are based on motifs which are both ancient and widespread in European literature.[24] Hence, if the *Contes* were indeed the object of justified criticism on moral grounds, such criticisms would necessarily have to encompass much of western literature at the same time. This point can be reinforced by a consideration of the attitudes towards morality and literature in the eighteenth century, and the particular place of nudity in French illustrated books of the period.

## iv. Nudity in French illustrated books of the eighteenth century

From what has been said already, it should be apparent that the *Contes* as such do not deserve to be more heavily criticised for their impropriety than many other significant works in the European literary landscape. It is also true that the engravings to be found in many of the editions prior to that of 1762 do not reflect the 'immorality' which the text was so often said to exemplify. Those earlier engravings are chiefly the work of De Hooghe and Cochin, who enjoyed considerable fame as illustrators of books, and as artists in their own right.[25] Nonetheless, a comparison of their engravings for the *Contes* with those of Eisen shows that they are rarely as inventive or as complex as the latter. It is of course true that they were labouring under practical constraints, such as the dimensions of the engravings which they were asked to provide. It is also true that the customs and manners of their times gave them less freedom in dealing with sexual matters. Consequently, in a more restricted space, they are more restrained in depicting the sexual activities which figure so prominently in the *Contes*. Time and again, Eisen shows in some detail physical activities at which De Hooghe and Cochin merely hint. It is true, as Gordon Ray observes (*The Art of the French illustrated book*, p.3) that eighteenth-century artists, including Eisen, were often indebted to De Hooghe

23. On La Fontaine's debt to these and other authors, see Lapp, *The Esthetics of negligence*.

24. See Catherine Grisé, 'Jean de La Fontaine's *Contes*: a poetic patchwork of folklore motifs', *Romance notes* 37:1 (1996), p.155-73.

25. See John Landwehr, *Romeyn de Hooghe, 1645-1708, as book illustrator: a bibliography* (Amsterdam and New York, 1970); Michel, *Charles-Nicolas Cochin et le livre illustré*.

for their inspiration. Even so, it is hard to agree wholly with his verdict that 'the elegance and relative decorum of the later rococo illustrations do not disguise their frequent dependence on his vigorous baroque inventions'.

'Decorum' is not the first quality that springs to mind in examining Eisen's illustrations for the *Contes*. If he clearly separates himself in some respects from the De Hooghe tradition, he is no less anxious to draw a distinction between his work for the *Contes* and that of Cochin *fils*. Ray asserts that Cochin's vignettes for the 1743/1745 edition 'are marked not only by the mastery of outline and firmness of composition which never deserted him, but also by acute observation and unpretentious humor' (p.28). One wonders, however, what 'firmness' means in this instance, when Cochin's often hesitant and sketchy designs are compared with those of Eisen; and how much more acute Eisen typically is at conveying the appetites, impulses and self-interest which are inseparable from La Fontaine's characters in the *Contes*.

What, perhaps more than anything, distinguishes Eisen from his two major predecessors is his use of nudity. The reason for this change of emphasis is not simply that Eisen was personally more inclined to the depiction of nudity than his predecessors (though from what we know of his private life, he was far from being strait-laced).[26] Nor were the Fermiers themselves more inclined than previous editors to take pleasure in the naked human form. It is, rather, that the eighteenth-century illustrated book gradually came to feature engravings in which nudity featured prominently. To find confirmation that this is so, we need go back no further than the beginning of the century. Some of the plates designed (and repeatedly used) for one or other of the innumerable editions of Fénelon's *Aventures de Télémaque* which flooded the market after its first appearance in 1699 contain nude figures. Those engraved by the Regent Philippe d'Orléans for an edition of Longus' *Daphnis et Chloé* (1718) likewise feature men and women who are naked, or partly so.[27] Yet in both cases, the nudity shown is as much a matter of scale as of decency. Works published in the first half of the eighteenth century are discreet in their depiction of the naked human form. The viewer is held at a considerable distance from these small-scale figures, or else they are shown modestly hidden by bushes, strategically-placed garments, and so on. But the same is not true after 1750, when nudity becomes much more common in illustrated books, and the viewer is rather closer to it.

Examples of this trend are not hard to find, both in works of literature and, perhaps surprisingly, in works of history. In 1757 there appeared in

26. See chapter 1 of this study, p.44, n.173.
27. Typical illustrations for these works are reproduced in Ray, *The Art of the French illustrated book*, p.8, 10.

Paris the five volumes of Boccaccio's *Il Decamerone*.[28] Both Cochin and Eisen (as well as other designers) contributed a number of plates, but most of the 110 engravings which are its chief glory were designed by Gravelot. They are noteworthy for offering numerous examples of the close-up view of nude figures (especially female figures) which we find in the *Contes*. Some clue to changing tastes in this regard is contained in a contemporary letter from Gravelot to his publishers, agreeing to provide a series of 'figures libres' to illustrate various scenes in *Il Decamerone*. This supplementary group, or *Suite libre* was, at their request, to be offered to the public separately from the engravings included in standard copies of the work:[29]

Ce que vous me demandez [he writes] se peut faire mais, pour rendre les choses suivant votre idée, cela exige de votre part une explication plus décidée et que je susse bien jusqu'à quel point je dois pousser la gaillardise [...] quant au fini que vous désirez, je vous promets d'y apporter mes soins, et enfin de mettre à ces desseins toute la correction et l'expression dont je puis être capable; moyennant quoi je ne vois pas que je puisse demander moins de soixante francs pour chacun.[30]

As the parallel illustrations reproduced by Stewart (*Engraven desire*, p.326-32) readily demonstrate, these additional engravings are much more sexually explicit than the standard series, in that they feature men with erections, couples having intercourse, etc. But Gravelot's letter is interesting at least as much for what it tells us about his own doubts and hesitations as for his willingness to provide material of this kind. He asks for more information ('une explication plus décidée') before embarking on these designs, and he is unsure how far he should go in depicting 'la gaillardise'. His reactions rather suggest that there was no commonly accepted standard in these matters among publishers at the time, and that he was unused to devising such designs. He is aware that such work is specialised, and is careful to stipulate that the price will be higher than usual (otherwise, he would presumably have accepted the same rate as he received for the standard illustrations). Gravelot was also the artist responsible for the twelve (anonymous) plates included in the first illustrated edition of Voltaire's *La Pucelle d'Orléans* in 1762. Here again, the viewer is permitted to see naked flesh, both male and female, and again is closer to the figures depicted than in works from the earlier part of the century.

28. See Cohen, *Guide de l'amateur de livres*, col.158-60. The imprint is 'Londra', but the Parisian origins of the book are beyond doubt, for documentary as well as bibliographical reasons. A French translation, using the same figures, was produced in 1757-1761; it has the imprint 'Londres'.

29. Hence, copies in eighteenth-century bindings can be found both with and without the 'suite libre'.

30. Quoted by Stewart, *Engraven desire*, p.324-25. Cohen (*Guide de l'amateur de livres*, col.159) states that these plates are indeed the work of Gravelot.

Even some works of history exhibit the same tendency at this time. In 1760, just as the Fermiers were preparing their edition of the *Contes et nouvelles en vers*, there appeared the first of six volumes edited by the abbé Aubert, with illustrations by Le Maire, and cumbersomely entitled *Les Traits de l'histoire universelle, sacrée et profane, d'après les plus grands peintres et les meilleurs écrivains. Dédiés à Monseigneur le duc de Bourgogne*. This collection, which has both an *Approbation* and a *Privilège*, ran to six volumes published between 1760 and 1762.[31] The two volumes of the *Traits* dealing with the *Histoire poétique* (1761)[32] contain in all 225 engravings and extracts, mostly based on paintings by well-known artists and drawn mainly from the *Odyssey*, the *Æneid*, and Ovid's *Metamorphoses*. The majority of the plates (some 160) depict men and women in various states of undress, including complete nakedness (though decency is preserved throughout). Hence, at the time when the illustrations for the 1762 *Contes* were being prepared, the royal imprimatur was given to a work dedicated to a prince of the blood, which used engravings to affirm its moralising aims. What is more, those engravings were frequently not dissimilar (in subject matter, if not in quality) to those produced by Eisen for the *Contes*.

When the Fermiers commissioned the illustrations for their edition of the *Contes* in the 1750s, there was a growing trend towards nude illustration in books. Nonetheless, their rejection of engravings which were considered to be too explicit (as well as for other reasons) shows that they were not willing to go down the same path as the publishers of *Il Decamerone*. There is no separate series of unbridled 'gravures libres' for their edition of the *Contes*.[33] The style of Eisen's engravings, with its emphasis on flowing draperies, abundant clothing, luxurious interiors and so forth, is undoubtedly characteristic of 'rococo' books. At the same time, the discreet use of nude figures which are seen in close-up is characteristic of books produced from the 1750s onwards, and it is to this new tendency that, to a large degree, the *Contes* bear witness. But this conclusion tells only part of the story, since nude illustrations, whatever their importance, are only one aspect of the role of engravings in French books at that period. Indeed, the whole question of the place of illustrations in books of this period needs fuller study than it has received hitherto; the following remarks are intended only as preliminary observations on this larger question, which needs to be dealt with in a separate study.

31. It is not recorded by Cohen, but is mentioned (slightingly) by Grimm in the *CL* for 1 May 1760 (vol.3, p.235).
32. These are the only volumes which I have been able to consult. Very few complete copies are recorded.
33. Compare Griffiths, *Prints for books*, p.22.

## v. The place of illustrations in eighteenth-century French books

Despite the high reputation of French illustrated books of the eighteenth century, it has to be remembered that many works of literature issued before 1750 were unillustrated; novels and historical works were plentiful and popular, and if they sold well without the expense of illustrations, the publisher's profits would accrue accordingly. In other cases, the same plates were used (or copied) time and again from one edition to another. The reason for this practice was essentially economic: good engravings cost money, and reusing them as much as possible reduced the publisher's outlay.[34] Even when the original plates became too worn to be pressed into service, they could be copied without significant differences to capitalise on the appeal of those used before.

This was of course a long-standing tradition. Holbein's original illustrations for the *Les Simulachres & histories faces de la mort* (1538), which was often reissued as *Le Triomphe de la mort*, were copied and recopied for hundreds of years.[35] And there are examples of the practice after 1700 too. Two prominent literary texts, *Les Aventures de Télémaque* (1699) and *Daphnis et Chloé* (1718), were repeatedly illustrated with the same plates.[36] In the case of poems, too, repetition of the tried and trusted was the order of the day. Hence, Voltaire's *La Henriade* (originally published without plates as *La Ligue* in 1723) was first illustrated, in quarto format in 1728, and the engravings, reduced in size, were copied for editions in 1741 and 1748.[37] In the case of La Fontaine's *Contes*, the repeated use of De Hooghe's illustrations between 1685 and 1743 is a striking example of this practice with particular relevance to our present concerns.[38] There is some evidence therefore that in the first half of the century, illustrations were used because they were already well known, and that those who bought books expected to find them illustrated with traditional plates, rather than with new and unfamiliar interpretations of the text. For this reason, it would not, on the whole, be true to say that this was a period of bold innovation or experimentation in the field of the illustrated book.[39]

34. Many works boasted nothing more than a frontispiece, and here again economies could be made. For example, the same frontispiece by Bernard Picart was used in Des Periers's *Cymbalum mundi* (Amsterdam, Prosper Marchand, 1711) and in Mme de La Fayette's *Histoire de la Cour de France pour les années 1688 et 1689* (Amsterdam, Jean-Frédéric Bernard, 1731).

35. For eighteenth-century French editions, see Cohen, *Guide de l'amateur de livres*, col.492.

36. See Cohen, *Guide de l'amateur de livres*, respectively col.379-90 and 649-55.

37. Cohen, *Guide de l'amateur de livres*, col.1025-26.

38. The most detailed list of the plates in the various editions is that of Hédé-Haüy, *Les Illustrations des Contes de La Fontaine*.

39. In *The Art of the French illustrated book*, Gordon Ray includes an appendix (p.530-32) of '100 outstanding French illustrated books, 1700-1914'. Only two are earlier than 1750, while twenty-three are included for the years 1750-1800.

This conservatism needs to be borne in mind when we come to assess the originality of the engravings for the 1762 edition of the *Contes*. At the same time, if engravings did not feature prominently in books of this period, the reasons were not purely economic, but aesthetic too, in that illustrations were not always well regarded as an artistic medium.

Much has been written on the role of truth and 'illusion' as terms of art criticism in the eighteenth century, but to a large extent the debates taking place at the time do not affect the artistic status of engravings. Marian Hobson observes that 'illusion' was a term applied essentially to the low genres, such as still-life painting, as a way of indicating that the painter had successfully rendered 'la chose même'.[40] But whatever the importance of 'illusion' as an aesthetic criterion at that time, Philip Stewart argues that engravings as a medium of artistic expression were exempted from these basic considerations: 'engraving [...] does not imitate objects themselves [...] but only their highlights and shadows [...] that is a highly privileged situation for any artistic medium in an era where illusion was arguably more crucial to the notion of æsthetic response than was reference' (*Engraven desire*, p.13). Even if it could be argued that engravings did occupy this privileged position in the artistic pantheon of the time, it is demonstrably true that, like low genres such as still-life painting, they were not universally regarded as having much intrinsic merit. In the words of one contemporary commentator whom Stewart quotes, illustrations in books were merely an 'agrément', and were not to be compared with the triumphs of the Dutch old masters.[41] Support for this view can be found in other writings of the time. While preparing his own edition of the works of Corneille in 1761, Voltaire wrote to Fyot de La Marche: 'je n'ai jamais trop aimé les estampes dans les livres; que m'importe une taille-douce quand je lis le second livre de Virgile, et quel burin ajoutera quelque chose à la description de la ruine de Troie? Mais les souscripteurs aiment ces pompons, et il faut les contenter.'[42]

What is significant, however, is that, despite this trenchant dismissal of the illustrated book, Voltaire acted on his belief that readers preferred their books to have plates, even when nothing useful was gained by such ornamentation. He therefore took considerable pains to commission plates of distinctive quality for *La Henriade* (1728), *La Pucelle d'Orléans* (1762) as well as for *Le Théâtre de Pierre Corneille*, which finally appeared in 1764.[43]

---

40. Hobson, *The Object of art*, p.69.

41. Stewart, *Engraven desire*, p.13. The reference is to Louis Doissin's poem *La Gravure* (1753). A similar view was voiced by Watelet in the article 'Gravure' in the *Encyclopédie* (1757).

42. D10062.

43. For details, see Cohen, *Guide de l'amateur de livres*, respectively col.1025, 1029-30, and 255-56. Cochin père designed the plates for *La Henriade*; those for *La Pucelle* and the works of Corneille are by Gravelot.

Voltaire's example in itself tells us that it would be simplistic to regard the role of illustrations in books of this period as consisting in 'mere' embellishment: on the contrary, there was a public demand for them, which authors ignored at their cost. Such a contention is difficult to justify, too, in the light of the enormous effort which the Fermiers and their artists invested in the engravings for the 1762 *Contes*, and especially when one considers their decision to reject so many of the initial designs. To understand more fully the purposes which the Fermiers were attempting to achieve in the *Contes* as a whole, we need to consider primarily not the theoretical importance of engravings, or the opinions of Voltaire, but the functions illustrations actually performed in French books of the eighteenth century.

From the very abundant evidence available to us, it is clear that engravings were intended to serve several distinct purposes.[44] Broadly speaking, three categories can be established.

The first comprises works of reference, such as the *Encyclopédie* (1751-1772), or the *Description des arts et métiers* which appeared in twenty-nine folio volumes between 1761 and 1778.[45] In works of this kind, copperplates have an explicative function, helping to clarify, through line drawings, diagrams and 'exploded' views of machinery and other equipment, many industrial and craft processes which would otherwise be all but incomprehensible to the uninitiated reader relying solely on printed accounts of what is involved.[46] Such engravings may also encompass physiological and other medical topics, serving as anatomical primers, as in the works of Gautier d'Agoty and others.[47] In this sense, they are linked to engravings of another significant type, namely those used in books dealing with natural history, such as Buffon's *Histoire naturelle*.[48] The plates found in works of this latter kind are essentially intended to inform, and to act as a quick, non-technical guide to the external, physical distinctions between one species and another. At the same time, they enable readers to identify fauna by their primary

44. No account is taken here of the numerous 'livres de colportage' which circulated at the time, and which were illustrated, often with poor-quality woodcuts of a very antiquated kind, rather than with copperplates. Some consideration of them can be found in Bassy, 'Le texte et l'image', p.158. On book illustrations at this period, see Griffiths, *Prints for books*, passim.

45. Accusations that Diderot had plagiarised from the plates for the *Description* prepared by Réaumur surfaced in the 1750s. On this question, see Jacques Proust, 'La documentation technique de Diderot dans l'*Encyclopédie*', *RHLF* 57 (1957), p.335-52.

46. See Stephen Werner: *Blueprint: a study of Diderot and the Encyclopédie plates* (Birmingham, AL, 1993).

47. See in particular Jacques Gautier [d'Agoty], *Myologie complette, en couleur et grandeur naturelle, composée de l'Essai et de la suite de l'Essai d'anatomie, en tableaux imprimés* (Paris, Gautier, Quillau père, Quillau fils, Lamesle 1746).

48. Georges-Louis Leclerc, comte de Buffon, *Histoire naturelle*, 36 vols, (Paris, Imprimerie royale, 1749-1778), with continuations by other hands published until 1804.

characteristics, even though they might never before have seen such examples themselves.[49]

The second major category comprises engravings which are, in the most neutral sense, the product of the imagination. In devotional works, for example, engravings could serve to inspire readers, or to reinforce their faith, by depicting objects or persons venerated for their spiritual values. Examples can readily be found in prayer books, books of hours and other works of spirituality, all of which were more common in pre-Revolutionary France than works of literature.[50] Their popularity offers a clue to the role played by illustrations in many books of the period, that of offering moralising lessons to their readers, and this is a function by no means limited to works of religious devotion. Indeed, both *Télémaque* and *La Henriade* point towards the use of illustrations to make broader philosophical points. Rather than simply to serve as embellishments, their function is to remind readers respectively of the need for rulers to act wisely, and of the dangers of religious fanaticism. This use of moralising engravings can also be seen in a number of contemporary works of history, such as the *Histoire des rois de France depuis Pharamond jusqu'à notre auguste Monarque Louis Quinze* (1722), which was mentioned earlier. Here, Benard, the son-in-law of the late geographer-royal Nicolas de Fer, sets out his intention to offer moral improvement to the young Louis XV through the medium of engravings (designed by Fer) depicting important events in the history of France:

le dessein de son auteur a été de faire passer a l'esprit par les yeux, d'une maniere agreable, les principales revolutions du Royaume et les actions les plus memorables. Persuadé que c'est dans l'histoire de leur monarchie que les roys de France doivent puiser les leçons du Gouvernement françois, il croioit qu'on ne pouvoit inventer trop de moiens pour la leur faire lire avec agrement et la graver plus avant dans leur memoire.[51]

Similar aims were voiced in works which were not exclusively literary or historical in content, and which drew on the resources of pagan mythology as well. The 1751 edition of Erasmus's *Eloge de la folie*, with plates by Eisen, is a case in point.[52] More significant still is the work mentioned earlier in relation to nudity in illustrations, the abbé Aubert's *Les Traits de l'histoire universelle, sacrée et profane*. The title also contains the following description of the book's intended purpose: *Ouvrage destiné principalement à l'éducation de la jeunesse, et propre encore à l'instruction ou à l'amusement des personnes de tout âge et de tout sexe. Par le Sieur Le Maire,*

49. See Pierre Gascar, *Buffon* (Paris, 1983).

50. Henri-Jean Martin, 'La tradition perpétuée', in *Histoire de l'édition française*, 4 vols (Paris, 1982-1986), vol.2, p.175-85.

51. *Histoire des rois de France depuis Pharamond jusqu'à notre auguste Monarque Louis Quinze* (Paris, J. F. Benard, 1722), 'Au roy', unpaginated. The work is described in the *Approbation* (18 July 1722) as 'un livre gravé'.

52. See Ray, *The Art of the French illustrated book*, p.51-53.

*graveur*. To judge from the high aspirations expressed on the title-page, Le Maire intended the work to have a moralising purpose for the benefit of all readers, particularly young boys and girls, and it was to be achieved by means of the engravings and the accompanying extracts (in Latin and French). At the time when the Fermiers were undertaking their edition, engravings of naked figures intended to serve a didactic purpose were being offered to the public, not as representations of actual events, or simply as decorative ornamentation, but as embodiments of more general truths and lessons.

The third category is made up of those books in which illustrations are intended neither to inform nor to moralise, but simply to embellish. It would, after all, be difficult to find any great moral significance (or, for that matter, any great moral danger) in the plates in *Daphnis and Chloé*,[53] for example, or in those relatively few novels which were illustrated.[54]

Thus, in the eighteenth century, illustrations in French books could broadly be said to serve three purposes: to inform, to moralise and to please. These three aims could overlap, in that informative and moralising engravings could also embellish; but it does not appear that engravings whose primary purpose was to inform (as in works of reference) were intended also to teach moral lessons, so that these two purposes remained essentially distinct. By the early 1760s, however, illustrations frequently serve a didactic purpose in works with a secular content, as well as in those of a more traditionally religious nature. And yet, if illustrations, including those of naked figures, could be used to teach moral lessons, the question arises of establishing the connection between what was shown and what readers were intended to read into them.

The engravings for the 1762 *Contes* are complex and diverse, in their subject matter, in their iconography and in functioning as vectors of the values which the Fermiers généraux wished to exemplify and communicate by means of their edition. Since they followed the customary order of the *contes*, the subject matter of each story was largely unrelated to what preceded and to what followed, and it would be pointless to try to trace any thematic progression or developmental coherence through the two volumes as a whole. It is true, as we observed in the first section of this study, that general ideas on the sexual conduct of women, or the behaviour of monks and nuns, or on the ability of the clever to outwit the stupid, are to be found throughout the *Contes*. Indeed, they provide themes to which La Fontaine recurs time and again. Nonetheless, the significance of the illustrations lies in the fact that they translate these ideas into visual form by means of a process which can only be the result of innumerable choices based on a particular view, a particular interpretation, of each

53. '[T]he main engraved series of illustrations cover the story clearly, relatively decorously and, to many modern eyes, with hardly a hint of the erotic.' Giles Barber, *Daphnis and Chloe: the markets and metamorphoses of an unknown bestseller* (London, 1989), p.35.
54. See below, p.399, for further discussion of this point.

story. It is in the nature of the differences between words and illustrations that no artist can interpret a story without adding something that is not in the text, or ignoring something which is. His interpretation also is guided by a set of values and assumptions which are built into the stories themselves, and which the Fermiers did not seek to alter textually, but which were inflected separately in each illustration. This is why Eisen's engravings do not automatically copy those of Romeyn de Hooghe or Cochin, though he may sometimes be indebted to them for suggesting an approach to illustrating particular *contes*.

Clearly, the changes made to many of the plates can only have been the outcome of discussions between the artist, the committee and the engravers. Many changes of a greater or lesser kind were introduced, and not a few of the plates went through several incarnations before a final version was approved. A study of this process leads unmistakably to the conclusion that some interpretations were rejected as unsuitable not for technical or artistic reasons, but because they did not provide an interpretation of the story which the Fermiers regarded as satisfactory; in practice, as we can often tell from internal evidence, this was because the initial version of a plate did not reflect the desired interpretation of the *conte* in question, or reflect the values which the Fermiers wanted to propound.

And it is precisely because the values, attitudes and beliefs of the Compagnie underlie each of the plates to varying degrees that a different kind of coherence must now be sought, based not so much on themes as on the reasons which govern the creation of the illustrations. In the search for this overall coherence, a variety of critical and analytical methods can be used. Primarily, we are dealing with the reader's perceptions of a visual image; and although an image is not a text, it can still be read and examined for what it communicates to the reader, and how it does so. While the earlier sections of this study have attempted to offer some answers to this question, there is a particular aspect of audience reception which we have not yet discussed. Modern criticism has tended to focus on what might be called a feminist reading of the values which the *Contes* are perceived to enshrine. It is at least arguable that such an approach misconstrues the aims and intensions of the 1762 edition (and no doubt other editions too) by putting ideologoy before facts and prejudice before understanding, and this is a point on which something needs now to be said.

## vi. The audience for the illustrations

The 1762 *Contes* appeared at a time when the question of the nature, status and role of women in society was being debated with some fervour. While earlier writers, such as Poulain de La Barre, had argued eloquently for the equality of the sexes,[55] it was generally the case that women were

55. Poulain de La Barre, *De l'égalité des deux sexes* (Paris, Jean Du Puis, 1673).

regarded as inferior to men in bodily strength, intellectual capacity and moral probity. It followed from this, and from the fact that female immorality was less easily forgiven than that of the male sex, that women must make greater efforts than men to resist the temptations of life and to set an example. The marquise de Lambert observed in her *Avis d'une mère à sa fille*, published in 1747: 'La honte est un sentiment dont on peut tirer de grands avantages en la ménageant bien [...] je veux dire celle qui nous détourne du mal par la crainte du déshonneur. Il faut l'avouer, cette honte est quelquefois le plus fidele gardien de la Vertu des Femmes: très peu sont vertueuses pour la Vertu même.'[56] The same concern for proper conduct is apparent, in another respect, in the *Conseils à une amie* of Mme de Puisieux (1749): 'Je ne vous conseille pas de vous livrer tout entiere à l'étude; cela ne convient ni à votre âge ni à votre sexe. D'ailleurs, quand vous sçauriez beaucoup, cela ne serviroit gueres que pour vous.'[57]

There is a good deal of evidence to support the view that these attitudes (many similar examples of which could be cited)[58] were predicated on a definition of femininity which was restrictive, reductive and prejudiced. It created a 'gendered' view of female behaviour based on purely biological factors, which served as a means of keeping women in subjection, of defining them as much by what they should not do as by what they should. The underlying principle of such beliefs was that female identity was a given, like female biology, and that the two were largely coterminous.[59] At the same time as women were meant to be kept in the sort of subjection to which these attitudes led, they were expected both to resist the seductions of men, for fear of losing their reputation, and to accept their dishonour once they had succumbed, while no concomitant blame attached to their seducer.[60] As Dena Goodman points out, whatever the merits of these views, there was no escaping the fact that men and women in mid-eighteenth-century France were expected to conform to different rules: 'The realm of virtue was not the same for women as it was for men, and the concern for female virtue was greater than the concern for male virtue, as attitudes towards adultery, for example, demonstrate.'[61]

It is of course true that the situation of women in pre-Revolutionary France was more complex than this picture allows. There were, for example, successful female novelists, such as Mme Riccoboni or Mme Le Prince de Beaumont; successful women painters like Elisabeth Vigée-Lebrun and successful women printers, such as the veuve Duchesne. And

56. *Œuvres de Mme la marquise de Lambert* (Lausanne, Marc-Michel Bousquet, 1747), p.62-63.
57. [Madeleine d'Arsant de Puisieux], *Conseils à une amie* ([Paris], no pub., 1749), p.23.
58. See Paul Hoffman, *La Femme dans la pensée des Lumières* (Paris, 1977).
59. See Judith Butler, *Gender trouble: feminism and the subversion of identity* (New York, 1990).
60. The classic analysis of the hypocrisy of these attitudes is, of course, Mme de Merteuil's bitterly realistic Letter LXXXII in Choderlos de Laclos's *Liaisons dangereuses* (1782).
61. Dena Goodman, *The Republic of letters* (Ithaca, NY and London, 1994), p.236.

if women officially played no direct part in the political process, it would be absurd to ignore the influence of, for example, Mme de Pompadour or, in another sense, of Marie-Antoinette. Even so, the restrictions and requirements under which the great majority of women laboured at the time – and indeed, have laboured since – is undeniable. Of particular importance for our present purposes is the fact that their situation has led to the gradual recognition in recent times of the sexist presuppositions inherent in the views outlined above; and this new perspective has in turn led to a number of innovative developments in literary and art criticism.

A significant consequence has been that the discussion of how women are represented in the literature and art of the eighteenth century has received a new impetus, and illustrated books have been looked at afresh. One of the most extensive critiques of such works undertaken in this perspective is that of Philip Stewart, who argues that the implied viewer or reader of books which contain engravings featuring nude figures, especially female figures, is 'paradigmatically male' (*Engraven desire*, p.12). He further claims that 'Although there is every reason to believe that a not inconsiderable female readership existed, and that it influenced literary production, all kinds of indirect evidence indicate just as clearly that the choices about what would be published and what would be purchased were made predominantly by men – who, in other ways as well, of course, controlled the artistic norms' (p.128-29). He asserts, from the evidence of such books, that the perspective adopted was 'commanded by thoroughly masculine preoccupations' (p.104), that it was essentially 'phallocratic' (p.132), and that 'the female conscience would have had to relate to erotic imagery essentially by espousal or reversal of a male perspective: in other words, in some way other than through direct identification with the *represented* point of view' (p.104; italics in original).

From these views a number of issues arise, which need to be distinguished carefully; some of them are of a general kind, and some relate specifically to the *Contes*. In the most obvious sense, women cannot identify with the male perspective, since they are biologically – and hence sexually – distinct, and do not regard men or women in the same way as men do; taken in this way, the statement would be so patently a truism as to be platitudinous. But this basic assertion is not really what is at issue here. Statements of the kind made by Stewart tend to proliferate in film criticism especially. They derive essentially from the work of the critic and filmmaker Laura Mulvey and her disciples, for whom the 'male gaze' is symptomatic of the objectification and (they would argue, consequent) subordination of women to men in the history of art and elsewhere.[62] What Mulvey is seeking to describe is the attitude of the male spectator

62. Laura Mulvey's edited volume *Visual and other pleasures* (London, 1989) contains a number of essays bearing on this topic, notably (p.14-26) 'Visual pleasure and narrative cinema'.

towards what can be seen on the screen, and *mutatis mutandis* her observations could apply to the viewer of the illustrations in the 1762 edition. But it should not be forgotten that a number of the plates also feature women looking at males who are the object of their desires, and vice versa, and this process occurs irrespective of how the viewer of the plate may react to the sight of the body in question. We have therefore a double sense of the 'gaze', both within and without the illustration, and we need to proceed with care if we are to distinguish the various implications of the term.

First, as a general point, Stewart is right to say that a large – and growing – female readership existed in France in the eighteenth century, and it is true that an (indeterminable) proportion of the novels, in particular, published at that time were written by and for women.[63] Hence, while men, for economic reasons, did have great influence in deciding what was published and what was purchased, they do not seem to have had any particular bias against publishing female authors, some of whom were successful with the public, which included a 'not inconsiderable female readership'. However, contemporary commentators expressed frequent fears that women might be led into moral corruption by reading books, especially novels, so that a tension existed between what women were offered and what they were supposed to be reading.[64] One could see in this prohibition the effects of what Stewart calls a 'phallocratic' attitude; that is, one which treated women differently from men, and sought to exclude them from some forms of knowledge. It is not clear, however, that this attitude had much effect at that time on women readers as such, except perhaps to make them more prudent in acknowledging what they read.[65]

This tendency to discourage women from looking at books which might corrupt them was not new, and it is given particular focus by the origins of the *Contes*. As Anne L. Birberick points out,[66] the suggestion (made in more than one early edition) that they were written in response to a request from Marie-Anne Mancini, duchesse de Bouillon, is given weight by the

63. It is difficult to arrive at any valid figure for the proportion of women novelists published in France in the eighteenth century. Many novels were anonymous; many claiming to be written by women were in fact written by men, and vice versa. Yet, as Anne Sauvy points out, female authors were numerous enough to justify the publication in 1769 of a five-volume *Histoire littéraire des femmes françaises* ('Une littérature pour les femmes', *Histoire de l'édition française*, ed. Roger Chartier and Henri-Jean Martin, 4 vols, Paris, 1983-1986, vol.3, p.445-53, here p.449).

64. See, for example, Georges May, *Le Dilemme du roman au XVIIIᵉ siècle* (New Haven, CT, and Paris, 1963), p.210-15, and Jenny Mander, *Circles of learning: narratology and the eighteenth-century French novel*, *SVEC* 366 (1999), p.164-67.

65. Mander reproduces (*Circles of learning*, p.165) a contemporary painting by Pierre-Antoine Baudoin, *La Lecture*, which shows the alleged 'moral' dangers into which the reading of novels could lure the female reader. Compare Stewart, *Engraven desire*, p.99-101.

66. Anne L. Birberick, *Reading undercover: audience and authority in Jean de La Fontaine* (Lewisburg, PA, and London, 1998), p.83-112.

fact that La Fontaine often refers to female readers. In point of fact, he closes the first part of the *Contes* in 1665 with a *Ballade* in which Cloris repeatedly admits: 'Je me plais aux livres d'amour' (*OCLF*, p.598-99).[67] La Fontaine had made the point, in the work itself, that women enjoying the contemplation of the erotic had to do so covertly to avoid censure: the example of Anne in 'Le cas de conscience' is instructive in this sense. She appreciates from her hiding-place the beauty of Guillot's body, and is upbraided by her priest when she admits to having done so (vol.2, p.146):

> C'est, dit-il, un très grand péché,
> Autant vaut l'avoir vu que de l'avoir touché.

Birberick comments that the story illustrates 'the dilemma faced by the "female" reader who is at once attracted to erotic subject-matter but forbidden to experience it because of *les bienséances* [...]. When this occurs, the "female" reader finds herself confronted with a moral authority that both discourages her behavior and actively seeks to condemn it.'[68] The 'female' reader, to whom many of the stories refer, must therefore transgress the unwritten social rules governing the conduct of her sex if she is to read the *Contes* for herself. From such evidence as we can glean from the text, it is debatable whether La Fontaine believed that women would necessarily have been less aroused than men by reading books which were forbidden to them. It is however undeniable that they were subjected to more rigorous criticism if they dared to do so. We ought therefore to ask whether the *Contes* show any concern with allegedly 'female' sensitivities, to enable women to risk reading them without encountering censure based on contemporary attitudes.

While the subject matter of many of the stories is bawdy and was often alleged to be blatantly immoral, La Fontaine did not cast aside a concern for propriety. Whether or not it is true that he particularly had female readers in mind, he avoided any crudity of language or description which might have caused them offence. As Birberick remarks: 'La Fontaine frequently modulates the sexual content of his tales by wrapping dangerous imagery in a discursive veil that insulates readers from the text's indecent material, even as it winkingly calls attention to it.'[69] Hence, if the *Contes* were likely to corrupt readers, whether male or female, this effect would result more from their content than from their language. Yet the leitmotivs of the stories, as we noted, are deeply engrained in the literature of western Europe as a whole. Hence, if the content is more or less universal and traditional, and the language is discreet, one wonders on what grounds La Fontaine can be more severely criticised than other authors who used the same material. Certainly, the virtue of female readers would have been at considerably less risk with

67. The *Ballade* was omitted from eighteenth-century editions of the *Contes*.
68. Birberick, *Reading undercover*, p.107, 110.
69. Birberick, *Reading undercover*, p.85. See also Fumaroli, *Le Poète et le roi*, p.372-75.

the *Contes* than with more overtly erotic writings of the sort for which the eighteenth century became notorious. Precisely because the *Contes* are largely concerned with human behaviour, and especially with the relationship between the sexes, the questions raised in them can apply equally well to men and to women. It is hard to see why, therefore, women should be less interested in them than men, especially as men are often shown in the stories as the victims, rather than the oppressors, of women.

If the accusation of phallocracy cannot properly be levelled at the text of the *Contes*, it may still be justified, as Stewart suggests, in regard to the illustrations which the Fermiers commissioned for their edition. Again, some general comments are called for before we look in detail at this question. First, a distinction needs to be made between books which were illustrated and books which were not. Illustrated works did not usually incur in their own right (that is to say, *because* of their illustrations) the censure on moral grounds which was so often directed at texts, and especially works of fiction. The continuing hostility that novels provoked was based fundamentally on their content, and on their tendency to blur the distinction between fact and fiction; it had little to do with the illustrations they contained.[70] In any case, before 1750 relatively few were illustrated, and of these hardly any contained engravings which would offend even the most sensitive reader.[71] Even in the second half of the century, it is hard to find many novels before the 1780s which contained any improper illustrations.[72] For this reason, it does not appear that illustrations *per se* in novels were usually regarded as especially perilous to female readers, so that such dangers as they might encounter in their reading logically derived from the printed word, rather than from the images based upon it. So far as the eighteenth century was concerned, then, illustrations in novels were not in themselves a significant source of moral corruption for readers of either sex.

But even if novels were not a danger because of their illustrations, erotic plates could be found in works of other kinds. Philip Stewart is concerned especially with such books, and it has to be said that some significant indicators run counter to his contention that women reading them would have had to adopt a 'male' perspective; that is, one which, by being 'phallocratic', was essentially oppressive to them. The evidence suggests, rather, that women not uncommonly collected and owned 'explicitly'

---

70. See May, *Le Dilemme du roman*, esp. p.23-46.

71. *Thérèse philosophe* (1748) was one of the few novels to gain some notoriety in the first half of the century as a result of its erotic illustrations. See Cohen, *Guide de l'amateur de livres*, col.733-35, and Françoise Weil, *L'Interdiction du roman et la librairie 1728-1750* (Paris, 1986), p.295-301. Neither May nor Mander reports any condemnation of illustrated books at this period.

72. See Jules Gay, *Bibliographie des ouvrages relatifs à l'amour, aux femmes, au mariage* (Paris, 1861).

illustrated books, and did not disdain them for the reasons alleged by modern commentators. Female bibliophiles possessed copies of the 1762 *Contes*, the ownership of which was immediately apparent from the fact that they bore the coat of arms of the lady in question. Cohen records such copies in the collections of Mme Du Barry, and the comtesse d'Artois (this latter copy, as it happens, was subsequently in the collection of Baroness James de Rothschild).[73] A copy of *Il Decamerone* with the 'suite libre' by Gravelot was in the library of the duchesse de Raguse.[74] In addition, the four-volume edition of Ovid's *Métamorphoses* (Paris, Hochereau, 1767-1771) which contained numerous nude engravings was in the collections of, among others, Mme de Laborde (the wife of a Fermier général), the duchesse de Grammont-Choiseul, the comtesse de Grammont d'Aster, and the comtesse de Provence.[75] For Montesquieu's *Le Temple de Gnide* (Paris, Le Mire, 1772), Eisen provided illustrations in which nudity plays as great a part as in his designs for the *Contes*. And yet the dedication copy from the publisher was offered to Sophie-Charlotte d'Angleterre, the wife of King George III; copies were also in the collections of Princess Marie-Béatrice d'Este, the comtesse d'Artois and the comtesse de Provence.[76] These copies are known because their armorial bindings testify to their provenance. It is likely that women also owned other, less illustrious copies whose provenance cannot be attested with certainty. It is therefore debatable whether an absolute opposition exists, or existed, between male and female attitudes towards the representation of sexual activity or nudity in illustrated books. And if we also allow with Anne Birberick, and *pace* Philip Stewart, that both men and women can take pleasure in the unclothed human form, then the 1762 *Contes* have something for everyone. The engravings include the naked male form as well as naked female figures, and they are always discreetly presented.[77] The Fermiers' conviction, attested repeatedly in the illustrations to the *Contes*, that women were equal partners with men in erotic adventures, would have encouraged the depiction of nudity designed to appeal to both sexes. Overall, then, it may be doubted that the 'male gaze' was a concept which the eighteenth century would have recognised. It is at least arguable, from the bibliographical evidence, that women would not have reacted very differently from men to nude illustrations, and that they could derive as much erotic pleasure as men from looking at them, without feeling that the depiction of nude females was oppressive or 'phallocratic'.

Women readers of the *Contes* (whether book collectors or not) would undeniably have found much in them to prompt reflection on the

73. For details, see Cohen, *Guide de l'amateur de livres*, col.561-62.
74. Cohen, *Guide de l'amateur de livres*, col.161.
75. Cohen, *Guide de l'amateur de livres*, col.771.
76. Cohen, *Guide de l'amateur de livres*, col.727.
77. On this general question, see Germaine Greer, *The Boy* (London, 2003).

depiction of their sex, both in the text and in the engravings. Some of the authors on whom La Fontaine drew for his inspiration (principally Boccaccio, Ariosto and Bonaventure Des Périers) often defined women, in their lustfulness, deceit and infidelity, in terms very different from the self-sacrificing, gentle, maternal model of womanhood offered by the Church through the person of the Virgin Mary.[78] Although this less charitable view of women has a long history, it has not be taken much into account, either in traditional literary criticism or more recently in film studies, despite the influence of Mulvey's work on the 'male gaze'. One commentator has concluded: 'If, however, "woman" is image – fantasy – is this not true of "man" too? The failure to put this question arises, I think, from the assumption that the fantasy of a popular work belongs to the dominant and therefore patriarchal imagination.'[79] To a considerable extent, and exceptionally, Eisen does indeed put the question, and uses the answer as the basis for many of his engravings. When one compares his work with that of Romeyn de Hooghe or Cochin, it is clear that he emphasises more than his predecessors not only the role of nudity but also of willing female acquiescence in sexual encounters, a willingness often indicated by the woman gazing raptly at her lover or seducer. In such cases, men are not seen as either symbolic of male domination, or as fetishistic substitutes for some displaced longing, but as sexually attractive beings in their own right.[80] In addition, as we noted in examining the differences between the rejected and the replacement plates designed for some stories (such as 'La servante justifiée' and 'Le diable en enfer'), Eisen sometimes altered the image to show precisely this feature in the females depicted in the revised version. In other instances (such as 'Le savetier' and 'On ne s'avise jamais de tout') the original engraving was replaced to show the female gaze indicating complicity in deceiving a male figure. Conversely, two engravings (for 'Le calendrier des vieillards' and 'La clochette') were altered to change the direction of the woman's gaze away from that of the man whose attentions she wishes to discourage. By these various means, Eisen and the Fermiers create a world in which sexual relationships are the norm, and women are both beautiful and available, if they choose to be. They are not so much the playthings of men, the subjects of their power, however, as their (usually) willing partners in erotic adventures.

The significance of the attitude expressed by La Fontaine, and echoed by Eisen, is that while it reflects the differing expectations which society has of men and women, it also makes clear that women are neither more

78. The idealised picture of saintly womanhood was given in one of the most frequently reprinted theological works of the century, Louis-François d'Argentan's *Conférences théologiques et spirituelles sur les grandeurs de la très-sainte vierge Marie mère de Dieu*, 2 vols (Rouen, F. Vaultier le jeune, 1680).
79. Christine Gledhill, 'Women reading men', in *Me Jane: masculinity, movies and women*, ed. Pat Kirkham and Janet Thumim (London, 1995), p.73-93 (here p.74).
80. See Laura Mulvey, *Fetishism and curiosity* (London, 1996).

nor less 'moral' than men. On the contrary, they are just as much given to sexual adventure, infidelity or 'gallantry' as men. While La Fontaine does not deny their maternal instincts, their love of jewellery and adornment, or their civilising influence, these qualities are ancillary to their role as sexual predators or participants. This disabused view of women is characteristic also of Eisen's illustrations, which depict females as seducers, or adulterers, as drunken, or cold-hearted, or sexually available even if, as nuns, they have taken vows of chastity. In the very few cases where they are the unresponsive objects of male lust, Eisen does not reveal any overt sympathy for them in a man's world. In this sense, the illustrations cut through the debate described by Goodman, to arrive at a less polarised and, paradoxically, more egalitarian view of women, though one bought at a high cost in moral and ethical terms.

Something has already been said about the theme of the sexual equality of men and women which recurs frequently in the *Contes*, and it is manifested equally by the illustrations. In itself, this idea is inseparable from the idea of personal freedom, since it allows women, in particular, to act in defiance of the restrictions traditionally imposed on their sex. While it would be otiose to repeat at length the points made in the analysis of the individual stories, it is useful to recall some examples of the way in which this theme is exemplified in the collection. In 'Le mari confesseur', Cochin shows worshippers at their devotions close to the couple. Eisen, in contrast, removes other worshippers almost entirely from the scene, reducing them to an anonymous mass in the background and concentrating on the way in which the wife outwits the 'priest', rather than on the social context of the encounter. The depiction of human sexuality within the confines of one story is changed from one edition to another in order to make the same point, as we can see from 'La servante justifiée'. Cochin's vignette, like Eisen's original illustration, shows the husband apparently pushing the servant to the ground, since her awkward posture cannot be sustained for more than a moment. In the revised Eisen engraving, the husband and the servant are presented much more obviously as two halves of one whole; the woman's role is no longer that of a passive recipient of the male's attention, but that of an equal partner in the encounter. The Cochin vignette for 'Le berceau', likewise, has little of the covert complicity between the sexes which we find in Eisen.

Because of the preconceptions and prejudices surrounding the status of women, Eisen's illustrations therefore often have the effect of startling the reader out of any lingering complacency about the female sex, and the technique of the plates emphasises this aspect of the work. Owing to the limited space at his disposal, Eisen almost always depicts figures whose beauty or ugliness, youth or age, health, wealth or poverty, are discernible at first glance, so that the contrast between them does not require a great deal of analysis. It is, rather, the context in which they are placed which determines how we react to their behaviour. It is this context which allows

Eisen to hint at the attitude which we may wish to adopt towards them, as, for example, when we are invited to determine whether an adulterous wife is to be praised or blamed. Such a woman may in principle deserve censure, but if (as in 'On ne s'avise jamais de tout' or 'Le calendrier des vieillards'), she is married to a much older (and usually unattractive) man incapable of satisfying her needs, her behaviour is understandable. It is even forgivable in the context of a work which does not condemn the satisfaction of the sexual impulse in either men or women. As Birberick notes, for La Fontaine 'there are no differences between husbands and wives in matters of sexual fidelity'.[81]

Indeed, contemporary medical opinion asserted that marriage was beneficial to the physical and psychological health of both sexes. The article 'Mariage (*Médec. Diete*)' in the *Encyclopédie* (1765) argued that since women were 'plus sensibles aux impressions du plaisir, [elles] en ressentent aussi davantage les bons effets. On voit des chlorétiques languissantes, malades, pâles, défigurées, dès qu'elles sont mariées, sortir rapidement de cet état de langueur, acquérir de la santé, des couleurs, de l'embonpoint, prendre un visage fleuri, animé; il y en a même qui naturellement laides, sont devenues après le *mariage* extrèmement jolies.'[82]

Even so, while female sexuality is generally presented in the *Contes* as active rather than passive, the Fermiers have to contend with tales which cannot readily be accommodated within this convenient framework. Their response is to veil unpleasant reality by suggesting that the victimisation of women is not as great a crime as might be thought. This is why the rape of a milkmaid in 'La clochette' is depicted not as the gross violation of a young, inexperienced girl by a man unable to control his lust, but as the expression of an urge which is part of nature. A cow with horns features in the revised version of the engraving, and the virginal halo of light which had surrounded the girl in the first version is absent from the second. Hence, the (anticipated) rape becomes no more than a fleeting episode in the relations between the sexes. The third illustration for 'La fiancée du roi de Garbe' similarly shows a woman who is about to receive the wholly unsubtle attentions of a violent 'galant', but whose face betrays neither alarm nor reluctance at the prospect. This tendency to depict women in the Eisen engravings as well able to take care of themselves in sexual matters adds a diegetic dimension to each individual illustration. Each paradigmatic episode therefore forms a thematic syntagm in which women are not oppressed even when they are the objects of rampant male sexual attention. This is the case, for example, in 'La servante justifiée', 'Le calendrier des vieillards', 'La fiancée du roi de

81. Birberick, *Reading undercover*, p.101.
82. *Encyclopédie*, vol.10, p.116. The author is identified only as '*m*', though modern research has established that this symbol designates Dr Ménuret de Chambaud (see Lough, *Essays on the 'Encyclopédie'*, p.465). See also Goodden, *Diderot and the body*, p.139-40.

400

Garbe', 'Le petit chien qui secoue de l'argent et des pierreries', 'Les Rémois', 'Le cuvier', and 'Nicaise'.

The depiction of men in the *Contes* is no more or less objectionable than that of women. They may be young, handsome and honest, or old, ugly and deceitful, just as women may be. Men are, moreover, as likely as women to display the vanity and jealousy traditionally ascribed to the female sex. It is true that Eisen, following La Fontaine, sometimes depicts male aggressiveness directed against women, but this is exceptional, and there is much evidence to support the view that, both in the text and in the illustrations, men are as much the dupes of women as vice versa. There is little sympathy for the woman who cannot cope with the sexual realities of life. Correspondingly, there is little indulgence for the man who allows himself to be cuckolded or otherwise misled by a woman: 'Joconde', 'Le cuvier', 'La gageure des trois commères' and 'Le calendrier des vieillards', for example, are illustrated by plates which do not re-dound to the advantage of husbands. On occasion, as in 'Le savetier', husbands and wives work together to defeat a threat to their marriage. Such stories are, however, rare in the *Contes* as a whole, where the mutual attraction of the sexes, and the problems to which it leads, are the central focus both of the stories and of the illustrations.[83]

The same wish to present a 'balanced' view of human sexuality leads Eisen to depict nuns and monks who isolate themselves from the world as only too ready to indulge in sexual adventure when the opportunity arises.[84] Yet this is not a matter of mockery, for he downplays the anti-clerical satire which, it has been argued, imbues at least three of the *contes*, and which is La Fontaine's own contribution to the stories.[85] Eisen's practice is, rather, to evoke the forbidden delights available in the cloister or the hermitage. He filters this primarily through the prism of female willingness to participate in the activities described in the text ('Le diable en enfer', 'Les cordeliers de Catalogne', 'Les lunettes', 'Le tableau', 'L'abbesse malade', 'Le psautier'). Even when no sexual activity occurs, as in 'sœur Jeanne', he depicts the eponymous nun seeming to cradle in her arms the child whom she bore before entering the convent. There is little in the illustrations, then, to suggest that the Fermiers felt sympathy for those who ignore what they see as the sexual realities of life, and who idealise either men or women.

83. Homosexuality, whether male or female, does not feature in the *Contes*, though lesbianism is a common theme in novels of the time. See May, *Diderot et 'La Religieuse'*, p.115-41.

84. Birberick comments perceptively on the 'false division between the cloister and the salon' in the *contes* which feature nuns ('From world to text', p.198). See also G. E. de La Fontaine, *La Fontaine dans ses Contes*, p.164-80.

85. See the comments on 'Mazet de Lamporechio', 'Les cordeliers de Catalogne' and 'L'hermite' in chapter 3 of this study.

Nor do the illustrations display much sympathy for the plight of a more specific section of society, namely the peasantry. The lower classes are shown in a way which conveys something of their misery, but without making them an object of pity. The gap between the lower orders and the wealthy is clearly an issue in the two versions of the plate for 'Les oies de frère Philippe', and in 'Le paysan qui avoit offensé son seigneur', in which Eisen depicts a toothless peasant grovelling before his handsome, wealthy young lord who is unconcerned at his plight. In this *conte* and again in 'Le baiser rendu', Eisen represents a peasant as gross and uncouth even when the text gives no basis for doing so. In this way, the illustrations point to a dislike of the lower orders of society which goes further than is necessary for the representation of the facts of the story. Neither De Hooghe nor Cochin (both of whom show the cruel treatment meted out to the re-calcitrant peasant) emphasises to the same extent the unattractiveness of the poor, their isolation from the rest of society, or the right of the rich to treat them as they please. By showing servants or peasants as swarthy and coarse-featured (in the second engraving for 'Joconde' and in the rejected engraving for 'Le tableau'), Eisen establishes an unfavourable connection between the lower orders and men of unprepossessing ap-pearance. When, as in 'Le tableau', they are also shown as energetic lovers, there is more than a suggestion that they are both morally inferior and sexually attractive to women.

This hard-headed refusal to sentimentalise men and women in general, or the lower orders in particular, has its counterpart in the Fermiers' rejection of the irrational. It is for this reason that Eisen domesticates the grotesque or the supernatural where the story will not permit such out-landish figures to be plausibly eliminated. This procedure is apparent in 'Belphégor', 'L'anneau d'Hans Carvel', 'Le diable de Papefiguière' or 'La chose impossible'. In these instances, the intrinsic absurdity of Devils and evil spirits is made manifest by their incongruity with the normal, con-temporary context in which they are placed. After being accorded ter-rifying powers and status in medieval and Renaissance art, such creatures are now reduced to objects of ridicule and scorn. Certainly there is nothing in the way they are depicted in the *Contes* to inspire sentiments other than mockery.[86]

So far, we have looked at the external factors intervening in the interpretation of the illustrations to the *Contes*. We have examined their relationship to the rococo book, the evolving role of illustrations in works of the period, the likely audience for the edition, and the attitude of the Fermiers towards human sexuality. These are what might be called cir-cumstantial considerations, in that they place the 1762 edition in the wider context of practices and attitudes of the time. They also create a framework within which the *Contes* can be placed in relation to other

86. See above, chapter 3, p.232, note 11.

works of the period, and which can offer some guidance in the interpretation of the illustrations. However, the *Contes* also have a specific history
and identity which unarguably marks them out from other contemporary
illustrated books. To grasp the nature of that specificity, we need first to
look at the underlying approach which La Fontaine adopted in writing
them, and then to examine how that approach accorded with the aims
and ambitions which the Fermiers nourished in underwriting the edition.

## vii. La Fontaine and the idea of personal freedom

The author of the *Contes* makes some effort to draw attention to this theme
in the work itself. The poet's unfettered right to use his sources as he sees
fit, and for his own purposes, is a point on which La Fontaine himself had
dwelt in the preface to the work in 1666. He claimed that his main aim in
writing the *Contes* was to 'attacher le lecteur, de le réjouir, d'attirer malgré
lui son attention, de lui plaire enfin [...] comme l'on sçait, le secret de
plaire ne consiste pas toujours en l'ajustement, ni même en la régularité.
Il faut du piquant et de l'agréable, si l'on veut toucher.' He goes on:

Venons à la liberté que l'Auteur se donne de tailler dans le bien d'autrui ainsi que
dans le sien propre, sans qu'il en excepte les nouvelles même les plus connues, ne
s'en trouvant point d'inviolables pour lui. Il retranche, il amplifie, il change les
incidents et les circonstances, quelquefois le principal événement à la suite; enfin,
ce n'est plus la même chose; c'est proprement une nouvelle nouvelle; et celui qui
l'a inventé auroit bien de la peine à reconnoître son propre ouvrage.[87]

He himself therefore makes much of his artistic freedom, for which he
offers neither apology nor excuse, since all is grist to the artistic mill.
Nonetheless, his assertion of his own freedom is in some respects puzzling.
As commentators have pointed out, at the time he was writing the *Contes*
he was closely associated with the Jansenists of Port-Royal.[88] In Pierre
Clarac's words: 'La plupart de ces contes, et les plus licencieux, parais-
saient entre 1665 et 1674; or, c'est précisément pendant cette décade que
La Fontaine est l'un des poètes presque officiels de Port-Royal.'[89] Marc
Fumaroli, too, has drawn attention to the religious aspects of the *Contes*,
though he sees not so much convergence as dissension between La Fontaine and the austere doctrines of the Catholic Church: 'La poésie de
La Fontaine [...] n'a jamais cessé pour autant d'avoir un horizon chrétien,
même si la vie du poète, "volage en amours", ses *Contes* anticléricaux et
licencieux, ses fréquentations et ses mœurs libertines, ont fait de lui, du
point de vue de l'Eglise, un scandaleux pécheur.'[90]

---

87. *OCLF*, p.603-604.
88. *Histoire de la littérature française au XVII<sup>e</sup> siècle*, ed. Antoine Adam, 5 vols (Paris, 1948-
1956), vol.4, p.21-22.
89. Pierre Clarac, *La Fontaine par lui-même* (Paris, 1961), p.70.
90. Fumaroli, *Le Poète et le roi*, p.549.

What these commentators have in common is the idea that a very perceptible tension exists between the role which religion played in La Fontaine's life when he was writing the *Contes*, and the manifestly irreligious content of the stories as a whole. As Catherine Grisé has shown,[91] individual tales, such as 'Mazet de Lamporechio', 'L'abbesse malade' or 'Le tableau', testify to an awareness of religious teachings and casuistic disputes of the sort which La Fontaine would have known from his acquaintance with Port-Royal. At the same time, it would be difficult to argue that he is a staunch defender of the rigorous spiritual values enshrined in the teachings of the Jansenists.[92] It has even been claimed that the *Nouveaux Contes* were so titled to offer a mocking parallel with the *Nouveau Testament* which had recently been published under the auspices of Port-Royal.[93] Furthermore, one eighteenth-century writer reported that La Fontaine had to be dissuaded by Racine and Boileau from dedicating one of the *contes* to Antoine Arnauld;[94] such irreverence is entirely characteristic of the author of the *Contes*. The treatment, and indeed the very presence, of Jansenist influences in a work of this kind indicates a somewhat *désinvolte* attitude on the part of La Fontaine towards the more severe prescriptions of the movement; overall, there is little evidence to suggest that he felt any great respect for the ethical debates in which the Jansenists played so large a part.

Commentators, up to and including those of Clarac's generation, reacted to the *Contes* with hostility, and professed themselves puzzled at this apparent dissonance between the work and the life. In contrast, more recent critics have tended to see in La Fontaine's assertion of freedom one of the chief characteristics of the work, and one which has implications for his poetic technique as well as for the content of the stories. In one of the earliest and most perceptive modern studies of the *Contes*, Lapp discusses at length (*Esthetics of negligence*, p.159-64) the 'vers libres' which are one of their essential characteristics, and which help to give them their air of studied negligence. He celebrates this quality as one of their most enduring features, and observes elsewhere that 'La Fontaine himself frequently declared his aversion to regularity in art' (p.30). Indeed, Lapp's study as a whole might properly be termed a celebration of the freedom with which La Fontaine wrote the *Contes*, and about which it is now time to say more.

91. Grisé, 'La casuistique dans les *Contes*'.
92. Compare Pierre Clarac, 'La Fontaine', in *Histoire de la littérature française*, ed. Antoine Adam, vol.1, p.240.
93. See *OCLF*, Introduction, p.xli.
94. See [Antoine Taillefer], *Tableau historique de l'esprit et du caractère des littérateurs français*, 4 vols (Versailles, Poinçot and Paris, Nyon, 1785), vol.2, p.190.

404

# viii. The theme of freedom as manifested in the *Contes*

The *Contes* are linked by their overriding concern with the idea of personal freedom, which takes a number of forms, and which creates multiple continuities throughout the text;[95] consequently, it is artificial to select any one group of stories for consideration in isolation from the rest.[96] Most often, the idea of personal freedom consists in a refusal to be bound by the constraints of marriage (for example, in 'Joconde', 'Le cocu battu et content', 'Le mari confesseur', 'La servante justifiée', 'La gageure des trois commères', 'Le calendrier des vieillards', 'A femme avare, galant escroc', 'On ne s'avise jamais de tout', 'La coupe enchantée', 'Le magni-fique', 'Le berceau', 'La mandragore', 'Les Rémois', 'Le roi Candaule et le maître en droit', 'Nicaise', 'Le cuvier', 'Le bât', 'Le faiseur d'oreilles et le raccommodeur de moules', 'Les quiproquo'). It may take the form of a refusal to conform to the dictates of the Church in the matter of celibacy ('sœur Jeanne', 'Les cordeliers de Catalogne', 'L'hermite', 'Mazet de Lamporechio', 'Comment l'esprit vient aux filles', 'L'abbesse malade', 'Le psautier', 'Le diable en enfer', 'La jument du compère Pierre', 'Les lu-nettes', 'Le tableau', 'La couturière'). It may consist in rejecting a parental prohibition against having sexual relations before marriage ('Les oies de frère Philippe', 'Le rossignol'). It may manifest itself in the rejection of legal norms ('Le juge de Mesle', and, in a different sense, 'Les deux amis', 'Les troqueurs' and 'Le contrat'). It may emerge in a refusal to conform to the social and sexual constraints imposed on women ('La fiancée du roi de Garbe', 'La courtisane amoureuse', 'Le cas de conscience', 'La cruche'), and sometimes on men too ('Le muletier', 'Pâté d'anguille', 'Le baiser rendu'). Occasionally, it might be said to be apparent in a wish to be free from the restrictions of superstition (as in 'Belphégor', 'Le diable de Papefiguière', 'La chose impossible'). It is true that a number of the *Contes* do not fit into any larger frame of reference of this kind, but even they are illustrated in a way which conveys a concern with personal free-dom, albeit in a sometimes perverse sense. Hence, 'Le paysan qui avoit

95. For the purposes of this thematic survey, the five *contes* included in the 1762 edition which are not by La Fontaine have been taken into consideration. They reflect many of the same preoccupations as those which are by him, and they were illustrated by Eisen on the same basis as the others.

96. Only in two instances (the prologues to 'Le psautier' and 'Les lunettes') does La Fontaine draw attention to the reiterated use of a specific topos, namely nuns in convents, which provides material for six tales. Birberick argues that this group needs to be seen separately, and that the presentation of the nun moves from a concern with social issues to a preoccupation with metafictional problems ('From world to text', p.181-201). This view is defensible, but ignores Eisen's repeated indications that sexuality is universal; monks and nuns are no different from other human beings when faced by sexual temptation ('Mazet de Lamporechio', 'Le diable en enfer', 'Le tableau'). Hence, to isolate one group of stories from the *Contes* may be legitimate if one wants to look only at how a group of related *contes* evolves, but there is a risk that their wider significance in the work as a whole will be lost from view.

offensé son seigneur' allows the 'seigneur' to behave without the constraint of ordinary human decency in order to recover his debt.

In some instances, La Fontaine warns against disregarding constraints. 'Le Gascon puni' recounts the effects of ignoring the feelings of others. 'Le faucon' and 'Autre imitation d'Anacréon' indicate the extent to which personal freedom may be lost, along with financial independence, if love is allowed to become a dominant passion. The unhappy consequences of another kind of unbridled self-indulgence are clear from 'Le glouton', the dangers of infidelity are illustrated in 'Les aveux indiscrets', and those of cruelty in 'Féronde, ou le purgatoire'. In turn, 'L'oraison de S. Julien' shows the effects of behaving with no concern for the law, as does 'La clochette'. Finally, there is a miscellaneous group which does not fit into any obvious category. This comprises 'Le savetier', 'La matrone d'Ephèse', 'Alix malade', 'Imitation d'Anacréon', 'Richard Minutolo', 'L'anneau d'Hans Carvel', 'Le villageois qui cherche son veau', 'Le fleuve Scamandre', 'La confidente sans le sçavoir', 'Le remède', and 'Promettre est un, et tenir est un autre'. Such broad categories inevitably group together *contes* which are widely separated in the text, and very disparate in their setting and in the characters who feature in them. The dozen or so stories (out of a total of sixty-nine) which do not readily fit into the general theme of personal freedom are a warning against any attempt at over-schematisation. They indicate that no one central idea, however widely it may be found in the work as a whole, informs every single story in the collection. But even with this reservation in mind, it is permissible to argue that the idea of freedom is sufficiently widespread in the stories to offer an area deserving particular attention, and that it is central both to the Fermiers' view of the *Contes*, and to Eisen's interpretation of them.

## ix. The Fermiers généraux, freedom and conventional values

The Fermiers could not avoid being aware of the controversies provoked by the relaxed view of conventional morality to be found in the *Contes*, for it had been a matter of adverse comment for nearly a century; indeed, it is paralleled in the illustrations which they commissioned for their edition. But they need not have echoed this attitude themselves, and could have downplayed it, as De Hooghe and Cochin did, or opted for uncontroversial, if elegant, engravings of the sort found in the Oudry edition of the *Fables*.[97] If they chose to do otherwise, it is because the idea of freedom which is central to the approach adopted by La Fontaine is fundamental also to an understanding of the aims and purposes of the Fermiers' edition

97. See my study 'Theme and technique in the "Oudry" edition of La Fontaine's *Fables*', *Bulletin of the John Rylands Library* 81:3 (1999), special issue *Text and image*, ed. David Adams and Adrian Armstrong, p.361-84.

of the *Contes*. They chose this work in particular as one which they wanted to promote because it is strongly based on the idea of freedom from social conventions, religious restraints and moral restrictions. Many of the individual *contes* take as their theme the conduct of men and women who flout sexual, religious or social norms in the conduct of their daily lives. It is characteristic of them that they readily indulge their appetites with scarcely a nod in the direction of the conventions which regulate the existence of their contemporaries. In this respect, the Fermiers could hardly have failed to see parallels between the *Contes* and their own conduct, free as they were in many ways to disregard the financial, political and legal strictures of pre-Revolutionary France in the pursuit of their own interest, power and advancement.

From what was said in the first part of this study, it should be clear that the Fermiers regarded freedom of action, at least for themselves, as a fundamental right. Even if they did not say so in as many words, their behaviour over many decades indicates that they were largely unconstrained in the pursuit of their economic and personal objectives. In addition, as we noted, informed commentators such as Naveau and Darigrand repeatedly accused the Compagnie of abusing its authority, of arrogating to itself the powers of the king and the state, and of nurturing the ambition to rule in its own interests.

The Fermiers' decision to withdraw and suppress the edition can most readily be accounted for by their concluding belatedly that the illustrations would be used, so to speak, as evidence against them. The depiction of immoral women, duplicitous clerics, bovine peasants and cuckolded husbands could easily be read not only as an interpretation of the text, but as a statement of the Compagnie's attitudes and moral values as well. Had the 1762 edition been widely available, therefore, these views could at once have become indelibly associated with the Compagnie, and could scarcely have enhanced either its popularity or its reputation for moral probity. Indeed, the Fermiers could have been accused of wanting to present a view of the world in which everyone else was as corrupt and unfeeling as they themselves were accused of being. At the very least, it could have been said of them that they were not content simply to exploit and oppress their contemporaries, but had to insult them as well.

Their emphatic assertion of their own independence was less appropriate and more offensive in 1762 than they could have realised when they embarked on their edition some years earlier. By that time, they had incurred virtually unanimous condemnation in the work of the *philosophes* and in the periodical press. This, and the hostility displayed towards them in government and in the *parlement*, meant that any further affirmation of their values through the *Contes* was likely to antagonise contemporary feeling still more. The only feature of their edition which distinguished it significantly from all its predecessors was the plates; these were expensive to commission and to produce, and to remove them from the book would have been unthinkable.

It is true that their edition of the *Contes*, as we noted earlier, shared some of the uninhibited characteristics of other illustrated books of the time, such as the *Decamerone* of 1757. Yet no other comparable publication was issued by an organisation which was so widely loathed and feared for its harshness, its oppression of the population at large, and its indifference to the sufferings which it caused. The process of reading, understanding and interpreting the text in relation to the illustrations constituted an appeal to, and depended on the acceptance of, the values which underlay the Compagnie's own activities. Readers who grasped the larger purposes of the plates and of the edition could scarcely fail to see in them evidence of the Fermiers' own predilection for freedom from undue restraint. In publishing the 1762 edition, replete with luxurious engravings, they might well have confirmed the worst suspicions as to their indifference to such commonly held beliefs. Whether this interpretation would always have been placed upon them is impossible to say, but the Fermiers chose not to run the risk, and sequestered most copies of the *Contes* for many years. They had, it seems, initially intended to market as many as 2000 copies of the work, a figure which was later reduced to 800. By then withdrawing the book altogether, they ensured that the subversive, satirical and libertarian message of the engravings was not made available to a wider audience.

There is an irony here, in that the Fermiers were asserting for themselves precisely those values of personal freedom, and the rejection of automatic deference to religious and secular authority, of which the *philosophes* also stood accused. The terms in which Christophe de Beaumont anathematised the latter, in his *mandement* of November 1758 against *De l'esprit*, might indeed be regarded as a summary of what the Fermiers represented. Helvétius's work, he declared, was to be condemned as 'anéantissant les notions primitives de vertu et de justice; établissant des maximes totalement opposées à la morale évangélique; substituant à la saine doctrine des mœurs l'intérêt, les passions, le plaisir'.[98] The difference, of course, lay in the fact that the Compagnie wished to assert these values at the expense of others, whereas the *philosophes* defended them on behalf of society as a whole. Had the Fermiers allowed the *Contes* to circulate freely, readers would have found in the engravings a less than flattering portrait of contemporary society painted by those who were aware of their own power, and determined to demonstrate it for their own ends. If the Fermiers did indeed take a more prudent course for the reasons given here, then we shall expect to find in the illustrations some evidence to explain their change of heart, and it is to that question that we now turn.

98. Quoted in Smith, *Helvétius, a study in persecution*, p.40.

# x. The assertion of the Fermiers' freedom in the illustrations

To start at the apex of society: both in the *Contes* and in Eisen's illustrations, there is a disinclination to bow before royal authority, and perhaps a contempt even for royal personalities and power. In 'Joconde' and in 'Le muletier', Eisen presents a king as a figure lacking in authority, and undeserving of respect for his person. In the second engraving for 'Joconde', the queen is shown on the same level as her dwarf, as if to suggest that they are, literally and metaphorically, equal. The Fermiers took this approach further still, and allowed Eisen to incorporate into the illustrations recognisable portraits of a number of exalted contemporary personalities, of whom Louis XV and Mme de Pompadour, in 'La chose impossible', are perhaps the best known.[99] Such apparently insubordinate behaviour suggests that they had little to fear from showing the king and his mistress as characters in a story which could scarcely be regarded as respectable. Owing to the close connections between the marquise and the Fermiers,[100] they must have calculated – correctly, so far as one can tell – that she would not retaliate against them after being depicted in this way. There is some evidence, then, that the Fermiers and their illustrators took the deliberate decision to depict royalty in ways which were not respectful of their dignity or of their allegedly superior status. Such a conclusion is not surprising in view of the commanding position occupied by the Compagnie, whose services were indispensable to the ruling elite for the proper functioning of government. A body so powerful did not need to defer to its supposed superiors. On the contrary: the opportunity to present its views on royal conduct was not to be missed, and the Fermiers took advantage of it.

The same willingness to mock personalities of the day would explain why, in the engraving for 'Le berceau', the figures of Mme d'Epinay and the marquis de Saint-Lambert are to be discerned.[101] Now, Mme d'Epinay had close connections with the Compagnie: she had married a Fermier in 1745, though by 1762 his fortunes had declined to the point where he was virtually bankrupt and was excluded from his offices under the Compagnie.[102] It cannot be assumed, therefore, that the reference to her was meant to be entirely jocular, or was not intended to wound her husband. Now, the personal conduct of the king and his mistress, as well as that of Saint-Lambert and Mme d'Epinay, was known not to be above reproach.[103] The fact that sly allusions could be made to such prominent

99. See Holloway, *French rococo book illustration*, p.25.
100. See the first chapter of this study.
101. Holloway, *French rococo book illustration*, p.25.
102. See Durand, *Les Fermiers généraux*, p.259.
103. According to the article by Gustave Charlier in the *Dictionnaire des lettres françaises* (Paris, 1995, p.457), Mme d'Epinay lived apart from her husband, and 'chercha une vaine

individuals adds to the impression that the Fermiers wanted the edition to have a mocking contemporary application,[104] by placing recognisable figures in incongruous situations. The implication of sexual licence contained in these illustrations would no doubt not have been lost on readers of the time, or at least not on those few readers who managed to acquire copies of the work.

In portraying some of their contemporaries as recognisably as they did, however, the Fermiers took care to select those who were either in positions of power but who were reluctant to take action against the Compagnie, or else those whose dissipation or licence mirrored their own. Louis XV, of course, fell into both categories. Hence, by means of these personal references, the Fermiers were indirectly commenting on their conduct, not necessarily because they disapproved of it, but because it was no different from their own, and those who were so depicted were therefore in no position to censure them. Essentially, then, these portraits were a sort of *tu quoque*, intended as much to reflect the general mores of society as to offer reproaches to selected individuals.

While the close links which they had long enjoyed with the Pompadour, and with Mme d'Epinay, undoubtedly gave them considerable licence, it has to be said also that the taste of the times was not averse to the satirical portrayal of those in power. In the *Correspondance littéraire* of 1 May 1761, Grimm observes:

Depuis quelque temps c'est la mode de faire des gravures satiriques, ou de graver même des satires, et de substituer le burin à l'impression. Le P. Elisée, carme déchaussé, s'étant fait dans ces dernières années une grande réputation par ses sermons, on a gravé contre lui une satire fort insipide intitulée *Saint Chrysostome ressuscité*. A l'occasion de la mort de M. le duc de Bourgogne, on a gravé une petite estampe représentant un grand chemin au bout duquel on voit les clochers de Saint-Denis. Les deux côtés du chemin sont bordés: l'un, par les médecins, ayant le premier médecin à leur tête; l'autre, par les chirurgiens, ayant à leur tête le premier chirurgien, et pour inscription on lit: *Le grand chemin de Saint-Denis*.[105]

The Fermiers were clearly aware of this trend, and did not disdain to follow it. Yet the *Contes* would scarcely have merited their enduring reputation if the interest of the illustrations had been confined to making fun of some of their better-known contemporaries. To understand the real significance of the 1762 edition, we need to look at more general characteristics of the plates. As we noted earlier, the majority of the engravings show individuals asserting their independence of mind and action, by behaving as

consolation dans une vie de plaisirs et de dissipations'. Saint-Lambert had become notorious for his affairs with, among others, Mme Du Châtelet and the comtesse d'Houdetot; the second of these relationships had, of course, been complicated by the (unrequited) passion which the comtesse inspired in Jean-Jacques Rousseau. See Maurice Cranston, *The Noble savage: Jean-Jacques Rousseau 1754-1762* (London and Chicago, 1991), p.55-103.

104. Lacroix lists half a dozen contemporary men of letters who, he claims, are recognisably depicted in other illustrations ('Les *Contes* de La Fontaine', p.261).

105. *CL*, vol.3, p.402-403.

their feelings, emotions and ideas dictate, in defiance of conventional religious, legal, sexual or social norms. Consequently, those readers who took the trouble to compare the 1762 edition of the *Contes* with earlier versions containing illustrations by De Hooghe and Cochin would have noted, in addition to the purely technical differences between them, a greater emphasis on the idea of personal liberty than previously. This new note struck in the depiction of human activities in the *Contes* is strengthened by the use of recurring motifs which insist on the revelatory nature of what is offered for our contemplation in the plates.

## xi. Revelations: the role of curtains and clothing

In a number of instances and for a variety of reasons, readers looking at the Eisen illustrations would have had the impression that they were being made privy to the lives of others. This tendency towards the revelatory extended to the exploration of topics which were often occluded in contemporary discourse or which, in the works of other authors, were often consigned to the obscene or the pornographic. The sense that the *Contes* are exposing what was often hidden is strengthened by at least one essential stylistic component of the plates, namely their use of curtains or draperies drawn back to disclose the actions of characters. The use of such objects had long been established in Dutch painting and engraving, often as a device to ennoble the sitters in portraits by placing them in a luxurious context.[106] It had never achieved the same popularity in French art, so that Eisen was free to use it for purposes of his own without implicitly invoking an established tradition. The curtain motif was a favourite of his, and it occurs in other works which he illustrated, such as La Morlière's *Angola* ([Paris], no pub., 1751), Boccaccio's *Il Decamerone* (1757), Dorat's *Les Baisers* (The Hague and Paris, Delamain, 1770) or Montesquieu's *Temple de Gnide* (1772).[107] It is also true that other contemporary artists, notably Marillier and Gravelot, use similar devices in their own designs for engravings.[108] Nonetheless, with the exception of *Il Decamerone*, it is difficult to find a parallel in other books of the time for so large a number of instances of its use. No other artist makes such extensive use of the open drapery motif to reveal the activities of characters from various levels of society. At the beginning of 'Le tableau', La Fontaine observes (vol.2, p.223):

106. See Martha Hollander, *An Entrance for the eyes: space and meaning in seventeenth-century Dutch art* (Berkeley, CA, Los Angeles, London, 2002), p.69-70.
107. Relevant examples are reproduced in Holloway, *French rococo book illustration*, respectively as plates 169, 223, and 63.
108. See Holloway, *French rococo book illustration*, plates 179, 208, 219.

On m'engage à conter d'une maniere honnête
Le sujet d'un de ces tableaux
Sur lesquels on met des rideaux.

Eisen might be said to have taken such 'tableaux' as the basis for the engravings, and to have seen it as his task, following La Fontaine, to 'raise the curtain' on scenes not normally exhibited for public perusal. One striking, if obvious, reason for the use of the motif is that the majority of the engravings depict scenes which are set indoors, and which would in normal circumstances take place away from the eyes of spectators. In this respect, it is wholly consistent with the purposes which the Fermiers set themselves in publishing their edition of the work. Nonetheless, the fact that other illustrators of the *Contes* (and indeed of other contemporary works) do not use the device to the same extent suggests that Eisen's use of it is significant as a leitmotiv. His habit of using draperies is so marked that it can scarcely be fortuitous, showing curtains which adorn the canopies of beds, or window-curtains which are open to throw light on the scene. A simple comparison will make clear the importance of this practice. De Hooghe uses drapes or curtains in the headpieces for nine *contes*,[109] and the motif occurs in eighteen of the engravings by Cochin.[110] Eisen, however, uses it in no fewer than thirty illustrations, out of a total of eighty or more.[111]

Of course, he had an advantage over his predecessors in that some of the *contes* are illustrated by more than one plate. But this is of no consequence for the interpretation of his designs, since he could have chosen to use motifs other than curtains in illustrating the stories. Unlike Cochin, he uses curtains or drapes even when their presence strikes one as incongruous. This incongruity is created in some instances because the luxurious furnishings contrast with the poverty shown in other aspects of the engraving (as in the rejected plates for 'La coupe enchantée', 'Imitation d'Anacréon', 'Le bât'). In others, the decorative purpose which curtains, placed as they are shown, would have served in reality is not

---

109. 'Joconde'; 'Le muletier'; 'Le Gascon puni'; 'Les deux amis'; 'Alix malade'; 'La mandragore'; 'Le remède'; 'Promettre est un, et tenir est un autre'; 'Le rossignol'.

110. 'Joconde'; 'La gageure des trois commères'; 'Le Gascon puni'; 'Le petit chien qui secoue de l'argent et des pierreries'; 'Le magnifique'; 'Les deux amis'; 'Alix malade'; 'Autre imitation d'Anacréon'; 'Richard Minutolo'; 'Le berceau'; 'La mandragore'; 'Le psautier'; 'La chose impossible'; 'Le bât'; 'Le faiseur d'oreilles et le raccommodeur de moules'; 'Le remède'; 'Le contrat'; 'Le rossignol'.

111. 'Joconde' 2, 3, 4; 'Le savetier'; 'La gageure des trois commères' 1, 2; 'Le Gascon puni'; 'Le petit chien qui secoue de l'argent et des pierreries' 1; 'Le magnifique'; 'Le glouton'; 'Alix malade'; 'sœur Jeanne'; 'Imitation d'Anacréon'; 'Autre imitation d'Anacréon'; 'Richard Minutolo'; 'Le berceau'; 'L'anneau d'Hans Carvel'; 'La mandragore'; 'La courtisane amoureuse'; 'Comment l'esprit vient aux filles'; 'L'abbesse malade'; 'Le psautier'; 'Le roi Candaule et le maître en droit' 1; 'Le diable en enfer'; 'Le tableau'; 'Le bât'; 'Le faiseur d'oreilles et le raccommodeur de moules'; 'Le remède'; 'Le rossignol'; 'La couturière'.

apparent ('sœur Jeanne', 'Richard Minutolo', 'Comment l'esprit vient aux filles', 'Le roi Candaule et le maître en droit', 'Le diable en enfer').

To the use of curtains must be added the fact that the clothes worn by the figures in the engravings are often those of the period at which the *Contes* were published. Indeed, the great majority of the illustrations show figures dressed in the clothing of the mid-eighteenth century, irrespective of the historical time in which the *conte* in question is set (and often La Fontaine provides no specific indications on this point). Only a handful of stories which are explicitly set in a precise historical period or place have engravings with characters dressed otherwise than in contemporary clothes: 'Joconde', 'La coupe enchantée', and 'Belphégor' are cases in point. In 'Le fleuve Scamandre', on the other hand, Eisen ignores the historical information given in the *conte*, which is set in Ancient Greece, in order to present the girl in modern dress. The *Contes* stand, in this respect, in marked contrast to *Il Decamerone*, in which the characters are shown for the most part in medieval or sixteenth-century garb. Since both De Hooghe and Cochin had shown characters dressed in the fashions of the time at which they were working, it cannot be argued that Eisen was departing from custom and practice in this respect. Even so, the consistent use of clothing which would have been worn by many readers of the *Contes* in 1762 does give the engravings a strong contemporary resonance, adding to the impression that the plates were intended to reflect the society of the times.[112]

By employing these means, the Fermiers suggest strongly that contemporary society is populated by adulterous wives, by girls avid for (further) sexual experience, or by lecherous monks and nuns. The clear implication is that, if the Fermiers are accused of licence, debauchery, self-indulgence and immorality, they are no worse than the figures depicted in the engravings; they can hold their own against those who criticise them for their heartlessness or cruelty by pointing to the failings of others. In this sense, virtually every *conte* takes its place in the generalised depiction of corruption, so that the work as a whole is a reflection of the Fermiers' wish to offer an unsentimental and often hostile portrait of the society of

112. Anachronistic contemporary dress is a feature of other illustrated books of the time, such as Moreau's *Œuvres de Molière*, 6 vols (Paris, Libraires associés, 1773). The practice was not however universal, and in other works artists did attempt, with varying degrees of success and accuracy, to clothe appropriately the characters in their illustrations. Sève, for example, depicts classical Roman or Greek dress in the illustrations to the *Œuvres de Racine*, 3 vols (Paris [Le Breton], 1760), as does Gravelot in the *Théâtre de Pierre Corneille*, 12 vols ([Geneva], no pub. 1764); Eisen and other artists show the same respect for classical antiquity in their work for Ovid's *Métamorphoses*, 4 vols (Paris, Hochereau, 1767-1771). Elsewhere, as in the *Contes moraux* of Marmontel, 3 vols (Paris, Merlin, 1765), Gravelot seems to have used ancient or modern dress, in accordance with the setting of the story, within the same series of engravings. The general rule with illustrators seems to have been that they would normally use contemporary dress, but would clothe characters in classical or 'historical' dress when the text required it.

the time. What is more, Eisen's illustrations testify to recent developments in art which distinguish them from the work of his predecessors. Attention was drawn, in the second part of this study, to the use of religious iconography in the engravings for 'Belphégor' and 'L'abbesse malade', and to the use of wild landscape in the second plate for 'La fiancée du roi de Garbe' and in 'Le fleuve Scamandre'. Slight though these indications are in the context of the engravings as a whole, they do show Eisen's keen awareness of contemporary art, and his wish to accentuate the links between the engravings and such developments, the better to appeal to the taste of his readers.

The use of recognisable personalities and clothing, and the references to fashionable trends in art, lead one to conclude that the Fermiers had a specific audience in mind in devising their illustrations. This audience was composed largely of well-informed readers who would understand the allusions and the responses to criticisms of the Fermiers which the plates contained. Initially at least, the Compagnie supposed that such readers would share the basic assumptions underlying the engravings, namely that they were not merely a reflection of the text, but an interpretation of it which embodied certain attitudes towards the poor, or towards women, or towards the Church. Those who did not share these views, or accept the suggestion that contemporary society as a whole was as corrupt as the engravings might lead one to suppose, would not have been inclined to share the joke with the Fermiers. This latter possibility seems to have occurred to the Compagnie only at a late stage, when its position was being assailed on all sides; prudence then prevailed, and the book was withdrawn. It should be noted that, whether or not these assumptions were widespread on the part of readers, they were not typical of the demands made on the public by the majority of illustrated books published at the time, and something needs now to be said about the place of the edition in the context of contemporary books embellished with engravings.

## xii. The significance of the 1762 *Contes* in the history of the eighteenth-century French illustrated book

It is clear from recent research that the *Contes* quickly became an inspiration to writers and illustrators because of the superior technical quality of their illustrations and the harmonious use of ornaments such as *culs-de-lampe*.[113] From an historical point of view, too, the use of illustrations for the *Contes* to embody a set of ideas and values dear to its publishers was a new departure for the eighteenth century. At least, it is hard to think of any previous example at that period of an illustrated book being used in this way. It is true, of course, that there was nothing intrinsically new in the idea of books as a way of affirming power and authority. The glory of

113. See Griffiths, *Prints for books*, esp. p.27-31.

French kings had been celebrated since the sixteenth century in the festival books which issued regularly from the presses. In the seventeenth and eighteenth century, royal weddings and triumphs were likewise commemorated, often in sumptuous folios bound in morocco with the king's arms emblazoned on the covers for all to see.[114] Yet, despite these antecedents, the 1762 edition of the *Contes* strikes out in a new direction, in that it celebrates the values not of majesty or kingship, but of financiers and tax-gatherers. For the first time at that period, an avowedly partisan group was using an illustrated book for (covertly) propagandist purposes. In later years, and during the Revolution especially, it was to become commonplace for illustrations of all kinds, both in books and in ephemeral productions such as cartoons, to carry a political message. At one end of the scale stand the three substantial folio volumes of the *Tableaux historiques de la Révolution française* (Paris, Pierre Didot l'aîné, 1798-1804), with some 150 plates depicting significant events and personalities of the time.[115] At the other, we find large numbers of cheaply printed pamphlets celebrating or attacking particular events and individuals. Many were produced, for example, to commemorate the execution of Louis XVI and Marie Antoinette. Others featured the demise, usually by violent means, of some leading figure who had fallen foul of his or her friends or enemies (the distinction between the two was not always apparent, and was subject to change without notice).[116] The Revolution provides the best example in French history up to that time of the link between illustration and political message. But it was not the first such example in the eighteenth century; that honour belongs to the edition of La Fontaine's *Contes et nouvelles en vers* published by the Compagnie des Fermiers généraux in 1762.

## xiii. Epilogue

If the analysis of the plates for the *Contes* and their history can tell us something about the aims and objectives of the Compagnie in 1762, it does not answer the question of why we still read them, and particularly why this edition is still sought after today. One essential, fundamental, reason for reading the text is that the *Contes* themselves give pleasure now as they have done for three centuries or more. However much the point may be disputed, there is a genius to them which is readily apparent when one reads the pale imitations of La Fontaine appended to the

114. See, for example, Cohen, *Guide de l'amateur de livres*, col.392-94. For an account of how the image of Louis XIV was created, see Peter Burke, *The Fabrication of Louis XIV* (New Haven, CT, and London, 1992).

115. See Cohen, *Guide de l'amateur de livres*, col.969-71; Michel Vovelle, *La Révolution française, images et récits*, 5 vols (Paris, 1985-1986), and Warren Roberts, *The Public, the populace and images of the French Revolution* (New York, 2000), p.59-192.

116. For many typical examples, see the *Chronique de la Révolution*, ed. Jean Favier (Paris, 1988).

edition. For more academic purposes, one can regard them as instances of universal themes present in folk-tales the world over, or because they tell us something of the mentality of the times at which they were written. In a world dominated by the Church, they were sceptical, even anticlerical; in a society where women had ostensibly little political power, they showed what power and influence women really could have by using their sexuality. For these and other reasons, the *Contes* have long been read, and will doubtless continue to be.

When we ask why the engravings to the 1762 edition of the *Contes* deserve attention, different considerations come into play. In the first place, Eisen may be said to have reclaimed by his illustrations a text whose status at that time was somewhat equivocal. Indeed, it was partly inspired by *Il Decamerone* of Boccaccio, a book which had recently been issued with engravings, for those who wanted them, of a distinctly erotic kind. But it is precisely because Eisen and the Fermiers remained within the bounds of conventional decency that the engravings were, and are, accepted as classics of the pre-Revolutionary illustrated book, rather than as specimens of erotic titillation. Though nudity and sexual activity do play a role in the illustrations, such qualities are hardly significant enough to constitute a major justification for studying them, and other reasons need to be found. One such reason is that Eisen offers an eighteenth-century interpretation of a seventeenth-century text. In doing so, he brings the values and attitudes of his own times to the depiction of stories which, in one sense, were at most a century old, but which in another sense are timeless. He makes them applicable to his own age, and in doing so reveals the values, preoccupations and prejudices which inform the view of the stories held by the Fermiers généraux. These indications tell us much about how the Fermiers used the *Contes* to present a *tu quoque* view of contemporary society which was unflattering, unsentimental and often unsparing in its dissection of the vices, hypocrisies and deceptions of the time. Some years ago, in a pioneering study, Robert Nicolich concluded:

The type of inquiry explored here for the illustrations of these six *contes* suggests the quantity of work that remains to be done in an area of complex and subtle inter-relationships. These interrelationships exist not only between the illustrations by De Hooghe and Eisen, but with La Fontaine's text, and with other *Contes* illustrations, too, as well as with the several textual sources and their illustrations.[117]

This study has attempted to indicate at least some of the directions in which these questions can be explored. But there are wider issues at stake too. We do not yet have anything approaching a comprehensive history of the illustrated book in France.[118] Still less do we have a detailed under-

117. Nicolich, 'Seventeenth and eighteenth-century illustrations for La Fontaine's *Contes et nouvelles en vers*', p.369.
118. Though a beginning has at least been made by Michel Vovelle, *Histoires figurales: des monstres médiévaux à Wonderwoman* (Paris, 1989).

## 4. *The lessons of the Eisen illustrations*

standing of its changing socio-cultural significance. It is to be hoped that through this study of the *Contes*, the door has been opened for further examination of the complex interrelationship which exists not only between texts and illustrations, but also between the illustrations and the society in which they were produced, and which they inevitably reflect in a multitude of ways.

# List of works cited

## i. Works published before 1800

Argentan, Louis-François d', *Confé-rences théologiques et spirituelles sur les grandeurs de la très-sainte vierge Marie mère de Dieu*, 2 vols (Rouen, F. Vaultier le jeune, 1680).

Bachaumont, Louis-Petit de, *Mémoires secrets pour servir à l'histoire des lettres en France, depuis MDCCLXII jusqu'à nos jours* [...], 36 vols (London, John Adamson, 1777-1789).

Blanchard, [?], *Les Partisans demasquez, nouvelle plus que galante* (Cologne, Adrien L'Enclume, 1707).

Bonaventure Des Periers, *Cymbalum mundi* (Amsterdam, Prosper Marchand, 1711).

Bure, Guillaume-François de, *Bibliographie instructive, ou Traité de la connoissance des livres rares et singuliers*, 7 vols (Paris, 1763-1768).

Chevrier, François-Antoine, *Testament politique du maréchal duc de Belle-Isle*, new edition (Amsterdam, Libraires associés, 1762).

Darigrand, Edmé-François, *L'Anti-financier, ou Relevé de quelques-unes des malversations dont se rendent journellement coupables les Fermiers généraux* ('Amsterdam' [Paris], no pub., 1763).

Dorat, Claude-Joseph, *Les Baisers* (The Hague and Paris, Delamain, 1770).

Erasmus, Desiderius, *Eloge de la Folie* (Paris, no pub., 1751).

Fer, Nicolas de, *Histoire des rois de France depuis Pharamond* (Paris, J. F. Benard, 1722).

Hénault, Charles-Jean-François, *Abrégé chronologique de l'histoire de France* (1744), 2 vols (Paris, Prault, 1768).

La Barre, François Poulain de, *De l'égalité des deux sexes* (Paris, Jean Du Puis, 1673).

La Bruyère, Jean de, *Les Caractères* (1688), 2 vols (Paris, Prault, 1768).

La Fontaine, Jean de, *Contes et nouvelles en vers*, 2 vols (Amsterdam, Etienne Lucas, 1731), with illustrations by Romeyn de Hooghe.

–, *Contes et nouvelles en vers*, 2 vols (Amsterdam [Paris, Barbou], no pub., 1745), with illustrations by Charles-Nicolas Cochin.

–, *Contes et nouvelles en vers*, 3 vols (Amsterdam [Lyon?], aux dépens de la Compagnie, 1762), illustrator unknown.

–, *Contes et nouvelles en vers*, 2 vols (Amsterdam [Paris], no pub., 1762), with illustrations by Charles Eisen.

–, *Fables de La Fontaine*, 4 vols (Paris, Desaint & Saillant, Durand, 1755-1759), with illustrations by Jean-Baptiste Oudry.

–, *Œuvres complètes de La Fontaine*, ed. Jean-Pierre Collinet (Paris, 1991).

Lambert, Anne-Thérèse, marquise de, *Œuvres de Mme la marquise de Lambert* (Lausanne, Marc-Michel Bousquet, 1747).

La Morlière, Charles-Jacques, *Angola* ([Paris], no pub., 1751).

Le Maire, Jean, *Les Traits de l'histoire universelle, sacrée et profane, d'après les plus grands peintres et les meilleurs écrivains*, 6 vols (Paris, Le Maire et al, 1760-1762).

*Mercure de France*, January 1763, 2 vols (Paris, no pub., 1763).

[Mirabeau, Victor Riqueti, marquis de], *L'Ami des hommes*, 6 vols (Avignon, no pub., 1756-1761).

–, *Théorie de l'impôt* ([Paris], no pub., 1760).

Molière, Jean-Baptiste Poquelin, *known as*, *Œuvres de Molière*, 6 vols (Paris, Libraires associés, 1773).

Montenoy, Charles Palissot de, *Œuvres complètes de M. Palissot*, 7 vols (Liège and Paris, Bastien, 1778).

[Montesquieu, Charles-Louis de Secondat, baron de], *Le Temple de Gnide* (Paris, Le Mire, 1772).

[Naveau, Jean-Baptiste], *Le Financier citoyen*, 2 vols ([Paris], no pub., 1757).

Ovid, *Métamorphoses*, 4 vols (Paris, Hochereau, 1767-1771).

Perrault, Charles, *La Vie des hommes illustres qui ont paru en France pendant ce siècle*, 2 vols (Paris, Dezallier, 1696).

Plato, *The Republic of Plato*, translated with notes and an interpretative essay by Allan Bloom (New York and London, 1968).

[Prévost d'Exiles, Antoine-François], *Histoire du chevalier Des Grieux et de Manon Lescaut* (1731), ed. Jean Sgard (Paris, 1995).

Pontas, Jean, *Dictionnaire des cas de conscience*, 2 vols (Paris, Le Mercier et al., 1715).

[Puisieux, Madeleine d'Arsant de], *Conseils à une amie* ([Paris], no pub., 1749).

Racine, Jean, *Œuvres de Racine*, 3 vols (Paris, [Le Breton], 1760).

*Recueil d'estampes pour la nouvelle Héloïse* (Amsterdam, Rey, 1761).

*Registres des privilèges et permissions simples de la librairie*, 1750-1763 (BNF n.a.fr. 21998-99).

Rousseau, Jean-Jacques, *Lettres de deux amans, habitans d'une petite ville au pied des Alpes*, 6 vols (Amsterdam, Rey, 1761).

[Roussel de La Tour, Pierre-Philippe], *Doutes modestes sur la richesse de l'Etat, ou Lettre écrite à l'auteur de ce système par un de ses confrères* (Paris, Ruinart, 1763).

[Saint-Cyr, Odet Joseph de Vaux de Giry, abbé de], *Catéchisme des Cacouacs* ('A Cacapolis' [Paris], 1758).

[Taillefer, Antoine], *Tableau historique de l'esprit et du caractère des littérateurs français*, 4 vols (Versailles, Poinçot and Paris, Nyon, 1785).

Voltaire, François-Marie Arouet de, *Correspondence and related documents*, ed. Th. Besterman, in *Œuvres complètes de Voltaire* [*OCV*], vol.85-135 (Geneva, Banbury, Oxford, 1968-1977).

–, *Le Siècle de Louis XIV*, 2 vols (Berlin, Henning, 1751).

–, *Œuvres complètes de Voltaire*, ed. Louis Moland, 52 vols (Paris, 1877-1885).

# ii. Works published after 1800

Adams, David, 'Politics and illustration: the lower classes as depicted in the "Fermiers généraux" edition of La Fontaine's *Contes* of 1762', *British journal for eighteenth-century studies*, 26:2 (2003), p.155-66.

–, 'Les premières illustrations de *La Religieuse*, ou la via non dolorosa',

in *La Douleur: beauté ou laideur*, ed. Angels Santa (Lleida, 2005), p.41-52.

–, 'Theme and technique in the "Oudry" edition of La Fontaine's *Fables*', *Bulletin of the John Rylands Library* 81:3, special issue *Text and image*, ed. David Adams and Adrian Armstrong (1999), p.361-84.

Baker, Keith Michael, *Inventing the French Revolution* (Cambridge, 1990).

Bal, Mieke, *Narratology*, trans. Christine van Boheemen (Toronto, 1985).

Barber, Giles, *Daphnis and Chloe: the markets and metamorphoses of an unknown bestseller* (London, 1989).

Barbier, Edmond-Jean-François, *Chronique de la régence et du règne de Louis XV (1718-1763), ou Journal de Barbier, avocat au parlement de Paris*, septième série (1758-1761) (Paris, 1885).

Barthes, Roland, 'Rhétorique de l'image', *Communications* 4 (1964), p.40-51.

Bassy, Alain-Marie, 'Le texte et l'image', in *Histoire de l'édition française*, 4 vols (Paris, 1983-1986).

Bautier, Roger, *De la rhétorique à la communication* (Paris, 1993).

Bernstein, Richard J., ed., *Habermas and modernity* (Cambridge, MA, 1985).

Birberick, Anne L., 'From world to text: the figure of the nun in La Fontaine's *Contes*', in *Refiguring La Fontaine: tercentenary essays*, ed. Birberick (Charlottesville, VA, 1999).

–, *Reading undercover: audience and authority in Jean de La Fontaine* (Lewisburg, PA, and London, 1998).

Birn, Raymond, 'The profits of ideas: *privilèges en librairie* in eighteenth-century France', *Eighteenth-century studies* 4:2 (1970-1971).

Blanckaert, Claude, 'Of monstrous métis? Hybridity, fear of miscegenation, and patriotism from Buffon to Paul Broca', in *The Color of liberty: histories of race in France*, ed. Sue Peabody and Tyler Stovall (Durham, NC, and London, 2003).

Boissais, Maurice, and Jacques Deleplanque, *Les Livres à gravures au dix-huitième siècle* (Paris, 1948).

Bredt, E. W., *Die drei galanten Meister von Valenciennes* (Munich, 1921).

Bryson, Norman, *Word and image: French painting of the Ancien régime* (Cambridge, 1983).

*Bulletin of the John Rylands Library* 81:3 (1999), special issue *Text and image: studies in the French illustrated book*, ed. David Adams and Adrian Armstrong.

Burke, Peter, *The Fabrication of Louis XIV* (New Haven, CT, and London, 1992).

Butler, Judith, *Gender trouble: feminism and the subversion of identity* (New York, 1990).

Calhoun, Craig, ed., *Habermas and the public sphere* (Cambridge, MA, 1992).

*Catalogue des livres de la bibliothèque de feue Mme la marquise de Pompadour, dame du palais de la reine* (Paris, Hérissant, 1765).

Charlier, Gustave, *Dictionnaire des lettres françaises* (Paris, 1995).

*Chronique de la Révolution*, ed. Jean Favier (Paris, 1988).

Clarac, Pierre, *La Fontaine par lui-même* (Paris, 1961).

Cobban, Alfred, *A History of modern France*, 3 vols (Harmondsworth, 1963).

Cohen, Henri, and Seymour de Ricci, *Guide de l'amateur de livres à gravures du XVIIIᵉ siècle*, sixième édition (Paris, 1912).

Conisbee, Philip, *Painting in eighteenth-century France* (Oxford, 1980).

Cranston, Maurice, *The Noble savage: Jean-Jacques Rousseau 1754-1762* (London and Chicago, 1991).

Darnton, Robert, *The Forbidden bestsellers of pre-Revolutionary France* (London, 1996).

–, *The Great cat massacre and other episodes in French cultural history* (Harmondsworth, 1984).

–, *George Washington's false teeth: an unconventional guide to the eighteenth century* (London and New York, 2003).

Davidson, Jane P., *The Witch in northern European art 1470-1750* (Düsseldorf, 1987).

Dawson, Robert L., *Confiscations at customs: banned books and the French* booktrade during the last years of the *Ancien régime*, *SVEC* 2006:07.

*Dictionnaire de biographie française*, ed. Jean-Charles Roman d'Amat (Paris, 1933-).

*Dictionnaire des lettres françaises: XVIIIᵉ siècle*, ed. François Moureau (Paris, 1995).

Ducourtieux, Paul, *Comment on devenait libraire à Paris au XVIIIᵉ siècle: les Barbou de Paris* (Paris, 1897).

Durand, Yves, *Les Fermiers généraux au XVIIIᵉ siècle* (Paris, 1971).

Fried, Michael, *Absorption and theatricality: painting and the beholder in the age of Diderot* (Berkeley, CA, 1980).

Fumaroli, Marc, *Le Poète et le roi: La Fontaine en son siècle* (Paris, 1997).

Gascar, Pierre, *Buffon* (Paris, 1983).

Gaxotte, Pierre, *Le Siècle de Louis XV* (Paris, 1974).

Gay, Jules, *Bibliographie des ouvrages relatifs à l'amour, aux femmes, au mariage* (Paris, 1861).

Gérard Genette, *Figures III* (Paris, 1972).

Gledhill, Christine 'Women reading men', in *Me Jane: masculinity, movies and women*, ed. Pat Kirkham and Janet Thumim (London, 1995), p.73-93.

Goldgar, Anne, 'The absolutism of taste: journalists as censors in eighteenth-century Paris', in *Censorship and the control of print in England and France 1600-1910*, ed. Robin Myers and Michael Harris (Winchester, 1992).

Goncourt, E. and J. de, *L'Art du dix-huitième siècle* (Paris, 1883).

Goodden, Angelica, *Diderot and the body* (Oxford, 2001).

Goodman, Dena, *The Republic of letters: a cultural history of the French Enlightenment* (Ithaca, NY and London, 1994).

Goubert, Pierre, and Daniel Roche, *Les Français et l'Ancien régime*, 2 vols (Paris, 1984).

Greer, Germaine, *The Boy* (London, 2003).

Griffiths, Antony, *Prints for books: book illustration in France 1760-1800* (London, 2004).

Grimm, Frédéric-Melchior, *et al.*, *Correspondance littéraire, philosophique et critique*, ed. Maurice Tourneux, 16 vols (Paris, 1877-1882).

Grimm, Jürgen, ' "Comment on traite les pervers": la satire anticléricale dans les *Contes*', *Papers on French seventeenth-century literature* 23:44 (1996), p.159-72.

–, ' "On ne vit onc si cruelle aventure": à propos du *Conte d'un paysan qui avait offensé son seigneur*', in *Car demeure l'amitié: mélanges offerts à Claude Abraham*, ed. Francis Assaf and Andrew H. Wallis (Paris, 1997).

Grisé, Catherine, 'Le jeu de l'imitation: un aspect de la réception des *Contes* de La Fontaine', *Papers on French seventeenth-century literature* 10:18 (1983), p.249-62.

–, 'La casuistique dans les *Contes* de La Fontaine', *Studi francesi* 97 (1989), p.411-21.

–, 'Erotic dimensions of space in La Fontaine's "La Fiancée du roi de Garbe" ', *Modern language review* 82 (1987), p.587-98.

–, 'Jean de La Fontaine's *Contes*: a poetic patchwork of folklore motifs', *Romance notes* 37:1 (1996), p.155-73.

Grosclaude, P., *Malesherbes, témoin et interprète de son temps* (Paris, 1961).

Haak, Bob, *The Golden age: Dutch painters of the seventeenth century* (London, 1984).

Habermas, Jürgen, *The Theory of communicative action*, trans. Thomas McCarthy, 2 vols (Boston, MA, 1984).

Hédé-Haüy, A., *Les Illustrations des Contes de La Fontaine: bibliographie, iconographie* (Paris, 1893).

Herrmann-Mascard, Nicole, *La Censure des livres à Paris à la fin de l'ancien régime (1750-1789)*, Travaux et recherches de la Faculté de droit et des sciences économiques de Paris 13 (Paris, 1968).

*Histoire de la littérature française au XVIIᵉ siècle*, ed. Antoine Adam, 5 vols (Paris, 1948-1956).

Hobson, Marian, *The Object of art: the theory of illusion in eighteenth-century France* (Cambridge, 1982).

Hofer, Philip, *Baroque book illustration: a short survey from the collection in the Department of graphic arts Harvard College library* (Cambridge, MA, 1951).

Hoffman, Paul, *La Femme dans la pensée des Lumières* (Paris, 1977).

Hollander, Martha, *An Entrance for the eyes: space and meaning in seventeenth-century Dutch art* (Berkeley, CA, Los Angeles, London, 2002).

Holloway, Owen, *French rococo book illustration* (London, 1969).

Hong, Ran E., 'La réécriture de deux *contes* de La Fontaine', *Papers on French seventeenth-century literature* 27:53 (2000), p.473-87.

Houle, Martha M., 'The play of *bienséances* in La Fontaine's *L'Abbesse*', *Papers in French seventeenth-century literature* 18:34 (1991), p.109-21.

Jollet, Etienne, *Figures de la pesanteur* (Nîmes, 1998).

Joly, Martine, *Introduction à l'analyse de l'image* (Paris, 1993).

Kwass, Michael, *Privilege and the politics of taxation in eighteenth-century France: liberté, égalité, fiscalité* (Cambridge, 2000).

Lacroix, P. L., 'Les *Contes* de La Fontaine. Recherches sur l'édition des Fermiers généraux', *L'Artiste* 44:2 (1874), p.255-56.

La Fontaine, Gilles E. de, *La Fontaine dans ses Contes* (Sherbrooke, 1978).

Landwehr, John, *Romeyn de Hooghe, 1645-1708, as book illustrator: a bibliography* (Amsterdam and New York, 1970).

Lapp, John, *The Esthetics of negligence: La Fontaine's 'Contes'* (Cambridge, 1971).

Laver, James, *A Concise history of costume* (London, 1972).

Leak, Andrew, *Barthes: Mythologies* (London, 1994).

Lebrun, Jacques, *La Jouissance et le trouble: recherches sur la littérature chrétienne à l'âge classique* (Geneva, 2004).

Leigh, R. A., 'Rousseau, his publishers and the *Contrat social*', *Bulletin of the John Rylands university library of Manchester* 66:2 (1984), p.204-27.

Levey, Michael, *Rococo to revolution* (London, 1977).

Lough, John, *Essays on the 'Encyclopédie' of Diderot and D'Alembert* (London, 1968).

–, *The 'Encyclopédie'* (London, 1971).

McEachern, Jo-Ann E., *Bibliography of the writings of Jean-Jacques Rousseau to 1800*, 2 vols (Oxford, 1993).

Malesherbes, Chrétien-Guillaume Lamoignon de, *Mémoires sur la librairie et sur la liberté de la presse* (1809), ed. Graham Rodmell, *North Carolina studies in the Romance languages and literatures* 213 (Chapel Hill, NC, 1979).

Mander, Jenny, *Circles of learning: narratology and the eighteenth-century French novel*, *SVEC* 366 (1999).

May, Georges, *Diderot et 'La Religieuse'* (New Haven, CT, and Paris, 1954).

–, *Le Dilemme du roman au XVIIIᵉ siècle* (New Haven, CT, and Paris, 1963).

Michel, Christian, *Charles-Nicolas Cochin et l'art des Lumières* (Rome, 1993).

–, *Charles-Nicolas Cochin et le livre illustré au XVIIIᵉ siècle, avec un catalogue raisonné des livres illustrés par Cochin, 1735-1790* (Geneva, 1987).

Milner, Max, *Le Diable dans la littérature française: de Cazotte à Baudelaire 1722-1861*, 2 vols (Paris, 1960).

Montagu, Jennifer, *The Expression of the passions: the origin and influence of Charles Le Brun's 'Conférence sur l'expression générale et particulière'* (New Haven, CT and London, 1994).

Mulvey, Laura, *Fetishism and curiosity* (London, 1996).

−, *Visual and other pleasures* (London, 1989).

Narkiss, Bezalel, 'On the zoocephalic phenomenon in medieval Ashkenazi manuscripts', in *Norms and variations in art: essays in honour of Moshe Barasch* (Jerusalem, 1983), p.49-62.

Nicolich, Robert N., 'Seventeenth and eighteenth-century illustrations for La Fontaine's *Contes et nouvelles en vers*: engraving designs by Romeyn de Hooghe and Charles Eisen', *Papers on French seventeenth-century literature* 13:24 (1986), p.221-82.

Norris, Christopher, *Deconstruction*, new edition (London, 2002).

Panofsky, Erwin, *Studies in iconology* (New York and London, 1972).

[Pereire, Maurice], 'Une circulaire du temps concernant l'édition des *Contes* de La Fontaine dite des Fermiers généraux', *Bulletin du bibliophile* (1922), p.272-75.

Perrault, Charles, *La Vie des hommes illustres qui ont paru en France pendant ce siècle*, 2 vols (Paris, Dezallier, 1696).

Portalis, Roger, *Les Dessinateurs d'illustrations au dix-huitième siècle*, 2 vols (Paris, 1877).

Proust, Jacques, *L'Encyclopédie* (Paris, 1965).

Quicherat, Jules, *Histoire du costume en France depuis les temps les plus reculés jusqu'à la fin du XVIIIᵉ siècle* (Paris, 1877).

Racinet, Albert, *The Historical encyclopedia of costume* (London, 1998).

Ravaisson, François, *Archives de la Bastille*, 17 vols (Paris, 1868-1881).

Ray, Gordon, *The Art of the French illustrated book from 1700 to 1914* (New York, 1986).

Riley, James C., *The Seven Years War and the Old Regime in France* (Princeton, NJ, 1986).

Rimmon-Kenan, Shlomith, *Narrative fiction: contemporary poetics* (London, 1983).

Roberts, Warren, *The Public, the populace and images of the French Revolution* (New York, 2000).

Rochambeau, René Lacroix de Vineux, comte de, *Bibliographie des œuvres de La Fontaine* (Paris, 1911; reprinted New York, 1970).

Rocquain, Félix, *L'Esprit révolutionnaire avant la Révolution 1715-1789* (Paris, 1878).

Rorty, Richard, 'Habermas and Lyotard on postmodernity', in *Habermas and modernity*, ed. Richard J. Bernstein (Cambridge, MA, 1985).

Rosenberg, Pierre, *Fragonard* (Paris, 1987).

Salomons, Vera, 'Charles Eisen', *XVIIIth century French book-illustrators* (London, 1914 [but 1921]).

Sauvy, Anne, 'Une littérature pour les femmes', in *Histoire de l'édition française*, ed. Roger Chartier and Henri-Jean Martin, 4 vols (Paris, 1983-1986), vol.3, p.445-53.

Sayce, R. A., *Compositorial practices and the localization of printed books 1530-1800*, Oxford Bibliographical Society occasional publications 13 (Oxford, 1979).

Schama, Simon, *Rembrandt's eyes* (London, 1999).

Schwab, R. N., W. E. Rex and J. Lough, *Inventory of Diderot's 'Encyclopédie'*, vol.3, *SVEC* 85 (1972).

Smith, D. W., *Bibliography of the writings of Helvétius* (Ferney-Voltaire, 2001)

−, *Helvétius, a study in persecution* (Oxford, 1965).

Stenger, Gerhardt, *L'Affaire des Cacouacs* (Saint-Etienne, 2003).

Stewart, Philip, *Engraven desire: eros, image and text in the French eighteenth century* (Durham, NC, and London, 1992).

Tucoo-Chala, Suzanne, *Charles-Joseph Panckoucke et la librairie française 1736-1798* (Pau, 1977).

Vovelle, Michel, *Histoires figurales: des monstres médiévaux à Wonderwoman* (Paris, 1989).
–, *La Révolution française, images et récits* (Paris, 1985-1986).

Weil, Françoise, *L'Interdiction du roman et la librairie 1728-1750* (Paris, 1986).
Werner, Stephen, *Blueprint: a study of Diderot and the Encyclopédie plates* (Birmingham, AL, 1993).
White, Eugene N., *France's slow transition from privatised to government-administered tax collection: tax farming in the eighteenth century*, available as Rutgers University Department of Economics working papers, online at: http://netec.mcc.ac.uk/WoPEc/data/Papers/rutrutres200116.html.

# Index

Note that words and names that occur very frequently in the text have been omitted.